L'ENFANT'S LEGACY

CREATING THE NORTH AMERICAN LANDSCAPE

Gregory Conniff, Edward K. Muller, and David Schuyler
Consulting Editors

George F. Thompson
Series Founder and Director

Published in cooperation with the Center for American Places
Santa Fe, New Mexico, and Staunton, Virginia

L'ENFANT'S LEGACY

PUBLIC OPEN SPACES IN WASHINGTON, D.C.

Michael Bednar

THE JOHNS HOPKINS UNIVERSITY PRESS : BALTIMORE

Printed in the United States of America on acid-free paper

2 4 6 8 9 7 5 3

The Johns Hopkins University Press
2715 North Charles Street
Baltimore, Maryland 21218-4363
www.press.jhu.edu

Library of Congress Cataloging-in-Publication Data

Bednar, Michael J.
   L'Enfant's legacy : public open spaces in Washington, D.C. /
Michael Bednar.
      p. cm—(Creating the North American Landscape)
   Includes bibliographical references and index.
   ISBN 0-8018-8318-0 (hardcover : alk. paper)
   1. City planning—Washington (D.C.)—History. 2. L'Enfant, Pierre
Charles, 1754–1825. 3. Public spaces—Washington (D.C.) 4. Open
spaces—Washington (D.C.) 5. Urban landscape architecture—
Washington (D.C.) 6. Plazas—Washington (D.C.) 7. Parks—
Washington (D.C.) 8. Washington (D.C.)—Buildings, structures, etc.
9. Washington (D.C.)—Description and travel. I. Title. II. Series.
   NA9127.W2B43 2006
   712'.5'09753—dc22   2005016599

A catalog record for this book is available from the British Library.

To my mother, Mary Rohal Bednar

CONTENTS

Acknowledgments

The concept for this book was developed out of a series of student research projects in my Design of Cities course at the University of Virginia School of Architecture. This led to a Web site, Washington Places, illustrating the evolution of many of the city's open spaces. A research sabbatical during the spring of 2002 enabled the development of the concept into book form.

In 1993 Elizabeth Barthold and Sara Amy Leach completed a series of reports on Washington's original public reservations for the Historic American Buildings Survey of the National Park Service. This led to the successful nomination in 1997 of the *L'Enfant Plan of the City of Washington* to the National Register of Historic Places. These reports were invaluable in providing a general background for my research on this book. My special gratitude extends to historian Sara Amy Leach, who also thoroughly reviewed the manuscript during its preparation.

Numerous highly regarded scholars have studied and written about the history, planning, and design of the nation's capital. Their writings have been sources of information and inspiration, knowledge and insight. In writing this book I relied on their work as a basis for interpretations regarding the expression of the nation's democratic ideals in the design of its physical environment. My perspective has been formed by four decades of architectural practice, teaching architecture and urban design, and civic service. The research method is eclectic in the best sense, relying on all available primary and secondary sources. I made extensive use of site visits, photography, and historical maps.

This project was generously supported by the Graham Foundation for Advanced Studies in the Fine Arts in Chicago. Additional generous support was provided by the Dean's Forum of the University of Virginia School of Architecture.

This book would not have reached fruition without the patient direction of the Center for American Places. President and publisher George F. Thompson and editor Randall B. Jones provided the consistent support, critical reviews, and publisher liaison that made the book possible. The highest standards of publication were provided by the Johns Hopkins University Press.

The staffs at the University of Virginia's Alderman Library and Fiske-Kimball Fine Arts Library provided necessary research materials, which were never due. In Washington, D.C., the staffs of the Department of the

Interior Library, the Washingtoniana Division of the District of Columbia Public Library, the Historical Society of Washington, and both the Geography and Map Division and the Prints and Photographs Division of the Library of Congress provided research sources and illustrations.

Numerous individuals provided invaluable comments and critiques, especially colleagues at the University of Virginia School of Architecture. Graduate student Meri Tepper created the excellent 1999 maps utilizing Geographic Information System data furnished by the District of Columbia Office of Planning. Finally, I thank my wife, Elizabeth Lawson, for her many helpful comments, her consistent encouragement, and her accompaniment on many trips to the nation's capital.

L'Enfant's Legacy

INTRODUCTION

IF THE WORLD is to contain a public space, it cannot be erected for one generation and planned for the living only; but must transcend the life-span of mortal men.

HANNAH ARENDT, *The Human Condition*

The role and purpose of public space in the American city has evolved from many traditions. Greece had the agora, a public place where citizens discussed and voted as a community to establish laws. Aristotle believed this activity should not be compromised by commercial interests.[1] In Rome there was the forum, a public place where citizens gathered and debated the political issues of the day. These ancient precedents formed the basis for many European civic places, where political activity occurred along with commercial, religious, and social functions. All of these precedents in turn formed the basis for public places in American cities, in particular the New England village green.

When Pierre Charles L'Enfant developed his 1791 plan for the City of Washington, he utilized these precedents to establish a network of public spaces of great variety linked together by broad, diagonal avenues. Some of these spaces were proposed for specific civic functions related to churches, academies, courthouses, markets, or the city hall. Others were designated the social centers of neighborhoods (appropriated spaces) and dedicated to the fifteen states for memorials. Still others, given no specified function (unappropriated spaces), were to evolve according to the future needs of the city. Most of these public spaces were realized; some were not (see the appendix). Finally, President's Park, Capitol Square, and the Mall were intended as national civic spaces, places where the democratic political ideals of the new nation were to be realized.

The subject of this book is the design of public open space in the City of Washington, the legacy of L'Enfant's innovative urban plan. Washington's public spaces fulfill several roles: political, social, functional, and design. Each space has evolved according to its specified roles in the city. The roles were shaped by forces surrounding each—the system of roads and paths, public amenities, memorials, the uses and styles of the surrounding buildings. This book emphasizes the political role, how the built form of public open space has or has not expressed the democratic freedoms of American citizens.

In his highly respected text *Democracy in America,* first published in 1835, Alexis de Tocqueville eloquently argues for individual liberty:

"Providence has given to each individual, whoever he may be, the degree of reason necessary for him to be able to direct himself in things that interest him exclusively. Such is the great maxim on which civil and political society in the United States rests . . . Extended to the entirety of the nation, it becomes the dogma of the sovereignty of the people."[2] This philosophical tenet expresses the intent of the U.S. Constitution and establishes a basis for the political role of public space in the city.

The political role of public space in the American city begins with the Bill of Rights of the U.S. Constitution. This fundamental document sets forth the relationships between individuals and the federal government, acknowledging the government's respect for its citizens as the source of political power.[3] The Bill of Rights establishes civil rights, basic human entitlements that individuals possess independent of those granted by government. Rights imply a duty not to impinge upon the rights of others. Spatial rights (access, action, control) are derived from these civil rights in order to govern personal behavior in public settings. U.S. citizens, as well as aliens and visitors, have many undeniable rights to freely pursue their public lives.

Many of America's democratic ideals are demonstrated in the public spaces of its cities. In these spaces people can freely participate in social encounters or assemble to celebrate an event or proclaim a cause. They can also assemble to protest government actions, often wars or social policies. They can erect buildings with unique architectural expression and engage in private activities in those buildings without fear. Groups can create memorials to heroic individuals or traumatic events.

America's democratic ideals are exemplified more in Washington, D.C., than in other American cities because Washington is the nation's capital, where citizens expect the highest design standards. Nowhere is this more evident than in the spaces of the federal city: Capitol Square, President's Park, and the Mall. At the Capitol citizens expect to encounter their government directly in a dignified setting, a symbolic public forum. At the White House they expect to meet the president where he works and lives. The Mall in particular is considered American's premier public place, its main square or park, its front lawn. There citizens are free to exercise their constitutional rights, to freely congregate, to peaceably protest, to celebrate their citizenship.

The public spaces of Washington are also political in the sense that each is subject to a power struggle for its control, an explication of the democratic process. The U.S. Congress has the most power, since Washington is a federalized capital city. The National Capital Planning Commission and the U.S. Commission of Fine Arts are powerful federal agencies responsible for policies and approvals. The National Park Service of the Department of the Interior has direct control of the *reservations,* the generic term for all federal public spaces. The political influence of the District of Columbia government has ebbed and flowed throughout its history, from a brief era of being a territory to direct federal control through appointed commissioners to home rule. Private political forces include real estate developers, land and building owners, and commercial interests. They often operate through advocacy groups or associations. Residents are potentially the strongest political force, voicing their concerns through advisory neighborhood commissions or neighborhood associations. Each of these groups competes for control of public space, which is contested territory wherein political influence is often made manifest in built form.

The dialectic between public and private behavior is fundamental to the changing social relationships between individuals in a public setting, as revealed in social historian Richard Sennett's *Fall of Public Man*, wherein he analyzes the history of behavior in public settings in specific periods of Western society. In Europe during the eighteenth century, there was a balance between public life in the cosmopolitan city and private life within the confines of the family. In spite of political repression, people inhabited public space to relax in parks, go to the theater, and use public transit. This changed in the nineteenth century, owing in large part to the forces of industrial capitalism, which provided mass merchandising and restricted leisure time. Sennett concludes that in Western society the balance has shifted toward private life, which has now become an end in itself. "Today, public life has also become a matter of formal obligation. Most citizens approach their dealings with the state in a spirit of resigned acquiescence, but this public enervation is in its scope much broader than political affairs." We no longer appreciate the significant value of being with strangers in public. "As in Roman times, participation in the *res publica* today is most often a matter of going along, and the forums for this public life, like the city, are in a state of decay."[4]

The changing relationships between individuals in public are the basis for the evolution of urban public space. In early-nineteenth-century Washington, there was a civility in people's public decorum and appearance. Spending time in the squares and circles of the city was both a form of passive recreation and a matter of enjoying social encounters between friends, acquaintances, or strangers.

In the early twentieth century these encounters became more formal, related to specific activities or events. Participation was deemed an obligation of being a good citizen. One went to political rallies, dedications, and meetings to be counted as present, not for a political or social experience. One neither expected nor desired social contact in a public place. In the latter part of the twentieth century, the advent of mass communication in print and electronic form obviated the need for attending public events; one received political news from television, radio, or the Internet. Social experience shifted to the private setting of one's family; one watched movies on videotapes or listened to concerts on compact discs rather than going to the movie theater or the concert hall.

The ways in which the City of Washington functions have changed significantly over the last two centuries. No longer is it a compact city for pedestrians with a large resident population. It is now an extensive metropolitan area whose population lives primarily in the suburbs and travels via automobile, bus, and subway. The people utilizing many of the city's open spaces are primarily office workers who are there on weekdays, and the numbers of visitors and tourists have greatly increased. Many of the public spaces no longer provide recreation for residents. Historic memorials have faded in significance. Conflicts between pedestrians and traffic limit access where roadways have intruded upon open spaces. The design of many public spaces in Washington must be reconsidered in the twenty-first century to accommodate new programs and purposes for a changing constituency.

The design character of a city is significantly shaped by its open spaces. These are the spaces where the city is perceived from a state of repose, where a memorable image can be developed. The extensive contiguous network of Washington's open spaces comprises the monumental core, diagonal avenues, and squares or circles. It is varied in geometry but consistent in its monumental scale, forming a complex spatial system for experiencing and using the city.

Public spaces serve an urban design role by providing relief from the dense urban fabric to achieve orientation and repose. To be recognized as outdoor rooms, they must have spatial definition, which can be achieved through the architectural context or landscape design. The number of diagonal avenues and orthogonal streets that intersect each open space in Washington make spatial definition difficult. The ways in which the buildings surrounding an urban open space (its architectural frame) relate to one another and to the open space characterize the spatial definition. Their architectural character, scale, and form have changed dramatically over the last two centuries. In Washington, the height limit for buildings, in effect for almost a century, has fostered spatial definition by forming strong street walls, although this ideal has not been achieved in all of the public spaces. Design is considered here in broad terms involving not only aesthetics but also circulation, access, functionality, vistas, and microclimates.

The focus of this study is the open spaces in the area defined by L'Enfant's 1791 plan for the nation's capital, those identified in the nomination of this plan to the National Register of Historic Places.[5] These include the monumental spaces of the federal city and the squares and circles of the constituent city as identified on L'Enfant's plan and subsequent plans. These are identified on a key map of central Washington (fig. I.1). Only urbanized open spaces, those defined by buildings on several sides, are analyzed. The extensive parklands along the Potomac and Anacostia rivers and Rock Creek Park are not part of this study. Nor are open spaces that have not been designed or developed, such as school or neighborhood playgrounds or minor public reservations.

The "Commentary" sections throughout this book analyze the present circumstances of a given public space and discuss its future. In many cases there are suggestions for design improvements or design intentions for both the open space and the immediate context. These are intended for the consideration of all persons concerned with or engaged in maintaining, improving, or changing the legacy of Washington's public spaces.

The terms *square* or *circle* and *park* are used somewhat interchangeably on historical and contemporary maps. The confusion lies in what is being designated. To maintain consistency of meaning, I use the term *park* or *plaza* in this text to refer to the actual open space, usually bounded by streets. The term *square* or *circle* refers to the entire context, which includes the blocks and buildings surrounding the open space. The term *urban block* refers to the site for buildings defined by streets. In general, only the specific architectural frame, or those buildings directly facing the park, is analyzed as the physical context.

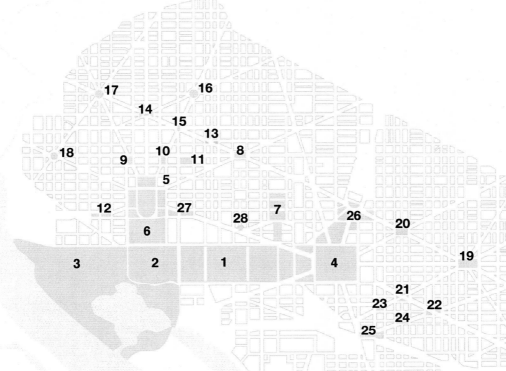

Fig. I.1. **Key map of central Washington with locations of public spaces**

Winston Churchill, the wartime prime minister of England, said, "We shape our dwellings, and afterwards our dwellings shape us."[6] This was after World War II, when England was contemplating rebuilding the Houses of Parliament in a new way. Churchill was concerned that the new building would change the nature of debate in unforeseen ways. He acknowledged the fact that human behavior is directly influenced by the design of the environment. He was also concerned with the legacy of an important civic place.

Washington, D.C., has a wealth of public open spaces in the form of broad avenues and parks. They represent the legacy of the city's founders and a resource for present and future residents and visitors to use and enjoy. These places serve as nodal points in the urban landscape and as focal points for communities. They evolved over many decades through active usage leading to developed forms, yet they face contemporary challenges from surrounding development, changing social contexts, and evolving cultural needs. The primary concern of this book is whether future generations will honor and continue to develop L'Enfant's legacy of public spaces as the expression of the nation's democratic ideals.

CHAPTER ONE

THE L'ENFANT PLAN

The Creation of the Plan, The L'Enfant Plan of Washington,
Nineteenth-Century Development, Twentieth-Century Development,
Extending the Legacy, Embodied Democratic Ideals

NO NATION had ever before the opportunity offered them of deliberately deciding on the spot where their Capital City should be fixed, or of combining every necessary consideration in the choice of situation, and although the means now within the power of the Country are not such as to pursue the design to any great extent, it will be obvious that the plan should be drawn on such a scale as to leave room for that aggrandizement and embellishment which the increase of the wealth of the nation will permit it to pursue at any period however remote.

PIERRE CHARLES L'ENFANT to George Washington, 11 September 1789

Great cities have great open spaces, which are used by residents and visitors for political action, socialization, recreation, and commemoration. In conjunction with the architectural context, the system of open spaces gives a city its image, that quality that makes it memorable to inhabitants and visitors. Pierre Charles L'Enfant understood this urban-design maxim from his experience with some great world cities. His plan for the new capital city of Washington would have as its hallmark a vast integrated system of public open spaces to express the democratic ideals of the new nation.

To create a capital city was a bold venture; it had never been done before. The national capitals of Europe were all located in existing cities. The constitution for the new nation authorized a capital city not more than ten miles square (one hundred square miles) that would be under federal control. President George Washington chose the final location, a site straddling the Potomac River at the mouth of the Anacostia River (also called the Eastern Branch), upriver from his own estate, Mount Vernon. In 1791 he determined the boundaries, with sides ten miles long running northeast and northwest from the mouth of Hunting Creek, a half-mile south of the Alexandria courthouse.[1] Three commissioners appointed by the president were to acquire the land and provide buildings for Congress, the President's House, and public offices by the first Monday in December 1800, when the capital would move from Philadelphia.[2] The Residence Act of 1790 did not specify that the capital should be located in a new city or town, although that was the general understanding.[3]

The Creation of the Plan

The creation of the new capital was a complex process involving interactions between President George Washington, Secretary of State

Thomas Jefferson, planner Pierre Charles L'Enfant, commissioners of the new city, and land proprietors. The president was preoccupied with how to get the capital constructed within ten years without congressional funding. Jefferson took a more active interest in the substance of the design until his own scheme was rejected, whereupon he acceded to Washington's wishes for the plan. L'Enfant played the role of visionary designer, paying scant attention to the exigencies of the situation and thus allowing his imagination to take advantage of the opportunity. The fascinating story of the creation of the city plan is described well by the planning historian John W. Reps in the first two chapters of his book *Washington on View*.[4]

President Washington decided to commission Major Pierre Charles L'Enfant, a French engineer, to develop the plan for the new capital city. He was a man capable of grand visions but without a sense of practicality; he had an artist's temperament and was enamored of his own work. Jefferson's description of L'Enfant's assignment is quite mundane: "You are desired to proceed to George town where you will find Mr. Ellicot employed in making a survey and map of the federal territory. The special object of asking your aid is to have drawings of the particular grounds most likely to be approved for the site of the federal town and buildings."[5] There probably were other, unrecorded communications from Washington and Jefferson to L'Enfant regarding their aspirations for the design of the capital. In any case, L'Enfant had his own intentions for the new capital, which he began to effectuate.

Early in 1791 Andrew Ellicott began to survey the site for the new capital city, a small portion of the original area of one hundred square miles chosen by President Washington.[6] Benjamin Banneker, a free African American who was skilled in mathematics, was employed as assistant surveyor.[7] Pierre Charles L'Enfant initially assisted with the surveying in order to familiarize himself with the site, particularly its diverse topography. The site was composed of river flats leading to the Wicomico Terrace, which was surrounded by the Sunderland Escarpment.[8] Crossing the peninsula between the two rivers were Tiber Creek (also called Goose Creek) and Rock Creek and their tributaries.

Thomas Jefferson was very interested in the design of the new capital. He developed a sketch plan for the capital on the site of a platted Potomac River town called Hamburgh before L'Enfant announced his plan. Jefferson's sketch showed public walks along the north side of Tiber Creek between two primary public buildings. In addition to sites for the Capitol and the President's House, he proposed that blocks be reserved for offices, town houses, market houses, public walks, and a hospital.[9] Surrounding this federal precinct was an orthogonal grid of streets forming large blocks that could be extended as the city grew. Jefferson gave his sketch to the president, who sent it to L'Enfant, who condemned the extensive uniform grid as inappropriate for the topography. Yet, elements of Jefferson's scheme were included in the final plan, albeit on a grander scale and in a different location.

In spite of L'Enfant's condemnation of his plan, Jefferson was supportive of L'Enfant and intended not to interfere with his work. L'Enfant solicited Jefferson's advice regarding the public buildings and requested European city maps.[10] Jefferson lent him the maps but said nothing about

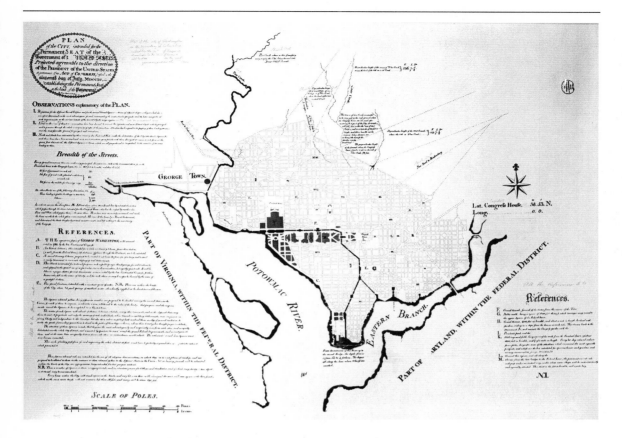

Fig. 1.1. Peter Charles L'Enfant, 1791 *Manuscript Plan for the City of Washington,* color facsimile (Washington, DC: U.S. Geological Survey, 1991). Library of Congress, Geography and Maps Division, 3730

the public buildings.[11] This is curious, since Jefferson held clear views about locating public buildings, which he tried to implement at Richmond, the state capital of Virginia. There he proposed separate buildings for the three branches of government (legislative, judicial, and executive), all to be located within the government precinct, making it the first state capital to physically express the American form of government.[12] By 19 August 1791, six months after he started work, L'Enfant had presented the president with a detailed plan, along with a report. This plan is what we now consider the L'Enfant Plan of Washington (fig. 1.1).

The commissioners proceeded with the sale of land that Washington had obtained from the original proprietors in exchange for city lots and ordered L'Enfant to have a map printed designating the east-west streets by letters of the alphabet and the north-south streets by numbers, both systems originating at the Capitol. They also determined that the capital would be called the City of Washington in the Territory of Columbia.[13] L'Enfant did not get the map printed in time, and the land sale went poorly. Events reached a crisis when L'Enfant had a house under construction demolished because it intruded six feet into one of the planned streets.[14] He also made no progress in designing the Capitol and the President's House, part of his original assignment, and he resisted the authority of the commissioners. Reluctantly, President Washington dismissed him in February 1792.

The surveyor Andrew Ellicott then assumed responsibility for drawing the revised city plan, aided by Thomas Jefferson's suggestions.[15] Elli-

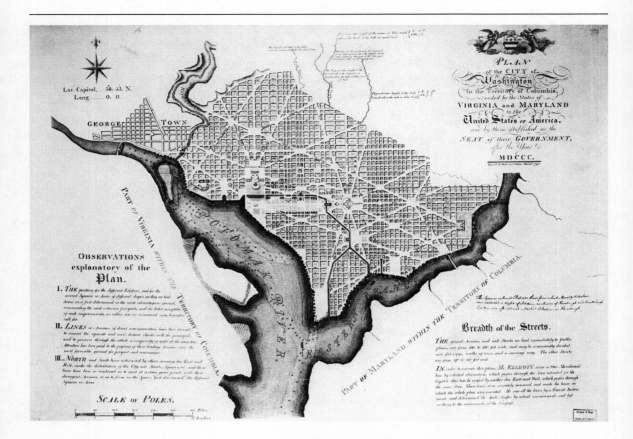

Fig. 1.2. Andrew Ellicott, *Plan of the City of Washington in the Territory of Columbia*, 1792. Library of Congress, Geography and Maps Division, 2440.1

cott drew this plan without the benefit of the original, which L'Enfant possessed. He added more landscape detail for the federal precinct and defined the shapes of all urban spaces (fig. 1.2). The most dramatic change was straightening Massachusetts Avenue, a long thoroughfare crossing the city from northwest to southeast. He also eliminated five short radial avenues and twelve civic spaces.[16] L'Enfant disagreed with these changes, but Ellicott said the road alignments would work better with the topography. Jefferson agreed with or suggested the simplifications made by Ellicott to eliminate open spaces and straighten Massachusetts Avenue. Unfortunately, he eliminated L'Enfant's name from the map, perhaps in retaliation, despite Washington's suggestion to keep it.

Based on Jefferson's scheme for a much smaller "town," as he called it, one can conclude that Jefferson was displeased with L'Enfant's monumental vision for the new capital. Yet he did not publicly criticize the adopted plan and acted to see it completed, becoming concerned with the architecture of the public buildings. Writing to L'Enfant on 10 April 1791, he advised: "Whenever it is proposed to prepare plans for the Capitol, I should prefer the adoption of some one of the models of antiquity, which have had the approbation of thousands of years, and for the President's House I should prefer the celebrated fronts of modern buildings, which have already received the approbation of all good judges. Such are the Galerie du Louvre, the Gardes meubles, and two fronts of the Hotel de Salm."[17] In Jefferson's view, good government did not depend upon a grand setting.[18] Perhaps not, but a grand setting can help to elevate the aspirations of

L'ENFANT'S LEGACY

lawmakers and the nation's citizens, as Washington undoubtedly believed when he approved L'Enfant's grand city plan for the capital.

By eliminating a dozen civic spaces Ellicott did not necessarily change the plan for the worse. Numerous urban places remained, which L'Enfant suggested should be defined by buildings bridging the streets to form gateways.[19] This would have created completely enclosed spaces resembling the European prototypes. Evidently L'Enfant recognized that it would be difficult to spatially define these urban places given the number of intersecting streets.

Washington waited until the end of his term of office to issue a proclamation designating the seventeen sites reserved for the federal government, totaling 541 acres (see the appendix).[20] These seventeen reservations formed the core of public space in the city. None of the squares or circles were part of this original federal land purchase. Along with others added over the years, the squares and circles became federal reservations as part of the street rights of way.

The L'Enfant Plan of Washington

The original plan, drawn in pencil in 1791 and now essentially illegible, is preserved in the Library of Congress. It has some colored areas—yellow for open spaces, red for buildings, and blue for water. For the two-hundredth anniversary of the plan the Library of Congress published both an exact-size, full-color facsimile and a computer-assisted reproduction of this original document. The latter is the plan reproduced here as figure 1.1. It contains numerous margin notations by L'Enfant, beginning with "Observations explanatory of the Plan":

I. The positions for the different Grand Edifices, and for the several Grand Squares or Areas of different shapes as they are laid down, were first determined on the most advantageous ground, commanding the most extensive prospects, and the better susceptible of such improvements as the various intents of the several objects may require.

II. Lines or Avenues of direct communication, have been devised, to connect the separate and most distant objects with the principal, and to preserve through the whole a reciprocity of sight at the same time. Attention has been paid to the passing of those leading avenues over the most favorable ground for prospect and convenience.

III. North and South lines intersected by others running due East and West, make the distribution of the city into streets, squares, etc, and those lines have been so combined, as to meet at certain given points with those divergent avenues, so as to form on the spaces "first determined," the different squares or areas, which are all proportional in magnitude to the number of avenues leading to them.[21]

Here L'Enfant explains how he derived the plan. He first chose the best locations for important buildings and squares and then connected them via avenues, which enabled them to be reciprocally viewed. Finally, he overlaid this network with a grid of streets oriented in the cardinal directions. The streets converged with the avenues at open-space nodes whose size was determined by the number of intersecting streets. The plan terminates at the base of the escarpment, which was then called Boundary Street and is now Florida Avenue.

The rationale for the layout of grid streets remains somewhat of a mystery. The streets vary in width and are spaced at varying intervals. Those spaced close together in both directions yield small blocks, whereas those spaced further apart yield larger blocks. The streets are more closely spaced on Capitol Hill, establishing its potential as a residential district. Certain streets were made wider and located to create axial relationships with squares or significant structures, such as K Street (Washington Circle and Mount Vernon Square), Eighth Street (national church), and Fourth Street (judiciary court). Sixteenth Street is the northern axial approach to the White House, connecting Scott Circle to Lafayette Square. North Capitol, South Capitol, and East Capitol streets, emanating from the dome of the Capitol, divide the city into four quadrants, with directional nomenclature used today: NE, SE, SW, and NW.

The most significant design feature of the plan for the nation's capital is the federal precinct. L'Enfant chose to locate the Capitol on the highest point, Jenkins Hill, with eight diagonal avenues leading to it. On its axis to the west is the "Grand Avenue," an esplanade four hundred feet wide lined with gardens and embassies. The President's House and park, intersected by six diagonal avenues, was located on a plateau with grounds sloping down to Tiber Creek. Thus the two most important buildings were linked formally through a series of gardens and functionally along the primary diagonal avenue. They were also geometrically linked by the two primary axes at right angles to each other, with Pennsylvania Avenue as the hypotenuse of the triangular figure. This is the hallmark of the plan, a monumental federal precinct that takes advantage of its topographic setting and its river location through grand vistas.

The manuscript plan also has an alphabetic key to certain features. *A* is an equestrian statue located at the intersection of the Capitol and White House axes. *B* identifies an itinerary column a mile from the Capitol on East Capitol Street, from which all distances on the continent would be measured. *C* is a naval itinerary column located on the Potomac River, and *D* is a nondenominational national church west of the proposed judiciary court to include monuments to heroes. *E* designates each of five grand fountains with a water spout, and *F* locates the grand cascade at the foot of Capitol Hill. *G* locates two public walks to the Capitol from the west. *H*, *I*, and *K* refer to the Grand Avenue, "President's Park," and a well-improved field, the series of contiguous open spaces that now comprise the Mall. *L* and *M* designate Capitol Square and the street leading to it, both to be lined with arcaded shops.

One of the most interesting aspects of the plan as it relates to the purpose of this book is the designation of squares as public open spaces:

> The squares colored yellow, being fifteen in number, are proposed to be divided among the several states in the union, for each of them to improve, or subscribe a sum additional to the value of the land . . . that purpose, and the improvements 'round the squares to be completed in a limited time.
>
> The center of each square will admit of statues, columns, obelisks, or any other ornaments, such as the different states may choose to erect; to perpetuate not only the memory of such individuals whose counsels, or military atchievments, were conspicuous in giving liberty and independence to the country; but also those whose usefulness hath rendered them worthy of general imitation;

to invite the youth of succeeding generations to tread in the paths of those sages or heroes, who this country has thought proper to celebrate.

The situation of these squares is such, that they are the most advantageously and reciprocally seen from each other, and as equally distributed over the whole city district, and connected by spacious avenues 'round the grand Federal Improvements, and as contiguous to them, and at the same time as equally distant from each other, as circumstance would admit. The settlements 'round those squares must soon become connected.

This mode of taking possession of, and improving the whole district at first, must leave to posterity a grand idea of patriotic interest which promoted it.[22]

The network of squares and circles numbered on L'Enfant's plan is among its most salient characteristics. There were fifteen appropriated squares because there were fifteen states in the union at the time. The states never adopted these squares, nor did the areas around them become colonies for residents from any given state. Rather they became the spatial centers of neighborhoods, serving as public parks.

Incorporated into L'Enfant's plan was a system for orderly growth and development that was to extend throughout the city. It would begin around several squares and then spread along the avenues. There would be a friendly competition among the various neighborhoods to attract residents and commercial enterprises. Federal buildings would also be distributed throughout the city so as to generate related functional districts. Evidently, L'Enfant was concerned that development would concentrate unduly near the federal precinct, which did initially occur, but over time squares located far away from the center became nodal points for neighborhoods. This system of distributed growth was farsighted, avoiding the congestion that comes with excessive concentration of a population.

Another important characteristic of this nodal system is the reciprocity of views: the squares provide points of orientation that are visible from other points of orientation. As places of identity in the spatial structure, they help residents and visitors find their way around the city. These park settings with fountains and statues are picturesque places in the urban fabric that create memorable images.

The squares and federal open spaces should not be considered in isolation from the network of avenues, which link the squares and circles together to form a coherent system of open spaces in "the city of trees." L'Enfant intended for the avenues to be seen as linear green spaces. They were designated to measure up to 160 feet wide, with 10-foot building setbacks and 30 feet for a walk under a double row of trees on either side of an 80-foot carriageway. Pennsylvania Avenue is the most important avenue because it connects the Capitol and the White House. But it also extends eastward through Seward and Eastern Market squares to the gateway bridge at the Anacostia River and westward around Washington Circle and over Rock Creek to Georgetown. Massachusetts Avenue parallels it to the north, connecting more public spaces—Dupont, Scott, Thomas, Mount Vernon, Columbus, Stanton, and Lincoln—than any other avenue. New York Avenue connects Mount Vernon Square to Lafayette Square, and Maryland Avenue connects Stanton Square to the

Capitol grounds. Connecticut Avenue relates Dupont Circle and Farragut Square to Lafayette Square, and Vermont Avenue relates Logan Circle, Thomas Circle, and McPherson Square to Lafayette Square.

Other notations to the plan establish the widths of streets and their layout, specifying that building lots would be perpendicular to the streets. Three churches are located, but burying grounds would be outside the city. A number of unappropriated squares are designated for colleges or academies. The plan has more than twenty additional open spaces in a variety of shapes at other intersections of the diagonal avenues, perhaps intended for appropriation by future states as the country grew in size.

The city plan is full of subtle features that may escape immediate notice, for example, the notched corners of Capitol Square and the civic square east of it, which form a transition to East Capitol Street, and the tapered street extending south from the Mall, which the early-twentieth-century urban designer Elbert Peets suggested was a grand water vista down a straight stretch of the Potomac River and may have been an earlier location for the President's House.[23] Another feature is the naval column that terminates the Eighth Street axis at the river. Some features that L'Enfant included in his astounding plan have been abandoned; others have not reached fruition two centuries later.

Almost immediately after the L'Enfant Plan was announced, the seemingly long distance between the President's House and the Capitol was criticized as unworkable for direct and efficient communication. But proximity could interfere with the operation of the legislature. L'Enfant explained that presidential messages should be delivered to Congress with decorum, thus requiring time and therefore distance.[24]

One common criticism of L'Enfant's plan is the lack of a prominent position in the scheme for the third branch of government, the judiciary. He did designate a judiciary court north of Pennsylvania Avenue near the Capitol, perhaps intended for the Supreme Court.[25] Did L'Enfant understand the importance of courts in the American system of government? At that time no one envisioned how important and powerful the Supreme Court would become two centuries later.

The plan for Washington can be placed in a category of city plans known as a network of squares. In the Mayfair, Bloomsbury, and Belgravia sections of London, England, a series of related squares was formed from the development of private housing estates. The plan of Philadelphia, Pennsylvania, has a large green square in each quadrant serving as a focal point for the neighborhood around it. The best city plan of this type is that of Savannah, Georgia, which has a square at the center of each twelve-block ward, or neighborhood. L'Enfant knew about all of these plans, and they likely influenced his design.

The most difficult aspects of L'Enfant's plan are the numerous awkward intersections between the diagonal avenues and the orthogonal grid, resulting in dangerous traffic junctions, parcels of unusual shape, disorderly relations of street wall planes, and difficulty in designing monumental buildings and shaping open spaces because of wide gaps between buildings.[26] These kinds of intersections are resolved in John Evelyn's third plan for rebuilding London after the Great Fire in 1666 and probably could have been resolved in L'Enfant's plan for Washington if he had had the opportunity.

L'Enfant's brilliant urban plan must be seen as a first draft since he never submitted a revised version. Speculation has focused on how he would have refined it. Would he have located additional public facilities facing the unappropriated open spaces? Could he have resolved the many awkward intersections of avenues and the grid to create better-defined open spaces?

The plan of Washington was inspired by the baroque concept of experiencing space through movement. The public spaces are outdoor rooms, avenues and squares defined by the walls of adjacent buildings. Modulation of these spaces—expansion through long vistas and contraction through visual closure—is the key to a memorable experience whether one is walking or riding at any of a variety of speeds. This baroque concept is difficult to achieve in Washington because the avenues are very wide in proportion to the heights of buildings abutting them, and the defining street walls of squares and circles have numerous interruptions. Axes are anchored by equestrian statues in the public reservations, not monumental buildings; one sees through these public spaces as in the squares of Savannah.

The L'Enfant Plan is without doubt one of the world's great urban plans. It bears this judgment after two centuries because of the inextricable relationships between its avenues, streets, building sites, and public spaces. They are ordered in a compositional structure that gives significance to a national capital. This composition was created in consort with the geographic circumstances of waterways and topography, utilizing the advantages of each to integrate plan and landscape. As Reps said of the plan, "L'Enfant thus brought elements of the natural landscape into the heart of the city. In doing so he combined garden and urban design in a civic composition of enormous scale, great complexity and almost bewildering variety. Although not without its faults, it surely ranks among the greatest of city plans in world history."[27]

Nineteenth-Century Development

The City of Washington developed slowly during its first few decades. L'Enfant's concept of distributed growth did not occur because there was no government money for all the necessary public improvements. Commercial development began on Pennsylvania Avenue, in the area of Center Market. Other growth concentrated around the Capitol and the President's House as private owners built lodging houses, shops, and dwellings. There were four types of housing: row houses (Wheat Row), villas with extensive gardens (Van Ness House), mansions with outbuildings (Octagon House), and temporary housing (boarding houses or hotels).[28] Government buildings included the Treasury Building, next to the White House, and the Patent Office Building and the Post Office on Eighth Street. These handsome white stone buildings designed by prominent architects dominated the red-brick residential areas. Buildings in the city were scattered, making it difficult to discern an urban pattern for the first half of the century. When Thomas Jefferson was president, he was concerned about the lack of a defined vista along Pennsylvania Avenue owing to a lack of buildings. To visually define the avenue, he planted rows of Lombardy poplars, which later were replaced with elms and other deciduous trees.[29]

Construction of City Hall at Fourth and D streets, NW, in 1820 was the first major departure from L'Enfant's plan. He had intended the municipal buildings to be located along the south leg of the canal (*E* on the plan), removed from federal buildings but near the port to better serve the city. The City Hall site was imposing, on a hill overlooking Pennsylvania Avenue on an axis with 4½ Street, which has a southern terminus at Greenleaf Point. The building is on the southern side of Judiciary Square, a location L'Enfant probably intended for the Supreme Court (see chapter 6).

The city continued to appear much as it had before the urban plan was conceived. The descriptions of visitors suggest that it looked like a distorted version of the hunting grounds at Versailles, a vast forest with angled avenues cut through it in a geometric maze. As Reps put it, "The scattered dwellings, the unbuilt-on public reservations, the streets that were muddy or dusty depending on the weather, the weed grown Mall, all contrasted markedly with the grandiose plan and the great area of the city. Visitors from home and abroad alike seldom failed to mock the pretensions of future grandeur held out by the supporters of the city and its imported plan."[30] Washington differed from other cities in that growth and development could not proceed ad hoc, following real estate economics or personal intentions. Everything had to follow the grand plan, resulting in an incomplete appearance for most of its first century.

British troops invaded the city during the War of 1812 and burned the federal buildings in August 1814. The White House, the Capitol, the War Building, the Treasury Building, and the Arsenal were burned, requiring almost complete restoration. The Navy Yard commandant destroyed that facility rather than have it fall into enemy hands. Spared were the Patent Office and the Post Office.[31]

Although the population continued to grow rapidly during the next two decades, visitors continued to comment on the lack of an urban appearance. Houses and public buildings were scattered over a large area lacking any sense of concentration. The city had no discernible street pattern or urban character. Constellations of buildings existed around the Navy Yard, the Capitol, the Patent Office, and the White House. By 1835 Pennsylvania Avenue was continuously lined with Federal-style row houses two to four stories high.[32] These were later combined to form hotels or office buildings. This avenue became the primary business corridor, lined with banks, newspaper offices, hotels, eating houses, and retail establishments.

Development of the Mall area, heretofore used for grazing, began in 1848 with the initiation of the Washington Monument and construction of the Smithsonian Institution the following year. Previously, the Botanic Garden had been created at the base of Capitol Hill. This development changed the concept of the Mall to an area of cultural institutions, not embassies as L'Enfant had intended.

In the early decades household water came from wells and springs in the public squares. Later, prosperous households had their own cisterns.[33] Built in 1853, the Washington Aqueduct, starting at Great Falls, on the Potomac River, provided a dependable water supply throughout the growing city. Due to geography, water was first available to the western and northwestern sections of the city, leaving the eastern sections with water shortages. Affluent citizens moved to areas with an adequate water supply, furthering patterns of social stratification that had begun with government officials' locating near the President's House and working-class residents' locating near the Navy Yard.[34]

During the initial decades of the nineteenth century most elected and appointed persons in the federal government resided in boarding houses and hotels. This started to change as affluent federal officials built permanent urban residences for the winter season. They brought their families to live in the city, necessitating places for education, worship, and entertainment. Following the Civil War, the city's cultural and scientific institutions, as well as certain departments of the federal government, attracted scientists, intellectuals, and artists to the city.

The extension of development to new areas depended on the transit system. Roadways continued to expand, and bridges were built over the Anacostia and Potomac rivers. Horse-drawn trolley lines were instituted in the early 1860s along Pennsylvania Avenue and Seventh, F, and Fourteenth streets.[35] By the 1880s the horsecar system provided public transit throughout the city. It was a democratic equalizer, utilized by everyone, including cabinet officials, congressmen, and generals.

The most complete and accurate survey of the city before the Civil War is the 1861 map by Albert Boschke (fig. 1.3).[36] It shows the concentration of development north of Pennsylvania Avenue between the White House and Capitol. Developed neighborhoods are also found west of the White House (Foggy Bottom), north of Mount Vernon Square (Shaw), and south of the Mall (Southwest). Otherwise, many blocks have only a few structures or are completely empty. Many of the streets, avenues, and parks existed only on the map, especially in the undeveloped areas.

During the Civil War, Washington was controlled by the military, which reallocated spaces and buildings for the war effort. Houses and office buildings around Lafayette Square became military headquarters, government buildings became hospitals, and parks were used as encampments. Prominent government buildings assumed value to the nation as patriotic symbols of the union. An extensive road network made the city vulnerable, as did the escarpment overlooking the city. Sixty forts and forty batteries were built to provide a line of defense in conjunction with the Navy Yard and the U.S. Arsenal, on the Anacostia River.[37] By the end of the war the city's permanent population was at least 50 percent larger than before the war because of government officials and freed slaves who had migrated there, finding it to be a safe haven. Affluent residents moved to higher ground, leaving the poor in row houses and alley dwellings near the rivers, resulting in further social and racial stratification.

The dispersed nature of the plan made the urban infrastructure expensive to develop and costly to maintain. The number of streets and their width far exceeded those in other cities. Even though the federal government owned all of the streets, the municipality was responsible for improving and maintaining them. Much of the urban land was owned by the federal government and exempt from property taxes, exacerbating the financial situation. The city government has been faced with this dilemma since its founding, having to continually negotiate with Congress for financial support to operate, develop, and maintain the nation's capital.

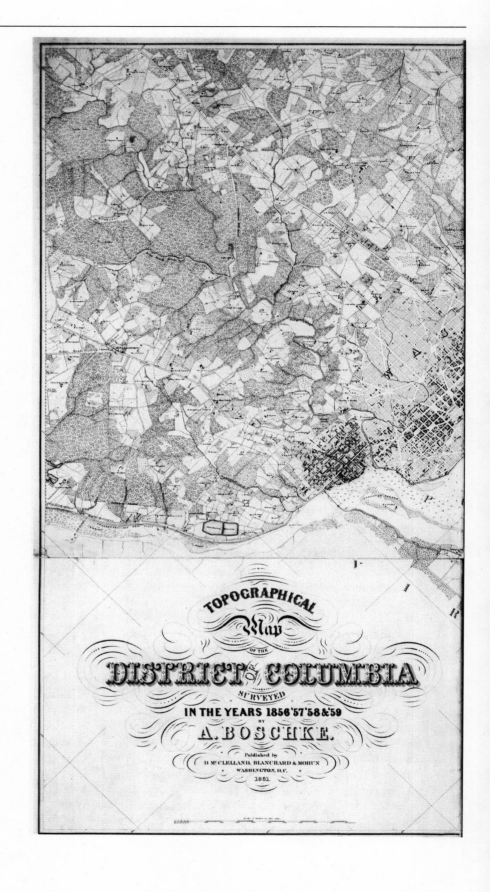

TOPOGRAPHICAL
Map
OF THE
DISTRICT OF COLUMBIA
SURVEYED
IN THE YEARS 1856 '57 '58 & '59
BY
A. BOSCHKE.
Published by
D. McCLELLAND, BLANCHARD & MOHUN
WASHINGTON, D.C.
1861.

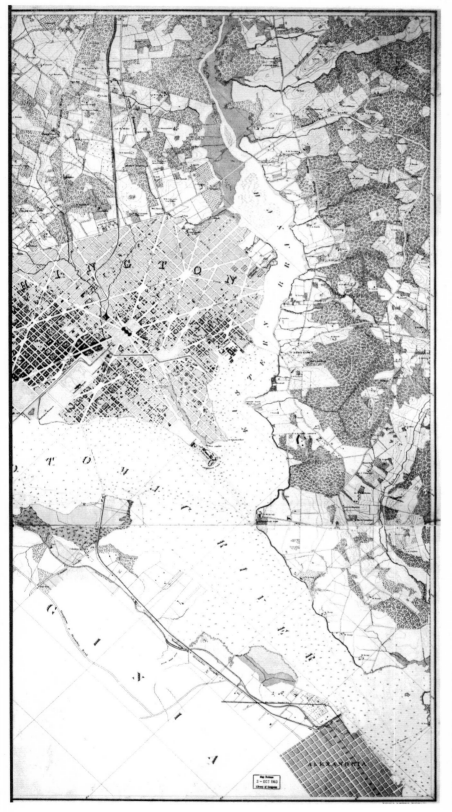

Fig. 1.3. A[lbert] Boschke, *Topographical Map of the District of Columbia, Surveyed in the Years 1856 '57 '58 & '59* (Washington, DC: McClelland, Blanchard & Mohun, 1861). Library of Congress, Geography and Maps Division, 1092

The District of Columbia had a territorial form of government from 1871 to 1874, with Alexander "Boss" Shepherd as the vice president of the Board of Public Works and later governor. As vice president, Shepherd had unparalleled power to undertake a comprehensive scheme of street and utility improvements, and he was relentless in his efforts. The streets were graded for the first time, so that sewer and water lines could be installed underneath them. At the same time, the privately owned gas company installed gas mains beneath the streets. Streetscapes were vastly improved by narrowing the carriageway and widening the tree lawn to make room for sixty thousand new street trees. In all, 119 miles of streets were paved and 38 miles of streets were graveled, 154 miles of curbs were installed, and 207 miles of sidewalks were laid. Many of the streets were paved with wooden blocks, as Pennsylvania Avenue had been earlier. Wooden blocks were not very durable and soon were replaced with granite blocks, concrete, or cobblestones.[38] The Washington Canal was encased in 3.5 miles of trunk sewer, with an additional 60 miles of street mains connected to 7 miles of interceptors.[39] This work was undertaken on a vast scale throughout the city, resulting in turmoil and frustration for the citizens. Costs escalated to four times the estimate, but the results were impressive. The territorial government was terminated in 1874, when Congress returned responsibility for city administration to three commissioners. Under Shepherd's brief direction, however, in both appearance and functioning Washington was vastly changed from a muddy village to a modern city.

Shepherd has been compared to Baron Haussmann in Paris, who had just completed the renovation of that city for Napoleon III. Frederick Gutheim summarizes Shepherd's influence as follows: "Shepherd did envision a physical plan that had exceeded in scale anything undertaken in the city since L'Enfant. Shepherd's legacy to the city was of consequence. In his concentration of effort on the business section of the city and on residential neighborhoods west of Capitol Hill, the eastern section of the city was ignored, reinforcing the pejorative characterization of that sector as limited to middle- and lower-income dwellings."[40] During this postwar era the Office of Public Buildings and Grounds of the Army Corps of Engineers improved many of the squares and circles throughout the central city by grading, seeding, fencing, planting trees and shrubs, placing walks, and providing utilities. The designs followed the picturesque tradition advocated by the landscape architect Andrew Jackson Downing, with curved paths in both symmetrical and asymmetrical patterns forming beds for flowers and shrubs.[41] Most parks had a watchman's lodge that had toilets for the public. Some parks featured fountains with sprays. Early wooden fences to keep out livestock were replaced by ornamental fences with cast-iron posts and heavy chains.

Many of these public reservations soon became locations for memorials to Union leaders: equestrian statues of generals and portrait statues of naval officers, both atop monumental granite pedestals. Usually private groups sponsored these memorials, chose the artists, and acquired authorization from Congress to use federal land. Site preparation and pedestals were paid for by the federal government.

The Mall had been developing on a project-by-project basis beginning with the Botanic Garden and the Smithsonian Institution. Chief of

Engineers O. E. Babcock drained the grounds around the Washington Monument, using the fill for the grounds south of the White House.[42] From 1882 to 1890 the Potomac River was dredged to form a shipping channel and tidal basin, with the fill used to create an extensive park area west and south of the Washington Monument. This was another major departure from the L'Enfant Plan, resulting in new public land that needed to be designed.

Capitol Hill is the vast area of the city on the plateau east of the Capitol (see chapter 9). The first residents were those who built the Capitol, followed by congressmen and their staffs living in boarding houses. In the decades after the Civil War the area of gridded streets burgeoned with the development of blocks of row houses with imaginative architectural variations. The area became home to black and white federal workers, who shopped at Eastern Market. This development was fostered by a permanent water supply in 1903, a water main supplied from the Howard University Reservoir, which in turn was supplied from the Potomac River above Great Falls.[43]

Twentieth-Century Development

At the turn of the new century Washington was in need of a renewed planning vision, particularly for the monumental core. The Mall area had developed as a series of uncoordinated buildings and grounds, with railroad tracks and a train station desecrating the city's most symbolic open space. Capitol Square was surrounded by mediocre residential and commercial development. Only the White House grounds and Lafayette Square were dignified, handsome landscaped settings, but they were unrelated to the Mall.

Many proposals were made to celebrate the centennial of the District of Columbia in the year 1900. Although nothing came of them, there was promise in the establishment of the Senate Park Commission, led by Senator James McMillan of Michigan, formed to study the park system and develop recommendations. When the commission finished its work in 1902, the city and country had a bold visionary plan for redesigning and expanding the monumental core and connecting it to a regional park system (see chapter 3).

The nation's capital needed to project an image of efficiency and power based on the physical expression of an ordered plan. The City Beautiful concept of the McMillan Plan was based on the design principles of ordered civic spaces formed by disposing monumental buildings in axial relationships. It was extended across the entire city to include parks, parkways, bridges, and streets, particularly those that served as entrances to the monumental core. The McMillan Plan, which demonstrated the value of sound urban planning, was intended to be a model of urban reform for the nation.

The vision of the McMillan Plan, which continued the design direction of L'Enfant's plan, received broad public and political support. In time the Mall was essentially completed according to this plan, including its westward extension to the Lincoln Memorial. The Jefferson Memorial was located on the White House south axis. Turning a large part of Capitol Square into the legislative complex was carried out as planned, but plans to make Lafayette Square the executive complex were only partly completed. The City Beautiful vision of neoclassical architecture in a sylvan landscape continues to reverberate in the present era, as seen in the dignified but conservative architecture of most federal buildings and many private ones.

The Public Buildings Act of 1926 was intended to complete more elements of the McMillan Plan, primarily the Supreme Court and the Federal Triangle. The latter was a large area, bounded by Pennsylvania Avenue, Constitution Avenue, and Seventeenth Street, around which the cross-axes of the L'Enfant Plan were formed. A tawdry area called "murder bay," it was focused on Center Market and the central post office. The McMillan Plan envisioned this area as a civic center, but instead it became home to the city's largest concentration of federal office buildings. The complex was well planned and designed (except for parking provisions), and it affirmed the presence of a strong federal core. It fostered the concept of government efficiency through coordination among departments.

The Federal Triangle supported the development of the Mall because it defined its northern edge and freed sites along the greensward for future museums. The actual reconstruction of the Mall and Union Square began in 1933 as a Public Works Administration project involving new roads, walkways, grading, and trees.[44] The Federal Triangle was deemed such a success that a similar area called the Northwest Rectangle was planned west of the White House bounded by E Street, Constitution Avenue, and Fifteenth and Twenty-third streets. This plan never received the same support or coordination. For example, instead of locating there, the War Department built the Pentagon in Virginia. The area along Constitution Avenue was claimed by a series of national organizations, leaving the remainder of the Northwest Rectangle for the General Services Administration, the Department of the Interior, and the State Department.

During the first few decades of the twentieth century the squares and circles were all redesigned following the neoclassical principles of the McMillan Plan, with symmetrical patterns of paths, hedges, and open lawns. This work was accomplished by Works Progress Administration labor under supervision of the National Park Service. Concrete coping replaced the post-and-chain fences around the parks, making them more accessible. New, classically inspired, iron urn-finial fences were installed around statues and flower beds to prevent pedestrian intrusion.[45] Victorian lodges were replaced with neoclassical lodges of the same design in several parks.

In the years between the two world wars the automobile began to establish its irreversible presence. Traffic congestion during the morning and evening rush hours was a daily event. If traffic was a big problem, parking was even worse. Curbside parking became ubiquitous, and parking garages disrupted the streetscape. In the 1920s people parked wherever they could, even on the White House grounds and the Mall.[46] Roads had to be redesigned for cars, widening them where possible. The nodal circles and squares became traffic bottlenecks, resolved by the construction of many underpasses. Street trolleys were discontinued in the 1950s, replaced by buses, which added to traffic congestion and air pollution.

After World War II the major planning issue became concentration versus dispersal. Suburbs of the District of Columbia in Virginia and

Maryland were rapidly drawing much of the resident population from the city. The concept of a compact federal core in the center of Washington was questioned for the first time. Large federal installations such as the Pentagon, the offices of the Central Intelligence Agency, the Bureau of Standards, Walter Reed Army Medical Center, and the National Institutes of Health were relocated to the suburbs, creating a new functional order. The polynucleated city envisioned by L'Enfant assumed another reality at a regional scale.

The downtown business district developed as a large zone bounded by Pennsylvania Avenue and M, Sixth, and Fourteenth streets in the northwest quadrant. F Street developed as Washington's primary shopping street, with its department stores and shops served by trolleys. After World War II, commercial development continued north to K Street, which became the primary commercial corridor, linking Mount Vernon, Franklin, McPherson, and Farragut squares and, to the west, Washington Circle. It became lined with office buildings built to the maximum height limit with street-level shops, restaurants, and services.

The 1950 comprehensive plan for the District of Columbia, developed by the nationally known planner Harland Bartholomew, was significant because of its highway component. It proposed three ring roads: an inner loop one mile from the White House, a middle loop three to five miles out, and an outer loop, or beltway, around the entire city six to ten miles out from the center. These roads would be connected by radial roads, nominally the avenues and their extensions. Mass transit was rejected owing to the low density of the city and the domination of the automobile.[47] Parts of the inner loop were realized with the Whitehurst Freeway and the Southwest/Southeast Freeway. The middle loop was never realized. The Beltway was completed in 1964 and exists today as one of the pernicious features of life in Washington. It is the source of almost constant reconstruction to try to improve its traffic-carrying capacity.

The 1950s were crucial for planning in the District of Columbia because the balance between the federal establishment and the private sector was seriously threatened. The role of planning itself was at stake because of the uncontrolled development taking place in the suburbs. There was a confrontation of values between the slowly evolving planned central city and the chaos of rapid growth in the outlying areas. In the view of the planner Frederick Gutheim, "What was at stake was the image of Washington, the entire metropolitan city regarded as a whole: its urban planning tradition of nearly two centuries, its careful regard for the natural setting and the continuity of its built environment, its specially designed entrances and carefully contrived vistas, its concept of parks and open spaces."[48] This observation was as true at the end of the twentieth century as it had been at midcentury.

The era of urban renewal impacted Washington primarily in the southwest quadrant, although there were renewal areas in Foggy Bottom and Adams Morgan as well. The plan for large-scale slum removal in the southwest by the architects Louis Justement and Chloethiel Woodard Smith received approval over the rehabilitation-and-infill plan of Elbert Peets.[49] The approved plan was based on closing streets to create superblocks of town houses and high-rise apartments around a town center. The Southwest/Southeast Freeway, connecting Fourteenth and South

Capitol streets, isolated this redevelopment area. Tenth Street became an esplanade linking the Mall with L'Enfant Plaza, crossing the railroad tracks and expressway, and terminating at Banneker Park, overlooking the waterfront.

Civil disturbances following the assassination of Reverend Martin Luther King Jr. in 1968 led to the destruction of property in African American neighborhoods along H, Seventh, and Fourteenth streets in the northwest quadrant. Community reconstruction efforts were soon initiated, resulting in new housing units and streetscape improvements.

The central portion of Pennsylvania Avenue exemplifies the tenuous bond between the federal city on the south side and the constituent city on the north side. At midcentury, it was a schizophrenic main street with an assortment of deteriorating hotels, office buildings, shops, theaters, and restaurants on one side and monumental neoclassical federal buildings on the other side. Planning for the renewal of Pennsylvania Avenue began when President John F. Kennedy commented on its dilapidated condition during his inauguration parade. Labor Secretary Arthur J. Goldberg began the renewal effort, but it was soon left to his assistant, Daniel Patrick Moynihan, to execute. Senator Moynihan became the long-term leader in this effort, providing political direction and civic inspiration for more than three decades.[50] He even moved into one of the apartments at Market Square as soon as they were completed. The 1964 visionary Pennsylvania Avenue plan, by Skidmore, Owings and Merrill, proposed the creation of a monumental corridor by redeveloping the north side of the street and completing the grand plaza of the Federal Triangle on the south side.

The redevelopment of Pennsylvania Avenue is one of the best recent examples of quality urban design in the District of Columbia. The Pennsylvania Avenue Development Corporation (PADC), a public-private entity formed in 1972 and given special powers, was charged with undertaking this process. In 1974 it produced its master plan, and in 1977 Congress provided the funds to carry it out. In two decades it leveraged public improvements to generate more than $1.5 billion in private investment.[51] PADC purchased sites in the twenty-one-block area, planned them, and sold or leased them to developers, who executed the PADC designs. The results are millions of square feet of offices, retail spaces, hotels, and apartments. PADC also redesigned the avenue's streetscape and seven public plazas. The only real failure was that it achieved only 50 percent of the housing goal.

The redevelopment of the avenue was a coming of age for the historic preservation movement in the city because the 1964 plan had called for demolition of all of the nineteenth-century buildings on the north side. Preserved and rehabilitated were the Willard Hotel, the National Theater, the Washington Star Building, and the Apex Building on the north side, as well as the District Building and the Old Post Office Building on the south side.

The north side of Pennsylvania Avenue accommodates an assortment of office buildings, mostly from the latter half of the twentieth century. They vary in their setback from the street line, their cornice height, and their facade materials. The most bombastic is the FBI Headquarters, a brutal concrete building with an inhospitable street-level facade. In terms

L'ENFANT'S LEGACY

of urban design, the most interesting is Market Square, comprising two buildings with curved, colonnaded facades that form a plaza for the Navy Memorial opposite the National Archives (see chapter 10).

The south side of the avenue was defined by the Federal Triangle projects of the 1930s, except for the eleven-acre gap behind the District Building, where the grand plaza was never completed. In 1998 the gap was filled by the ten-story Ronald Reagan Building, an international trade center. A primary intention of this project was to revitalize the federal precinct with a public pedestrian system and public-program components. It completes the Federal Triangle with an architectural statement of civic dignity.

The streetscape of Pennsylvania Avenue was also redone to form a visually handsome and dignified parade route with wide, brick paved sidewalks and new planters, lights, benches, and trees. Although there are now some street-level restaurants and shops, the primary design intention of visually unifying the schizophrenic nature of Pennsylvania Avenue has only partially succeeded. It is not yet a great or memorable street that can favorably compare with such streets in other major cities. A big part of the problem is the eight traffic lanes, which cannot be divided with a planting strip because all the street elements must be removable for the quadrennial inauguration parade.

The redevelopment of Pennsylvania Avenue has fostered the redevelopment of the old downtown north to Massachusetts Avenue. It is once again becoming a thriving neighborhood, with mixed-use projects in adapted historic buildings. Located in the center of this district is the MCI Arena, a new venue for professional basketball and hockey. Only one department store, Hecht's, remains amid efforts to bolster retail uses. Chinatown continues to exist as a distinct precinct as Gallery Place, a large, mixed-use project is built adjacent to it. Now this area is on the way to becoming a "living downtown," with cultural facilities, housing, and shops attracting a wide variety of residents, including artists, government workers, and professionals.[52]

Planning for Washington's subway system began in the 1960s, and in 2001, after thirty-two years of construction, it was substantially completed, with eighty-six stations and 103 miles of track.[53] The stations are well distributed throughout the downtown area, many located at the public squares, each bolstering adjacent real estate development. The Metro subway system represents a nodal development pattern similar to L'Enfant's but at a different geographic scale. With five lines extending into outlying communities along the radial corridors, the Metro has dramatically changed the way Washington functions. The stations are linked to bus and auto commuter routes, creating an extensive and efficient public transit system. Ridership is high and continues to grow, but the system continues to have financial difficulty. The biggest problem is the planning assumption that most trips would be between the center city and the suburbs, when in fact there are as many trips between suburban locations. This problem needs to be addressed in future public-transit planning and Metro line extensions.[54]

Construction of the Metro system wreaked havoc on the city's streetscape for many years. Some station entrances were located in public spaces; others were built into new or old buildings. One early policy deci-

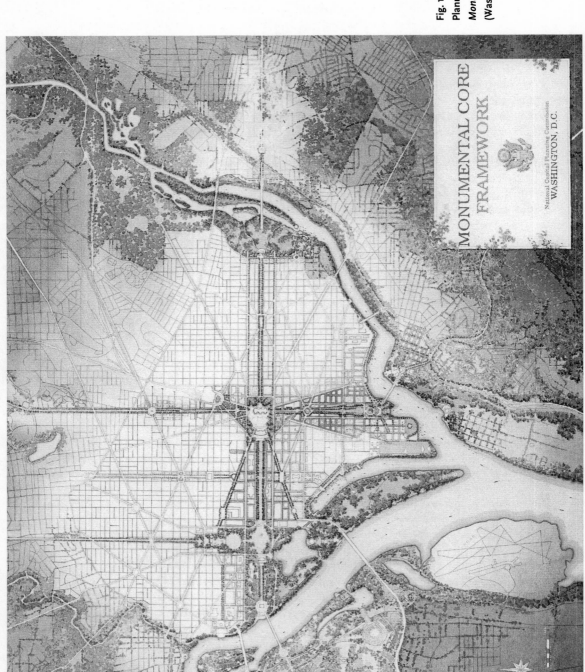

Fig. 1.4. National Capital
Planning Commission,
Monumental Core Framework
(Washington, DC, 1997)

sion was to make the underground stations alike in design to project a consistent image. The exemplary design scheme created by the Chicago architect Harry Weese featured barrel vaults of coffered concrete with subdued indirect lighting. The underground stations, free of advertisements, have an aura of uncluttered tranquility. Excellent maintenance has reduced litter and graffiti, and consistent policing keeps crime to a minimum. Washington's Metro system is not like subways in other cities; it bespeaks the decorum one expects in the nation's capital. The depth of the stations below ground has caused many maintenance problems with the long escalators. This should be alleviated when canopies are installed over the entrances to keep out precipitation.

Although the role of the federal establishment as an employer in the Washington region has been waning, its economic influence will always continue to dominate. Office growth in the city has boomed in the last two decades as lobbyists, organizations, law firms, and research groups have sought a presence near the seat of federal government. Many of these new buildings surround and define the squares and circles, as well as the K Street corridor and Pennsylvania Avenue. Now corporate headquarters for aerospace, communications, and computer technology are locating in the region, mostly in the suburbs. As Frederick Gutheim concludes, "However one defines growth or city building difficulties, Washington suggests measurable success in the chief problem, maintaining the metropolitan city itself as a unity and securing from one historical period to another, continuity over nearly two centuries."[55]

Extending the Legacy

In 1997 the National Capital Planning Commission (NCPC) announced its twenty-first-century plan for Washington, entitled *Extending the Legacy,* which recenters the city on the Capitol and its axes. As described by the NCPC, "Extending the Legacy represents the third act in a continuing planning drama that began over 200 years ago, when President George Washington commissioned Pierre L'Enfant to lay out the new capital. Like the L'Enfant and McMillan plans, it looks ahead 50 to 100 years. And like them, it offers a framework for future development."[56] The plan builds upon the maxims of the McMillan Plan by reinforcing the significance of the monumental core via the elimination of expressways and railroad tracks and the enhancement of public transit (fig. 1.4). It establishes guidelines for accommodating new museums, memorials, federal buildings, and embassies and invigorating the extensive natural waterfront.

Extending the Legacy expands the concept of the monumental core east, north, and south along the axes of the Capitol. South Capitol Street would be developed as a new gateway into the city, with a prominent new location for the Supreme Court on a waterfront site at its southern end. This relocation of the Supreme Court could revitalize the historic neighborhoods on the southeast side of the Anacostia River when the freeway there is placed below grade, providing access to the waterfront. North Capitol Street would continue to develop as a tree-lined boulevard. East Capitol Street would become a link to an ecological park along the Anacostia River, with the existing stadium site becoming a major memorial location. New federal office buildings along these corridors would incorporate mixed uses so as to enhance streetscape activity.

The area along the Anacostia River south of M Street would be a focal point for redevelopment. An estimated five thousand employees have been added at the Navy Yard, and expansion has begun at the adjacent Southeast Federal Center with construction of the new Department of Transportation, accommodating another five thousand employees. These employment centers are fostering adjacent private commercial and housing development that could easily extend to the south side of the river. A proposed new baseball stadium on south Capitol Street would provide additional development opportunities.

One of the planning themes is to connect the city to the waterfront to make it useful for passive recreation and events. The waterfront, most of which is now owned by the government, would become a continuous open space from Georgetown to the National Arboretum. Similar urban design trends are occurring in other river cities, such as Providence, Cincinnati, Boston, and Pittsburgh. A water-taxi system would create a new mode of functional and recreational transit between popular points along both sides of the two rivers. One such stop would be at the Kennedy Center, where a new plaza will create riverfront access. A new transit system called the "circulator" would carry tourists and commuters around the monumental core above ground on electric-powered vehicles connected to other transit stops.

In the southwest quadrant the goal is to improve access to a redeveloped waterfront. The Southwest/Southeast Freeway would be removed, and railroad tracks would be laid underground. This would allow historic streets in the L'Enfant Plan—Maryland, Virginia, and Delaware avenues and F Street—to be restored, creating numerous new development sites.

Preserving and enhancing the Mall by limiting the number of memorials is another of the planning themes. The NCPC's subsequent Memorials and Museums Master Plan proposes thirty-eight new sites, many along the waterways and none along North Capitol and South Capitol streets as originally proposed.[57] These sites have the potential to foster new stores, hotels, and restaurants in locations not currently frequented by tourists.

Extending the Legacy relates well to its two predecessor plans, building upon their themes. It seeks to correct a perceived weakness in both plans, providing a location for the Supreme Court that is symbolically equal to those for the executive and legislative branches of government. The proposed site at the end of South Capitol Street may be compromised by plans for a new baseball stadium just north of this location. L'Enfant's plan had an active waterfront since it was necessary for transit and commerce; the McMillan Plan did not enhance the waterfront except as it related to new memorials. A beautiful and vital waterfront that is physically and visually accessible could be the grandest vision of the twenty-first-century plan. The NCPC has since undertaken more detailed studies of waterfront development in six areas along the two rivers.

Extending the Legacy is a bold and visionary plan to guide the future development of the city. The long-term participatory planning process has garnered support from many constituencies, especially politicians. Like its predecessors, this plan will take decades to enact, and this test of time will demonstrate its validity. The recommended economic development corporation to provide leadership and funding has not been initiated. As the plan concludes, "Fears that visionary plans such as Legacy are too expensive and cumbersome, a distraction from the urgent business of making cities safe and livable, evaporate when compared with the extraordinary benefits that such planning has already bestowed on Washington. The capital is the product of bold plans, conceived in optimism and carried out with conviction. Inertia is the agent of urban decay. Cities that cannot anticipate the future will be run over by it."[58]

A large-scale urban design initiative that the twenty-first-century plan did not anticipate was brought about by the September 11 terrorist attacks on the World Trade Center and the Pentagon in 2001. Since that event security has become a primary concern in Washington. City streetscapes have been cluttered by a multitude of temporary security measures in the form of concrete vehicular barriers, guard stations, and concrete bollards, which are visually offensive and disrupt the pedestrian environment.

Utilizing appropriate urban design measures, an Interagency Security Task Force developed a comprehensive approach to providing perimeter security to buildings.[59] The primary intent is to prevent a bomb-laden vehicle from approaching these buildings; security issues in the buildings themselves are not addressed. On-street parking spaces would be removed and replaced by parking garages. The plan employs a kit of parts for replacing existing street furniture with reinforced planters, benches, light poles, parking meters, and drinking fountains. These would be placed less than forty inches apart so as to create a continuous vehicular barrier on required streets, including Pennsylvania Avenue from the White House to the Capitol. Low walls at curbside, along with rows of bollards, would be installed in the Federal Triangle. The devil is in the details: what will this security system look like when it is completed? If this plan is implemented, it will prevent the vast majority of attacks that take the form of past terrorist attacks, but it will not prevent other forms of terrorist activity. The architect Roger K. Lewis believes that the greatest value will be the placebo effect, the psychic comfort that comes from reduced fear.[60] Specific security design schemes have been developed for the major monuments and federal sites.

Recognition of the power of L'Enfant's brilliant plan for the city has been a long time coming. Much of the city was completely built at a residential scale by the turn of the twentieth century, and most of the lots had been built upon. For the first time all of the spaces and streets were defined by buildings. Much of the city has been rebuilt since then, and at a denser scale, one even better suited to L'Enfant's grand vision (fig. 1.5). But the city is not yet completed; many blocks and sites await redevelopment. It will never be completed because the city is a changing entity utilizing the capacity of its visionary plan to adapt to new realities.

Planning is far more complex in Washington than in most cities because of the federal government's role. The NCPC and the U.S. Commission of Fine Arts exercise strong control. Committees of the U.S. Congress must approve major planning initiatives and provide funding. After languishing for many years, local planning has been reactivated under Mayor Anthony Williams. There is also a great deal of politics—federal and local, business and civic, neighborhood and personal.

Ultimately, the problem with open-space planning in Washington is that it is federal land surrounded and served by local infrastructure. All

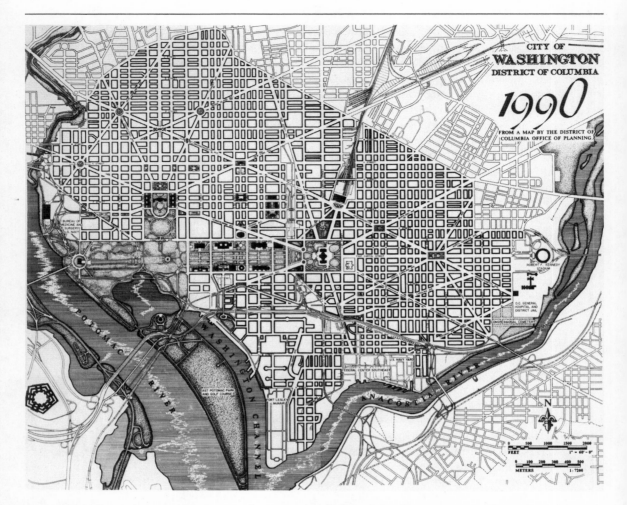

CITY OF
WASHINGTON
DISTRICT OF COLUMBIA
1990
FROM A MAP BY THE DISTRICT OF
COLUMBIA OFFICE OF PLANNING

Fig. 1.5. Plan of the City of Washington, 1990. Library of Congress, Prints and Photographs Division, HABS No. DC 612-22

of the reservations are owned by the federal government and maintained by the National Park Service. The surrounding streets are also owned by the federal government but maintained by the District of Columbia. The reservations are protected by the National Park Service Police, whereas the streets are protected by the Metropolitan Police. These jurisdictional situations require extensive planning coordination for improvements and funding cooperation for maintenance (see the conclusion).

Embodied Democratic Ideals

The democratic form of American government is a balance of powers among the legislative, executive, and judicial branches. The monumental core of Washington is based on the triangular relationship between the Capitol, the White House, and the Washington Monument. The most important public building, the Capitol, is given prominence by its location on the highest hill, with no building higher than the dome. This hierarchy is preserved by enforcement of a strict ordinance limiting building height. The Capitol is more than a mile from the second most important public building, the White House. These two sites symbolically express the balance of power between the legislative and executive branches of government. The ceremonial connection along Pennsylvania

L'ENFANT'S LEGACY

Avenue also expresses the separation of power with reciprocal views. The western vista from the Capitol along the Mall anticipates the country's growth and expansion; the southern vista from the White House aligns with a long stretch of the Potomac River, providing a direct view to the seat of political power for those approaching the city on the river. The intersection of the western axis of the Capitol and the southern axis of the White House locates the monument to George Washington, the military leader of the Revolutionary War and the first president.

Many questions have been raised regarding the lack of an equally prominent site for the judicial branch of government. Reps says that Thomas Jefferson could have corrected this oversight if he had responded to L'Enfant's request to locate the "number and nature" of public buildings.[61] L'Enfant proposed a judiciary court on a hill north of Pennsylvania Avenue, but Congress did nothing to provide a courthouse, forcing the Supreme Court to meet in the Capitol. There it remained until 1935, when the present neoclassical building was constructed across from the Capitol on First Street, NE, not a very important location and one too near the Capitol to express a balance of powers. Speculation regarding this longstanding issue focuses on the early Supreme Court's lack of equal political status. *Extending the Legacy,* the twenty-first-century plan, proposes a new prominent site for the Supreme Court at the end of South Capitol Street, a location that would physically express the balanced constitutional triangle of powers.

The government draws its authority from the people, who are represented by the constituent city, the largest land area in Washington. Along the Grand Avenue (the Mall) L'Enfant proposed a public walk, "all along side of which may be placed play houses, rooms of assembly, academies and all such sort of places as may be attractive to the learned and afford diversion to the idle."[62] He was trying to make a city that would be both beautiful and convenient for the residents, an expression of respect for their important role in a democracy. The system of walkways and gardens of the Mall connected to the White House grounds and Capitol Square form an egalitarian place for the general public to recognize their equality as citizens of a constitutional democracy.

L'Enfant envisioned a capital city where the public buildings of government would be integrated with the functional city of the people. He intended the Capitol to be surrounded by shops extending along East Capitol Street. The functional connection between the Capitol and the President's House would be Pennsylvania Avenue, where the government precinct on the south side would be contiguous with the constituent city on the north side.

The L'Enfant Plan includes proposed locations for other functional elements, such as markets, academies, colleges, and churches. There is even a proposed site for a national church: "This Church is intended for national purposes, such as public prayer, thanksgiving, funeral orations etc. and assigned to the special use of no particular Sect or denomination, but equally open to all."[63] This is a most interesting proposal because it indicates his awareness of the First Amendment to the U.S. Constitution, which prohibits Congress from making laws establishing religion.

L'Enfant's constituent city was planned as a series of squares as neighborhood centers linked by avenues forming a network of public space.

Here the residents could meet to acknowledge their common bond and purpose, their sense of being a community of equal citizens. The reciprocal views related each neighborhood to the larger community of the entire city. The network of diagonal avenues was overlaid by a functional network of streets arranged in an orthogonal grid with differentiated spacing. This facilitated freedom of movement to encourage both commercial and social exchange. Both networks were without hierarchy, creating an equal and abundant distribution of access potential and development opportunity.

But L'Enfant's squares were not intended solely for the residential neighborhoods. He proposed that they be dedicated to the states of the Union, with statues, columns, or ornaments in the center, thus politicizing them. They served as lively neighborhood social centers until after the Civil War. Then the federal government assumed greater control of the squares by permitting veterans and special-interest groups to place memorials dedicated to military or political heroes. Since most of these memorials are dedicated to Civil War generals, they also served the political purpose of the Union in proclaiming victory. Their presence produced an inherent tension between the neighborhood and the federal government, which supported their placement. The squares now had a monumental role in the nation's capital that detracted from and compromised their social role as community places.

Unfortunately, the baroque axial scheme that L'Enfant proposed for the new national capital had its precedents in the absolutist capitals of Europe, such as Louis XIV's Paris or Pope Sixtus V's Rome. The American task was to disassociate this urban design from its historical connotations, to utilize it in a new way to express the ideals of a new democratic republic. Spiro Kostof points out that the grid city form is equally undemocratic since it has been utilized by absolute, royal, and utopian forms of government. It is best seen as a practical, functional planning device that rapidly initiates urban land development and transfer of ownership.[64]

Embodied in L'Enfant's plan for the capital city are the political ideals of the new nation. Many of these urban design intentions were not written or discussed by the nation's founders. Yet they are expressed in the plan that has guided development of the capital city for more than two centuries. They are so embedded in this urban plan that many are not recognized without explicitly focusing on their existence, a testimony to the value of L'Enfant's enduring legacy to America.

CHAPTER TWO

PUBLIC SPACE AND DEMOCRATIC IDEALS

Spatial Rights, The U.S. Constitution,
Memorials and Politics

FREEDOM OF RELIGION; freedom of the press; freedom of person under the protection of the habeas corpus; and trial by juries impartially
selected—these principles form the bright constellation which has gone
before us, and guided our steps through an age of revolution and refor-
mation.

THOMAS JEFFERSON, First Inaugural Address, 4 March 1801

Urban public space in a democratic society mediates relationships between individual citizens and between these citizens and the state. Some
of these relationships are legally codified in the U.S. Constitution. Others
are spatial rights implied by the principles of democracy. Their basis is
the fundamental understanding of public versus private, aspects of the
public common and the private household. As Hannah Arendt elucidates
in her insightful book *The Human Condition,* there cannot be a public
realm without there first being a secure private realm, a household where
basic human needs are achieved. Only then can man become a social or
political animal in public through action and speech.[1]

Spatial Rights

Providing for democratic user rights and values is one of the most
significant purposes of public spaces in a democratic society. The freedom to engage in public life is a basic American democratic right, the
resultant of a free society. As stated in a book entitled *Public Space:* "With
the assembly of people, a sharing and unity are possible that can give
expression to communal feelings and an exercise of rights, sometimes
leading to political action."[2] I am concerned here with the spatial rights
of access, freedom of action, and claim as outlined in that book.[3]

Public spaces are freely accessible to all people all of the time. Access
can be physical, visual, or symbolic, types that are interrelated. Physical access might be available but involve restrictions such as fencing or
busy streets. In the 1870s the seemingly benign issue of fences around
the public reservations became divisive. The chief of engineers installed
high iron or wooden fences around the squares and circles in Washington, D.C., wherever and whenever possible. Without fences, cows, chickens, and dogs ran wild, destroying ornamental plantings and disrupt-
ing use of the parks. Without fences, youths went into the parks at night
to cause damage and disrupt the peace. But the fences did not promote
the democratic ideal of free access to public places for all citizens. The

U.S. Congress debated this issue in a bill in 1877 requiring removal of the fences because "these grounds are committed to the care of the people."[4] Comparisons were made with public spaces in other countries that did not have fences. But the bill failed, and the fences remained for some time before they were removed to create the freedom of access we now enjoy.

Visual access is a paramount concern for safety, to be balanced against the desire for seclusion. The landscape design in Washington's public reservations has dramatically changed since the nineteenth century, when dense foliage up to eye level defined secluded outdoor spaces. The landscape design strategy has since evolved to leave the understory open, with tree limbs pruned high to permit easy visual surveillance by individuals or police. It now may be difficult to find areas of seclusion for privacy, but personal security has improved.

Symbolic access relates to freedom of inclusion, a welcoming ambiance. Its denial is communicated through the presence of inimical groups or guards, both making one wary of free use. Thus, homeless persons or groups of teenagers may implicitly prohibit some individuals from using a park. Women, the elderly, and children are particularly sensitive to these aspects of symbolic access.

Freedom of action is conditional, based on responsible use of the space following rules of conduct. The lack of posted regulations in Washington's public reservations is a good thing, granting users a sense of freedom, although the regulations are still in effect. Although freedom of speech is honored, National Park Service regulations are in effect. These regulations were first developed to cope with demonstrators who camped in Lafayette Square for weeks on end, impinging upon the rights of other users. The National Park Service decided to restrict the size of signs and the duration of protests. For larger political demonstrations a group must first obtain a permit, which specifies restrictions as to location and timing. Spontaneous political demonstrations are now only possible in municipal public spaces (the streets), but still with the risk of arrest.

Spatial control or claim is another aspect of user rights: who actually uses the space? Ideally, public space is freely accessible, but realistically it may be controlled by certain groups at certain times. This is a form of territoriality, a basic human instinct, which can be practiced even in public places, albeit on a temporary basis. Groups such as joggers, dog walkers, children with caretakers, or elderly men lay claim to certain areas of a park at certain acknowledged times of the day. These groups may informally negotiate occupation of certain areas of a park, or they may all use the same area but at different times of the day or week. On a larger scale, the neighborhood may lay claim to the space and protect it through security watches or improvement initiatives. The residential squares of Capitol Hill are spaces that promote neighborhood identity and are used primarily by nearby residents. They are territorial places.

Public spaces can foster meaningful social relationships by providing opportunities to participate in communal activity. Encounters with strangers in public settings can vitally contribute to people's development of self-identity. Public spaces afford a supportive context in which diverse cultural groups can encounter one another. Stereotypes are diminished, allowing people to respond to others who are different from them, creating temporary human bonds. Public spaces can acquire positive communal meaning, encouraging the formation of an egalitarian society. They reinforce cultural norms of tolerance between disparate economic and social groups.

The U.S. Constitution

The U.S. Constitution enumerates the civil rights of citizens, set forth primarily in the first ten amendments, the Bill of Rights, ratified collectively in 1791. These amendments enumerate the individual rights of citizens guaranteed by the national government (by 1791 many state constitutions already had their own bill of rights). These rights can be considered moral claims or entitlements, that is, human rights. The Bill of Rights acknowledges the government's respect for its citizens by according legal protection of their unalienable rights. Rights also imply duties; each has consequences, and none are absolute.[5] Twenty-seven civil rights are enumerated in the Bill of Rights. Additional rights are granted by subsequent amendments. The primary rights related to actions or privileges in public spaces are examined here.

Amendment I applies most directly to the freedoms we enjoy in public spaces: "Congress shall make no law respecting an establishment of religion, or prohibiting the free exercise thereof; or abridging the freedom of speech or of the press; or the right of the people peaceably to assemble and to petition the Government for a redress of grievances."

Freedom of religion is directly expressed in many of Washington's public spaces by religious structures facing them. The gathering of worshipers before and after services often expands into the squares and circles. The separation of church and state is a corollary of Amendment I, but special permits are granted for religious services held in the public parks. Religious services have been held at Stanton, Judiciary, Lincoln, Franklin, Lafayette, and Rawlins parks.[6]

Freedom of speech and assembly is witnessed in the countless demonstrations, rallies, parades, and festivals held in Washington's public spaces. These all have an implicit or explicit agenda to influence government policy or public opinion. Democracy in America begins and ends with the power of the people, as Alexis de Tocqueville argues in his highly regarded book: "In our day, the spirit of the city seems to me inseparable from the exercise of political rights."[7] Public opinion in a democracy is very influential in guiding the actions of elected representatives. Thus, public opinion needs to be made known to them through meetings and public forums, which are most effective when they occur in public spaces. The true functioning of a democracy requires debate and discussion to select government leaders and influence legislation. Freedom of speech and of the press is one of the strongest characteristics of American society, acknowledging the capacity of the citizenry to engage and challenge the government. The right of assembly is essential to a democratic society based on the free exchange of information and ideas.

During the unpopular Vietnam War in the 1960s and early 1970s the public spaces of Washington were in use continuously for demonstrations and protests. These events occurred primarily in Dupont Circle, Lafayette Square, Capitol Square, and West Potomac Park, in full view of the elected leaders of government. Reports of these events on television and in newspapers helped shape public opinion and thus public policy regarding the war. In recent years these public spaces and others have been increasingly utilized to protest government policies on a wide variety of social and political issues. A march down Pennsylvania Avenue or a rally on the Mall brings high visibility and prestige to a group and its cause.

The right to freedom of assembly was intended for political purposes, but it also enables citizens to gather for social reasons. Among the most democratic events in the public reservations of Washington are the numerous ceremonies celebrating holidays—Independence Day, Labor Day, Washington's Birthday, Columbus Day, Decoration Day, Navy Day, Flag Day, May Day.[8] These celebrations were very popular during the 1920s and 1930s, when they were marked by parades, speeches, fireworks, and concerts. Ceremonies were also held at specific memorials especially the Grant Memorial, at the east end of the Mall. At some reservations there were Christmas trees, community singing, and tree dedications. Many such events continue to the present day. For example, Inauguration Day is actively celebrated every four years.

The Grand Army of the Republic, a Civil War Union veterans' organization, was a powerful patriotic force in the aftermath of this terrible conflict. In addition to sponsoring numerous statues and memorials in the city, it held encampments, or reunions, in the public reservations, which were authorized by Congress and the secretary of war.[9] These began in 1866 and continued until almost all the veterans had died. They were held primarily on the White Lot (White House grounds), on the grounds of the Washington Monument, and in Lafayette Square. In 1892 they centered on Garfield Park, where ten large wooden buildings and a number of tents were erected. The numerous encampments of Civil War veterans were both social and political events.

Freedom of speech includes symbolic speech (e.g., performances) and commercial speech (e.g., signs and advertisements). Free summer band concerts have been held in the city's public reservations for many decades. First formally scheduled in 1904, they have featured the U.S. Army Cavalry Band from Fort Myer, the Engineer Band from the Washington Barracks, and the U.S. Marine Band. One could attend a band concert every evening in one of the following parks: Dupont Circle, Iowa Circle, Franklin Park, Judiciary Park, the Smithsonian grounds, Garfield Park, Lincoln Park, the Capitol grounds, or the White House grounds.[10] The tradition of Marine Band concerts on Wednesday afternoons on the Capitol grounds and Saturday afternoons on the White House grounds began long before 1904. In the 1920s the band concerts increased in number to more than one hundred, with additional neighborhood band concerts. Some of these concerts continue to the present day.

Freedom of expression applies to aesthetics and art, as seen in the variety of architectural designs surrounding public spaces and the variety of memorials in them. The complete exercise of freedom in architectural design is lawfully restricted in the City of Washington. Numerous historic districts require aesthetic review of building designs to ensure compatibility. The U.S. Commission of Fine Arts reviews the designs of all public and private buildings facing public reservations. Other design restrictions are applied according to the provisions of the zoning and building codes.

L'ENFANT'S LEGACY

Amendment IV of the U.S. Constitution proclaims "the right of the people to be secure in their persons, houses, papers, and effects, against unreasonable searches and seizures." This is a right to privacy of one's person and property unless search warrants are legally obtained. Although privacy is not mentioned in the Bill of Rights, it is strongly implied by many stipulations. One's home is one's castle, although one's office may not be protected from intrusion. Personal privacy is an essential freedom that allows one to occupy public places without fear of confrontation by government officials or others.

After the Civil War, the park watchmen in Washington spent most of their time caring for the grounds and the park users. As the city developed and the density increased, they became more concerned with protecting citizens and enforcing rules, especially in the evening. They performed a useful function in maintaining order and mediating disputes. In 1904 they were upgraded to park policemen and given uniforms, revolvers, and bicycles so that they could be more effective in enforcing laws. The Office of Public Buildings and Grounds annual reports provide lists of arrests, mostly for disorderly conduct, drunkenness, trespassing, vagrancy, indecent exposure, violating park regulations, or fast driving of horses.[11] Persons of objectionable character were ejected from the parks, an action that ignored personal rights.

Amendment V stipulates that no person shall "be deprived of life, liberty, or property, without due process of law; nor shall private property be taken for public use without just compensation." The condemnation of private property for public use (eminent domain) must be justly compensated. Liberty of contract enables the ownership of private property for commercial activity in buildings that front public spaces. These property rights are subject to certain rules and regulations for the common good. Zoning laws establish relationships between public and private property to create a coherent physical community, and building codes protect public health, safety, and welfare.

Amendment VI guarantees the right to a speedy and public trial. Trials are open to the scrutiny of the general public or the press to protect those on trial and the integrity of the judicial process. The location of courthouses on or in public places assures this right, enabling the people and the press to assemble and discuss the judicial proceedings.

Amendment XIV guarantees "equal protection of the laws," which is interpreted by the courts to include equal access to all public places, thus denying all forms of segregation.[12] Equal access is demonstrated in the public spaces of a city, which are common ground freely accessible to all people all of the time. This basic definition of public space guarantees accessibility subject only to limited restrictions such as laws against loitering or soliciting. Americans' equality as citizens means that their relationships in public are symmetrical and reciprocal: communication can be initiated by either party in an encounter. The very presence of public space is an expression of our equality as citizens.

Memorials and Politics

The plethora of memorials in the nation's capital is among the most visible expressions of the right to freedom of speech. Every memorial has a message and an intended audience. That message was intended by those who sponsored the memorial and those who allowed it to be installed on government property, thus making it a public monument. The memorial may tell us more about the sponsors than about the subject, for example, why they created the memorial and how they got it approved and constructed. But the original message may be lost in history and/or reinterpreted by future generations. Memorials with specific messages do not allow reinterpretation and thus often fade into obscurity. Universal memorials that speak through metaphor allow future generations to view them with fresh eyes, making their message new again. Memorials do not necessarily seek to achieve consensus; they may be intended to provoke debate.

Memory is individual, but commemoration belongs to a community. It is a public action requiring public space for its realization. It usually requires an object, such as a statue, a plaque, or a sculpture, to signify the person or event being commemorated, and after that object is placed and dedicated, it becomes valued. Naming can also be a form of commemoration. Usually when the statue of an individual was placed in a Washington public reservation, the reservation too was named after that person.

A memorial is a public place in the city, not a mere object. Its location in relation to other monuments, open spaces, avenues, or public buildings indicates its significance. It requires access for contemplation and distance for viewing, as well as space for gathering during public ceremonies. Successful memorials engage us in reflection through evocative form or significant inscriptions. They can also have an educational purpose, reminding us of historical figures or events that have been forgotten. In this way, memorials represent a continuum, contributing to the repository of buildings and places that constitute the historical city. They help Americans celebrate their democratic values and form civic identity.

Many memorials were dedicated in the District of Columbia in the decades following the Civil War. They were primarily cast-bronze equestrian statues of Union generals on high neoclassical stone pedestals. These were located in the centers of circles or squares within the original L'Enfant Plan, changing the social configuration of the space from centripetal, focused on the center, to centrifugal, focused on the perimeter. These are heroic memorials, larger than life, towering over the observer with postures depicting historic narratives. Notable exceptions are the marble fountain dedicated to Admiral Dupont and the granite shaft of the Stephenson Grand Army of the Republic Memorial.

The great number of these memorials indicates the preoccupation with the Civil War. They also serve as a solemn reminder of a period in the city's history when it was the center of Civil War operations, dominated by military equipment and personnel, who utilized many of the open spaces. The statues are placed in the most prominent urban locations, the junctures of avenues, as a constant reminder to subsequent generations of the great national trauma.

Although the Civil War memorials were largely funded by private patriotic groups, the pedestals and site preparation were often funded by the federal government since they were placed on federal land. This tacit federal support proclaims that the Union army prevailed, and the unity of the nation was preserved. The Grand Army of the Republic, founded in 1866, became the largest Union veterans' organization to work with sponsors and win approval for many of these memorials. It was a strong political organization with many supporters in Congress.[13]

A generalized procedure was followed for the creation of public memorials in the decades following the Civil War. A private group interested in sponsoring a memorial formed a committee that solicited members of Congress to sponsor a bill allowing the memorial to be installed on federal land. As part of the bill, Congress formed a memorial commission, which often included the secretary of war; this enabled his designate, the chief of engineers, to be responsible for installing the memorial. There was usually little debate associated with these bills if the memorial committee had garnered political support. When the bill was passed, Congress appropriated funds for the pedestal and site preparation. Sometime during the process the memorial commission selected a site coordinated by the chief of engineers. The memorial commission sponsored a competition for artists or sculptors to provide designs. The design selected usually went through a series of revisions and approvals before the final piece was cast. The design was executed, and the memorial installed, in cooperation with the Office of Public Buildings and Grounds. The process concluded with acceptance by the memorial commission and a dedication ceremony.

The motives of the memorial commissions were varied and interesting, not necessarily stated but implied in the final design. The pose of the statue, the supporting figures or elements, and the inscriptions help convey the message behind the memorial. Most memorials honor military heroes and were sponsored by veterans' organizations who wanted to promote the patriotism or valor of native sons from particular states. For example, the statue of General McPherson was sponsored by the Society of the Army of the Tennessee. Other memorials are more philanthropic, dedicated to individuals such as Daniel Webster or Abraham Lincoln for their contributions to statesmanship or political leadership. Some are related to causes, such as homeopathic medicine (Dr. Samuel Hahnemann) or labor unions (Samuel Gompers). Although it appears that there was a government policy to support memorials dedicated to the Civil War, each was a unique enterprise. The large number of Civil War memorials is the result of strong political support of those groups and the timing of their proposals when the public reservations were being fully developed after the war.

Location was critical because it helped to establish the prestige of the memorial. The best locations were the squares and circles, where the memorial could be approached and seen from many vantage points via the nexus of avenues. Thus the memorial extended to the place itself, which assumed the name of the memorial. Only in Stanton Square, where there is a statue of General Nathanael Greene, is there a memorial honoring someone other than the space's namesake, in this case Edwin Stanton.

The location of a memorial in Washington, D.C., automatically places it on a level of national significance. Most groups interested in creating a memorial seek a site on or near the Mall. In recent years the city has been overrun with memorials of all shapes and sizes, and more proposals are pending. To control this process and its political nature, Congress passed the 1986 Commemorative Works Act. Congress must approve a memorial's concept and its site in separate acts. In addition, the design and the site must be approved by the U.S. Commission of Fine Arts, the National Capitol Planning Commission, and the secretary of the interior. Persons honored must have been dead for twenty-five years, and wars must have been over for ten years, before a memorial may be erected.[14] The intent of this legislation was to take politics out of the memorial process, but of course this is never completely possible.

The process of building a memorial on the Mall has always depended on political influence and persuasion. That has not changed very much in spite of legislation to prevent it. What has changed is the power of the regulatory bodies to control the location and design. The approval process is long, difficult, and open to wide public debate. This is in addition to selecting a design and raising the funds. Needless to say, placing a memorial on the Mall is an arduous process, but there are many groups who are not easily dissuaded (see chapter 3).

Building a memorial is so very difficult because the memorial endeavors to convey conclusive meaning about an event or a judgment about the value of an individual. Human nature makes us reluctant to cast these conclusive meanings in stone or bronze, and rightly so. Eras want to interpret meaning from the perspective of their own history. Commenting on the new World War II Memorial, the cultural critic Philip Kennicott writes: "In a democratic society, there is a natural, healthy resistance to any kind of compliance with a final understanding of history. Historical understandings change. Good wars and good men don't necessarily seem so to later generations. And nothing, even a just war or a great man, is entirely good."[15]

CHAPTER THREE

THE MALL

L'Enfant's Grand Avenue, Nineteenth-Century Development,
The McMillan Plan, Building the Grand Scheme, The Architectural
Context, Ground Zero, Memorials and Meaning, America's
Democratic Front Lawn

IT IS SOMETIMES called the City of Magnificent Distances, but it might
with greater propriety be termed the City of Magnificent Intentions . . .
Spacious avenues, that begin in nothing, and lead nowhere; streets, mile-
long, that only want houses, roads, and inhabitants; public buildings that
need but a public to be complete; and ornaments of great thoroughfares,
which only lack great thoroughfares to ornament—are its leading features . . . To the admirers of cities it is a . . . pleasant field for the imagination to rove in; a monument raised to a deceased project, with not even a
legible inscription to record its departed greatness.

CHARLES DICKENS, *American Notes*

The monumental core of Washington, D.C., is composed of six large areas:
the White House grounds, Capitol Square, the National Mall, the Washington Monument grounds, West Potomac Park, and East Potomac Park.
In this chapter I discuss the National Mall, the Washington Monument
grounds, and West Potomac Park, collectively referred to by the National
Park Service as the Mall area. The National Mall is a large greensward defined by Constitution Avenue on the north side, First Street, NW, on the
east, Fifteenth Street, NW, on the west, and Independence Avenue on the
south. The Washington Monument grounds are between Fifteenth and
Seventeenth streets, NW. West Potomac Park is defined by Constitution
Avenue on the north side, the Potomac River on the west, the elevated
railroad bridge on the south, and Seventeenth Street, NW, on the east.

Within the National Mall are several national museums and a part
of the Department of Agriculture. The Washington Monument grounds
focus on the obelisk dedicated to George Washington. They include the
original lockkeeper's house (1837) for the Washington Canal (also known
as the Tiber Canal), at the corner of Seventeenth Street and Constitution
Avenue. The primary features of West Potomac Park are the Lincoln Memorial and the Reflecting Pool, on axis with the Washington Monument.
To the south are the Tidal Basin and the Jefferson Memorial. Scattered
throughout this area are other memorials of varied size, including the
Vietnam Veterans Memorial, the Korean War Veterans Memorial, and the
Franklin Delano Roosevelt Memorial.

L'Enfant's Grand Avenue

L'Enfant's primary design intention for the federal precinct was to relate the President's House to the Capitol utilizing two means. The urban relationship was established along Pennsylvania Avenue, which afforded a direct physical connection and reciprocal views. The landscape relationship was established via large, related open spaces that terminated at the Potomac River. L'Enfant describes these spaces in the margins of his 1791 plan as follows: "Grand Avenue, 400 feet in breadth, and about a mile in length, bordered with gardens, ending in a slope from the houses on each side."[1] It extended west from the "Congress House," his name for the Capitol, to the monument dedicated to George Washington. This avenue is dotted on the plan and connected to the surrounding city north and south by perpendicular streets of varying width. The Grand Avenue runs through the "well improved field, being part of the walk from the President's house, of about 1800 feet in breath, and 3/4 of a mile in length. Every lot, deep coloured red with green plots, designates some of the situations which command the most agreeable prospects, and which are the best calculated for spacious houses and gardens, such as may accommodate foreign ministers."[2] Grand Avenue was bordered on the north by a canal formed from Tiber Creek that turned south in front of Capitol Hill. It linked the Potomac and Anacostia rivers and was intended to support commercial activities along its banks. A cascade fed by Tiber Creek from the north was proposed at the foot of Capitol Hill.

When Andrew Ellicott redrew the city plan for printing in 1792, he articulated the outlines of buildings on both sides of the Grand Avenue (see fig. 1.2). One of these buildings, on the north side of the canal at a turning basin, is the market. A monumental building is shown two blocks west of the market on the south side of the canal, possibly the theater L'Enfant mentioned in his report to President Washington.[3] On Ellicott's plan the Grand Avenue was formalized with a row of trees on each side.

Nineteenth-Century Development

Washington, D.C., was slow to develop in the first decades of the nineteenth century. There were only a few dwellings scattered among the "Magnificent Distances" observed by Charles Dickens in his visit to the city in 1842. Some roads were only swaths cut through the forest; most were muddy and unpaved. None of the public reservations, including the Mall, as it was soon called, had been improved in any manner.

The Washington Canal, built in 1802 according to a design by the architect Benjamin Henry Latrobe, formed the north edge of the Grand Avenue. Financial considerations forced him to eliminate L'Enfant's turning basin at Eighth Street, as well as the cascade and basin at Capitol Hill.[4] The eighty-foot-wide canal did not serve shipping and commerce well, being much used for the dumping of garbage and sewage. It often filled with silt, creating stagnant water with foul odors. Wood was used to form the canal and locks, but they were frequently damaged by heavy storms. Operations at the Center Market, built in the location shown on Ellicott's plan, only exacerbated this noxious situation.

In the early decades the Mall was used for grazing and agriculture. In 1812, in an effort to improve the land, Congress authorized leasing it for public purposes.[5] At the foot of Capitol Hill the Columbia Institute initiated a botanic garden in 1820. It did not last long, and the government built its own Botanic Garden in 1850, an octagonal greenhouse. In 1870 it became the eastern end of a Victorian conservatory three hundred feet long with a domed central palm house. A decade later the Bartholdi Fountain was brought to Washington from the Centennial Exposition in Philadelphia and placed nearby, in the center of the Mall.[6]

The concept of the Mall was changed forever when Congress accepted the bequest of the Englishman James Smithson for an institution devoted to research and the diffusion of knowledge. The Grand Avenue would become the site of cultural institutions, not foreign ministries as L'Enfant had proposed. (There was an earlier proposal to place a national university on the Mall.)[7] Robert Mills, the architect asked to design the institution, imagined the entire Mall as the site for horticultural, botanical, and zoological facilities.[8] His design was not built, but his site concept prevailed, resulting in a Smithsonian Institution that at the end of the twentieth century occupied the majority of buildings on the Mall.

The Smithsonian Institution was the first building on the Mall, built in 1847 according to a design by James Renwick Jr. Its picturesque style and medieval inspiration departed from the neoclassical designs of other public buildings in the city. The medieval style was reminiscent of that of European universities founded during the Middle Ages.[9] The appearance was also the by-product of a search for a new architectural expression based on eclecticism. The building of rough red sandstone was composed as a central two-story block linked by hyphens to asymmetrical wings. Distinctive towers in the center and corners were varied in height and expression, creating a unique profile and garnering the nickname "Castle" (fig. 3.1). Sited on a slight rise on the Tenth Street axis, the Smithsonian Castle has a prospect over the rolling land and adjacent waterways. Its placement honored L'Enfant's Grand Avenue but encroached upon the future vision of a wider Mall.

The central feature of L'Enfant's plan, at the crossing of the White House and Capitol axes, was to be an equestrian statue of George Washington. The statue was later deemed inappropriate, resulting in the scheme for a grand monument by the architect Robert Mills. Mills proposed an obelisk six hundred feet high with a colonnaded building at the base (a pantheon 250 feet in diameter and 150 feet high) for honoring other Revolutionary heroes. He had completed a monument to George Washington in Baltimore in 1815.

L'Enfant's location for the large monument proved to be unsatisfactory because of poor soil conditions, and it was moved 370 feet east and 123 feet south, a location that would lead to future design difficulty.[10] If his scheme of an equestrian statue had been followed, this would not have occurred. Perhaps L'Enfant surmised that this marshy site had poor subsoil. Construction was initiated in 1848 but halted in 1854, at a height of just 152 feet, owing to inadequate funds raised through public subscription.[11] It rose to 156 feet in the next two years. Throughout the course of construction many alternate schemes were suggested, but Mills's scheme prevailed, though without the pantheon. Work commenced after the Civil War in 1876, utilizing public funds to complete a simplified design. The completed obelisk (1884) has a width-to-height ratio of 1:10;

Fig. 3.1. Smithsonian Institution Castle, north side. Library of Congress, Prints and Photographs Division, HABS No. DC 520B-1, photo by Jack Boucher, 1968

Fig. 3.2. Washington Monument, view to northeast. Library of Congress, Prints and Photographs Division, HABS No. DC 2-1, photo by Jack Boucher, 1971

it is 555 feet tall with a square base 55 feet on a side. It was built of marble from many states, with a 50-foot-tall pyramid top of Maryland marble and an aluminum tip (fig. 3.2).[12] In the words of John W. Reps, "No one seeing this majestic obelisk for the first time can fail to be moved by the Washington Monument's simple beauty, its smooth, tapering faces bereft of any ornamentation and its immense scale fitting perfectly the grand spaces of the city plan."[13]

The Mall needed a comprehensive landscape design to guide future development. In 1850 President Millard Fillmore asked the prominent American landscape gardener Andrew Jackson Downing to develop designs for the Mall, Lafayette Park, and the White House grounds (fig. 3.3). Downing was a proponent of the naturalistic approach to landscape design that originated in England. He also was the first advocate in America for public parks like those in England and Germany. He wanted the Mall to become an "extended landscape garden, to be traversed in different directions by graveled walks and carriage drives, and planted with specimens, properly labeled of all the varieties of trees and shrubs which will flourish in this climate."[14]

In Downing's 1851 scheme the Mall was divided into six precincts by city streets, with the canal adjusted to follow the diagonal of Missouri Avenue at the east end. Within each precinct curvilinear roads and pathways were placed over undulating topography supported by picturesque groupings of trees and plants. The precincts had different features. President's Park had a large circular parade ground encircled by a row of elms and a carriage drive. This was surrounded by a dense zone of plantings and paths for private use. A large marble arch at the end of Pennsylvania Avenue was the principal gateway to the grounds. An iron suspension bridge spanned the Tiber Canal to the Washington Monument grounds, where a meadow of American trees was planted around the obelisk. East of this was Evergreen Garden, a series of concentric elliptical paths formed by evergreens of every species from the local geographic region. The Smithsonian Pleasure Grounds were an arrangement of botanical specimens to enhance the Castle. East of the Smithsonian was Fountain Park, with a fountain and a small lake. The sequence ended with another bridge across the Tiber Canal for a drive through the Botanic Garden to a gateway at the Capitol grounds.[15] Downing's death two years later stalled the impetus to follow his master landscape plan. Only the Smithsonian grounds were executed according to his design, although other parts of the Mall and the White House grounds were improved in the picturesque manner. Downing's design approach did impact other reservations in the city, which were redesigned according to the naturalistic landscape tradition.

During the Civil War most of the Mall was used for military purposes, such as camping, training, slaughtering cattle, and storing equipment. Armory Square Hospital, at Sixth Street, was composed of fifty temporary wooden structures near the armory.[16] Without the authority of an accepted comprehensive plan, the Mall continued to develop in an ad hoc manner. When the Department of Agriculture needed a new building in 1868, it was located west of the Smithsonian almost at the centerline of the Mall.[17] The large grounds in front of this building, which extended to the canal, were designed in a more formal manner than the

Fig. 3.3. *The Altograph of Washington City*, by James T. Dubois, 1892. Library of Congress, Geography and Maps Division, 1119.1

adjacent picturesque Smithsonian grounds. The gardens included a pair of summer houses and a large Victorian greenhouse.

Fig. 3.4. Arts and Industries Building, view to southeast

Similarly, the National Museum (now the Smithsonian's Arts and Industries Building) was located east of the Castle but further back from the Mall to preserve views to the Capitol. It was built to house objects of American manufacture and arts exhibited at the 1876 Centennial Exposition in Philadelphia.[18] Designed by local architects Adolph Cluss and Paul Schulze, its appearance derives from the original exposition building. The plan is a Greek cross with a central octagonal rotunda within a square footprint. All the facades are in the same Victorian style, with elaborate polychrome brickwork and large arched windows encasing an exposed iron structure (fig. 3.4). The 1881 building presently serves as an exhibition space on the Mall.

The massive flood of 1881 was caused by melting snow from a severe winter, along with increased river sedimentation. It inundated the Mall and Pennsylvania Avenue, providing Congress with incentives to fund the Army Corps of Engineers to correct this problem. A deeper channel would be formed in the Potomac River, and the dredged material would be used west of the Washington Monument grounds to elevate the tidal flats six feet above low water and enclose them with masonry and riprap edges. This construction improved river navigation, eliminated malarial marshes and created new parkland. The dredging operation created the land area for West Potomac Park, stretching a mile west from the Washington Monument, and East Potomac Park, a new island two miles long to the south. The new parks surround the Tidal Basin, a newly formed tidal reservoir with gates at either end to provide water for a deeper Washington Channel. This construction work continued until the end of the century, providing 621 acres of new parkland and 118 acres of tidal reservoir.[19]

The creation of the new land led to a significant departure from the L'Enfant Plan. So did abandoning the canal and replacing it with a trunk sewer during the era of territorial government from 1871 to 1874. The stage was set for a new plan, a new vision that would soon be developed. In a sense this was the beginning of the modern city of Washington.

Fig. 3.5. View of the Mall from
the Capitol with the Botanic
Garden *(lower left)* and the
railroad station *(upper right)*,
1885. Washingtoniana Division, DC Public Library

The greatest imposition on the Mall as a picturesque open space was the Baltimore and Potomac (later the Pennsylvania) Railroad (fig. 3.5). In 1872 Congress allowed tracks to cross the Mall at Sixth Street to the station on B Street (now Constitution Avenue), with a train shed extending halfway cross the Mall itself.[20] The trains and their tracks constituted a noxious presence of noise and soot, ruining the tranquility of this public space and the vista to the Capitol. The massive brick Victorian Gothic station with an elaborate clock tower was the site of President Garfield's assassination in 1881.[21]

During the nineteenth century the federal government divested itself of Mall acreage by selling or donating tracts. In 1820 the area between First and Third streets at the base of Capitol Hill was given to the Columbia Institute to create a botanic garden. The area between Third and Sixth streets, four parallelogram-shaped parcels bordered by Pennsylvania and Maryland avenues, were sold to the city government for development in 1822 and quickly filled with residences, stores, and boarding houses. In 1846 the parcel between Ninth and Twelfth streets was given to the newly formed Smithsonian Institution. The thirty-seven-acre tract west of Fourteenth Street was given to the Washington National Monument Society in 1848. After the Civil War the tract between Twelfth and Fourteenth streets was given to the Department of Agriculture. The last divestiture was a fourteen-acre parcel at Sixth and B streets given to the Baltimore and Potomac Railroad in 1872 for construction of a depot. In

L'ENFANT'S LEGACY

the twentieth century all these tracts were reclaimed to develop the present National Mall.

At the turn of the century Downing's romantic vision of a series of parks forming the Mall was in place. Starting at the base of Capitol Hill and moving west, there were the Botanic Garden, Armory Square, the Smithsonian Pleasure Grounds, the Department of Agriculture grounds, and the Washington Monument grounds. L'Enfant's vision of a continuous green space from the Capitol to the Potomac River had also been realized, albeit in fragmented form with multiple landowners.

The McMillan Plan

The year 1900 marked the centennial of Washington, D.C., as the nation's capital. Several suggestions were made for improving the city, particularly the federal district. Senator James McMillan of Michigan, chairman of the Senate Committee on the District of Columbia, saw this as an opportunity to study the monumental core. He sponsored passage of a Senate resolution to study the entire park system of the District of Columbia. A Senate subcommittee formed an expert group made up of Daniel H. Burnham, an architect from Chicago; Frederick Law Olmsted Jr., a landscape architect from Boston; and Charles F. McKim, an architect from New York. Burnham acted as the chairman, and Charles Moore, clerk of the Senate Committee on the District of Columbia, acted as secretary.[22] Later the sculptor Augustus Saint-Gaudens joined the group. In 1901 work on a new comprehensive plan began. The study process and the resulting plan are thoroughly explained by Reps's book *Monumental Washington*.[23]

Burnham, McKim, and Saint-Gaudens had worked together on the White City at the World's Columbian Exposition in Chicago in 1893. The project that initiated a national architectural movement termed City Beautiful, the White City was a monumental grouping of neoclassical buildings around a lagoon, all with common Beaux-Arts design characteristics, such as symmetry and axiality. Built in less than two years, it was stunning under nighttime lighting. The City Beautiful movement espoused the coordinated relationship of classically inspired buildings forming monumental civic spaces with sculpture and fountains set within a controlled landscape. "However eclectic it became in its borrowings and whatever the style of particular buildings within its plans," Thomas Hines writes, "the thrust of City Beautiful planning was predominantly baroque in its emphasis on processional sequences of spaces and buildings arranged as a unified group."[24]

The comprehensive McMillan Plan (also called the Senate Park Commission Plan) grouped legislative buildings around the Capitol and executive buildings around Lafayette Square. The Mall was extended west to the river, with a memorial to Lincoln at the end. The Washington Monument grounds would be expanded, and the White House axis terminated in a group of memorials. The Mall itself would be lined with buildings of public purpose. L'Enfant's L-shaped Mall would be reformed into a cruciform (fig. 3.6).

At the east end of the Mall would be Union Square, intended to join the Mall to Capitol Square. This space would be a great plaza with fountains, terraces, and green parterres. The chief feature would be the Grant

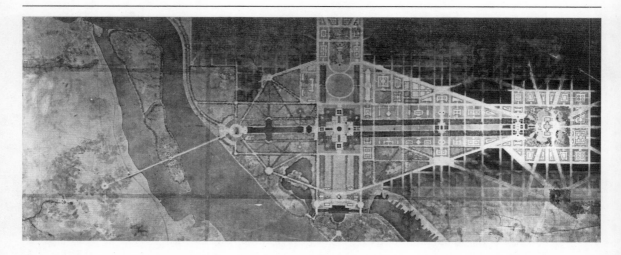

Memorial and statues of General Sherman and General Sheridan. It was likened to the Place de la Concorde in Paris.[25]

The primary design intention for the Mall was to develop it for public use. B Street would be extended eastward on the north and south sides, forming a uniform sixteen-hundred-foot width for its entire length. This would create large building sites on both sides of the Mall for great museums or buildings devoted to scientific purposes. The axis of the Mall would be shifted to line up with the existing Washington Monument. Pairs of parklike roads with paths, along with four rows of formally spaced elm trees, would frame the central lawn. The resulting greensward would be three hundred feet wide and one and a half miles long. All north-south streets would pass through the space on grade in order to make it a place of movement. The cross-axial space between Seventh and Ninth streets would be designed similar to Union Square.[26] The intended character was likened to that of the Mall in New York City's Central Park, except that there the roads are depressed into underpasses, separated from the pedestrian paths. The infringement of the Smithsonian Institution and the Department of Agriculture are not mentioned, nor are they shown on the plans.

The crucial part of the monumental-core plan was the Washington Monument grounds, the area the Senate Park Commission studied the most. The grand monument needed an appropriate setting from which visitors could have expansive views in all directions. West of the obelisk would be a sunken garden with a round pool marking the true north-south axis to the White House. It would be forty feet below the Mall, reached by stepped terraces and fountains three hundred feet wide on three sides of the monument. Large groves of elms would define these spaces at the corners. From the sunken garden, "the gem of the Mall system," the view of the monument would now be even more magnificent.[27]

South of this monumental central space, the Senate Park Commission proposed a place of recreation called the Washington Common. It would contain a stadium for athletic contests and festival occasions, ball grounds, tennis courts, open-air gymnasiums, and playgrounds for children. The Tidal Basin would be used for boating, swimming, and skating in winter. At the intersection of the White House axis and Maryland

L'ENFANT'S LEGACY

Avenue would be a memorial, a pantheon for statues honoring a group of men or a single individual.[28]

The last element on the newly created parkland between the Washington Monument and the river would be the Lincoln Memorial. The Mall would be extended at its sixteen-hundred-foot width with a canal thirty-six hundred feet long and two hundred feet wide with arms at its center. This formal element, recalling the canal at Versailles, would lead to a rond-point, a gateway to the city's park system. It would access drives leading to Potomac Park, to Rock Creek Park, and via a new memorial bridge to Arlington Cemetery. This bridge, on axis with the Custis-Lee mansion (Robert E. Lee's home), was seen as a symbolic reconnection of the northern and southern regions of the country. At the center of the rond-point, and at the same elevation as the base of the Washington Monument, would be a memorial dedicated to Abraham Lincoln. Areas north and south of the canal would be planted as woods with formal roads and paths.[29]

The Senate Park Commission recommended that the triangular area between Pennsylvania Avenue and B Street be used for municipal buildings: a District building, a new city market, an armory, police and fire headquarters, and an emergency hospital. (Plans for legislative buildings around Capitol and Lafayette squares are discussed in chapter 4 and 5, respectively.)

The primary criticism of the Senate Park Commission lies in its failure to rectify the lack of symbolic expression of the three divisions of the federal government. Emphasis is given to both the legislative and the executive branch by grouping buildings for these purposes around the Capitol and the White House, respectively, but the new building for the Supreme Court was sited as part of Capitol Square, only exacerbating the problem. Since the role of the Supreme Court has become equal in importance to the roles of the other two branches, it should have had an equally important symbolic position in the plan. John W. Reps thinks it should have been located at the site of either the Lincoln Memorial or the Washington Common.[30]

To be sure, there were flaws in the visionary plan, but as Reps concludes, "With all these objections considered, the Park Commission plan still emerges as a composition of civic design unmatched in American history and surpassed by few comparable efforts elsewhere in the world. This sweeping and noble plan carried the stamp of those who created it in the belief that a distinctive image of urban grandeur could be achieved in the nation's capital by underlining and reemphasizing the original baroque character of the L'Enfant design."[31] The McMillan Plan for Washington was the first and perhaps the best embodiment of the City Beautiful movement, which was to sweep the country as Cleveland, Denver, St. Louis, and San Francisco all adopted and built City Beautiful plans.

Building the Grand Scheme

All grand plans take time, patience, and perseverance to achieve. Before the plan was drawn, Frederick Law Olmsted Jr. left the 1900 convention of the American Institute of Architects in Washington with these words: "In great undertakings requiring centuries to mature the one hope of unity and harmony, the one hope of successful issue, is the establishment of a comprehensive plan and the consistent adherence to it."[32]

Fig. 3.7. World War I and
World War II temporary
buildings around the Lincoln
Memorial reflecting pool.
Library of Congress, Prints
and Photographs Division,
LC-USZ62-11934, courtesy of
Washingtoniana Division, DC
Public Library

With the death of Senator McMillan in 1902, Glenn Brown, secretary
of the American Institute of Architects, became the chief proponent of
the plan. Finally, in 1910 the U.S. Commission of Fine Arts was formed
to oversee the execution of the McMillan Plan, along with other duties.
Gradually, political leaders became convinced of the validity of following
a comprehensive plan in order to produce an ordered result. The new
Department of Agriculture building was sited on the Mall in accordance
with the master plan, as was the new National Museum. New office buildings for the Senate and House were sited to form a new Capitol Square.
Construction of the new Union Station, designed by Daniel Burnham,
proceeded on a site north of the Capitol.

World War I caused delays in development progress, as well as incursions into the Mall space. Temporary buildings, or "tempos," served as
barracks and offices on the north side of the Reflecting Pool at the Lincoln Memorial. The Navy and Munitions buildings provided 1.8 million
square feet of floor space for fourteen thousand workers in seventeen
buildings, each five hundred feet long, separated by courtyards.[33] The ad-
age that temporary buildings are really permanent comes from the fact
that many of these buildings remained in place until World War II. More
"tempos" were built during that war to house sixteen thousand more
workers south of the Reflecting Pool and east of the Smithsonian Castle.
These identical two- to four-story concrete structures marred the vistas
of the Mall until the 1970s (fig. 3.7).

One crucial aspect of implementing the McMillan Plan was placement of the Lincoln Memorial at the Potomac River on the extension
of the Capitol axis. Many other sites were suggested and studied before
the U.S. Commission of Fine Arts prevailed and recommended the river
site.[34] Henry Bacon's design was chosen for the memorial, which included a long reflecting pool. Pamela Scott and Antoinette Lee comment:
"The sense of quiet and repose essential to the experience of the Lincoln

Fig. 3.8. Lincoln Memorial, east side. Library of Congress, Prints and Photographs Division, HABS No. DC 462-10, photo by Jet Lowe, 1991

Memorial derives from its placement in the extended landscape created especially for it and from the perfectly balanced relationship between Daniel Chester French's great statue of Lincoln and the equally great architecture that Henry Bacon designed to shelter and display it."[35]

The memorial design is a metaphor for the United States, with thirty-six Doric columns of white Colorado marble representing the number of states at the start of the Civil War (fig. 3.8). The visitor arrives at a terraced plaza before mounting a great flight of stairs to the cella and the great statue. The interior is suffused with daylight through narrow marble skylights in a high attic. On the end walls of the east and west chambers are murals and inscriptions from the Gettysburg Address and the Second Inaugural Address.[36] The awesome Georgia marble statue of Lincoln seated on a large throne atop a pedestal, by Daniel Chester French, is in the central chamber.

Another crucial element of the McMillan Plan was anchoring the southern axis of the White House by locating a memorial structure at its intersection with Maryland Avenue. This memorial was dedicated to Thomas Jefferson, and John Russell Pope was commissioned to design it. His scheme was based on the Pantheon in Rome, which Jefferson had used as his design precedent for the main library at the University of Virginia.[37] The white marble memorial is a circular colonnade of Ionic columns with a deep portico facing north to the White House. Within are circular wall segments with inscriptions, all covered with a dome, creating a monumental chamber for the heroically scaled statue. The nineteen-foot bronze portrait statue by Rudulph Evans is in the center on a six-foot base.[38] The impression is astounding: a superscale figure standing alone within a platonic space (fig. 3.9).

The circular form of the Jefferson Memorial relates well to the rectangular form of the Lincoln Memorial. Both are elevated on plinths with colonnaded exteriors. Both are also related to water bodies that create reflections for picturesque images. Both are also isolated at the termini of axes. The procession to the Lincoln Memorial is a noble experience,

Fig. 3.9. Jefferson Memorial,
view to south

but the land approach to the Jefferson Memorial from the north is quite awkward. The McMillan Plan proposed to reshape the Tidal Basin to create a broad landscape connection to this memorial, but the plan was not followed. The most dramatic way to approach the Jefferson Memorial is from across the water via a paddleboat.

Perhaps the greatest failure in executing the McMillan Plan lies at the center, the Washington Monument grounds. Subsoil investigations concluded that the sunken garden could not be executed without seriously jeopardizing the foundations of the obelisk. This certainly could have been determined when the master plan was created. Thus, the area the Senate Park Commission studied the most remains virtually unchanged a century later. The visual connection between the White House and the Jefferson Memorial suffers the most from this situation since the eye wants to make the obelisk part of this axis, which is perceptually false.

Key elements of the McMillan Plan were now in place. The ends of the two great axes each terminated with a significant memorial. The Mall had been cleared of intrusive development and nonconforming structures. The larger architectural frame was formed with compatible buildings along the streets, which defined the great green space. Development of the Mall with landscaping and cultural buildings could now commence.

President Roosevelt's public works program in 1933 resulted in implementation of the Mall development plan as prepared by the landscape architect Frederick Law Olmsted Jr. and the planner Charles Eliot II.[39] The old Department of Agriculture building near the middle of the Mall was finally removed, and the four parallelogram-shaped blocks of boarding houses, stores, and residences were cleared. Constitution Avenue was cut through to Pennsylvania Avenue, necessitating the demolition of the American Colonization Society Hall.[40] The Mall had been divided into three strips by four parallel roads running east-west. After grading and removal of obstructive trees, the two outer strips were planted with four parallel rows of equally spaced elm trees along the entire length from Third Street to Fourteenth Street. More than anything else, these uniform

Fig. 3.10. Grant Memorial,
view to east

rows of trees establish the ambiance of this greensward and define the axial lawn, the *tapis vert*. They also serve to isolate the rows of buildings on either side, making the Mall more of a park setting than an urban boulevard.

The Senate Park Commission recommended Union Square as the location of the Grant Memorial. This required relocation of the Botanic Garden to a site south of Maryland Avenue. After almost a decade of political battles, the government-sponsored Grant Memorial was completed, although the setting was not. The sculpture, by an unknown New York artist, Henry Merwin Shrady, was completed in pieces from 1909 to 1920. Measuring 252 feet by 71 feet, it is the largest sculptural memorial in the city, with groups of bronze military figures at either end of a marble platform—the dramatic cavalry at the north end and the austere infantry at the south end. In the middle is the bronze equestrian statue of General Grant on a tall marble pedestal surrounded by four bronze lions on smaller pedestals (fig. 3.10).[41] Memorials to the two great Union leaders, Grant and Lincoln, now anchored opposite ends of the Mall.

Finally in 1934 Union Square was completed as designed by Frederick Law Olmsted Jr., a formal connecting space between the Mall and his father's earlier design for the romantic Capitol grounds. There was no cross-axis as in the McMillan Plan, only a simple landscaped oval traffic island as a transition between the Mall and the Capitol grounds.[42] The monument to General George Meade was added in 1927 but has since been moved. The Peace Monument (1877), an allegorical, vertical monument in a traffic circle at the intersection of Pennsylvania Avenue and First Street, was retained, as was the portrait statue memorializing President James A. Garfield (1887), located in a traffic circle at the intersection of Maryland Avenue and First Street.[43]

The U.S. Botanic Garden, based on a French conservatory for exotic plants and palms, was designed by Bennett, Parsons and Frost from 1931 to 1933.[44] From 1997 to 2001 all the plants were removed, and the building was restored and rebuilt with an addition along Independence Avenue for services and another entrance. A three-acre National Garden consisting of a Rose Garden, a First Ladies Water Garden, and the Senator John Heinz Environmental Learning Center will be added south of this building in the future.[45]

The Mall

West Potomac Park was programmed for recreation and leisure activities. This included a polo field, a bathing beach, a nine-hole golf course, an archery field, volleyball courts, and baseball fields. The city of Tokyo donated three thousand Japanese cherry trees, which were planted along the Tidal Basin in 1912.[46] The construction of the World War I temporary buildings altered development plans and eliminated the cross arms from the Reflecting Pool. And the completion of the Lincoln and Jefferson memorials required new roads and footpaths to access them and new bridges over the Potomac River.

East Potomac Park is south of the Tidal Basin between the Washington Channel and the Potomac River, separated from the Mall by four bridges. It was designated as a recreation park in the McMillan Plan. After dredging completed the 330-acre land mass in 1911, a roadway was built around the entire perimeter and lined with Japanese cherry trees. During World War I the area was used for barracks and victory gardens. Afterward a golf course, a teahouse, a tourist camp, and stables were constructed. A four-mile promenade along the water was completed in 1931. Congress designated Hains Point, at the tip, for a National Peace Garden in 1988. There are currently no memorials, but several sites have been recommended. At Hains Point a large, five-part bronze sculpture called *Awakening* depicts a man emerging from the earth. There are a number of National Park Service buildings throughout the park, including the National Capital Region Headquarters.[47]

The last comprehensive plan for the Mall was completed in 1965 by Skidmore, Owings and Merrill (SOM) with landscape architect Dan Kiley (fig. 3.11).[48] Interstate 395 was routed beneath a six-acre reflecting pool adjacent to the Grant Memorial, thus introducing the water feature L'Enfant wanted in this location. The plan also recommended placing the cross streets under the Mall, as Twelfth Street had been in 1959. The Mall itself was to be embellished with fountains, small plazas, pavilions, kiosks, and additional rows of trees. The plan included better pedestrian connections to the Jefferson Memorial and eliminated the traffic circle around the Lincoln Memorial. These design proposals enhanced those of the McMillan Plan, but most of them have not been implemented.

For the nation's bicentennial, Constitution Gardens was installed on the north side of the Reflecting Pool, as designed by SOM. Its design reverts to Downing's landscape tradition, with undulating topography, meandering paths, and a free-form lake, a counterpoint to the formality of the Senate Park Commission scheme. A memorial to the signers of the Declaration of Independence was placed on an island in the lake in the following decade.[49]

In recent decades the National Park Service has been trying to control incursions of auto and bus traffic into the Mall. In 1960 traffic was eliminated from Washington and Adams drives, and they were converted to gravel walkways. Parking is now available only on Madison and Jefferson drives and on the cross streets. Location of the Smithsonian Metro station at the corner of Twelfth Street and Adams Walk has alleviated some parking problems.

The McMillan Plan extended the spirit of L'Enfant's intentions and combined them with new exigencies and programs to create a future vision for the Mall. Frederick Law Olmsted Jr.'s plans for the Washington

L'ENFANT'S LEGACY

Fig. 3.11. Washington Mall master plan, 1965. Courtesy of Skidmore, Owings and Merrill

Monument grounds and Union Square were more realistic in terms of budget and circumstances. The SOM plan proposed a more active pedestrian Mall with enhanced western grounds. With all of the recent building and memorial activity, perhaps it is time for a revised master plan for this, the most crucial area of the monumental core in the nation's capital.

The Architectural Context

The northern boundary of the Mall was originally established by the Washington Canal. When the canal was encased in a sewer and covered over, it became B Street, now Constitution Avenue. The triangular area between Fourteenth Street, B Street, and Pennsylvania Avenue focused on Center Market at Seventh Street. The Old Post Office was here, as was the District Building, the seat of city government. It was a bustling area that deteriorated and became known as "murder bay" because of its criminal activities.

In 1926 the area was planned by the Office of the Supervising Architect as a federal building precinct, not a municipal precinct as recommended by the Senate Park Commission. Ohio and Louisiana avenues were eliminated, as were some cross streets, to create sites for seven major buildings grouped around two courtyards.[50] Each building in the Federal Triangle would be designed by a different architect, with eclectic variations according to Beaux-Arts design principles. Edward H. Bennett's master plan dictated setbacks, cornice heights, and limestone facades to foster aesthetic coherence. The Federal Triangle was to be the ideal City Beautiful complex, a coordinated group of harmonious buildings that expressed cooperation among government departments. It established

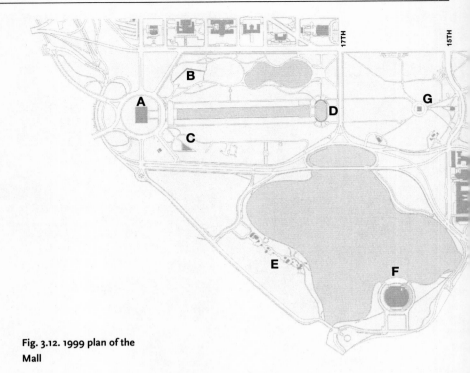

Fig. 3.12. 1999 plan of the
Mall

a monumental federal office core for the city and defined Constitution
Avenue as the northern architectural frame for the Mall with consistent
Beaux-Arts architecture. (Fig. 3.12 shows the location of all elements dis-
cussed below in this chapter.)

Between 1926 and 1938 the Federal Triangle was completed, except
for the Grand Army Plaza, which remained a parking lot. Anchoring the
short leg of the triangle is the mammoth U.S. Department of Commerce
building, which defines the east side of the White House grounds. Between Fourteenth and Twelfth streets, facing Constitution Avenue, with a
great portico entry and government auditorium, is the U.S. Customs Service and Interstate Commerce Commission building. The Internal Rev-
enue Service building is in the next block, but one quadrant was never
completed because the Old Post Office, built in 1899, was not demolished
according to the master plan. Next along Constitution Avenue is the
U.S. Justice Department building. On the Eighth Street axis, facing both
Pennsylvania and Constitution avenues, is the National Archives and Records Administration, with the largest public program component. At
the apex of the complex is the Federal Trade Commission building, with
its rounded end.[51] Each building has a public component and/or a grand
lobby with displays and exhibits.

Along Constitution Avenue west of the White House grounds a series
of pavilions were built in the 1920s and 1930s to house national organizations that wanted a prestigious location. These pavilions continued the
scale, street relationships, and landscape treatment of the organizational
buildings along Seventeenth Street. Starting at the corner and moving
west are the Organization of American States (1908–10), the Pan Ameri-

L'ENFANT'S LEGACY

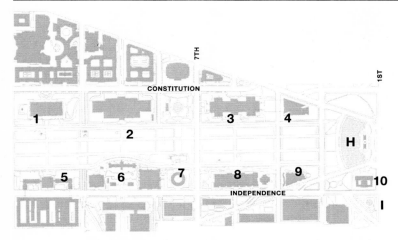

1: National Museum of American History
2: Natural History Museum
3: National Gallery of Art West Building
4: National Gallery of Art East Building
5: Agriculture Department
6: Smithsonian Institution
7: Hirshhorn Museum
8: National Air & Space Museum
9: National Museum of the American Indian
10: Botanic Garden

A: Lincoln Memorial
B: Vietnam Veterans Memorial
C: Korean War Veterans Memorial
D: World War II Memorial
E: Roosevelt Memorial
F: Jefferson Memorial
G: Washington Monument
H: Grant Memorial
I: Bartholdi Fountain

can Union (1910), the Department of the Interior / South Building (1933), the Federal Reserve (1937), the National Academy of Sciences (1924), and the American Pharmaceutical Association (1933).[52] This is a handsome series of low-scale symmetrical buildings with formal front gardens and axial approaches. Unlike the eastern segment of the avenue, along the Federal Triangle, this part of Constitution Avenue does not have a monumental urban edge. The generous landscaping around these pavilions does, however, forge a continuum with the open landscape of West Potomac Park, on the south side of the avenue.

During the urban-renewal planning for the southwest quadrant of the city in the 1950s, Tenth Street was to be the connector north to the Mall. About the same time, the area between Independence Avenue and the railroad tracks was planned as a new federal office building precinct. Along Independence Avenue, which had been extended to the Capitol grounds in the 1940s, new federal buildings were built that served as a larger architectural context along the south side of the Mall. These include the Forrestal Building, which bridges Tenth Street (1969), Federal Office Building No. 10 (1963), the former National Aeronautics and Space Administration building (1963), the Department of Education building (1961), and the two Department of Health and Human Services buildings (1941 and 1976). Earlier, a mammoth Department of Agriculture building (1937) was constructed at the corner of Fourteenth Street. Most of these buildings align to create a clearly defined southern edge to Independence Avenue. They serve as a neutral modern architectural background for the more elaborate architecture on the north side.

These new buildings followed the design guidelines formulated by Daniel Patrick Moynihan in his celebrated 1962 memorandum "Guiding Principles for Federal Architecture," which stated that "design must flow from the architectural profession to the government, and not vice versa." The designs "must provide visual testimony to the dignity, enterprise, vigor, and stability of the American Government. Special attention should be paid to the general ensemble of streets and public places of which Federal building will form a part. The development of an official style must be avoided."[53]

Along the north side of the Mall, on the superblocks between Fourteenth and Third streets, are four monumental museums and a sculpture garden. The oldest of these is the Natural History Museum, built from 1901 to 1911, as designed by Hornblower and Marshall. This huge white, granite-clad, four-story structure has a Corinthian portico leading to a three-story octagonal entry hall covered by a dome. The three wings have open-plan exhibition halls with skylights.[54] A part of the Smithsonian Institution, the museum houses a vast collection of natural artifacts.

To the west is the smaller National Museum of American History, also a part of the Smithsonian Institution. Built from 1955 to 1964, it has a modern design by the venerable proponent of classicism McKim, Mead and White and its successor firm, Steinman, Cain and White. Efforts to get the distinguished firm of Saarinen and Saarinen to design a more modern building failed.[55] The long, low modernist temple sits on a one-story plinth with a recessed attic story. All the facades are of identical precast concrete panels clad with pink marble set in two different planes. It houses a vast collection of American historical and cultural artifacts.

Separating these two Smithsonian museums from the West and East buildings of the National Gallery of Art is the National Gallery of Art Sculpture Garden. To maintain the bilateral symmetry of the Mall, a circular pool whose diameter is the same as that of the Hirshhorn Museum was placed on the Eighth Street axis in the late 1960s, defined by two concentric rows of linden trees. In winter it serves as a skating rink, serviced by the adjacent concession stand. The sculpture garden was designed around the pool and the concession stand by the landscape architect Laurie Olin in 1999 as a place of contemplation and relaxation. It accommodates seventeen modern sculptures on the six-acre site in a picturesque landscape of winding paths and free-form plantings. The National Gallery of Art Sculpture Garden is juxtaposed on axis with the Hirshhorn Sculpture Garden, across the Mall, which has three times as much sculpture formally composed in one-quarter of the space.[56] The two pedestrian-scale outdoor spaces within the monumental Mall complement each other with similar artwork.

The National Gallery of Art West Building (1936–41) is one of the best-designed edifices on the Mall. It was donated by Andrew Mellon along with his superb art collection to form the national art gallery. The building was designed by John Russell Pope, the same architect who designed the nearby National Archives and the Jefferson Memorial. The Jefferson Memorial design is based on the Roman Pantheon, which was also the inspiration for the central space of the West Building; one is open, the other closed.

The National Gallery West Building has entrances from the Mall and

Fig. 3.13. National Gallery of Art West Building, view to northeast

Constitution Avenue. Long stairs from Madison Drive lead to a deep Ionic portico (fig. 3.13). On the north side, one enters through a solid base, with the portico above. Both approaches lead to the grandly scaled rotunda with its double circle of enormous Ionic columns of dark green marble. A circulation spine passes through the rotunda, linking all the galleries and two skylit garden courts. Since much of the art in the National Gallery West Building is from the Italian Renaissance, the building exterior was designed in a modernized Renaissance style. The building is detached from its urban context by landscaped courts and low walls. The museum is not only a superb work of architecture but a glorious setting for the world-class collection of artwork from all ages and cultures contained within.

The National Gallery of Art East Building opened in 1978 on a prominent site on Pennsylvania Avenue, facing the Capitol to the east. The building design needed to relate directly to the existing, neoclassical West Building. The program required a variety of flexible galleries for temporary and twentieth-century exhibitions and a Center for Advanced Study in the Visual Arts.[57] The architect of the East Building, I. M. Pei, resolved the site restrictions and program requirements with a brilliant design concept. He divided the trapezoidal site into an isosceles triangle for the museum and a right triangle for the study center, with a gap in between (fig. 3.14). A concourse below the Fourth Street plaza physically connects the West and East buildings. The exterior cladding of Tennessee marble, from the same quarry as that for the West Building, is in pieces of the same size and color gradation, from brown at the bottom to pink at the top.[58]

The East Building demonstrates unequivocally that modern architecture could contribute to a neoclassical context, albeit through different stylistic expression, owing to the clear geometric relationship to the site and the axial relationship to the West Building. The two buildings are also equally monumental, befitting the scale of the federal core. When

President Jimmy Carter opened the East Building in 1978, he stated that
it symbolized the connection between art and public life in the United
States. The design makes the museum available to the public through its
welcoming openness; the transition from the Mall to plaza to porch to
lobby to atrium is smooth. Accessibility is manifested by the dramatic triangular atrium, which turns pedestrian circulation into choreographed
movement, making every visitor a public dancer. Not all of the museum's
art is confined to separate exhibition spaces; some is in the atrium, where
visitors can freely mingle with it.

The south side of the Mall had an earlier beginning than the north
side with the 1846 Smithsonian Castle and the 1881 Arts and Industries
Building, which have been handsomely renovated. The old Department
of Agriculture building of 1868, which also infringed upon the Mall open
space, was removed in the 1930s, long after a new building was built in
1902–8 according to the proper alignment. The 750-foot-long building
started as two L-shaped wings of offices and laboratories; the higher
central mass was built in 1930. Designed by the firm of Rankin, Kellogg
and Crane, it is the only government office building facing the Mall. The
wings follow neoclassical design principles for this building type, but the
central piece does not relate well to the wings.[59]

East of the Department of Agriculture building is the Freer Gallery of
Art, with its main entrance on Independence Avenue. Completed in 1928 as
designed by Charles Adams Platt, it was conceived as a Renaissance Italian
palazzo of gray granite. The main entry leads to a large square courtyard.[60]
The museum's rusticated exterior expression relates to its neighbor to the
west but stands in contrast to those to the east. This is a gem of a building,
much smaller than most of the other museums on the Mall but wonder-
fully suited to its fine collection of Asian paintings and arts.

Along Independence Avenue, adjacent to the Freer Gallery and south
of the Smithsonian Castle, are three pavilions (1987) that give access to
two underground museums and the S. Dillon Ripley Center. The two pa-

vilions form a gateway to the Enid A. Haupt Garden, the southern quadrangle of the Smithsonian, with fountains and sculpture that recalls the art exhibited below them. The west pavilion accesses the Arthur Sackler Gallery, connected underground to the Freer Gallery. The east pavilion gives access to the National Museum of African Art.[61] The third pavilion, a circular folly between the Freer and the Castle, grants access to the S. Dillon Ripley Center, three stories of underground offices, an auditorium, classrooms, and support spaces. The intimate garden and three modern pavilions in a carefully composed landscape are a great design success.

Until recently the most controversial building on the Mall was the Hirshhorn Museum (1974), centered on the Eighth Street axis. The first proposal was to locate it underground on the north side of the Mall to form a garden space. Joseph Hirshhorn rejected this scheme for a museum dedicated to the private art collection he donated to the Smithsonian. Gordon Bunshaft, of Skidmore, Owings and Merrill, then created a modern monument that makes no compromise with its prominent context. Its form is that of a doughnut raised above an elevated plaza on four sculptural concrete piers. The only exterior opening is a slit for an observation room and a balcony facing the Mall (fig. 3.15). It was to be sheathed in travertine, but budget considerations resulted in pink precast granite aggregate panels.[62] Inside are three floors of offices and galleries with large glazed openings that face a circular courtyard. It is scaleless, monolithic, and introverted, a large piece of inhabitable, minimalist sculpture. It does somehow relate to the circular forms on the Mall—the domes atop buildings on the north side, the Capitol dome, and the Jefferson Memorial. The walled plaza with its fountain is unfortunate, for it is an enclave rather than an outdoor place openly accessible from the Mall and Independence Avenue.

This great circular museum anchors the southern end of the Eighth Street axis, which the McMillan Plan highlighted as a formal break in the

Fig. 3.15. Hirshhorn Sculpture Garden and Museum, view to south

long axis of the Mall. Part of the Hirshhorn Museum is the sunken sculpture garden, which protrudes into the Mall and emphasizes this cross-axis. Located in the zone of trees, fourteen feet below the Mall grade, the garden is reached via stairs on the Mall side. It is a very tectonic garden with minimal plantings and a long reflecting pool. The sculpture has been adroitly chosen and placed to form a coordinated visual experience (see fig. 3.15).

Adjacent to the Hirshhorn Museum is the National Air and Space Museum, designed by Hellmuth, Obata and Kassabaum in 1976, the most popular museum on the Mall, with 10 million to 12 million visitors annually. The four solid boxes joined by three glass galleries do not adequately express the power of their program, the history of American aviation and space exploration (fig. 3.16).[63] One expects more exciting architecture to relate to the exciting contents: the Wright brothers' airplane, the *Spirit of St. Louis,* and the *Apollo* moon-landing module. The design relates to that of the National Gallery of Art West Building, across the Mall, in having the same seven-part massing and pink Tennessee marble facades. The symmetrical scheme with a central entry from a two-level terrace has classical overtones. But it does not have the detail of the National Gallery of Art West Building to give it human scale. Only its size, not its architectural expression, makes it monumental.

On the Mall side, the glass galleries were intended to evoke accessibility but fail to do so because of the heavy brown tinting. On the Independence Avenue side, the visual transparency in these zones is denied by additional marble masses. The solid blocks contain exhibits on two levels, whereas the glazed galleries are primarily for circulation. These sixty-two-foot-high galleries have acrylic roofs, with exhibits suspended from white pipe trusses. For many years the most exciting experience of

this building was to enter under the Wright brothers' first airplane, which was suspended overhead. In 1988 a crystal-shaped restaurant featuring the same pipe trusses with bronze glazing was added to the east end of the museum.

Fig. 3.17. Aerial view of the National Mall from the Capitol. Library of Congress, Prints and Photographs Division, HABS No. DC 615-6, photo by Jack Boucher, 1992

Perhaps the Mall's most unusual building opened in 2004 on the trapezoidal site facing the Capitol and opposite the National Gallery of Art East Building. The National Museum of the American Indian accommodates a vast collection of artifacts. The curvilinear design utilizing water and light by the Native American architect Douglas Cardinal is meant to evoke eroded cliffs and to express reverence for nature. The main entry leads to a full-height circular gathering space surrounded by sinuous galleries on five levels.[64] This highly noncontextual scheme with an exterior of rough yellow limestone is surrounded by Native American–inspired gardens.[65] Many have considered this to be the last museum on the Mall, but other sites are being considered for other museums. While they may not abut the great open space or have the same prominence, these sites still have the attraction of proximity to the Mall.

The architecture critic Donald Canty once commented, "Sometimes it has seemed that over the years the Smithsonian has devoted itself to seeing how different . . . its buildings on the Mall could be from one another."[66] The assortment of buildings along the Mall may be considered a museum of architecture, reflecting the changing architectural styles in the city and nation during the last century and a half (fig. 3.17). Most of these buildings were approved by the U.S. Commission of Fine Arts, and yet little other than light-colored exteriors and similar heights relate them to one another. The long rows of deciduous elm trees visually separate the sides of the Mall and ameliorate the visual cacophony. Likewise, the buildings are usually seen obliquely as one approaches them along Madison or Jefferson Drive. The Mall as a generous monumental landscape has the capacity to absorb a great deal of disparity yet maintain its integrity. But there is a limit, as the historian Richard Longstreth asserts: "The Mall can even hold its own against the few architectural banalities that have been inflicted on it; however, any precinct can only tolerate so much intrusion before the underlying spirit is compromised beyond retrieval, leaving little more than an assemblage of varied opinions about design cast in three-dimensional form."[67]

Ground Zero

The Washington Monument stands at ground zero in the nation's capital, at the intersection of its two primary axes. This spot is the literal and figurative spatial anchor of L'Enfant's superb plan. The soaring obelisk, the tallest element in Washington and the tallest masonry structure in the world, at this location serves as a reference point from all points in the city and many in the suburbs. The expansive views from the observation room atop the monument provide one of the city's best visitor experiences. The power of this symbol at this critical location is immeasurable. The city and even the nation revolve around it. The actual spot where the axes cross is still unoccupied because the monument was built to the southeast of that point because of its poor soil.

After 114 years of wear and tear the National Park Service embarked on the restoration of the Washington Monument in 1998. The refurbished monument reopened in July 2000. Visible still is the change in stone color at 156 feet, where construction stopped before the Civil War.

Robert Mills's original design for the Washington Monument included a huge colonnaded base for a pantheon of heroes. It is fortuitous that this base was omitted because too costly, for its absence gives the monument a formal clarity. As *Washington Post* critic Benjamin Forgey states, "Part of the significance of the Washington Monument is its abstraction. It remains a tribute to the man himself but, lacking direct reference such as a statue, it also can be read as a statement about the founding of the nation as a whole."[68] Like a Greek Doric column, it sits on a simple concrete plaza without a base.

The site of the monument has remained unresolved since the Senate Park Commission's design for a grand sunken plaza was rejected because of poor soil conditions. In 1999 the monument sat on a mound in a circular plaza within a circular drive ringed with flags. The site is basically an open lawn with trees clustered around the perimeter. Paths lead from all sides, but parking is off of Constitution Avenue, south of the German American Friendship Garden. A stone survey lodge was erected in 1886 near Fifteenth Street. South of the obelisk is the outdoor Sylvan Theater, completed in 1917. The Christopher Columbus Memorial is on the west side.

Even before the terrorist attacks on 11 September 2001 the Washington Monument was viewed as a security risk. It is a symbolic, open target, the kind of highly visible structure terrorists could attack to make a statement. Concrete barriers encircled the monument as a temporary security measure. The permanent solution by landscape architect Laurie Olin is based on the English garden concept of the ha-ha, a hidden trench to keep wandering animals away from the manor house. In this scheme the ha-has are curved low walls and sunken paths looping around the obelisk at the base of the mound to prevent vehicles with bombs from approaching the monument.[69] Visitors enter the historic stone lodge along Fifteenth Street before proceeding along the sunken paths to the monument. This satisfies National Park Service criteria of providing a four-hundred-foot perimeter of security while preserving the existing cultural landscape. A tunnel approach and underground visitors' center have been put on hold.

The Washington Monument is as much a symbol of the nation as the White House and the Capitol. Its pure geometric form standing alone evokes the strength of the nation as a democracy. The monument is rooted in its mounded site, uncompromised at its base, visible from all directions. It follows the ancient Egyptian and Roman traditions of using obelisks to mark important locations and honor heroes.

Memorials and Meaning

A significant number of plans for improving the Mall have been produced since L'Enfant's initial scheme. None of these plans adequately considered the placement of memorials, and no one was able to predict the growing desire to memorialize individuals or events at this epicenter of American democracy. The McMillan Plan provided the locations of some memorials. No one anticipated the major memorials built at the end of the twentieth century. The result has been a series of ad hoc decisions on memorial placement, many of them prudent, some questionable.

I shall discuss only the major memorials here. The three memorials in Union Square were previously addressed. Other earlier memorials on the Mall were dedicated to Joseph Henry, first secretary of the Smithsonian, and the landscape architect Andrew Jackson Downing. Memorials to Louis Daguerre and Dr. Samuel Gross are no longer on the Mall. Minor memorials in West Potomac Park are listed below in chronological order of completion:

Commodore John Paul Jones Memorial (1912), south end of Seventeenth Street

John Ericsson Monument (1926), Independence Avenue and Ohio Drive

Japanese Lantern, 1651, gift of the governor of Tokyo (dedicated 1954), Independence Avenue and West Basin Drive

Japanese Pagoda, 1600, gift of the mayor of Yokohama (dedicated 1958), Ohio Drive and West Basin Drive

District of Columbia World War I Memorial (1931), south side of Reflecting Pool

Signers of the Declaration of Independence (1981), Constitution Gardens Lake

George Mason Memorial Garden (2002), north of Roosevelt Memorial

The contemporary era of memorials on the Mall begins with the Vietnam Veterans Memorial, sponsored by the Vietnam Veterans Memorial Fund. This is a memorial like no other, for it is not an object in the landscape. It is the landscape, an enigmatic gash in the ground itself. Most war memorials honor the victors and/or their leaders. Focusing on the lives lost and not the war was the design intention of Maya Lin, who won the design competition while an architecture student in 1981. Almost everyone was astonished by the memorial form, an angled wall inscribed with fifty-seven thousand names (more than a thousand more have since been added) of those killed in the order in which they fell, set into the ground with one end pointing to the Washington Monument and the

other pointing to the Lincoln Memorial. Here is how Lin describes the scheme: "I imagined taking a knife and cutting into the earth, opening it up, an initial violence and pain that in time would heal. The grass would grow back but the initial cut would remain a pure flat surface in the earth with a polished, mirrored surface. The need for the names to be on the memorial would become the memorial; there was no need to embellish the design further."[70] The experience of the memorial is profoundly engaging because the polished black granite wall reflects the living who encounter the dead along a narrow paved path. One descends into the earth, the realm of the dead, and then emerges again into the sunlight (fig. 3.18).

This minimalist memorial, completed in 1982, was difficult for the conservative establishment in Washington and elsewhere to accept. Some saw it as a negative statement, a black wall in a ditch. The seemingly apolitical design was in fact a political statement. But a controversial war deserved a controversial memorial. Opponents of the design had three representational figures and a flagpole added at one end. Now an underground exhibition center is planned to help people understand the Vietnam War. But the public has accepted and appreciated this poetic memorial, thronging to it for one of the most memorable visitor experiences in the nation's capital.

Next to be built was the Korean War Veterans Memorial, which combined the concept of memorial as landscape with the tradition of figurative representation. Its intent was to honor patriotic duty by means of a representation of a platoon of soldiers marching uphill toward the American flag and a circular pool of remembrance defined by linden trees (fig. 3.19). A team from Pennsylvania State University won the competition, but the memorial design was completed by Cooper-Lecky Architects in 1995. Frank Gaylord was the sculptor of nineteen cast-steel figures, larger than life-size, wearing ponchos over military gear.[71] It was sponsored by the American Battle Monuments Commission, formed by Congress in 1923. The triangular hill is defined by a dark gray granite wall with an inscription and facial images of war personnel lit by fiber optics, which personalizes the memorial in a manner similar to that of the Vietnam Veter-

Fig. 3.19. Korean War Veterans Memorial, view to east

ans Memorial. The granite wall, the angular geometry, and the changes in topography positively relate this memorial south of the Reflecting Pool to the Vietnam Memorial on the north side.

The Franklin Delano Roosevelt Memorial was dedicated in 1997 after thirty-seven years of design competitions, delays, and design changes. In form it is a landscape rather than a structure, occupying 7.5 acres on the west side of the Tidal Basin. Sponsored by the FDR Memorial Commission, it follows the Senate Park Commission "kite diagram" for locating memorials in relation to the Mall axes and the locations of other monuments. Designed by the noted landscape architect Lawrence Halprin, it was constructed of four thousand blocks of rusticated carnelian granite from South Dakota, the heaviest weighing thirty-nine tons.[72] Conceptually it is a didactic narrative representing Roosevelt's four terms in office: four sequential spaces with progressively rougher granite surfaces, separated by four gardens. In each space the story is told by statues, inscriptions, and bas-reliefs (fig. 3.20). Water features in many forms—falling, flowing, splashing—in juxtaposition with the placid edge of the Tidal Basin add much to the aesthetic experience. The memorial has been fitted well to its odd site in spite of the difficult underpinning necessary to support the large stone elements on fill land. In appearance it differs vastly from anything else near the Mall, relating instead to primitive stone structures and/or ruins of antiquity. The choreographed processional experience is provocative and engaging, encouraging the visitor to encounter the spaces and their artifacts. Protests from disabled citizens that Roosevelt's disability had been hidden resulted in the addition of a sculpture of him in a wheelchair even though he never appeared in a wheelchair in public.

Almost nothing is built or changed on the Mall without years of debate and controversy. This has been the case with almost every memorial constructed thus far. In the case of the World War II Memorial there was a higher level of contentiousness in Congress, in committee hearings, and in courtrooms, as well as among veterans and the media. There was disagreement on the site, the design, and the process for approval. The site

Fig. 3.20. Roosevelt Memorial, third-term space with seated statue and pet dog

at the east end of the Reflecting Pool surrounding the existing Rainbow Pool is one that J. Carter Brown, chairman of the U.S. Commission of Fine Arts, thought would conform with the McMillan Plan.[73] The design in essence is two apsidal colonnades of granite piers north and south of a smaller Rainbow Pool, defining a plaza recessed into the ground surrounded by acres of gardens. On the north-south axis of the memorial are two tall temple forms commemorating the Atlantic and Pacific theaters of war with imperial bronze sculptures by Raymond Kaskey. The process involved modifying Friedrich St. Florian's winning competition design until everyone involved was reasonably satisfied except the opponents who contended the memorial would intrude upon the vista between the Washington and Lincoln memorials and thus violate local historic preservation laws.

The World War II Memorial, sponsored by the American Battle Monuments Commission, honors the greatest conflict of the twentieth century in the nation's most visible public place. Ground was broken on Veterans Day in 2000, and the 7.4-acre memorial was dedicated amid great fanfare on Memorial Day in 2004. The reality of its existence may not settle the controversy, but everyone can now judge the results with a personal visit. Joseph Cannon, the Republican Speaker of the House of Representatives from 1903 to 1911, bitterly opposed the site for the Lincoln Memorial. After it was dedicated he reflected on his political battles: "I have been in many fights, some I have lost—many I have won—it may have been better if I had lost more. I am pleased I lost the one against the Lincoln Memorial."[74] The World War II Memorial is a fine addition to the Mall that will be cherished by future generations (fig. 3.21).

But the controversy continues with a multitude of critiques. Negative criticisms include that it lacks originality as public art since it is an assemblage of known neoclassical elements and symbols without meaning, that it relies too much on words to memorialize the sacrifices of those

Fig. 3.21. World War II Memorial, view to west

who fought and won the war for democracy,[75] and that it is not emotionally engaging. A positive critique is that the components enhance the setting, frame views, and encourage pedestrian occupation.[76] The neoclassical elements, the rows of pillars and the biaxial symmetry, integrate it with the Jefferson and Lincoln memorials. Most critics and visitors (except those who view the Mall as sacrosanct) agree that the memorial has not harmed the view between the Washington and Lincoln monuments. It is a well-designed urban place, defined and yet open, a focus for gatherings within the Mall. It satisfies the designer's intentions of creating a space full of life-giving water in which to celebrate the freedom earned by those who sacrificed; it is a heroic tribute to those who died. The public place in this auspicious location is the true memorial, a place to experience freedom within the nation's civic center.

Still to come is the Martin Luther King, Jr. National Memorial on the northwest edge of the Tidal Basin. ROMA Design Group won the competition to honor the civil rights leader with a memorial sponsored by Alpha Phi Alpha fraternity.[77] However, the design will undoubtedly be modified during the review-and-approval process.

The Mall is no longer the pleasure ground intended by L'Enfant. The hidden issue behind the controversies regarding memorials is the nature of the Mall itself, which will continue to change as Americans' cultural values change. J. Carter Brown thought it should be more than a recreational space. "It's important that we bring intellectualism and gristle and armature to our national symbols. We really need to understand what people have gone through before us to make it possible for us today."[78]

Brown cites a comment made by the Bauhaus painter Joseph Albers while touring Washington: "Washington is a city of space but not spaces."[79] The Vietnam War, Korean War, and Roosevelt memorials have made human-scaled spaces in this monumental landscape that can be inhabited. Visitors can easily relate to them and their commemorative content. The architect Roger K. Lewis is concerned that long, high walls are being used to shape these spaces, thus separating them from their context. "Does erecting such walls make sense, given one of the Mall's most unique attributes is its continuity and horizontal sweep, which allows us to see extraordinary distances and enjoy extraordinary vistas?"[80] He has a point, especially with regard to the Roosevelt Memorial and the future King Memorial. The Vietnam and Korean memorials utilize walls that shape space without obstructing vistas.

The competition to locate memorials in the Mall area led the National Capital Planning Commission, the Commission of Fine Arts, and the National Capital Memorial Commission to become proactive and develop a Memorials and Museums Master Plan.[81] It establishes a moratorium on new memorials in a zone called the Reserve, along the east-west axis of the Mall, Lafayette Park, the White House grounds, the Washington Monument grounds, the Tidal Basin, and the Capitol grounds. A large zone adjacent to this area would be reserved for works of "preeminent historic and national significance." A total of 102 potential sites are identified along the waterfront crescent, monumental corridors, and North Capitol, South Capitol, and East Capitol streets. These sites are all within an easy distance of public transit stops, one of the plan's criteria. The plan also encourages the creation of new types of memorials in the form of plazas, fountains, gardens, and even renovated buildings.

This master plan may be challenged by groups proposing additional memorials. Congress has passed legislation for a memorial to President John Adams and his family to be located on federal land. The sponsors are seeking a site related to the Washington Monument and the Jefferson Memorial because of Adams's associations with Washington and Jefferson.[82] Additional memorials to President Ronald Reagan, African Americans, and Disabled American Veterans have been proposed, but no sites have been approved. Once again the primary issue is prestige; every group wants its memorial to be located on the Mall, the single most important public space in the country. In this location it can be directly associated with the democratic ideals of the nation.

America's Democratic Front Lawn

On Easter Sunday, 1939, seventy-five thousand people came to hear Marian Anderson sing on the steps of the Lincoln Memorial after she had been prohibited from singing at the Daughters of the American Revolution Constitution Hall (fig. 3.22).[83] This event helped to establish the Lincoln Memorial steps and grounds as a rallying place for African Americans struggling for civil rights. This culminated with the 1963 march on Washington, the centennial of emancipation, when Martin Luther King Jr. gave his inspiring "I Have a Dream" speech.

When the United States escalated the unpopular war in Vietnam, protestors utilized the Mall as a forum for political demonstrations. These events strained its physical fabric and necessitated police protection to maintain civil order. Public-transit schedules were adjusted, and streets were closed. The National Park Service began to require permits for demonstrations and protests. In 1991 alone more than two thousand permits were issued for exhibits, demonstrations, and festivals on the Mall.[84]

In the year 2000 nearly three thousand permits were issued for every conceivable kind of event or exhibition protected by the First Amend-

ment on the Mall. These included annual events such as Earth Day, the Millennium March for Equality, and the Names Project Quilt. Thousands of participants inevitably leave mounds of garbage that must be cleaned up by sponsoring groups. This level of pedestrian activity has destroyed the turf, resulting in sections of the Mall being closed for six-month periods to renew the grass and walkways.[85] To control this deterioration, liquor has been banned and vendors have been moved to the perimeter. Yet authorities are sensitive to keeping the Mall freely accessible as a symbol of the nation's open democracy.

Many Mall events are political, intended to communicate to the president or Congress the people's views. Such is the Million Mom March, calling for gun control; Solidarity Day, to protest President Reagan's labor policy; and Stand for Children, to spotlight health and poverty problems. While these political gatherings have had little direct influence on legislation or policy, their indirect influence is difficult to measure. This may be because there are now too many of these events to focus anyone's attention in a compelling way, as did the civil rights marches of the 1960s. Or they need to be part of a sustained political movement, such as the antiabortion and gay rights movements.

Some of these events, such as the Million Man March, the African American Family Reunion, the Million Family March, and the Promise Keepers assembly, are personal gatherings rather than protests.[86] The estimates of attendance are no longer made by the National Park Service but are undoubtedly inflated by the organizers. Although these events may not draw a million, they do draw hundreds of thousands, proving the appeal of making a statement in the nation's premier democratic forum.

Fig. 3.22. Marian Anderson at the Lincoln Memorial, 1939. Library of Congress, Prints and Photographs Division, LC-USZ62-130159, photo courtesy of *New York World Telegram and Sun*

The Mall is also a cultural forum. There are annual events such as the Fourth of July concert and fireworks and the Smithsonian Folklife Festival. Screen on the Green presents free classic films on a giant screen one night a week during the summer.

And the Mall area is used daily by thousands of sports enthusiasts. From dawn to dusk on the weekends and holidays, as well as after work during the week, there are games of rugby, soccer, softball, volleyball, polo, flag football, Frisbee, and lacrosse. This is in addition to the thousands of joggers and walkers all day, every day, everywhere throughout this precinct (fig. 3.23).

The terrorist attacks on 11 September 2001 have had many repercussions, not the least of which is protecting monuments on the Mall. A scheme of trenches and low walls has been constructed to protect the Washington Monument. The Lincoln and Jefferson memorials would be encircled by low, concrete walls faced with stone to match the monuments. These would give way to planters and bollards where pedestrians enter the memorials themselves. Measures such as street closures, limited vehicular access and restricted parking, in addition to increased police patrols, are also likely.

The Mall itself should remain available to the public, with free access and use as expressions of freedom in an open democracy, despite fears to the contrary. For the festivities there on the Fourth of July in 2002, several areas were fenced off, and people entering them passed through metal detectors. An incident in March 2003, when a man drove a purportedly bomb-laden tractor into Constitution Gardens, led to a forty-eight-hour standoff and resulted in the closing of major streets. In the aftermath several authorities said that the Mall would remain open despite such abuses.[87] Freedom of public access must be preserved at all costs.

We must hope that the terrorist threats that have impacted the nation's capital will not diminish the public's desire to be on the Mall or to visit its many attractions. The class trip to Washington has been a rite of passage for thousands of U.S. high-school students. More and more foreign tourists are coming to Washington to experience this unique capital

South Capitol, and East Capitol streets to form four urban quadrants (see fig. 1.1). The Grand Avenue forming the Mall was the equivalent of a West Capitol Street. The angled Delaware and New Jersey avenues north and south of the Capitol also crossed at its center. At the base of Capitol Hill along the Tiber Canal, labeled *F* on the map, he proposed a "Grand Cascade, formed of the water from the sources of the Tiber," a falls forty feet high and one hundred feet wide flowing from under the base of the Congress House.[1] Labeled *G* are two walks described in the key as "Public walk, being a square of 1900 feet through which carriages may ascend to the upper square of the Federal house." These two walks were extensions of Pennsylvania and Maryland avenues leading up Jenkins Hill past four gatehouses. Curiously, a footprint for the Capitol is not shown on the map, though one is shown for the President's House. Labeled *L* is Capitol Square, and labeled *M* is East Capitol Street. The key reads: "Around this square, and all along the Avenue from the two bridges to the Federal house, the pavement on each side will pass under an arched way, under whose cover, shops will be most conveniently and agreeably situated. This street is 160 feet in breadth, and a mile long."[2] L'Enfant proposed arcades around Capitol Square and along East Capitol Street to provide access to commercial spaces. He envisioned the eastern extension of the plateau as the future commercial center of the new capital city.

When Andrew Ellicott redrew the city plan in 1792, he retained all of L'Enfant's design features around the Capitol. He did, however, show a footprint for the Capitol set within a formal square defined by small urban blocks (see fig. 1.2). The two avenues leading up the hill were formalized and terminated by green spaces with gatehouses at their corners. There was also an axial green space aligned with the cascade. Ellicott described the origins of the city grid as follows: "In order to execute this plan, Mr. Ellicott drew a true Meridienal line by celestial observation which passes through the area intended for the Capitol; this line he crossed by another due East and West, which passes through the same area."[3] Thus, the grid of Washington is oriented to the true cardinal directions utilizing the center of the Capitol as the origin. The location of the Capitol is given on the map as latitude 38°53′ N and longitude 0°0′

The Capitol was the second federal building to be constructed in Washington (following the White House); George Washington laid the cornerstone in 1793. The north wing was completed by 1800, in time for the capital to be relocated from Philadelphia. Capitol Square developed as a residential and commercial precinct, providing lodging for members of Congress and services for the neighborhood. The blocks to the east were lined with an assortment of small-scale buildings, such as Carroll Row, a boarding house for members of Congress that was later demolished to make way for the Library of Congress.[4] The Sewall-Belmont House (1800), on the northwest corner of Constitution Avenue and Second Street, NE, is the only Capitol Square structure remaining from that era.

Few sites in the city served as many different uses as First and A streets, NE (fig. 4.1): it has been the location of a tavern, a meeting place for Congress, a prison, a school, a boarding house, a National Women's Party headquarters, and the Supreme Court, in that order. The Old Brick Capitol was located on the site of an old tavern-hotel that was demol-

ished in 1815 to build a temporary meeting place for Congress while the Capitol was rebuilt after the British burned it in 1814. Congress met in this large, four-story Federal-style brick building for four years. During the Civil War it was a prison for a wide assortment of inmates, including two infamous female Confederate spies.[5] It was demolished in 1932 to make way for the New Supreme Court building.

Andrew Jackson Downing's 1851 plan for the Mall did not extend to Capitol Square. Development of this area during the nineteenth century occurred without benefit of a master plan, resulting in an unfortunate deviation from the L'Enfant vision. The Library of Congress was built in 1886 on First Street, at the southeast corner of Capitol Square. To form this large site, one block of A Street and one block of Pennsylvania Avenue, SE, were eliminated, interrupting an important vista toward the Capitol along this avenue from the southeast.

The Thomas Jefferson Building of the Library of Congress, designed by John L. Smithmeyer and Paul Pelz and built from 1871 to 1897, is one of Washington's most magnificent edifices.[6] Established by Congress in 1800 for its own use, the Library of Congress is now open to the public as one of the best research libraries in the world. It was the city's first Beaux-Arts building, standing alone on its landscaped site, an elongated, five-part stone structure facing First Street, SE (fig. 4.2). Large-scale exterior stairs lead to the arcaded entry of a grand central pavilion. The processional sequence through the great stair hall to the octagonal reading room establishes the hierarchical purpose of the library. The three-story stair hall is flooded with natural light from windows and a stained-glass ceiling. Light from the 160-foot-high dome suffuses the reading room, which is similar in form to the reading room of the British Museum in London (1823–47). Closed stacks are hidden from view in three-story wings. Corner pavilions, containing smaller reading rooms, mimic the form of the main pavilion. An addition at the rear of the building in the 1930s provided space for a rare-book library along with other service functions.

In figure 4.3, a map of Capitol Square in 1903, all of the blocks sur-

L'ENFANT'S LEGACY

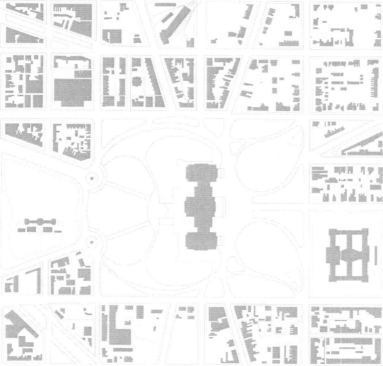

Top: Fig. 4.2. Jefferson
Building of the Library of
Congress, view to southeast.
Library of Congress, Prints
and Photographs Division,
HABS No. DC 461A, photo by
Jack Boucher, 1975

Bottom: Fig. 4.3. Capitol
Square in 1903 (north is to
the top)

rounding the Capitol have been developed with row houses, commercial buildings, or service functions. It also shows the new Library of Congress. The blocks west of the Capitol along Pennsylvania and Maryland avenues are also developed. The Botanic Garden buildings on the west side are located just south of the Capitol axis.

The Capitol

The centerpiece of Capitol Square and the capital city is the Capitol building itself. Symbolically, it is also the centerpiece of the nation, a monumental representation of the United States' democratic form of government. It has a complicated architectural history spanning more than two centuries.[7]

When the design competition for a new Capitol resulted in no clear winners, Thomas Jefferson created a compromise design composed of Dr. William Thornton's elevation and Stephen Hallet's plan. The resulting design featured a central domed rotunda adjacent to a circular space topped by a high domed temple on the west side. The north wing had a semicircular chamber for the Senate, and the south wing had an elliptical chamber for the House of Representatives. The three-story structure had a rusticated ground floor, a tall principal floor, and a third story with a low, sloped roof hidden behind a deep entablature and balustrade. When the federal government first moved to the District of Columbia, the Senate, House, circuit court, and Supreme Court all met in the north wing. A temporary chamber for the House was built in 1801 on the foundations of the south wing, connected by a wooden passageway to the north wing.[8]

Benjamin Henry Latrobe assumed architectural responsibility in 1803 and completed the building according to his own redesign. He rebuilt the already completed interior of the north wing, added a low saucer dome over the central rotunda, and built east and west facing porticoes. He also completed the Supreme Court chamber and the Library of Congress space, rebuilt the Senate chamber, and erected the House wing before the British partially burned the building in the War of 1812. Subsequently, the House chamber was redesigned as a semicircular room, and the space for the Library of Congress was enlarged to face the Mall. These sophisticated chambers, formed by layers of space, are still among the best rooms in the Capitol. Charles Bulfinch was appointed in 1818 to complete the building according to Latrobe's design. He redesigned the west portico and the rotunda, the latter with a high-profile dome. He extended the east terrace around the building and landscaped the grounds, enclosing them with a fence and gatehouses. The Capitol was finally completed in 1829, as illustrated in an 1844 daguerreotype (fig. 4.4).

The first major expansion occurred in 1851, when Thomas U. Walter's scheme adding north and south wings connected to the original building by passageways was accepted. The wings were pushed eastward, with grand stairs above carriageways leading to porticoes with pediments in front of colonnades extending across the entire east facade. Porticoes on the other sides did not have pediments. The north wing accommodated the rectangular Senate chamber, and the south wing accommodated the rectangular House of Representatives chamber. Montgomery C. Meigs, of the Army Corps of Engineers, was the supervising engineer for six and a half years, working closely with Walter to make design and construction

changes. Walter also designed a much higher dome with a great upward sweep, a peristyle at its base, a windowed attic, and a tholus at the top, intended to balance the long facades of the expanded building. It was actually two domes of fireproof cast iron held together by iron trussed ribs. Meigs was greatly instrumental in having the new dome constructed. The allegorical statue *Freedom,* sculpted by Thomas Crawford, was placed on top in 1863.

Fig. 4.4. Daguerreotype of U.S. Capitol, east side, by John Plumbe Jr., 1844. Library of Congress, Prints and Photographs Division, LC-USZ62-46801

Two additional extensions of the Capitol were completed in the twentieth century. The east front was expanded by thirty-two feet in 1962, replicating Latrobe and Bulfinch's facade in Georgia marble. Not only did this add space but it moved the dome back from its precarious position at the edge of the building. The basement-level courtyards on the west side between the building and terrace were roofed to provide additional office space in 1991.

During the 1960s the Capitol came to be seen as a historic landmark rather than just a functional structure.[9] Architect of the Capitol J. George Stewart planned a west-front extension in 1965 that would essentially mimic the east-front extension but would destroy the Olmsted terraces. The furor over this project was highly contentious and political. Stewart's successor, George M. White, also favored the extension of the west front, but Congress finally responded to political pressure in 1983 and denied the extension in favor of the restoration, replacement, and repair of the original sandstone facades. The work, which was completed in 1987, involved replacing 40 percent of the damaged sandstone with Indiana limestone.[10] This was a victory for historic preservation in America, a movement dedicated to promoting architectural history as an important cultural value.

The Capitol precinct is unique in being directly supervised by Congress. During the early years the architects working on the Capitol were employed by the commissioner of public buildings, who was responsible for the Capitol and the other federal buildings in the city. When the commissioner's role was abolished in 1867, the Architect of the Capitol became responsible to Congress for the maintenance, operation, development, and preservation of the Capitol, the Capitol grounds, Capitol Plaza, the Senate and House buildings, the Supreme Court, the Library of Congress, the Botanic Garden, and sundry other support buildings and open spaces. The Capitol precinct is not subject to the same kinds of design checks and balances as other parts of the federal core.[11] The president appoints the Architect of the Capitol, whose office is funded by Congress.

In spite of the Capitol's long history and many architects, its exterior exhibits considerable architectural harmony. This is because of the overarching agreement by everyone involved to rely on the classical design tradition, with minor individual interpretations. There is variation in proportions and three-dimensional details. The repeated use of Corinthian columns, both fluted and unfluted, on all facades greatly contributes to the visual unification.

Ten individuals have served as Architect of the Capitol, a remarkable and dedicated group who have shouldered the awesome responsibility to oversee this important federal precinct. They have had to work in the arena of politics, where professional judgment and advice are not always followed. The professional agendas of the architects to improve the edifice have also influenced the Capitol's history. It is thus remarkable that the Capitol is a building of such quality, worthy to be the symbol of the American nation.

The Capitol Grounds

The grounds of the Capitol were at first much smaller than they are today. The eastern edge was First Street, with A Street on the north and south extending west and looping around the base of Capitol Hill. During the Capitol's first decades the grounds were used for construction staging. In 1816 the east grounds were landscaped, and an ornamental iron fence was installed to enclose them and to keep away cows, goats, and hogs. It was not until 1826 that Charles Bulfinch developed a design for the grounds that included vaults under the west terrace for wood and coal storage, courtyards for privies, and lodges for a fire engine, porters, and guards.[12] He also extended the fence around the entire grounds, providing carriage gates at the north and south entrances. Bulfinch designed handsome stone gatehouses and gateposts for the western entrances. These were removed in the 1870s and are now on the White House grounds along Constitution Avenue. The grounds themselves were used for band concerts and croquet games.

The Capitol was expanded in 1851 with large wings extending very close to A Street on the north and south dividing the grounds into east and west parcels. Large portions of the Capitol grounds were used for construction staging, and portions of the iron fence were removed. Afterwards, the grounds were left in a sorry state, ungraded and unlandscaped.

From 1865 to 1872 Congress debated whether to expand the grounds to a size befitting such a grand edifice. The commissioner of public buildings lobbied for this expansion and improvement, saying that "no building, be it ever so beautiful, has a finished appearance if the grounds around it are rough, uncouth and unenclosed."[13] He also wanted the railroad running past the east grounds removed because the trains could be heard in the halls of the Senate.[14] Finally, in 1872 legislation was passed to expand the grounds to fifty-eight acres, extending to B Street on the north and south. All private buildings on the newly acquired urban blocks would be demolished.[15]

The first comprehensive effort to plan the Capitol grounds occurred in 1873, when Senator Justin S. Morrill, chairman of the Committee on Public Buildings and Grounds, secured an appropriation to improve them and asked Frederick Law Olmsted to provide the design.[16] Olmsted was America's preeminent landscape architect, having completed designs for Central Park in New York and for major parks in Brooklyn, Boston, Detroit, and Buffalo. His primary concerns about the existing Capitol context were the lack of visibility of the grand structure, particularly from the west, and the location of numerous trees unrelated to the Capitol's design. He was also concerned that the building did not rest solidly upon its hilltop site owing to the lack of a substantial base.

Olmsted's design proposal of 1874 was illustrated with a single drawing (fig. 4.5). From the west, the Capitol would be approached via shaded walks as extensions of Pennsylvania and Maryland avenues. These would lead to a grand stepped west terrace that would serve as an appropriately scaled base for the recently enlarged Capitol. The marble terraces would wrap around the north and south sides. Secondary curved walks scaled the hill, offering changing perspectives of the edifice and its landscape. The main approach from the east was an extension of East Capitol Street lined with tulip trees and flanked on either side by curved walkways defining spacious oval lawns. Low walls with seats would line this carriageway. Two large red granite planters, each with a bronze vase and fountain, terminated this approach. The main carriage approaches to the east plaza continued to emanate from B Street on the north and south.

Olmsted's master plan maintained the symmetrical order dictated by the Capitol's design within a landscape that followed the picturesque tradition. According to the Olmsted historian Charles E. Beveridge, "In his parks, Olmsted subordinated architecture to the landscape, but in planning the grounds for a great structure like the Capitol, the landscape design was subordinated to the building."[17] The grounds were conceived as a precinct wherein all but one of the fifteen converging streets (East Capitol Street) were visually and physically stopped at the periphery by a thick edge of trees. All walks except the three formal approaches were curved to afford varying vistas of the Capitol.

Work commenced on the Olmsted design the same year it was approved, with the removal of trees to create vistas and the removal of earth to establish the required grading. After new gas, water, and sewer lines were laid, new walks and roads were installed.[18] Work on the west terrace was delayed while Congress debated a western Capitol extension for a larger library. When appropriations for construction of the west terrace were assured, Olmsted resigned in order to let the Architect of the Capitol supervise construction. At the behest of Congress, the upper terrace was redesigned to provide windows for committee rooms, whereas the lower exedra terrace received a series of niches surrounding an octagonal fountain. Work continued throughout the 1880s on both the terrace and the grounds, where a variety of paving materials were utilized for the roads and pathways. A beautifully crafted brick summerhouse (the Grotto) was also constructed on the western grounds, a secluded cool retreat set into the hill amid lush planting. It is the most intriguing place on the Capitol

General Plan
for the
Improvement
OF THE
U. S. CAPITOL GROUNDS.

grounds, like an open-air chapel reached through arched openings with seating around a small fountain.

When completed, the west terrace anchored the magnificent structure to its hilltop site as predicted. Its neoclassical design of white Vermont marble was contextually appropriate for the Capitol (fig. 4.6). Moreover, it provided a wonderful promenade around the building and a spectacular place from which to view the Mall and the surrounding city. The terrace became like the Piazza di Spagna in Rome, a public gathering place to meet, greet, and view. In time the presidential inauguration was shifted to this location since it afforded a viewing platform and large spectator grounds. During the first century of the Capitol the east facade was considered the front. After the completion of the west terrace, the west facade came to be known as the front of the Capitol, and the Mall became the Capitol's front yard.

Little of positive value was done to the Capitol grounds during the twentieth century. The west grounds have been reasonably well maintained as Olmsted designed them, including the low stone walls, the Grotto, and many of the handsome copper lanterns with their elaborate stone bases. To preserve the integrity of Olmsted's plan, the placement

L'ENFANT'S LEGACY

of memorials on the grounds has been opposed.[19] The east grounds have
suffered many incursions because of security and vehicular access. Some
of the handsome red granite balustrades installed by Olmsted along the
walkways were removed, although the beautiful fountains remained until
recently. Security gates were located on the north, south, and east approaches, with access controlled by large concrete planters. The entire
east plaza became an asphalt parking lot with meager landscape relief
adjacent to the building, a setting similar to that of a shopping mall.

Fig. 4.6. U.S. Capitol, west
terrace. Library of Congress,
Prints and Photographs
Division, HABS No. DC 1-11,
photo by Jack Boucher, 1975

Capitol Square

The 1902 McMillan Plan proposed a unified Capitol Square defined
by a series of monumental buildings for the Senate on the north side
and the House of Representatives on the south side, along with a new
Supreme Court on the east side. These buildings would create a formal
architectural frame for the Capitol grounds and a dignified setting for
the Capitol. Capitol Square would have strongly defined corners that included two proposed buildings on the western corners forming a gateway
from the Mall (see fig. 3.6). Quoting from the McMillan Plan, "The construction of the above-mentioned buildings as planned will make it in
the highest degree appropriate that fronting the entire square occupied
by the Capitol grounds only public buildings bearing a common relation
to legislative work shall be erected. If the reciprocal relations of the new
buildings shall be studied carefully, so as to produce harmony of design
and uniformity of cornice line, the resulting architectural composition
will be unequaled in magnitude and monumental character by any similar group of legislative buildings in the modern world."[20]

The urban designer Elbert Peets has compared the McMillan Plan
for Capitol Square with L'Enfant's plan.[21] The original city plan divided
the square into a western half, which made a transition to the Mall, and
a smaller eastern half surrounded by arcaded shops, which made a connection to the plateau. The eighty-foot difference in elevation made this
a natural spatial division. In trying to form the square into one coherent

space defined by uniformly scaled monumental buildings the McMillan Plan does not acknowledge the grade change. The scale of the space,
which is eighteen hundred feet wide, twice the width of the Tuileries Gardens in Paris, also makes its definition difficult to perceive.

The McMillan report decried the existing conditions of Capitol
Square and its context of squalid private buildings. It also criticized the
closing of Pennsylvania Avenue to make way for the Library of Congress
and strongly recommended that all existing avenues focus on the dome
of the Capitol. On the western side, Olmsted's design was altered in order
to insert Union Square, which included a water feature as L'Enfant originally intended.

Most of the McMillan Plan for Capitol Square has been completed as
proposed. During the 1930s and 1940s the blocks around the square were
cleared of private buildings, one by one, as new construction projects
were initiated for the Senate, the House of Representatives, the Supreme
Court, and the Library of Congress. Only one small, triangular block
remains north of the Supreme Court. The proposed design for Union
Square was altered by Frederick Law Olmsted Jr., who designed it to be a
transition space between the Mall and the Capitol grounds designed by
his father. The biggest departure from the McMillan Plan was the creation of a landscape connection between Union Station and the Mall that
involved the urban blocks between North Capitol and First streets, NE.

With the McMillan Plan for Capitol Square accepted, albeit not officially approved by Congress, the Architect of the Capitol began planning
two new congressional buildings. In the interest of economy the prestigious New York firm of Carrere and Hastings was hired only to design the
exteriors of the two new buildings on the identically shaped sites.[22] The
Cannon House Office Building (1908) is on a large trapezoidal site at the
southwest corner of First Street, SE, and Independence Avenue, SE. The
building occupies the entire site, with three-story neoclassical facades at
the street lines and a large open-air courtyard. The building's principal

Fig. 4.8. Russell Senate Office
Building, view to northeast

spaces are expressed by the projecting corner pavilion with its two-story
arched windows diagonally facing the Capitol dome (fig. 4.7).

The Russell Senate Office Building (1908) is located on the northwest
corner of First Street, NE, and Constitution Avenue, NE (fig. 4.8). The
plans and elevations are similar to those of the Cannon Building. The
fourth side, enclosing the courtyard along First Street, NE, was not completed until 1933, at which time the C Street, NE, side was given a new,
dignified facade since it faced the park fronting Union Station.[23]

These first two buildings according to the McMillan Plan for Capitol
Square established design precedents for buildings to come. Their street
walls created a strong architectural frame for the Capitol grounds, and
their architecture was suitably elaborate, while deferring to the Capitol.
Each building was connected to the Capitol via a tunnel with a subway
for congressional use. A power plant to provide heat and electricity for
these buildings, as well as the Capitol and the Library of Congress, was
also constructed at this time south of Capitol Square. Although it no longer provides electricity, it has been expanded five times to provide heat-
ing and air conditioning.[24]

The Senate Park Commission chose the trapezoidal site at the northeast corner of First Street, NE, and East Capitol Street for the Supreme
Court. Although disagreeing with this site choice, the eminent architect
Cass Gilbert designed a dignified and compelling classical edifice.[25] The
steel-frame Supreme Court building (1935), faced with white marble, is
in the form of a Roman temple flanked by two lower wings, each with
two courtyards (fig. 4.9). The Corinthian portico facing the Capitol is on
axis with the latter's north-wing portico. Its strength and purity of form
set the Supreme Court apart from its flamboyant southern neighbor, the
Library of Congress, while establishing its hierarchical importance as second only to the Capitol. The figural form is set off from the urban context
by terraces and low walls surrounded by lawns and hedges that establish
its significance.

The Longworth House Office Building (1933) occupies the sloping, narrow trapezoidal site west of the Cannon Building. The neoclassical design by Allied Architects of Washington has three-story flat marble facades above a two- to three-story rusticated granite base, with two additional stories on the roof recessed behind a marble balustrade.[26] Facing the Capitol is an imposing Ionic portico with a pediment above an arcaded base. Because Independence Avenue slopes down at this point, the cornice line of the Cannon Building was maintained on the Longworth Building in spite of the latter's greater building height. The Longworth Building's simpler design with sparse ornament, sometimes referred to as stripped-down classical, indicates the growing influence of modern architecture.

Although the location of a new Union Station was known to the Senate Park Commission, the landscape connection to Capitol Square was not planned. This changed in 1910 with plans for extending the Capitol grounds to Union Station Plaza, in front of the railroad station. The design concept was to create a grand entrance to the Capitol and the Mall for those arriving by train. Over a period of three decades, twelve urban blocks of hotels, residences, and commercial buildings were acquired and cleared to form this large open space called Capitol Plaza.[27] During World War I the area was used for temporary barracks and hotels for government employees. The Chicago firm of Bennett, Parsons and Frost developed the master plan in 1927 with a small underground garage under a raised terrace and a streetcar viaduct in line with C Street. On axis with North Capitol Street is a broad esplanade with a large pool at D Street, and there is a ceremonial fountain on the terrace above the garage (fig. 4.10). On the triangular block bounded by Constitution, Louisiana, and New Jersey avenues is the Robert A. Taft Memorial, dedicated to the former senator and Speaker of the House. His bronze statue stands at the base of an unadorned, marble-faced rectangular tower one hundred feet high and incorporating a twenty-seven-bell carillon.[28] The remain-

L'ENFANT'S LEGACY

ing area is a series of lawns with trees and walks, a greatly underutilized space in a very important location.

After the 1930s era of multiple building projects there was a hiatus until 1948, when the New York firm of Eggers and Higgins was retained to design a modern building that would fit the classical Capitol Square context. Located east of the Russell Senate Office Building, the E-shaped Dirksen Senate Office Building (1958) faces First Street, NE. A seven-story structure with colonnades implied by tall vertical windows, its design broke new ground with the introduction of modern architectural language to Capitol Square.[29] Its most disappointing feature is the false entrance portico on First Street, NE; the real entries are on Constitution Avenue. The building's visual impact on Capitol Square is presently minimal. If and when the last commercial buildings on the triangular site to the south are removed, its impact will be more significant.

The Rayburn House Office Building is located along Independence Avenue west of the Longworth Building on a large site created by closing off Delaware Avenue. Harbeson, Hough, Livingston and Larson, of Philadelphia, designed the four-story building that encompasses more than 1 million square feet, 25 percent more floor area than in the Capi-

Fig. 4.10. Aerial view of Capitol Plaza, view to south along North Capitol Street. Library of Congress, Prints and Photographs Division, HABS No. DC 612-16, photo by Jack Boucher, 1992

tol. There is a central courtyard, and large courtyards open to the streets on the east and west sides. The white marble exterior was designed in a classical modern style similar to that of the Dirksen Building, with an understated base, middle, and top. However, the base is very high on the downhill side, the middle has vertical openings mimicking a colonnade, and the top is too large. The design lacks human scale because of poor proportions and architectural details.

In 1982 the Hart Senate Office Building was completed on the half-block site east of the Dirksen Building, to which it is attached. The new building, which faces Second Street, NE, was given re-entrant corners so as to preserve the Sewall-Belmont House. It appears to have four stories, it is actually eight stories high with a floor area similar to that of the Rayburn Building. The Hart Senate Office Building was the first building on Capitol Square of truly modern design, with gridded facades of white marble and tinted glass. The architect, John Carl Warnecke, created a new kind of office building, with circulation organized around a skylit atrium one hundred feet tall featuring an Alexander Calder stabile-mobile entitled *Mountains and Clouds*.[30]

Proposals for a memorial to President James Madison were realized in a single building on the urban block south of the existing Jefferson Building. The Library of Congress James Madison Memorial Building (1980) was designed by DeWitt, Poor and Shelton with an enormous footprint (500 feet by 400 feet) encompassing 1.5 million square feet.[31] The six-story building (with a recessed seventh floor) has six-story colonnades of rectangular columns on all four facades, negating a sense of orientation. It is surrounded by raised planters dissociating it from the streetscape. This marble-clad block with massive, unarticulated corners has even less human scale than the Rayburn Building. The architectural expression can only be described as banal monumental.

The Bartholdi Fountain was originally located near the Botanic Garden at the base of Capitol Hill when it arrived from the Centennial Exposition in Philadelphia in 1878. When both the fountain and the garden were removed to create Union Square, a separate Bartholdi Park was created in 1932 on the triangular site bounded by Independence Avenue, First Street, SW, and Canal Street. The fountain was sculpted by Frederic Auguste Bartholdi, whose most famous work is the Statue of Liberty. The elaborate fountain sits in a large-diameter marble basin.[32] The park itself is heavily planted with annuals and perennials in beds reminiscent of the 1870s. At its south end is a residence originally intended for the director of the Botanic Garden but now used for offices.

After all of the building sites facing the Capitol were occupied, Architect of the Capitol George M. White commissioned a master plan to guide future growth. To avoid intrusions upon the Capitol Hill neighborhood, the Senate was envisioned as growing to the north, and the House was envisioned as growing along South Capitol Street. The 1981 master plan also envisioned the relocation of the Supreme Court to its own judicial campus away from Capitol Square.[33] Large numbers of visitors would be accommodated at a visitors' center in Union Station, with transit via a people mover in a tunnel. Parking would be eliminated from the east plaza of the Capitol.

The McMillan Plan vision of a legislative precinct around the Capitol

L'ENFANT'S LEGACY

with "harmony of design and uniformity of cornice line" has resulted in a setting of strong visual unity based on consistent cornice lines, street setbacks, monumental scale, and facade materials. The building design expressions vary in style and quality. The Jefferson Building of the Library of Congress, built before the McMillan Plan, is the most architecturally aggressive because of its large dome and articulated massing. The first two Senate buildings and the first two House buildings, with their reserved neoclassical expression, are contextually the most appropriate. The strong form of the Supreme Court announces its hierarchical significance in spite of its smaller size. The Rayburn Building is the most bombastic because of its large size (the facade is 720 feet long) and its lack of detailed articulation. The Library of Congress Madison Building, with its awkward modernistic classical design, does not strongly encroach upon the precinct.

Figure 4.11 shows the McMillan Plan as it was realized with the addition of Capitol Plaza. The architectural frame of Capitol Square is complete except for one triangular block north of the Supreme Court. Although the McMillan Plan shows this site as vacant, the existing structures are not obtrusive and could remain.

The biggest variation from the McMillan Plan occurs in the northwest corner, where a landscape connection to Union Station was created, significantly weakening the spatial form of Capitol Square as a coherent public space. A landscaped edge of trees, plantings, and low walls would strengthen this spatial definition. This design treatment is clearly illustrated in the renderings produced by William Parsons in 1927 for this enlargement of the Capitol grounds.[34] At present the Capitol grounds tend to merge with Capitol Plaza, there being no clear delineation between them.

Capitol Plaza is a poorly utilized open space that should be developed for additional memorials or civic uses as shown on the original 1927 plan.[35] The recently completed Memorials and Museums Master Plan does not recommend sites in this area because memorials are restricted on the Capitol grounds, of which this is an extension.[36] This should be changed because the area is ideally suited for memorials, with high visibility and easy access from the Mall, the Capitol, and Union Station.

Access to Government

Starting with Andrew Jackson in 1829 the presidents were inaugurated on the east side of the Capitol, first on a platform and later on a neoclassical inaugural stand.[37] The inauguration date was 4 March until 1937, when it was changed to 20 January to reduce the period during which the outgoing president was a lame duck.[38] Inaugurations most often took place in the open air on the east side of the Capitol until President Ronald Reagan's first inauguration in 1981, when the ceremony was shifted to the west side. During his address the new president said, "Standing here one faces a magnificent vista, opening up on this city's special beauty and history. At the end of this open mall are those shrines to the giants on whose shoulders we stand."[39] The west front is an awe-inspiring inauguration setting, with the new president addressing thousands of spectators on the west lawn of the Capitol from a podium constructed on the west terrace.

Olmsted's scheme for the Capitol grounds, with its series of open and closed spaces linked by gracious walkways, physically expressed the dem-

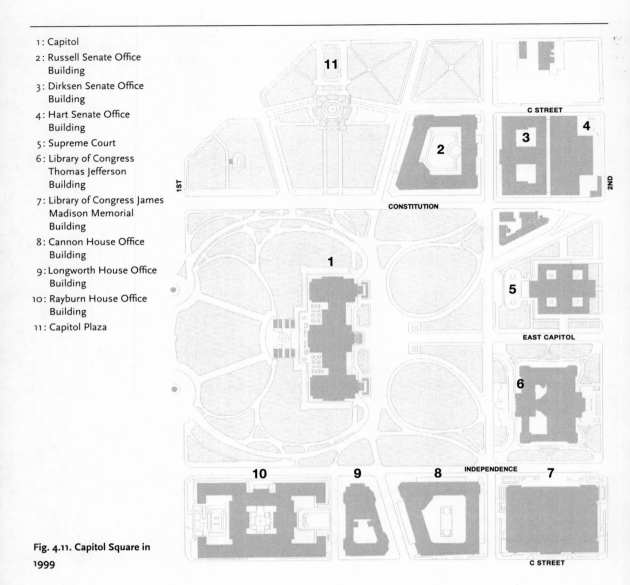

Fig. 4.11. Capitol Square in 1999

ocratic ideals of free access to government. The elegant eastern promenade enabled citizens and lawmakers alike to approach the Capitol with dignity. The expansive terraces linked this place where laws are made to the surrounding city where they are enacted. Many people consider the western grounds of Capitol Square to be the most symbolic public open space in the country. It is the scene for grand public events such as the concert on Independence Day.

Among the rights the Constitution affords to U.S. citizens is access to the government. Physical access to the legislative chambers is of primary importance, with physical and visual access to the grounds secondary. The reason for this access right is to enable citizens to influence the legislative process, to make their petitions known to their elected democratic representatives. To deny this access even symbolically is a serious matter in a democratic society.

The west terrace of the Capitol and its steps are America's favorite grandstand, the single best place in Washington from which to view the totality of the Mall within its urban and natural context. "Sit on the front stoop of democracy and listen to the National Symphony Orchestra or the U.S. Marine Band or Leontyne Price or Johnny Cash. Watch the fireworks, applaud the speech, join the protest, get a suntan, walk the dog, jog the steps."[40] The stairs also proclaim access to the government in architectural language that is hard to deny. Numerous protest groups have stood on them to plead their cause, be it women's liberation, an end to the Vietnam War, gay rights, stopping abortion, or saving the environment. It is a right of passage in visiting the city or residing there to climb the Capitol steps. And yet they were closed indefinitely in fall 2001 for security reasons, to protect Congress and its staff. This is an enormous symbolic statement resented by many as giving in to the terrorists at the expense of maintaining an open society. A proposed fence around the entire Capitol grounds, similar to the one around the White House grounds, would permit access to the Capitol steps, but this proposal is also highly controversial.[41]

One continuing activity on the west plaza is the concerts held four days a week in the summer by the bands of the four military services, a tradition dating to 1863. In addition, the National Symphony Orchestra performs starlight concerts on the west lawn of the Capitol on Memorial Day, Independence Day, and Labor Day.

Heightened security since the terrorist attacks of 11 September 2001 has strongly impacted the Capitol, which is considered a likely future target of a truck bomb. There have been previous incidents, such as the 1983 bombing outside the Senate chamber and the 1998 shooting of two Capitol policemen. The current rows of concrete planters restricting vehicular access to the east plaza will soon be replaced with iron bollards three feet tall surrounding the grounds on three sides. The fourth side will be similarly secured when the visitors' center is completed.[42] Construction has commenced on security protection around the House office area with retractable vehicle barriers, reinforced planters, steel bollards, and police shelters.

The need for a U.S. Capitol visitors' center has long been recognized and studied. In 2002 construction was finally started on the 588,000-square-foot Capitol Visitor Center, located on the east side, which will include auditoriums, an exhibition hall, congressional facilities, and visitor amenities in a footprint larger than that of the Capitol itself. The complex will be largely invisible, located on two underground levels and a third, service level reaching fifty feet below ground. Funded by a public-private partnership, it will provide better security for the Capitol staff and will improve the experience for 3 million annual visitors through education and exhibits. The thirty-foot-high central space will be a great hall with skylights spatially related to the Capitol rotunda. Visitors will access the Capitol via stairs, elevators, and escalators located under the 1962 east-front extension. Designed by RTKL Associates, of Baltimore, the center is scheduled to be completed in 2006.

The center area on the east side of the Capitol grounds will be significantly changed by the new visitors' center. Most of the change will be undoing the intrusions of the last several decades to create a dignified setting with a formal, stone-paved plaza. Access to the underground center will be via pedestrian ramps on both sides of the East Capitol Street approach, thus altering the Olmsted landscape. Digging an enormous, deep hole for the new facility has necessitated the removal of numerous trees, including some that Olmsted planted and five memorial trees. Some will be transplanted, and the memorial trees will be replaced.[43] When the project is complete, there will be more trees than before, mostly conforming to Olmsted's plan. The Capitol Visitor Center is indeed far too expansive, but the improved visitor experience is a reasonable trade-off for modification to the landscape. It does represent restricted access to the place of government, a restriction that many U.S. citizens find difficult to accept.

Alan M. Hantman, Architect of the Capitol since 1997, observes that "for more than 200 years it has been a work in progress."[44] Even a quick study of the evolution of the nation's most venerated building reveals the remarkable changes that have taken place in response to changing circumstances and the growth of the new nation, as well as changing views of how this architectural symbol should represent the nation and its ideals. Will this tide of change subside in subsequent decades? Probably, since a completed building can undergo only so many changes and retain its design integrity.

Greater changes are likely to take place on the Capitol grounds and around Capitol Square. The entire issue of security and access control will be considered many times in future decades, necessitating both management and landscape changes. This will also involve the perimeter streets around Capitol Square, where vehicular closure is already being considered. The architectural frame of Capitol Square is completely built, but there will be numerous internal changes to these federal buildings. New buildings for growing functions will need to be located north and south, as outlined in the 1981 master plan.

Capitol Square is not a square in the traditional sense of a social or recreational public place. It is more like a garden for the use of those who work or visit there. It is defined on the north and south by the Senate and House office buildings, which generate a great deal of employee pedestrian traffic between them and the Capitol. Visitors and tourists come to view the Capitol and stroll the grounds. There are often protests in front of the Supreme Court, where the public is welcome to view trials. The nation's premier research library is also there, generating even more pedestrian traffic. The low wall and fence surrounding Capitol Square have been removed in many places, creating freer access.

The U.S. Capitol is often called "the people's house," and the people need to be able to access it. Improved but controlled access will certainly be engendered by the Capitol Visitor Center. Probably more significant for the general population is free access to the grounds, the public space of Capitol Square. Ever since Bulfinch fenced the grounds and installed gates with gatehouses, this place has been more of a sacred precinct than a true public place. Indeed, it must be construed as both, and it must function as both. The people should be allowed to freely access the grounds of the U.S. Capitol for dignified use with civic decorum.

L'ENFANT'S LEGACY

CHAPTER FIVE

PRESIDENT'S PARK

Lafayette Square, The White House Grounds

HERE WAS THE common meeting ground of so many historical personages that it could be called, perhaps, the center of the political history
of the nation. More than any single spot in America, this little plot of
ground was still animate with the past, still quietly redolent of by gone
days, still preserving the faint echo of the footsteps of those who led the
country to greatness. The past is still mirrored in the historic residences
that surround it, where so many of these people lived or visited. American life owes much to La Fayette Square.

MARIE BEALE, *Decatur House and Its Inhabitants*

Lafayette Park and the White House grounds were called President's Park
on L'Enfant's plan for the city. Reservation Number 1 was divided by
President Thomas Jefferson into a public park to the north and the mansion grounds to the south. Lafayette Park is now the public space north of
the White House. It has also been called President's Square and at times
Jackson Square, after the statue at its center.[1] The White House grounds
are the enclave of the executive branch of the federal government and
the private gardens of the president and his family. Linking these two
precincts is the Pennsylvania Avenue corridor.

In design terms this precinct of the federal core is organized by the
axis of Sixteenth Street. For more than two centuries, maintaining a
symmetrical balance about this axis has been the ruling design motiva-
tion. This symmetry is evident in the landscape design of Lafayette Park,
the buildings forming Lafayette Square, the executive mansion, and the
White House grounds.

Lafayette Square

Lafayette Park is bounded by H Street and Pennsylvania Avenue to
the north and south and by Jackson Place and Madison Place to the west
and east. From this seven-acre park there are vistas to the northwest along
Connecticut Avenue to Farragut Square and northeast along Vermont
Avenue to McPherson Square. The White House and Lafayette Park, both
on axis with Sixteenth Street, have a northern vista to Scott Circle.

A Prestigious Neighborhood

Lafayette Square literally resonates with the history of the United
States, as Marie Beale, a former owner and resident of Decatur House,

states in her book *Decatur House and Its Inhabitants.* Every U.S. president
has visited the square, and all, except George Washington, lived in the
White House. When George Washington visited his namesake city in 1797
a sixteen-gun salute was held on the lawn north of the White House.[2]

To be a neighbor of the president is a special privilege. This simple
fact has led numerous significant individuals to take up residence nearby
or to in some way inhabit this locality in order to be close to the source of
political power. In the past, more so than in the present, Lafayette Square
was the epicenter of politics and diplomacy in the nation's capital.

Benjamin Ogle Tayloe, the first chronicler of Lafayette Square, wrote
a short book published in 1872 called *Our Neighbors on LaFayette Square.*
He knew all the presidents from John Quincy Adams to Abraham Lincoln
during the forty years that he lived there, and his book contains com-
mentaries about each of them. Tayloe was the son of the Virginia planter
John Tayloe III, who built the nearby Octagon House. The intimacy of
the situation is illustrated by one observation he recorded: "While I write,
President Lincoln is passing by my window, followed by a cavalry escort
with drawn swords."[3]

The people who chose to live near the White House often had a close
relationship—political, commercial, social, even romantic—with the
president and/or other neighbors. They often visited one another's homes
and met in the park. If and when they moved, it was to another location
nearby, as is aptly illustrated by Jeanne Fogle's fascinating book *Proximity
to Power: Neighbors to the President near Lafayette Square,* wherein she
chronicles the residents of each house facing the park.[4] Lafayette Square
held a strong, almost magnetic attraction. Residents were senators and
congressman, secretaries of state and cabinet officers, generals and foreign ministers. Many vice presidents lived on the square since there was

L'ENFANT'S LEGACY

no official residence for them. Moving was common given the continual change of power with the election or death of each president.

The first structure on Lafayette Square was the White House, begun in 1792 (see below). It was followed on the opposite side of the square, at Sixteenth and H streets, by St. John's Church in 1816. The church was designed by the prominent architect Benjamin Henry Latrobe, who was supervising the reconstruction of both the White House and the Capitol after the War of 1812.[5] The original church had a Greek-cross plan with an octagonal cupola atop a shallow dome. Four years later, in 1820, the transept was extended to the west by George Bomford, creating a Latin-cross plan with a Roman Doric portico. A triple-tier steeple was added to the stuccoed brick church, which had a main entry on Sixteenth Street and a secondary entry facing the park on H Street. In 1883 James Renwick Jr. extended the east end with Ionic columns and a Palladian window, provided two service wings, and inserted new, larger windows for stained glass (fig. 5.1). Two of the windows memorialize six former presidents.

The original interior was arranged in a series of interlocking circles radiating from the center of the Greek cross. The twenty-eighth of the eighty-eight original pews was selected by President Madison and has since been reserved for the nation's leader. Called the "Church of the Presidents," it has been visited by every chief executive since 1816. St. John's has been the scene of numerous significant events, including the funerals of President William Henry Harrison and Dolley Madison.

Commodore Stephen Decatur and his wife retained Benjamin Henry Latrobe to design the first residence on the square, at the northwest corner, in 1818. Soon after, a street called Jackson Place was created along the west side of the park to provide access for the properties there, nineteen of which were owned by Decatur. Latrobe's design was reserved yet imposing, a nearly cubic mass with a hipped roof and planar brick facades with elegant windows (see fig. 5.6). The exquisite entrance vestibule leads to a stair hall that leads to the primary, second-story rooms. Behind the house on H Street were the stuccoed slave quarters and stables. Although many changes have been made to the house, it retains its Federal grandeur.

Decatur House became a social and diplomatic center of Washington. After Commodore Decatur's life was cut short in 1820, when he was mortally wounded in a duel, the house was occupied by the minister of France, the Russian Legation, Secretaries of State Henry Clay and Martin van Buren, the statesman Edward Livingston, and the British Legation.[6] The house was occupied by the military during the Civil War, before the house was acquired by the Beale family in 1871. In 1944 Marie Beale had the facades restored to their original design, with some changes.[7] The last and longest resident of Decatur House, she donated it to the National Trust for Historic Preservation in 1956 in order to preserve it for posterity. Today it is a house museum dedicated to the lives of the Decatur and Beale families.

The Ewell House was built next, in 1820, south of the Decatur House on two midblock lots. After the mid-1820s it was occupied by three secretaries of the navy and two senators.[8] Between the Decatur and Ewell houses is a Victorian town house with a grand entry that was purchased in 1845 by William Learned March, secretary of state for Presidents Polk and Pierce.[9]

A dramatic incident occurred near the Ewell House in 1858 involving Representative Daniel Sickles, his wife Theresa, and Philip Barton Key, a district attorney. Sickles and his wife were living in the Ewell House. Key and Theresa met at a dinner party and fell in love; though the affair was widely known, it was not known to Sickles. Theresa would signal Philip from her window, and he would signal back from the park. When Sickles finally learned about the affair, he confronted Key in the park and mercilessly shot him three times. Sickles's attorney, Edwin M. Stanton, managed to have him acquitted based on a plea of temporary insanity.[10]

In the early 1820s Surgeon General Joseph Lovell built his elegant house facing the White House at the corner of Pennsylvania Avenue and Jackson Place. In 1837 Francis Preston Blair, editor of the *Congressional Globe* newspaper, purchased the dwelling, and it has since been known as Blair House.[11] The house was later occupied by four cabinet secretaries before the Blair family returned in 1852. In 1858 Francis Preston Blair built a handsome three-story town house next door for his daughter and son-in-law, Samuel Phillips Lee. In the 1940s the government purchased and combined the Blair and Lee houses to serve as the official guesthouse of the president.

In 1822 Richard and Anna Cutts built their modest, three-story brick and stucco Federal house across the park from the Decatur House. A street called Madison Place was created between Pennsylvania Avenue and H Street to give Cutts and his neighbors access. Cutts subsequently had financial difficulties and sold the house and adjoining lots to James and Dolley Madison so that Dolley's sister Anna and her children could live there. In 1837 Dolley Madison herself moved there and the house became known as the Dolley Madison House. Owing to financial problems she leased the house to Senator William C. Preston, of South Carolina, from 1840 to 1844, after which the elderly Dolley returned to continue her social life and died there in 1849. Captain Charles Wilkes purchased the house and dramatically changed the exterior. During the Civil War it became the residence of the commanding general of the City of Washington, George B. McClellan, who remained in the house until Wilkes returned after the war.[12]

Diagonally across the intersection from Decatur House, Thomas Swann built a simple three-and-one-half-story brick house in 1828. The Massachusetts statesman Daniel Webster lived there in the 1840s. The banker William Wilson Corcoran bought the house in 1848 and retained the New York architect James Renwick Jr. to enlarge it into one of the most fashionable Renaissance-style mansions in the city.[13] Founder of the Corcoran Gallery and the Riggs Bank, Corcoran was a great philanthropist and an avid art collector.

Over the years Corcoran's art collection became so large that he built the first Corcoran Gallery of Art (1858) just west of Blair House. Renwick designed it in the French Second Empire style, with an elaborate slate mansard roof and many exaggerated architectural elements. Niches around the exterior hold statues of great European artists and the American sculptor Thomas Crawford. The Quartermaster Corps of the U.S. Army utilized the building during the Civil War, delaying the gallery opening until 1871. The first building in this style in Washington, it greatly influenced subsequent architecture. From 1899 to 1964 the U.S.

Court of Claims occupied the structure. It was renovated in 1967 to become the Renwick Gallery, for the decorative arts, part of the Smithsonian Institution.[14]

East of his house on H Street, W. W. Corcoran built a fine rental property in 1845.[15] It was home to many, but it was named for Senator John Slidell, of Louisiana, later minister to France for the Confederacy, who lived there from 1853 to 1861. The Slidell House was also leased to the author Henry Adams, grandson of John Quincy Adams. He became friends with the statesman and author John Hay, who was President Lincoln's private secretary and wrote a biography of Lincoln. The building's last occupant was the American Association of University Women, and it was razed in 1922 to make way for the U.S. Chamber of Commerce Building.

Adams and Hay purchased lots adjacent to the Slidell House and in 1884 retained the Boston architect H. H. Richardson to design a double house.[16] The two dwellings of red brick and sandstone were designed as one in the unique Richardsonian Romanesque style. Hay's asymmetrical house faced Sixteenth Street but occupied the corner. It was larger than Adams's symmetrical house, which faced H Street. The massive facades were replete with deep-set windows, arched entrances, turreted towers, and recessed balconies. These two houses, among the best works of nineteenth-century architecture in Washington, were the city's center of literary life for two decades. In 1906 Adams proclaimed, "La Fayette Square was Society. Beyond the square, the country begins."[17]

Benjamin Ogle Tayloe built his three-story brick house on the east side of the park in 1828. It was one of the important social centers in Washington.[18] In 1887 Senator J. Donald Cameron of Pennsylvania purchased the house, which he later leased to Garret Hobart, President McKinley's vice president, and Senator Marcus Alonzo Hanna of Ohio. The house is now part of the U.S. Court of Appeals, with the Tayloe Café on the second floor.

South of the Tayloe House, the U.S. naval hero Commodore John Rodgers built a large, thirty-room house in 1831 on lots that Henry Clay traded him for a prize jackass.[19] President Polk lived there in 1845 while the White House was being renovated. William Seward, Abraham Lincoln's secretary of state, rented the house, and the president visited frequently. On 14 April 1865 President Lincoln was assassinated at Ford's Theater by John Wilkes Booth. Seward was recovering in his house from a carriage accident when Lewis Payne, a member of Booth's conspiracy, broke into the house, attacked his family members, stabbed Seward, and left him for dead.

East of St. John's Church, Matthew St. Clair Clark built a spacious, five-bay mansion in 1836. In 1842 Alexander Baring, the British minister to America, moved there. His title was Lord Ashburton and the house acquired this name. In time this would become the parish house. It was significantly rebuilt by Thomas U. Walter in 1854 as an Italianate-style mansion with elaborate sandstone window frames.[20]

This fine group of town houses lining the streets around the park constituted the nineteenth-century architectural frame of Lafayette Square. They also created the social setting for a vibrant and influential neighborhood whose most notable resident was the president of the United States.

Memorial Park

On Ellicott's city plan of 1792 the width of President's Park was reduced at the north end by inserting additional city blocks on the east and west sides, thus establishing the present form of Lafayette Park. When construction of the White House began, workers built their huts in the park. During the War of 1812 troops camped there, and later workers rebuilding the executive mansion used the park as a construction staging area.

When Thomas Jefferson moved into the White House in 1801, he was concerned with both its size and the vast grounds. He had a road called Executive Way cut through the lawn north of the house, thus creating a separate public park. In time this route became a part of Pennsylvania Avenue. Each year President Jefferson held an Independence Day celebration in the park with a fair, gun salutes, military parades, band music, and a reception.[21]

President's Park was one of the first open spaces improved in the city. In preparation for the visit of the Marquis de Lafayette in 1824 the park was graded, trees and shrubs were planted, paths were laid, and a wooden fence was installed to keep out grazing livestock.[22] The celebration for Lafayette was a grand event, including a procession leading to the White House, where he was greeted by President James Monroe. Large crowds gathered in the park to pay tribute to the elderly Revolutionary War hero. Thereafter this public space was called Lafayette Park.

W. W. Corcoran and Joseph Henry, the first secretary of the Smithsonian, convinced President Millard Fillmore to hire the landscape architect Andrew Jackson Downing to redesign the Mall and Lafayette Park.[23] The romantic landscape scheme of 1851 included many small, elliptical flower beds, larger free-form planting beds, and winding pathways leading to the center, where a memorial was planned. The park would be heavily planted with trees and exotic plants donated by Corcoran. Jackson's death in 1852 and the Civil War delayed completion of this design until 1872.

When Congress authorized an equestrian statue of Major General Andrew Jackson for Lafayette Park it had the original plan, two lawns bordered with trees and divided by a broad path the width of the Sixteenth Street axis. There were only nine buildings facing the park, and many of the vacant lots were used as gardens or yards for outbuildings.[24] The Jackson memorial was located at the center of the park on an elliptical plot surrounded by a tall cast-iron fence. It was dedicated amid great fanfare by President Franklin Pierce in 1853. The statue, by the sculptor Clark Mills, faces west, and there are four Spanish cannon captured by Jackson in Pensacola, Florida, around the base. Jackson is depicted tipping his hat while reviewing his troops on a precariously balanced, rearing mount; the granite pedestal is inscribed, "The Federal Union, It Must Be Preserved" (fig. 5.2). James M. Goode describes the statue as follows: "This work, with its fine attention to naturalistic detail and fiery tension of pose, has about it an air of naïve, almost primitive, exuberance."[25] Mills later produced the equestrian statue of George Washington that is in Washington Circle. During President Franklin D. Roosevelt's first term it was suggested that the two statues be exchanged so that all of the memorials in Lafayette Park would be related to the Revolutionary War.

L'ENFANT'S LEGACY

During the Civil War, Union troops camped in Lafayette Park and left it in shambles. In the era of territorial government Downing's design was implemented, with numerous lawns and trees, along with curved pathways and flower beds. In addition, a watchman's lodge with toilets was built on the north side. Two large, handsome bronze urns from the U.S. Navy Yard were placed on granite pedestals east and west of the Jackson statue. Figure 5.3, a map of Lafayette Park in 1903, shows the Downing design. All the town houses are shown, along with St. John's Church, the Corcoran Gallery of Art, and the Second Bank of the United States.

Fig. 5.2. Statue of Andrew Jackson, Lafayette Park

Lafayette Park continued to grow in popularity as a refuge from the bustling city. Here residents could see exotic plants and animal exhibits. Streetcar lines on the north and south sides provided easy access. In 1897 gas lamps were replaced by electric lamps to discourage criminal and immoral nocturnal activity. The following year, the iron fence was removed to facilitate pedestrian access from all directions, an effort to promote the democratic right to freedom of access.[26]

A program to honor four foreign heroes of the Revolutionary War was initiated in 1891 with a south-facing bronze statue of French Major General Marquis Gilbert de Lafayette. Congress sponsored the statue, which was to be positioned south of the Jackson statue in the center of the park, thus blocking the northern view of the statue. Wisely, it was actually located in the southeast corner. Lafayette is depicted in civilian attire atop a high pedestal, with portrait statues of four French compatriots (including Rochambeau), two cherubs, and a female figure gathered around the base (fig. 5.4). In 1902 Congress also sponsored a complex sculpture honoring French Major General Comte Jean de Rochambeau, placed in the southwest corner of the park. He faces south atop a high granite pedestal, pointing with his right hand while holding a battle plan in his left hand. This is a copy of a memorial in his birthplace, Vendôme, France (fig. 5.5).[27]

In the northwest corner is a memorial honoring German Major General Friedrich Wilhelm von Steuben, dedicated in 1910. Facing northwest,

President's Park

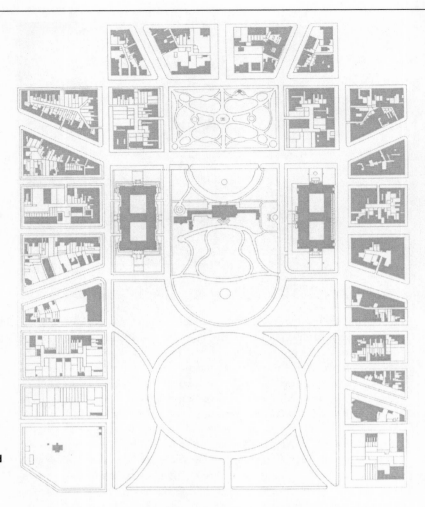

Fig. 5.3. Lafayette Square and the White House grounds in 1903

the eight-foot-high bronze portrait figure atop a high pedestal shows him at Valley Forge in a heavy cloak. Sponsored by Congress, it is a heroic memorial with classical figures all in repose (fig. 5.6). The last of the four memorials, in the northeast corner, was dedicated in 1910, to Polish General Thaddeus Kosciuszko; it was sponsored by the Polish National Alliance of America. Facing north, the young military engineer, in the uniform of the Continental army, stands atop a granite pedestal. On the east face of the pedestal, Kosciuszko is in an American uniform freeing a bound soldier symbolizing the American army. On the west face of the pedestal, the fallen general is in a Polish uniform directing a peasant soldier symbolizing the Polish army (fig. 5.7).[28]

In the 1930s Downing's romantic park design was changed to follow the Senate Park Commission's formal, classical recommendations. The watchman's lodge had already been replaced with a classical design in 1914 (this is the only one remaining of identical lodges in Franklin, Lincoln, and Judiciary squares). Utilizing Works Progress Administration labor, the National Park Service replaced picturesque pathways in 1937.[29] The new scheme was a continuous oval path with two additional parabolic paths joining the memorials in the corners to the center. Parallel axial

L'ENFANT'S LEGACY

Top: Fig. 5.5. Statue of Major General Comte Jean de Rochambeau, Lafayette Park, with New Executive Office Building

Bottom: Fig. 5.4. Statue of Major General Marquis Gilbert de Lafayette, Lafayette Park

Fig. 5.6. Statue of Major
General Friedrich Wilhelm
von Steuben, Lafayette Park,
with Decatur House

Fig. 5.7. Statue of General
Thaddeus Kosciuszko,
Lafayette Park, with old
Cosmos Club in background

paths were aligned with the sidewalks of Sixteenth Street to form wide, seasonal planting beds north and south of the Jackson statue, which was surrounded by an evergreen hedge and an iron-spear fence. Many of the existing trees were retained, and the urns were relocated to the south entrance.

As the park became more formal, so did the events held there. In the 1930s it was the site of the national Christmas tree and of memorial trees with plaques. Arts-and-crafts shows were held there, as were annual ceremonies honoring the individuals depicted in the statues.

Changing Uses

After the Civil War, high real estate prices forced residents to move from Lafayette Square to more desirable locations north and west of the business district. Banks, government departments, law firms, labor unions, and national organizations recognized the advantages of being close to the White House. Many residences on the square were converted to office use or razed and replaced with new, larger buildings.

In 1869 W. W. Corcoran demolished his residences on Vermont Avenue to construct the extravagant, six-story Arlington Hotel. A year earlier, Senator Charles Sumner of Massachusetts had built a dignified, four-story brick home east of Ashburton House. In 1889 Corcoran bought the Sumner House and the adjacent Pomeroy House and connected them to the hotel as an annex.[30]

The Cosmos Club, founded in 1878 to advance science, literature, and art, moved to the Ingersoll House, on the east side of the square, in 1882. From there it moved to the nearby Dolley Madison House, later constructing an addition on the south side. The National Geographic Society, formed from some of the membership of the Cosmos Club, utilized a part of the Madison House, with a separate entrance on H Street. The Cosmos Club continued to expand by razing the Ingersoll and Windom houses in 1909 and replacing them with a five-story clubhouse (see fig. 5.7).[31] In 1917 it purchased the Tayloe House, converting it into a women's annex and the stable into an assembly hall. The Cosmos Club now owned half of the block, but in 1939 it was forced to sell to the federal government, which wanted the site for offices.

The trend of conversions from residential to office uses continued around the square. In the 1850s a group of Victorian town houses were built at the southwest corner of the park, on Jackson Place. They were purchased by Andrew Carnegie in the 1890s and combined for use as the International Bureau of the American Republics.

The area near the Treasury Building became desirable for banking institutions. A branch of the Second Bank of the United States was built at the northwest corner of Fifteenth Street and Pennsylvania Avenue in 1824. Designed by George Hadfield, its neoclassical brick and stucco exterior was scored to resemble stone; an adjacent cashier's house was built later. In 1898 the Riggs National Bank razed the cashier's house to build a neoclassical structure. The original bank was sold to the American Security and Trust Company in 1904, which demolished it to erect a neoclassical marble building.[32]

In the late 1820s Dr. James Gunnell built an elaborate, five-story brownstone for his large family at the corner of Madison Place and Pennsylvania Avenue. The house was taken for military use during the Civil War and was razed in 1869 to construct the Freedman's Savings Bank. The bank was intended for use by former slaves and their descendants. When the bank failed in 1874, the building was purchased by the federal government for use by the Department of Justice and the U.S. Court of Claims. The John Rodgers House was razed in 1884 to build the six-story Lafayette Square Opera House, which changed the scale of Jackson Place. Changing ownership in 1906, the renamed Belasco Theater, with its eighteen-hundred-seat auditorium, was a center for opera, theater, and ballet in Washington until the Depression. During World War II it reopened as the Stage Door Canteen for entertaining servicemen, closing in 1946. During the Korean War it reopened again as the USO Lafayette Square Club.[33]

The Twentieth Century

The Senate Park Commission report of 1902 proposed a scheme to unify Lafayette Square by replacing all of the buildings with neoclassical white marble structures.[34] The scheme followed the French academic ideal of uniform buildings defining an urban place. The model for this design concept is Place Vendôme in Paris, the royal square with uniform facades designed by J. H. Mansart for King Louis XIV in 1699.[35]

Few people criticized the McMillan Plan concept for Lafayette Square since it followed the design approach for the entire Mall and Capitol Square. But the urban designer Elbert Peets later questioned its ultimate wisdom: "Purely as a matter of design, it is surely to be regretted that the residence scale and atmosphere of Lafayette Square cannot be maintained to connect the White House with the residence district of the city. It seems an ideal location for those unofficial White Houses, the national headquarters of clubs and societies—all of red brick, to preserve for the White House its dominance of scale and color."[36]

Two components of the McMillan Plan were completed. The U.S. Treasury Annex, designed by the distinguished architect Cass Gilbert, was built on the site of the Freedman's Bank in 1917. It was intended to take up the entire block and define the east side of the square, but only one segment was constructed. The identical limestone facades on Madison Place and Pennsylvania Avenue show a rusticated basement supporting a giant, three-story Ionic colonnade. The deep entablature hides another story, and a recessed attic is hidden behind the balustrade. The Ionic columns are different from those on the main Treasury Building, to the south, but the Greek Revival details are similar.[37]

Another piece of the grand plan was put into place when the U.S. Chamber of Commerce Building replaced the Slidell and Corcoran houses in 1929. It was designed by Cass Gilbert utilizing the same scheme as the Treasury Annex: identical street facades, each with a giant colonnade of Corinthian columns, on H Street and Connecticut Avenue. However, the Chamber of Commerce Building is more elegant, with better proportions and more refined details.[38]

During World War I the federal government purchased and demolished the Arlington Hotel and replaced it with the Department of War Risk (now the Department of Veterans Affairs) in 1919.[39] It occupies the full block along Vermont Avenue between H and I streets, and the narrow end faces Lafayette Park on H Street. Although it could have been another part of the Senate Park Commission vision, it does not have the colonnade motif of the Treasury Annex or the Chamber of Commerce Building. The facades of gray limestone are not refined, and its ten-story height is twice that of the other two Beaux-Arts buildings.

In 1927 the Hay-Adams double house was demolished, and a new, eight-story luxury hotel, the Hay-Adams Hotel, was constructed by the developer Harry Wardman. The H Street and Sixteenth Street facades have very similar projecting bays, but the entrance is on 16th Street.[40] The almost cubic mass with articulated elevations of limestone defines the street corner well. Throughout the years the Hay-Adams Hotel has maintained its reputation as a luxury lodging with a direct view of the White House.

In the late 1940s many labor organizations and unions located around Lafayette Square to improve their visibility and prestige. The Congress of Industrial Organizations (CIO) moved to Jackson Place, as did the United Auto Workers (UAW) and the United Steelworkers. The American Federation of Labor (AFL) built its current headquarters next to St. John's Church on Sixteenth Street in 1954.[41]

Along Jackson Place several new, higher office buildings were built during the first three decades of the twentieth century. The walled garden of the Decatur House was replaced by an eight-story office building in 1929. It housed the Institute for Government Research, which became the Brookings Institute. When the Brookings Institute built its own headquarters nearby, the National Grange purchased this building. South of the National Grange Building, the Marcy House became home to the Women's City Club, and the Glover House was leased to a number of organizations over the years. The Ewell House also had a series of tenants, most notably the National Women's Party, which used the location to promote women's suffrage. In 1932 the Brookings Institute demolished the house and built a nine-story building in its place. North of this building, the Parke House was demolished to make way for the eight-story International Bank building.

Preserving the Square

The Senate Park Commission scheme to rebuild Lafayette Square with federal buildings was forsaken by the Commission of Fine Arts in the 1930s when it planned the Federal Triangle along Pennsylvania Avenue. After World War II the federal government purchased all the buildings facing Jackson Place and Madison Place for expansion. The General Services Administration (the real estate arm of the federal government) proposed to demolish most of the historic buildings and construct a new executive office building on Jackson Place and a court of claims on Madison Place.[42] The American Institute of Architects and the Committee of 100 on the Federal City both strongly opposed the plan.[43]

During the 1950s the historic preservation movement was being discussed in the city as a strategy for urban redevelopment. Marie Beale gave the Decatur House to the National Trust for Historic Preservation in 1956, and other buildings around the square were declared historic landmarks. The time was right to make a stand for limiting further destruction of the cultural heritage of Lafayette Square.

In 1962 President and Mrs. John F. Kennedy expressed their interest in preserving the historic buildings around Lafayette Square. The concept for doing this and erecting new federal buildings can be attributed to the architect Grosvenor Chapman, who published a design sketch in the *Washington Post* in 1961.[44] The Committee of 100 on the Federal City had asked Chapman to study the problem. Chapman's sketch showed the new buildings behind the old ones, which were preserved and converted to government offices. Nonconforming buildings between the historic ones were replaced with "new Federal-style" ones. The sketch was given to William Walton, an artist and friend of the Kennedys, who showed it to Mrs. Kennedy, who then showed it to the president.

The president discussed the proposal for new federal government buildings with the architect John Carl Warnecke, whom he met at a cocktail party. After Warnecke was given the design commission, he used Chapman's strategy to preserve the historic buildings by placing taller, new office buildings behind them. He also decided to use the same design treatment on both sides of the square to balance the visual effect. The new slab-shaped, dark red brick buildings were intended as unobtrusive backgrounds for the lighter-colored brick historic buildings.

The National Courts Building, on the east side of the square, was completed in 1967 to house the U.S. Court of Claims and the U.S. Court of Appeals. The Dolley Madison House, the Cosmos Club, and the Tayloe House were incorporated, with a courtyard between the old and new buildings. The Belasco Theater was demolished to make way for an arcaded entry court opening onto Madison Place. This part of the new building mediates the scale between the Treasury Annex and the historic row houses. The new nine-story slab building was placed behind, with a narrow facade on H Street (fig. 5.8).

The ten-story New Executive Office Building, on the west side of the square, was completed in 1969 at a height near that of the Old Executive Office Building, south of it. Four taller office buildings dating to earlier in the twentieth century were demolished and replaced with new row-house office buildings (see fig. 5.5). One has an open base to serve as an entry to the New Executive Office Building via a courtyard. The historic structures were preserved and rehabilitated for smaller federal agencies. The New Executive Office Building has an offset, H-shaped plan with a long, blank brick facade along Seventeenth Street.

The new, taller federal buildings were the first modern designs on Lafayette Square. They were also among the first in Washington to use a design strategy termed *contextualism*, accommodating a new building to its context by utilizing compatible design features. The use of red brick as a facade material was the primary means of relating to this historic context, although the colored mortar joints mask the wall texture. The metal mansard roofs that hide mechanical equipment relate to the roofs on the Renwick Gallery and the Old Executive Office Building. The bay windows were claimed as contextual features, although there are no other buildings with bay windows in this area and their two-story height makes them too prominent along the top of each tall building. Up close, the scale of details in the new buildings, particularly of the windows, does not relate well to the context.

Subsequently, First Lady Ladybird Johnson initiated changes to the

landscape of Lafayette Park as part of her city beautification program. The 1969 park scheme by Warnecke preserved the existing paths in brick, incorporated two large elliptical pools with water jets, and added a few new paths to provide informal landscaped areas.[45]

Figure 5.9 illustrates contemporary conditions around Lafayette Square. The historic row houses along Jackson Place are utilized by executive committees. The two new buildings on the site of the former Ewell and Blair houses are part of the New Executive Office Building and serve as an entry to the midblock courtyard. The Townsend and Parker houses are now part of the president's guesthouse. There have been very few changes to the architectural frame of the square since 1969 except for the new office building at the northwest corner of H Street and Connecticut Avenue.

Scale is one of the primary urban design issues at Lafayette Square. The early-nineteenth-century houses were small in scale relative to the size of the park, although the consistent facade planes on the east and west side had clarity and balance. The City Beautiful scheme introduced a larger scale, which would have produced a stronger definition of the open space had it been consistently carried out. This definition is best seen along H Street with the street wall created by the Chamber of Commerce Building, the Hay-Adams Hotel, and the Department of Veterans Affairs building. The new high-rise buildings introduce an even greater scale, but their location impacts the skyline of the city more than the park itself.

Cities should exhibit their physical history, and Lafayette Square reflects well its three primary eras of development. This is evident in the scale and architecture of the early row houses, the white neoclassical buildings, and the modern high-rise structures. This design expression manifests the vitality of the place, a living part of the city that has evolved through two centuries of change.

Changes in architectural design accompany changes in building use.

Fig. 5.8. National Courts Building, view to east from Lafayette Square

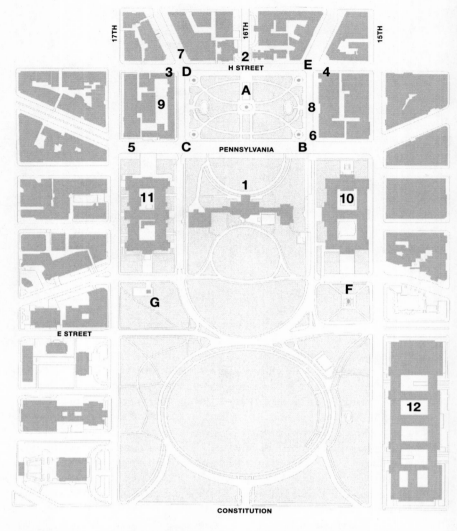

Fig. 5.9. Lafayette Square and the White House grounds in 1999

This prestigious residential neighborhood gave way to a zone of political influence made up of labor unions and lobbyist organizations. Now it is primarily the enclave of the executive branch, similar in purpose to Capitol Square.

Federal employees dominate the park during the week, but there is a population vacuum in the evening, when only the Hays-Adams Hotel provides people to occupy the space. On weekends only St. John's Church, the Renwick Gallery, and Decatur House are occupied. Special events would make the park an exciting destination for more pedestrians. There will always be tourists in front of the White House, and their numbers would be increased by the proposed "circulator" transit system. But gone is the real vitality engendered by traffic on Pennsylvania Avenue before it was blockaded.

Today the park is heavily utilized by tourists, business people, city residents, and homeless people, all of whom enjoy its amenities. Security is provided by the Secret Service and the National Park Service Police. The park is a handsome oasis of grass and trees at the front door of the executive branch of the federal government. As a visual image, it continues to be an extension of the president's front lawn, a part of the original President's Park.

The White House Grounds

The White House grounds are bounded by Pennsylvania and Constitution avenues to the north and south, respectively, and by Seventeenth and Fifteenth streets to the west and east. From these grounds there is a northern vista to Lafayette Square, and there are spectacular southern vistas to the Mall, the Washington Monument, and the Thomas Jefferson Memorial.

The Executive Mansion

The White House grounds and the President's House are clearly delineated on L'Enfant's plan as a contiguous open space bordered by Tiber Creek to the south. None of the intersecting streets penetrate these grounds. The site for the President's House was chosen for its direct relationship to the Capitol along Pennsylvania Avenue to the southeast. It also provided direct views to the Potomac River and the City of Alexandria to the south.

The dominant architectural element of this entire precinct is the White House. Its geometric center is at the crossing point of New York Avenue, Pennsylvania Avenue, and Sixteenth Street as the north-south axis. In spite of its significance as a seat of political power and its positional significance in the L'Enfant Plan, it is not an imposing building. Its power is in the symbolic representation of the office of president of the United States.

Construction of the White House was initiated as soon as possible after the plan for the new city was approved. The Irish-born architect James Hoban won the design competition in 1792, and the cornerstone was laid in October of that year. His design was a simplified, two-story rectangular Palladian palazzo with a tetrastyle Ionic portico on the north and a colonnaded porch on the south facade. This porch bowed out in the center around an oval reception room. It was built of light-brown Aquia, Virginia, sandstone, which had to be sealed with whitewash for preservation.[46] In 1901 it became known officially as the White House.

President John Adams was the first to occupy the house, in 1800, and there has been almost continuous alteration and/or expansion since then. Benjamin Henry Latrobe redesigned the north and south porticoes in 1807, but they were not constructed until two decades later. Latrobe also added single-story wings on the east and west sides and landscaped the grounds with terraces. The house was partially burned by British troops in 1814, requiring a completely new interior, designed by Hoban. The exterior walls remained sound, and their white paint hid the scars from the fire.

In 1901, during Theodore Roosevelt's presidency, the New York firm of McKim, Mead and White designed office wings connected by colonnades. They also renovated the attic story for domestic use. In 1909 the architect Nathan C. Wyeth extended the west wing, creating the famed oval office to reflect the oval reception room in the main house. During Harry Truman's presidency (1945–53) the building was gutted and reconstructed to make it structurally stable.[47]

Fig. 5.10. White House, view
to south from Pennsylvania
Avenue

The initial design for the President's House was not intended to project political power, as was the design for the Capitol. The generations of alterations to the building have resulted in a compromised albeit fascinating piece of architecture (fig. 5.10). This is well documented in William Seale's book *The White House: The History of an American Idea.* "Excellence of design, however, is not the issue with the White House. Ideas put it up, and ideas have shaped it year by year, until the house itself is a unique and uniquely American place for the presidency."[48]

The Landscape Design

The White House grounds were located on a plateau called Wicomico Terrace overlooking the Potomac River at the juncture of Tiber Creek. Vistas from this site, directly south along the Potomac River, were impressive. Ships sailing north to Washington or Georgetown would see the President's House directly ahead. L'Enfant's vision for the site was a series of terraced gardens stepping down to a pond at Tiber Canal. Between canal and river there would be additional gardens around the monument to George Washington. President Thomas Jefferson was concerned with improving the grounds, which he thought too large. Around the private grounds he built a fence with an arched entry from Pennsylvania Avenue on the southeast side.[49]

After the War of 1812 the grounds again became a construction site during the rebuilding of the White House. President Monroe surrounded the mansion with a serpentine iron fence with tall, heavy gates.[50] During the presidency of John Quincy Adams (1825–29) significant improvements were finally made to the mansion grounds. Paved paths were placed among formal gardens with hundreds of tree seedlings.

Under President Andrew Jackson (1829–37) the south lawn was graded and more paths were established. The serpentine fence was replaced with a straight one, with two gates on the north side at either end of a curved driveway. Fresh water was conveyed from springs in Franklin Square through wooden pipes and stored in a reservoir east of the mansion. In the 1830s additional trees of many species were planted, and a two-acre flower garden was created south of the house.

After the Treasury Building, on the east side, burned in 1833, President Jackson reputedly instructed that it be rebuilt to block the line of site to the Capitol because he was angry with Congress.[51] This unfortunate placement thwarted one of L'Enfant's most important design precepts, that of reciprocal views between the two most important buildings in the nation's capital. Obscuring this vista was exacerbated when the Treasury Building was later expanded to the south and Jefferson's arched entry to the grounds was eliminated.

The grounds south of the mansion were shaped by Downing's 1851 landscape plan (see fig. 3.3). This plan added a southern parabolic drive to the existing northern one beginning at the intersection of Pennsylvania Avenue and Fifteenth Street and ending on Seventeenth Street. The grandest proposal for the southern grounds was a circular drive defined by thick planting inscribing a large lawn, which Downing labeled "Parade or President's Park."[52] This led to the formation of The Ellipse, which exists today. However, the Civil War intervened, and this area became a cattle and horse corral called the "white lot" because of the white fence around it. Its swampy character was unpleasant, and there were even proposals to relocate the White House to a higher and healthier site.

When Ulysses Grant became president in 1869 he decided to leave the White House where it was and improve the southern grounds by filling and grading them. Over the next two decades this area was developed. The circular road was lined with elms and electric lights. In 1876 a fountain with a bowl seventy-five feet in diameter with jets and sprays was placed on the south lawn.[53] Two sandstone gatehouses designed by Charles Bulfinch in 1828 for the Capitol grounds were moved to the southeast and southwest corners of the Ellipse in 1880. The four companion gateposts were relocated south of Constitution Avenue.[54]

The private grounds near the mansion were only opened for the annual Easter egg hunt, which began in 1879, but the great lawn became a place of public refuge from the city, used for religious revivals, band concerts, and sports, including archery, baseball, croquet, and tennis. Cyclists raced around the oval roadway, and nighttime security became a problem.

The Senate Park Commission had significant influence on the White House itself but little impact on its grounds. Woodrow Wilson's wife, Ellen, had the flower gardens redesigned, creating the now-famous Rose Garden. In 1936 Fredrick Law Olmsted Jr. redesigned the grounds, planting masses of trees to ensure visual privacy while creating a southern vista to the Jefferson Memorial. Roadways were realigned to the present-day configuration.[55]

The tradition of utilizing the White House grounds for memorials began in 1848, when a statue of Thomas Jefferson was moved from the Capitol to a location near the north entrance. This was followed in 1903 by an elaborate memorial to the Civil War General William Tecumseh Sherman on its own parcel south of the Treasury Building. This large memorial, sponsored by Congress and the Army of the Tennessee, features a fourteen-foot-tall equestrian statue and two bronze groups representing

War and Peace on a tall pedestal. The stepped base has corner figures representing the four branches of the armed forces. Carl Rohl-Smith was the primary sculptor; however, the memorial was completed by others after he died.[56]

In subsequent decades the prestige of the White House grounds was sought for memorials, but only groups with political influence succeeded in placing their memorials there. Many of the smaller memorials were randomly placed without benefit of a master plan, including the following:

Butt-Millet Fountain (1913)—Ellipse
Zero Milestone Shaft (1923)—Ellipse
Alexander Hamilton (1923)—south of the Treasury Building
Settlers of the District of Columbia Memorial (1936)—
    Fifteenth Street
Albert Gallatin (1947)—north of the Treasury Building
Boy Scout Memorial (1964)—Fifteenth Street
Haupt Memorial(1969)—Constitution Avenue

The larger memorials assumed significant positions within contexts redesigned for them. An elegant memorial honoring the soldiers of the First Division of the American Expeditionary Force in World War I was placed south of the Old Executive Office Building in 1924. This sixty-five-foot column, made of a single piece of granite, supports a fifteen-foot gilded bronze statue of Victory designed by Cass Gilbert and his son and sculpted by Daniel Chester French. A memorial honoring the Second Division in World War I was placed along Constitution Avenue. This huge granite portal has a gilded bronze sword symbolically blocking the German advance.[57]

The White House grounds near the mansion are highly restricted for security reasons. All roads are closed to public vehicular traffic, and Executive Drive has recently been closed to public pedestrian traffic. There are a multitude of walkways and benches along the roadways and throughout the grounds. The grounds feature many picturesque plant ensembles and specimen trees, many planted by the presidents (fig. 5.11). The most well known are the East Garden and the Rose Garden, outside the Oval Office. These are only accessible to the public during tours or via the media. The only regular public event is the century-old annual Easter Egg Roll, which draws more than one thousand spectators to the South Lawn. The public has access to the president mostly away from his place of residence.

The Ellipse is now a site for both passive recreation and active sports such as softball, football, and soccer. The national Christmas tree, a live blue spruce, is located on the north-south axis at E Street. Every year there is a ceremonial illumination during the winter holiday season. During the Vietnam War era many protests and demonstrations were staged on the Ellipse so as to gain the attention of both the president and the press. These have continued on a more limited basis during the current era of conflicts.

The Architectural Context

The immediate architectural context for the White House comprises the two large, flanking buildings on the east and west sides. President George Washington insisted that these executive department offices be

Fig. 5.11. White House, view to north with gardens. Library of Congress, Prints and Photographs Division, HABS No. DC 134-96, photo by Jack Boucher, 1985–92

located in close proximity to the executive mansion. East of the White House was the first State Department building, occupied in 1800, and west of the mansion was the first War Department building, occupied in 1811. Both were aligned with the White House facing Pennsylvania Avenue, and both were designed by George Hadfield.[58] The British burned both in 1814, but James Hoban rebuilt them within the remaining outer walls.

Two additional executive office buildings, also designed by Hoban, were built in 1818–19 on the lawns north of these two buildings. All four buildings were similar in footprint and elevation, built of brick with Ionic porticoes supporting pediments. The older Treasury Department building burned again in 1833, and the State Department building was demolished in 1866. The Navy and War Department buildings were demolished in 1879 and 1884, respectively. The stage was set for construction of the present context.

East of the White House, the new Treasury Building was constructed incrementally beginning in 1836. The architect Robert Mills initiated the process with an E-shaped form comprising a spine facing Fifteenth Street and three wings with porticoes facing the White House. One of the city's most impressive buildings, it was built utilizing fireproof brick vaulting. The most impressive feature is the monumental Fifteenth Street facade, a three-story, 466-foot-long Ionic colonnade of brown sandstone that was rebuilt in granite in 1908.[59] In 1855 Thomas U. Walter added wings on the west side to enclose the courtyards. He also added entry porticoes in the Ionic order on the south, west, and north sides, along with pediments at the ends on the east side. After the Civil War, Alfred B. Mullet added a north wing that had a sunken forecourt because of the terrain (fig. 5.12).

West of the White House, Mullet designed a magnificent new State, War and Navy Building, erected between 1871 and 1888. This masterpiece of Second Empire design was the finest office building in the city, although some officials considered it too flamboyant for a government of-

fice building.[60] It relates to the Renwick Gallery, of similar style, across Pennsylvania Avenue. A sculpted gray granite building of bold presence, the massive, five-part form has three pavilions (one for each department) joined by straight segments. The projecting pavilions have stepped porticoes. An articulated mansard roof of slate and copper gives the building additional height and mass. The predominant Doric order is mixed with Ionic columns to create an elaborate architectural scheme on all sides. Now named the Eisenhower Executive Office Building, it has outstanding preserved interiors (fig. 5.13). In the past, many have criticized its appearance in relationship to the Treasury Building and called for alterations to bring it into conformity with the neoclassical context.[61]

The larger architectural frame of the White House on the west side of Seventeenth Street begins to impact the grounds south of New York Avenue. The three blocks north of this are opposite the Eisenhower Executive Office Building.

On the block opposite the First Division Memorial is the second Corcoran Gallery of Art (1897), built after the original became too small. The rounded north end accommodates the Corcoran School of Art, which turns the corner onto New York Avenue. An 1928 wing facing E Street was built to house the Clark art collection. A spectacular new wing by the architect Frank Gehry is planned along New York Avenue. Continuing south, the American Red Cross National Headquarters (1915) is a memorial to the women of the Civil War. Together with separate buildings facing E and Eighteenth streets it forms the headquarters complex grouped around a rectangular green space opening onto D Street.[62]

The Daughters of the American Revolution Continental Memorial Hall (1910), a monument to the founders of the nation and the headquarters for the organization, occupies the next block of Seventeenth Street. The original white marble building features a large concert hall, a library, and a memorial room.[63] The last building in this group is the Organization of American States Building (1908), located in the middle of the block with a curved drive on Seventeenth Street, large lawns on C Street and Constitution Avenue, and an expansive rear garden on Eighteenth Street. This was the site of the grand, Greek Revival Van

L'ENFANT'S LEGACY

Ness house designed by Benjamin Henry Latrobe in 1813, completed in
1816, and demolished in 1908.[64] The stuccoed carriage house is extant at
Eighteenth and C streets.

Fig. 5.13. Eisenhower (Old)
Executive Office Building,
view to northeast

An eclectic group of buildings forms the streetscape of this part of
Seventeenth Street. The 1903 map shows the early commercial buildings
between Pennsylvania and New York avenues, the Corcoran Gallery, and
the mostly vacant three blocks between E and B streets (see fig. 5.3). The
1999 map shows the assortment of commercial buildings along the northern section and the set of pavilions along the southern section (see fig.
5.9). The neoclassical pavilions defining the west side of the Ellipse are a
handsome architectural group of similar form, with mediating landscape
relating them to their urban context.

The larger architectural frame on the east side of Fifteenth Street
begins to impact the White House grounds south of E Street. The two
blocks north of this mostly face the Treasury Building. On the southwest
corner of F and 15th streets was Rhodes Tavern, built in 1797, a prominent
gathering place that served as an unofficial town hall. The tavern and
additions to it survived until preservationists lost a long battle in 1984
and it was demolished. All that remains is a plaque at the corner.[65] The
block between E Street and Pennsylvania Avenue is now Pershing Park
(see chapter 10).

Defining most of the east side of the Ellipse and forming the short leg
of the Federal Triangle is one gigantic building, the Commerce Department Building. Designed and built between 1926 and 1932 by York and
Sawyer of New York City, this three-block-long building contains thirty-
seven acres of floor space formed around six courtyards that are accessed
by driveways from Fourteenth and Fifteenth streets.[66] The main facade,
on Fourteenth Street, is composed as three distinct masses. The Fifteenth
Street side has four projecting Doric colonnades with pediments containing sculptural groups. The primary limestone facades have a rusticated
base, a three-story middle, and an attic story set behind a balustrade.

The 1903 map shows the numerous banks, theaters, and office buildings that existed along Fifteenth Street between New York and Ohio avenues. In the two blocks south of this were an automobile livery and a lumberyard (see fig. 5.3). All of these structures south of Pennsylvania Avenue were demolished to construct the Commerce Department Building and the Federal Triangle to the east. All the streets in this area were also eliminated, as shown on the 1999 map (see fig. 5.9).

Design analysis of the architectural context for the Ellipse reveals that there is an imbalance in the way the west side is defined relative to the east side. On the west side the spatial definition is erratic because of the individual building pavilions surrounded by formal landscape. On the four blocks only the Corcoran Gallery occupies the full block face. On the east side the Commerce Department Building forms a powerful and definitive edge to the Ellipse. Its monumental neoclassical design relates well to the Treasury Building and to other buildings around Lafayette Square, but it erases the urban block pattern of streets present on the west side. The east elevation, which appears as three distinct masses, should have been carried through to the west elevation to recall this street pattern. Fortunately, the thickly planted landscape on both sides of the White House grounds around the Ellipse tends to obscure this imbalance.

Saving a Democratic Place

On Inauguration Day an extensive parade passes in front of the White House on Pennsylvania Avenue. The design of the inaugural viewing stands used by the president and guests reflects the wishes of the new president and are paid for by his political party. The design of these reviewing stands has varied considerably, from earlier neoclassical styles to recent modern styles.[67]

Between inaugurations Pennsylvania Avenue in front of the White House is a zone of contention. Visitors and tourists come here to be near the president's house, to see where one of the world's most politically powerful persons lives. Protestors come to express their views on government policies in the hope of influencing the president. Others come because they are employed by the federal government.

During the 1970s the area of Lafayette Square near Pennsylvania Avenue was the scene of many civil rights demonstrations and Vietnam War protests. Large group events occurred on specific days by permission and with police protection. Across from the White House there were live-in protests, long-lasting vigils, and demonstrations involving large signs. Tourists and park users complained about the restricted views of the White House. In 1984 the National Park Service developed rules limiting each individual to one sign measuring four feet square and requiring that individuals stay with their signs at all times.[68] And a court decision in the same year restricted the sidewalk in front of the White House to stationary signs in the central zone. This reduced the number of protestors but did not eliminate them. These restrictions are a curtailment of citizens' First Amendment rights to free speech.

On 20 May 1995 Pennsylvania Avenue between Fifteenth and Seventeenth streets in front of the White House was closed to vehicular traffic with concrete barriers. The U.S. Secret Service closed the avenue on orders from President Clinton to prevent a vehicle with a bomb from exploding and endangering the president, his family, staff members, and the White House itself. Madison Place and Jackson Place were also closed to traffic. This was done one month after a truck bomb destroyed the federal building in Oklahoma City. The impact on city traffic was severe since twenty-six thousand vehicles used this primary east-west route each day.[69]

The symbolic implications of closing Pennsylvania Avenue were even greater than the traffic problems. Some say the city has now been divided physically and psychologically. No longer is the White House on a street (1600 Pennsylvania Avenue) where residents and tourists can drive by to view it. The president now lives in an enclave fortified by fences, gates, and numerous police forces. Thomas Jefferson's fear that the White House might be an isolated palace has come to pass; during all the past wars and insurrections Washington's main street has never before been closed.[70] Now, a symbolic aspect of America's open society and accessibility to government has been curtailed, and the result is visible to everyone. The closed avenue gives the appearance of bowing to the terrorists.

The positive side of the closing is the benefit to pedestrians, who no longer have to dodge vehicular traffic in front of the White House. The area is now heavily used by skateboarders and joggers, cyclists and strollers, who use the space leisurely in a quiet atmosphere without cars, trucks, and busses. The number of protestors has decreased owing to the lack of passing traffic to witness their messages. Interestingly, John Carl Warnecke, the architect who last redesigned Lafayette Park, had proposed turning the avenue into a pedestrian mall with circular fountains at the gateways and plantings.[71]

Everyone in Washington, official and unofficial, took sides in the wake of the closing of Pennsylvania Avenue. Not in recent history has an urban design change caused such a furor in the nation's capital. Those favoring reopening do not believe that closing the avenue will prevent terrorist attacks utilizing means other than a truck bomb. They also cite the concession to fear, which they consider an affront to an open democracy. Those favoring the closing cite the continued need for security for the president's family, the White House staff, and tourists.

In 1996 the National Park Service proposed a new design for the Lafayette Park precinct.[72] The intent was to return to a design similar to one during Thomas Jefferson's presidency. In 2002 the landscape architect Michael Van Valkenburgh won the competition to produce a final design scheme for the closed stretch of Pennsylvania Avenue. Van Valkenburgh's design, though simple, creates a place of dignity.[73] At the Fifteenth and Seventeenth Street gateways there are double rows of bollards (some retractable) and gatehouses. These block-long entrance zones are defined by elm trees and large granite paving blocks. The area in front of the White House, with a new granite sidewalk, remains visually open to Lafayette Square. Pennsylvania Avenue is unfortunately paved with brown tinted asphalt extending along Jackson Place and Madison Place to H Street. Nothing in this scheme impedes reopening the avenue in the future. This minimalist design was completed in time for the January 2005 presidential inaugural.[74]

Advocates for reopening the avenue were making progress in Congress and President George W. Bush was ready to consider it until 11 September 2001, when terrorists violently attacked the World Trade Center in New York City and the Pentagon in Arlington, Virginia, using hijacked airplanes. The result of the attacks was a declared world war on terrorists and extreme security measures nationwide, especially in the federal precinct of Washington. It is doubtful that reopening the avenue will be considered in the near future.

Since 2001 Lafayette Square has had the aura of a military zone. The White House compound is highly guarded. Both East Executive Drive and West Executive Drive are closed, as is E Street. Bollards and guardhouses restrict access to the closed portion of Pennsylvania Avenue for all but special vehicles. Secret Service agents and U.S. Park Police are everywhere on foot, bicycle, horseback, and motorcycle and in cruisers. Nevertheless, there still are many pedestrians, primarily dressed in business attire, walking to meetings, talking on cellular phones, or taking a lunch break in the park. There are also tourists, joggers, and homeless persons, but few protesters.

The community consensus is that Pennsylvania Avenue should be reopened to automobile traffic once the war against terrorism subsides. Placing footbridges as gateways at Fifteenth and Seventeenth streets may be necessary to restrict other kinds of vehicles. Other design enhancements in the Van Valkenburgh design could remain to make this a special part of the avenue. E Street should be reopened, probably with two-way traffic in four lanes. These measures would balance the interests of security and openness. Allowing auto traffic to pass the White House would introduce vitality to this place, allowing it to once again function as a part of the city rather than a high-security zone.

Lafayette Square and the White House grounds are two of the most hallowed public places in the capital city. They have a long and cherished history as sites where citizens exercise their First Amendment rights of free speech and free assembly. Pennsylvania Avenue mediates between these two places, providing literal and symbolic access to the executive branch of the federal government and the president. Design and security changes in this zone must be highly scrutinized, for they challenge the democratic ideals of this great nation and the freedom of its citizens.

CHAPTER SIX

EARLY SQUARES

Judiciary Square, Mount Vernon Square

IT IS INTERESTING to see how faithful colonial and frontier America was to the early Renaissance practice of according more dignity to the building than to the square in front of it. The eighteenth-century belief was that the square, however large and imposing, derived its dignity from its association with the building, and was in fact merely the place where inhabitants gathered to pay homage to the authorities within.

J. B. JACKSON, "The American Public Space"

Judiciary Square and Mount Vernon Square are among the oldest public spaces in Washington outside the federal precinct. Their historical precedents are the Renaissance civic square and the medieval market square of Europe. But they have been shaped by the specific exigencies of their neighborhood contexts and the uses prescribed by their functional roles in the city. These squares are distinct among public spaces in Washington in terms of their relationship with their architectural context.

At the center of one of Washington's oldest neighborhoods, Judiciary Square has undergone more change than most of the city's urban places in both landscape and architectural frame. It is unlike any other original square in that it is not at the nexus of radiating avenues and intersecting streets. It is near the Capitol and the Mall yet isolated from them as an enclave. Before the construction of the Metro station and the National Law Enforcement Officers Memorial this park was not a place visitors frequented. It is the judicial center for the District of Columbia, inhabited mostly by individuals who work there or have official court business.

Mount Vernon Square is also located in one of Washington's oldest neighborhoods, being the site of the city's first market in the 1840s. It is becoming one of Washington's newest neighborhoods, with extensive large-scale development in the 1970s and the recent construction of a new convention center. In the middle of the park was the District of Columbia Library, which was converted to the City Museum, devoted to the history of Washington's neighborhoods.

These two squares embody many American democratic ideals, albeit in different ways. Judiciary Square follows the American precedent of courthouse squares. The memorials there demonstrate freedom of speech by their variety of subject matter and artistic expression. The public library at Mount Vernon Square was one of the few unsegregated places in the city throughout the twentieth century, exemplifying the democratic ideal of equality. The City Museum continues that tradition, celebrating the diversity of the city's cultures, people, and neighborhoods.

Judiciary Square

The park at Judiciary Square, located in the northwest quadrant, is bounded by Fourth, Fifth, D, and G streets, an area of about eighteen acres. To the south is John Marshall Park, a public space with four buildings defined by Third, Sixth, and D streets and Pennsylvania Avenue.

The Nineteenth Century

Judiciary Square appears on the L'Enfant Plan as one of the original seventeen federal reservations, set on a slope above Pennsylvania Avenue (see fig. 1.1). Between the Capitol and the President's House, it was L'Enfant's designated location for federal courts so as to form a triangular spatial relationship among the three primary branches of government. Two avenues radiate from the south end. The western one, Indiana Avenue, provided a vista to the Washington Monument until the Federal Triangle was constructed and blocked the view; the eastern one, Louisiana Avenue, now nonexistent, appears on early maps as a vestigial avenue only four blocks long. Judiciary Square is also designated on Ellicott's 1792 plan for the city, where it is centered on a street extending south to Fort McNair (see fig. 1.2).

In the early years Judiciary Square's uses and architecture were varied. By 1801 there were vernacular wooden buildings on the park, but the first government building was a jail erected in 1802.[1] Built north of E Street, the two-story brick building was designed by George Hadfield. Next was the Greek Revival City Hall on D Street, also by Hadfield, constructed in 1820, with east and west wings added later (fig. 6.1). Robert Mills designed a new jail of brick with stucco in the Gothic Revival style, which was built in 1839 on the northeast corner facing G Street.[2] In 1845 a public school was built on the site. The old jail then became the Washington Infirmary Hospital, operated by the medical faculty of Columbian College; enlarged in 1853, it had more than one hundred patient rooms.[3] When the Civil War began, this was the only available hospital for wounded soldiers. Unfortunately, it burned in 1861, and a large military hospital was built in the park the following year.[4]

During the middle decades of the nineteenth century this location was becoming a place of civic importance, yet nothing was done to develop it as a public park. A stream ran from the northwest to the southeast corner to join Tiber Creek, and the area remained ungraded. In spite of its condition, a tradition of holding inaugural balls in Judiciary Square was born. Presidents Zachary Taylor, James Buchanan, Abraham Lincoln, and Ulysses Grant all held their inaugural balls there in temporary buildings.[5]

The first public monument honoring the slain Abraham Lincoln was placed on the south side of City Hall in 1868.[6] The life-size marble statue by Lot Flannery, paid for by citizens, was placed atop a thirty-five-foot column. The old frame buildings and brick school remained in the park until 1874, and the jail until 1878. Improvements to the park were ongoing from 1873, prompting Chief of Engineers Thomas Lincoln Casey to comment in 1877 that "this park has proven an agreeable place of resort for residents of this part of the city, and is daily visited by large numbers of

Fig. 6.1. Drawing of old City Hall, c. 1866. Library of Congress, Prints and Photographs Division, LC-USZ62-24214

persons. When the trees planted have attained a more advanced growth, and the improvements at present in contemplation have been fully carried out, it will not be second to any other park in its advantages."[7]

Finally, during the era of territorial government the landscape of the park was improved. The schoolhouse was removed, followed by the old jail, with a large marble fountain installed in the jail's former location. In 1873 the old City Hall became a federal court with an 1881 addition.[8] By 1875 the park was graded and sodded, paths were graveled, and the park was fenced. Elms and tulip poplars were planted around the perimeter.[9]

On the north side of the square, construction of the massive Pension Building starting in 1882, created a strong defining presence. This grand building, designed by General Montgomery C. Meigs, encompassed a great hall scaled as a civic square. The building first housed the Pension Bureau, followed by the General Accounting Office and other federal agencies. With the form of a Roman palazzo, containing the largest atrium in the city, it became the new location for presidential inaugural balls.[10] The highest roof element, a great gabled clerestory, is on axis with the square. The red brick mass, with its twelve-hundred-foot terra cotta frieze depicting Civil War troops, stands in contrast to the limestone courthouses around Judiciary Square, although their common classical features give this public space a measure of unity (fig. 6.2).

A map of Judiciary Square in 1888 (fig. 6.3) shows that most of the lots on adjacent streets were developed. The continuous buildings along Fourth and Fifth streets are mostly residences interspersed with offices for lawyers and doctors or, along Fifth Street between D and E streets, buildings for Columbian College (now George Washington University). Those along the east side of Fourth Street were built in pairs in the 1850s; their plain, four-story facades clearly define the urban space. On Indiana Avenue south of the square was Blagden Row, a particularly handsome

Fig. 6.2. Pension Building, south elevation, from Judiciary Square

group of town houses designed by William Baldwin and built by Thomas Blagden in 1852. This group of five four-story ashlar houses was occupied by prominent figures, including Senator Robert Toombs of Georgia and Chief Justice Roger Taney. Two other structures shown on the map—Metropolitan Methodist Church, at C and 4½ streets, and Freemason's Hall, at D and 4½ streets—were subsequently demolished to create John Marshall Park.[11] The map shows the Pension Building and the U.S. courthouse (old City Hall), along with the fountain, the watchman's lodge, and the Lincoln statue. E and F streets are wide paths or carriageways rather than streets; the other pathways are a series of free-form curves almost symmetrical in layout.[12]

The Twentieth Century

After the turn of the century new public buildings were erected to complete the present-day architectural frame. The District of Columbia Court of Appeals was erected on the southwest corner of the square in 1910. Old City Hall was renovated with a limestone facade and converted to the District of Columbia Courthouse in 1916–19.[13] The Lincoln statue was removed briefly, but public protest caused it to be returned and placed on a pedestal on the south side of the courthouse.

The Senate Park Commission proposed that the area now called the Federal Triangle be developed as a municipal center. When the federal government reserved the area for its own use, the urban blocks between D Street and Pennsylvania Avenue were designated for the municipal center formed around the axis of the old 4½ Street. The 1934 master plan by municipal architect Nathan C. Wyeth proposed two new municipal buildings there, with additional courts around Judiciary Square.[14] This resulted in the construction in 1937 of the Police Court north of the Court of Appeals and of the Municipal Court on the opposite side of the square. To complete the complex, a juvenile court was added on the east side of the square to complement the 1910 Court of Appeals.

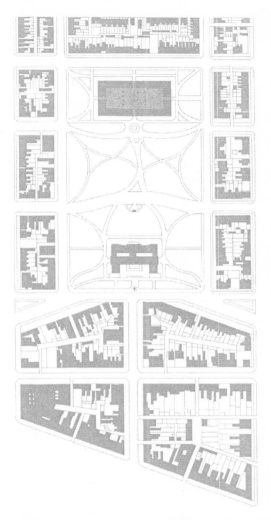

Fig. 6.3. Judiciary Square in 1888

The courts that define Judiciary Square are a beautifully coordinated set of buildings following idealized Renaissance precedents for a civic square. They all defer to the old City Hall, considered to be one of the finest Greek Revival buildings in the city. The designs are all based on classical architecture, with common cornice heights, roof forms, and limestone facades. Moreover, the buildings on opposite sides of the square are balanced in terms of location and size to form an ordered composition.

Additional improvements were made to the park, including a concrete coping to replace the fence and the Victorian watchman's lodge to replace a classically styled structure. A memorial fountain with a life-size gilded nymph and fawn honoring the esteemed Washington lawyer Joseph James Darlington was placed at the southwest corner in 1923, and a bronze equestrian statue on a granite base honoring the Latin American General Jose de San Martin was placed in the center of the park in 1924.

As the new court buildings were completed, the park became less of a neighborhood amenity and more of a formal civic place. There were frequent gatherings and protests. As automobile use became prevalent, more areas of grass were paved with asphalt for parking. F Street was straightened, the fountain removed, and the watchman's lodge demolished.

The initial element forming John Marshall Park was the municipal administration building and plaza on the east side of the 4½ Street axis, completed in 1940. The six-story limestone building, designed by Nathan C. Wyeth, has a pink granite base with a setback on the upper three stories. The proposed twin municipal building on the west side was abandoned in favor of the U.S. Courthouse, an eight-story building with two floors of underground parking, completed in the 1970s.

Two more buildings were added near Pennsylvania Avenue to complete the definition of John Marshall Park. The E. Barrett Prettyman U.S. Court, a rectangular, eight-story building, was completed in 1952. Since the building does not align with the angle of Pennsylvania Avenue, a plaza was built in front of it that contains a statue honoring General George Meade moved from the east end of the Mall. A large annex designed by Michael Graves is under construction on the east side. On the west side is the Canadian Chancery, designed by Arthur Erickson in 1989, with a raised courtyard that opens onto the public space. The light gray marble building, although modern in expression, incorporates references to its context, such as a rotunda and fluted columns.[15] The completed buildings defining Judiciary Square and John Marshall Park, along with the landscape designs, are shown in figure 6.4.

The public space at John Marshall Park was designed by Carol R. Johnson in 1983 as three handsomely landscaped terraces stepping up from Pennsylvania Avenue.[16] It maintains the visual axis from the Mall to old City Hall and the Pension Building. The processional sequence from Pennsylvania Avenue through John Marshall Park is varied, as the paths shift from being on axis to being on the perimeter (fig. 6.5). In a plaza at C Street is the bronze statue (1884) of John Marshall, former chief justice of the Supreme Court, atop a marble base, relocated from the Capitol.

The construction of the Metro system in the 1960s and 1970s transformed the way much of the city functioned. The great hope was to alleviate traffic congestion and the ever-increasing need for more parking. Location of a Metro stop in Judiciary Square has kept it from becoming one big parking lot. Unfortunately, the parcel south of E Street remains just such an eyesore. The Metro station, with twin escalators and twin elevators, is near F Street on the park's axis. The San Martin statue was relocated to a federal reservation on Virginia Avenue.

One of the great victories for historic preservation in Washington was saving the Pension Building, restoring it, and converting it to the National Building Museum in 1985. The federal government paid for the extensive restoration and continues to own the building. It is a private museum dedicated to the man-made world, showcasing American achievements in architecture, urban planning, construction, engineering, and design. It presents permanent and temporary exhibitions, films, lectures, concerts, symposia, and workshops.

In 1989 Judiciary Square was selected as the site for the National Law Enforcement Officers Memorial. The architect Davis Buckley chose an oval geometry to unite the disparate elements while maintaining a clear north-south axis. Michelangelo utilized an oval geometry in the same way more than four centuries ago at the Campidoglio in Rome.[17] The

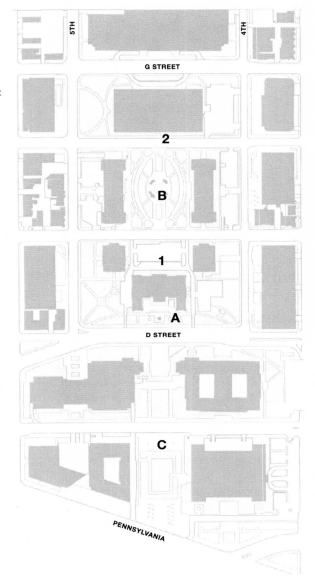

1 : District of Columbia
    Court House
2 : National Building
    Museum

A : Abraham Lincoln Statue
B : National Law Enforcement
    Officers Memorial
C : John Marshall Park

5TH

4TH

G STREET

2

B

1

A

D STREET

C

PENNSYLVANIA

Fig. 6.4. Judiciary Square in
1999

primary space-defining elements are two three-hundred-foot curving
marble walls originally inscribed with the names of more than twelve
thousand (now fifteen thousand) police officers killed in the line of duty.
The scheme recalls the Vietnam War Memorial on the Mall. The walls are
reinforced by two curving rows of clipped linden trees, which define an
oval space for ceremonies (fig. 6.6). The existing Metro elevator towers
were built into two curving steel pergolas. The escalators at F Street are
on axis opposite a cascading pool on the south side of the space. The most
intriguing features are bronze sculptures of lions and cubs by Ray Kaskey
at the ends of the curved marble walls. They are metaphors for the protectors and the protected, the police officers and the citizens. Completed
in 1991, this memorial in a place where laws are adjudicated honors those
who have enforced them. It is a landscape memorial both unified in de-

Top: Fig. 6.5. John Marshall
Park, view to north

Bottom: Fig. 6.6. National
Law Enforcement Officers
Memorial, view of memorial
wall and lion sculptures

sign composition and subtle in its design execution; it has given Judiciary
Park new public purpose and renewed pedestrian vitality.

The contrast between the north and south sides of Judiciary Park is
surprising. The south side remains a surface parking lot. The landscaped
area on the east side of the old City Hall is tawdry in appearance, defined
by an incongruous split-rail fence. It contains a provocative sculpture
called *Guns Into Plowshares,* constructed of old pistols. The space on the
west side is a maintained landscape with new brick walkways. The Dar-

lington fountain is set within a low hedge enclosure there. The Lincoln statue remains in place on the axis.

Commentary

The future direction for Judiciary Park is quite evident. The south portion needs to be redesigned to give it a quality commensurate with this dignified setting. A big part of the redesign will be the excellent design proposed for an underground police museum to complement the existing memorial, by the same architect.[18] The museum will be entered through two glass pavilions within a landscaped plaza adjacent to the old City Hall. The privately funded museum will be a national center for law enforcement history, as well as an additional memorial to the fallen officers.

The larger architectural context for Judiciary Square, bounded by Third, Sixth, H, and D streets, has been completely rebuilt in the last few decades. The urban design intention to create a neutral backdrop for the smaller-scale neoclassical buildings facing the square has not been consistently developed. The parking lots behind the court buildings along Fourth and Fifth streets should be either removed or redesigned.

Judiciary Square is an enclave within the city fabric. Through traffic has been thwarted by the lack of a direct connection to Pennsylvania Avenue and the dead-end streets at the I-395 underpass. On the other hand, the Metro provides direct pedestrian access. The absence of traffic helps to create the ambiance of a dignified public space.

The courthouse square as a public space is a hallowed part of the American townscape. Amendment VI of the U.S. Constitution guarantees the right to a speedy and public trial; attendance by the press and/or the general public makes trials open to scrutiny. Courthouse greens enable people and the press to assemble freely and discuss the judicial proceedings. Fortunately, Judiciary Square continues to be surrounded by courthouses that are actively engaged in the judicial process. When City Hall was also located there, it was an even more meaningful place. This historic building is being renovated for the D.C. Court of Appeals.

L'Enfant's vision of a judiciary square on a hill overlooking the Mall has generally been fulfilled. The ordered setting of neoclassical buildings gives this open space the requisite dignity. It bustles during the day with people from all walks of life doing business in the courts. The National Building Museum is a popular attraction drawing many visitors to interesting exhibits and concerts. The National Law Enforcement Officers Memorial provides new pedestrian vitality in the evening and on weekends, and the proposed new police museum will extend this activity to the south side of the park.

Mount Vernon Square

Mount Vernon Square, two blocks wide, lies at the intersection of Massachusetts and New York avenues and K and 8th streets in the northwest quadrant. The reasons for naming it after George Washington's home are obscure. It was later called Carnegie Library Square because of the library built on the site. On L'Enfant's 1791 map it appears as number 2, a rectangular appropriated open space, one of the original seventeen public reservations (see fig. 1.1). The square also appears on Ellicott's 1792 map in the same configuration (see fig. 1.2). It is located on the Eighth Street axis, which is emphasized on L'Enfant's plan by the location of five grand fountains at Pennsylvania Avenue and the location of a nondenominational church for national purposes and monuments. The axis is the location of the old U.S. Patent Building, now two national museums. This urban space is somewhat remote from all of the others, making reciprocal vistas difficult to perceive.

The Nineteenth Century

Prior to the Civil War the area around Mount Vernon Square became known as the Northern Liberties, being the northernmost limit of the developed city. Seventh Street was the primary north-south transit route after being chartered by Congress in 1810 as a turnpike. It was macadamized in the 1870s, and streetcar lines were placed on Seventh and Ninth streets and along New York Avenue.[19] Seventh Street developed into one of the city's earliest commercial corridors. The area grew rapidly during the first half of the nineteenth century to become one of the most densely populated neighborhoods (see fig. 1.3). It was an integrated neighborhood, with white residents living in dwellings facing the main streets and African American residents living along the alleyways. By the early twentieth century these alley dwellings were outlawed, and their residents migrated northward to the U Street neighborhood.

As first developed, the park was four triangular parcels formed by the intersection of the two avenues. The first intrusion upon the open space was a two-story fire station built there in 1840.[20] It served the civic purpose of safety but also provided a meeting space for community groups. In 1846 a brick market building was built on the triangle along Seventh Street.[21] It was a considerable nuisance, with many animals and wagons, much garbage, and constant commotion. By 1856 the fire station had been demolished, and neighbors wanted the offensive market removed as well.

The public space was used as a polling place. During the city's 1857 mayoral election a riot broke out there between the Know Nothing Party and local immigrant residents. Having lost the previous election, the Know Nothing Party imported gang members from Baltimore to intimidate voters with knives, rocks, and guns. To quell the ensuing riot President Buchanan summoned two companies of U.S. Marines, which the mob confronted. The mayhem resulted in dead and wounded on all sides, but the Marines prevailed and the polls reopened.[22]

The Northern Liberties Market grew into an even bigger nuisance, and neighbors petitioned for its removal. Alexander "Boss" Shepherd was determined to demolish it despite controversy that pitted the residents of the neighborhood against the merchants.[23] On the night of 3 September 1872 Shepherd dispatched the wrecking crew; unfortunately, the bodies of a young boy and a butcher were discovered in the rubble the next morning.[24] Shepherd finally developed the park in 1872, when the roadways were paved in concrete over new sewer and gas lines.[25] The triangles of land were planted, and an elaborate cast-iron fountain honoring Commodore Thomas Truxton, a Revolutionary War naval hero, was placed at the juncture of the intersecting streets.[26]

L'ENFANT'S LEGACY

Fig. 6.7. Mount Vernon
Square in 1888

The open space was not formed into a coherent rectangle until 1882, when the roadways were removed and replaced with gravel paths and two hundred trees and six hundred shrubs were planted. In his annual report Chief of Engineers A. F. Rockwell stated, "The improvement of this square was undertaken at the request of a majority of the property-owners and residents around it, which request was embodied in a petition signed by them and now on file in this office, recommending the removal of the concrete carriage-ways and the closing of the park to vehicles. It is believed the alteration made in the grounds have the approval of all who now resort to it, as in its former condition the constant passage of vehicles of all descriptions through the park made it unpleasant and oftentimes dangerous for those frequenting it."[27] The residents effectively utilized the democratic process to instigate the development of this park.

Figure 6.7, a map of Mount Vernon Square in 1888, shows an area in which virtually all the lots have buildings upon them, forming continuous street walls. These are mostly row houses, although many shops and services are identified east of the park on Sanborn maps. In many cases shopkeepers lived above their enterprises. In the northwest quadrant are Mount Vernon Place Church, the House of the Good Shepherd, and McKenorge Church. The park itself has a symmetrical pattern of curved pathways from the corners and straight pathways from the sides, all meeting at a circular fountain.

The Twentieth Century

At the turn of the century Mount Vernon Square was dramatically altered by the construction of a building at its center, the only square of the original L'Enfant Plan with such an intervention. In 1899 Andrew Carnegie donated funds for the first District of Columbia public library. The idea of building upon a federal reservation was initially opposed by several members of Congress, but Senator James McMillan, chairman of the Senate Committee on the District of Columbia, settled the issue. The library was completed in 1903 as designed by the New York firm of Ackerman and Ross (fig. 6.8).[28] The Beaux-Arts, white marble structure has a high cen-

tral mass with a monumental arched south facade and two lower wings. Narrow vertical windows on the north facade express the book stacks inside. One of the few racially unsegregated places in the city, the library served all of the residents. Additions to the library were proposed from 1929 to 1953 but were opposed by the National Park Service, which did not want to sacrifice any more public park lands.[29] This library closed after a large new library was built at Ninth and G streets in 1972. The site was transferred to the District of Columbia, and the building was used by the city university to house its library and the architecture department.

Mount Vernon Park was severely altered by the presence of the new library. Although it does not have a large footprint, the large terraces, planters, and walkways surrounding the library occupied approximately half the park's acreage. It was essentially divided by the library building into two parcels along Ninth and Seventh streets. The park was minimally redesigned in 1913.

In 1917 the Mount Vernon Place Southern Methodist Church decided to invest in the neighborhood by building a new structure across the intersection from its current location. The southern branch of the Methodist Episcopal Church, formed in a schism over slavery, wanted a national church in a prominent location. Located on the triangle of land at Massachusetts Avenue and K Street, the neoclassical building of Georgian marble has an imposing Doric portico and stairs facing the square. This church had the largest congregation in the city during the 1930s. It has a very positive architectural relationship with the library building and its presence validates the democratic ideal of freedom of religion.

During the Depression of the 1930s the neighborhood began to decline. Through traffic increased along Seventh Street and New York Avenue. Residents moved to other neighborhoods, leaving vacant buildings that became home to secondary commercial uses such as garages, laundries, and warehouses. The park was occupied by vagrants and the unemployed, who intimidated library users and staff. Commercial activ-

L'ENFANT'S LEGACY

ity continued in the buildings around the park, with two banks, a hotel, a theater, and a large department store.

The area around Mount Vernon Square was one of the centers of rioting in the aftermath of the murder of Martin Luther King Jr. in 1968. Many of the buildings along Seventh Street and adjacent streets were burned. All the buildings in the four blocks north of the square were demolished when the site was purchased by the city for a new University of the District of Columbia campus. The first new building to be erected after the riots was the seven-story American Security Bank headquarters on its previous site at Seventh Street and Massachusetts Avenue.

During the past three decades the District of Columbia government has been investing in the redevelopment of the Mount Vernon Square area. In 1977 four blocks southwest of the square were purchased by the city under eminent domain; residents were relocated and businesses closed. A banal concrete convention center was completed there in 1983. This induced the development of other office buildings and hotels. Located directly south of the square is Techworld (1989), a high-tech trade center and eight-hundred-room hotel on two blocks, with an enclosed pedestrian bridge crossing Eighth Street between the sixth and eighth floors.[30] This incursion was opposed by preservation groups because of the significance of the Eighth Street axis and vista on the L'Enfant Plan. The twin reflective glass structures with splayed corners create a bleak streetscape and a brutal architectural frame for the historic library and square.

The next big decision for Mount Vernon Square was how to utilize the vacant blocks north of the park. The most serious proposal, in 1978, was for a downtown campus for the University of the District of Columbia, which failed to gain congressional approval because of a declining student enrollment and the construction of a Van Ness campus.[31] Attempts to interest private developers in building a Mount Vernon campus also failed.

In the early 1990s Washington needed a larger convention center in order to compete with other cities and generate income from hotel rooms, restaurants, travel, and shopping. It was not feasible to enlarge the existing one. After much deliberation, the site north of Mount Vernon Square was chosen because it was vacant, because it was close to downtown, and because there was a Metro stop at Ninth and L streets. The big disadvantage was the imposition of traffic and activity on the redeveloping Shaw and Mount Vernon neighborhoods.

The design for the new Washington Convention Center was unveiled in November 1996. It would be the largest building in the city and would occupy the most ground area: six city blocks from K Street to N Street and from Ninth Street to Seventh Street (fig. 6.9). The proposed building was also long (1,500 feet) and high (130 feet) and bulky (2.3 million square feet), threatening to overwhelm the Shaw and Mount Vernon neighborhoods, which protested the incursion. A revised design in October 1997 placed the exhibition hall entirely underground to lower the building's height, increasing the project cost by 20 percent.[32] Costs continued to escalate during construction, from 1998 to 2003, which included an expanded Metro station and new utilities. The construction period was

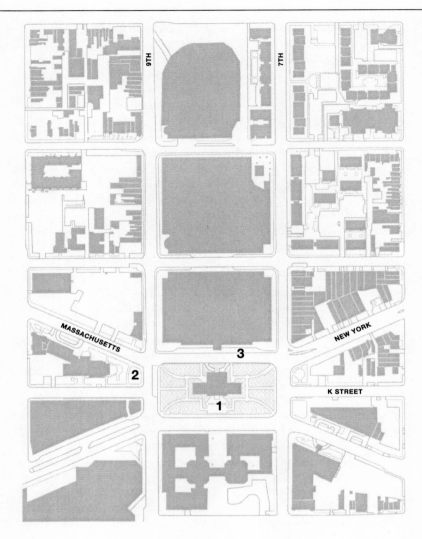

**Fig. 6.9. Mount Vernon
Square in 1999**

contentious and troublesome for businesses and neighbors alike, with
many instances of protest and complaint, which authorities tried to as-
suage.

The exterior of the mammoth building was designed to look like a
series of smaller buildings in order to reduce the visual impact of its scale.
Glazed pedestrian bridges over L and M streets allowed those streets to
remain open. Everything possible was done to relate the building's dyna-
mism to its urban context, such as putting the circulation on the perimeter and revealing it with large expanses of glass, transparent for people
and translucent for trucks. The design was by Thompson, Ventulett,
Stainback and Associates, of Atlanta, with Theodore R. Mariani and Dev-
rouax and Purnell, of Washington. Limestone and granite were utilized
on the two-block-long facade facing the park, relating it to the federal
city, whereas brick facades faced the residential neighborhood. The largest element, a multitiered lobby with a curved glass facade and two limestone pylons marking the axis of what once was Eighth Street, faces the
park (fig. 6.10). The points where the building meets the neighborhood

L'ENFANT'S LEGACY

Fig. 6.10. Washington Convention Center, view to northwest. Photo by Brian Gassel, courtesy of TVS & Associates

are less satisfactory. The long Seventh Street facade is a series of projecting bays, designed to reduce the scale, and there are shops and restaurants along Ninth Street, but the N Street facade is a screen covering seventy loading docks directly across the street from the Victorian-era Immaculate Conception Church.

The front part of the new convention center, containing the grand lobby and ballroom, completed in 2003, is monumental (ninety feet tall) but mostly transparent along its subtly concave facade facing the park. It is an interior analogue to the open space, a great gathering place with wonderful views of the park and the monumental city beyond. At night it becomes an urban theater featuring the choreography of people meeting and moving along stairways, bridges, and balconies. It does not overwhelm the historic marble Carnegie Library but frames and reflects it in a symbiotic relationship.[33]

Washington is a capital city, but the capital part always receives more attention than the city part. For a time there was a City Museum dedicated to telling the story of the city's neighborhoods, arts, sports, businesses, and education. Located in the beautifully restored Carnegie Library, the long-awaited museum opened in 2003 with a multimedia theater, galleries, archives, education center, and research library.[34] The central feature was a large contemporary floor map of the original area of the District of Columbia created from satellite images. Neighborhoods were featured on a rotating basis in the changing exhibits gallery. Conventioneers from across the street, as well as tourists and residents, had the opportunity to learn about the constituent city that makes the federal city function. Unfortunately, the museum closed after eighteen months for reorganization. The park itself has been minimally redesigned. It may need to be redone in the near future to accommodate increased foot traffic.

Commentary

Critics of the new convention center have accepted its presence and are now concerned about the lack of room for expansion. The old convention center was too small just seven years after it was built, losing conventions to other cities with bigger facilities. Every major city with a convention center has had to expand it two or three times. The present site is landlocked, surrounded by a neighborhood with many historic structures. On the west is the Blagden Alley Historic District, a Victorian middle-class neighborhood with extant alley dwellings. On the east is the Mount Vernon Square Historic District with some frame dwellings dating from the 1840s. Along Seventh Street is an existing block of affordable housing units called the McCollough Terrace Apartments. Many families and individuals have recognized the value of these historic structures by buying them and restoring them as private residences, but they feel threatened by the negative consequences of the new convention center. Destruction of additional urban fabric for expansion will cause even more contention than did construction of the new convention center.[35]

The neighborhood is undergoing significant changes. Increasing rents and building redevelopment are forcing residents and businesses to relocate. The convention center authority would like them to stay to give the center a context of local flavor that is different from that of convention centers in other cities.

Redevelopment of the old convention center site (the building has been demolished) remains in limbo. Mayor Anthony A. Williams has outlined a proposal for hundreds of housing units with retail stores and a public library around a large public plaza.[36] Development of the site is crucial to the success of this area, balancing economics with public uses to create a thriving place. The city government is also seeking developers for a large convention hotel on private land, which is critical to the success of the new convention center.[37]

Mount Vernon Square has had more physical changes during its history than any other city square. For the first century it was home to a bustling market within a burgeoning commercial neighborhood. During most of the second century it served as a civic space occupied by the public library. Now in the third century, it continues its civic role with the city museum in the shadow of an enormous new convention center. It is unique among the city's public reservations in having a building at its center, with only the periphery for pedestrian uses. It continues to serve a democratic purpose since the city museum, not unlike the library, is an institution devoted to educating residents to be informed citizens.

CHAPTER SEVEN

OFFICE SQUARES

Farragut Square, McPherson Square, Franklin Square,
Rawlins Park, Gompers-Burke Park

THIS PHYSICAL AND PSYCHOLOGICAL function of the square does not depend on size or scale. The village green in a small New England town, the central square of a residential quarter within a larger city, the monumental plaza of a metropolis—all serve the same purpose. They create a gathering place for the people, humanizing them by mutual contact, providing them with a shelter against the haphazard traffic, and freeing them from the tension of rushing through the web of streets.

PAUL ZUCKER, *Town and Square*

After early development near the White House, urban growth extended to the neighborhoods around the next group of proximate squares in the city's northwest quadrant, fulfilling L'Enfant's prediction of a multinodal city wherein nodes would compete with one another. After the Civil War the prestigious residences around these squares were either converted to or replaced by offices for federal agencies, law firms, organizations, and other entities seeking proximity to the government's executive branch. Currently, these squares function as focal points in the commercial city north and west of the White House. They are all nodes of intense pedestrian, social, and commercial activity.

Another of L'Enfant's growth precepts was to intertwine the federal and local functions so that they would positively interact with each other.[1] Federal buildings would induce private development, thereby strengthening the economy of the city. This is borne out by the squares discussed in this chapter, which have a federal presence through government buildings or tenancy in private buildings.

Development of these parks was promoted under the territorial government from 1871 to 1874. Governor Alexander Shepherd's legacy to the city was not only extensive public works but the formation of these five public spaces. The consequence of his efforts was the promotion of commercial development in these sectors of the city.[2]

Pierre Charles L'Enfant recommended that building heights be the same as the widths of the streets the buildings abutted. This recommendation was refined and modified by the District of Columbia building regulations in 1910, with additional restrictions for buildings around public reservations.[3] Since private developers usually try to erect the largest buildings allowable, in time all edifices around a square came to assume the same mass and height. In this regard the buildings around

Farragut, McPherson, and Franklin squares approach the City Beautiful ideal of urban space defined by uniform buildings.

Each of these five urban spaces has undergone at least one transformation in the last two centuries, from residential uses to commercial and/or government uses. Each accommodates diverse use: the luxury apartment building at McPherson, the Army Navy Club at Farragut, the Crowne Plaza Hotel and the Almas Club at Franklin, the Octagon House at Rawlins, and the housing at Gompers-Burke. All except Rawlins Park have street-level commercial space. Diverse uses improve security around these open spaces by making them active nodes beyond business hours. They also enhance their image, fostering use by more people.

Each space also has a memorial purpose. At Farragut and McPherson the statues are imposing and centered, dividing these spaces into two triangles. At Franklin and Rawlins the statues are smaller in scale and at the periphery of undivided spaces, allowing the parks to assume their primary role as places of social gathering. At Gompers the memorial is well integrated, whereas at Burke it is not.

Use of these public spaces at the end of the twentieth century exemplifies the democratic ideals they embody. These are unprogrammed places available for free use by all citizens and visitors, demonstrating the right to equal protection of the law. These are places of free assembly and association with opportunities for casual meetings. The architecture and memorials defining them exemplify freedom of expression. Performances and events are held in these spaces, demonstrating freedom of speech.

Farragut Square

Farragut and McPherson are twin open spaces of the same size and shape, both located two blocks north of the White House. They each intercept a diagonal avenue that terminates at Lafayette Square. Farragut Square (1.6 acres) is located between I and K streets and is intercepted by Connecticut Avenue. Seventeenth Street is divided by the park forming block-long east and west segments. There are southern vistas to Lafayette Square, the White House, and the Washington Monument.

The Nineteenth Century

Farragut Square appears on both the L'Enfant and Ellicott plans of the city. In spite of its proximity to the White House, there was little development around the square until after the Civil War, when it became the location of prominent residences such as the large Gothic Revival home built for Ellisha Riggs Jr. on the southeast corner in 1858.[4] The southwest corner was the location of the Western Academy, an early public school, from 1805 to 1825.[5] During the Civil War, Union troops camped in this space and several temporary buildings were built.

The park was first improved in 1873, when Connecticut Avenue bisected it and created two triangular parcels. Connecticut Avenue was improved by the territorial government with a wide concrete pavement lined with aspen trees extending from Lafayette Square to the city boundary at Florida Avenue. Brigadier General Nathaniel Michler, of the Army Corps of Engineers, Office of Public Buildings and Grounds, did not want the road to bisect the park, but his successor, Orville Babcock, prevailed since he was a friend of "Boss" Shepherd.[6]

The original park improvements were completed in conjunction with plans for a statue of Admiral David Glasgow Farragut, the first admiral of the U.S. Navy. Congress had named the park in his honor, and an elliptical area in the middle of the avenue was prepared.[7] At the same time, the triangular parcels were improved with walks, water and drainage pipes, an iron fence, and flowers, shrubs, and trees. When the statue was installed in 1881, the Connecticut Avenue pavement was removed to reshape the entire open space as a rectangle. The portrait statue of Farragut, on a high granite base, faces the White House. It was sculpted by a woman, Vinnie Ream, and cast from the metal of a propeller from the USS *Hartford,* the ship to which Farragut lashed himself during the battle of Mobile Bay.[8] He is remembered for his famous words, "Damn the torpedoes, full speed ahead!" (fig. 7.1). This first monument in the nation's capital to a naval war hero was authorized and funded by Congress.[9] Vinnie Ream and her husband later bought a brick mansion on the square overlooking her famous work.[10]

In the 1870s and 1880s the area around Farragut Square became a social and diplomatic hub, an extension of uses from Lafayette Square. The British minister rented the house built for Riggs, which was later purchased by Brigadier General Albert Myer in 1877. In 1883 Captain Nathan Sargent built an ornate brick house on the east side of the square. On the north side were three stone-faced row houses built in 1873, the site of lavish entertaining. "Boss" Shepherd lived in the towered corner house, next to the architect Adolph Cluss, who had designed the houses.[11] The unofficial use of the park as a military gathering place became official when the Army Navy Club built a five-story Romanesque Revival structure on the southeast corner of Seventeenth and I streets in 1891.

A map showing the square in 1888 (fig. 7.2) shows the Riggs House and the three row houses on the north side, the western one labeled as the Russian Legation on the Sanborn map. Additional row houses are

Fig. 7.1. Statue of Admiral David Glasgow Farragut with children, view to north, 1880–90. The Historical Society of Washington, D.C. / City Museum

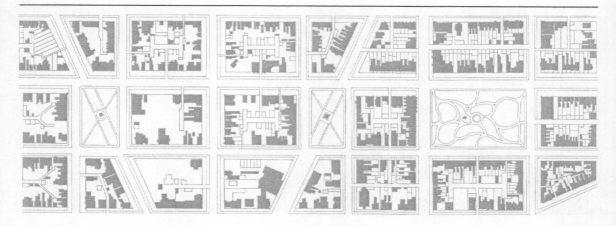

Fig. 7.2. Farragut, McPherson, and Franklin squares in 1888

shown lining the west, south, and east sides of the square, but the south-east quadrant is almost vacant.

The Twentieth Century

After the turn of the century the area around Farragut Square began to change from residential to commercial. Trolley tracks placed along Connecticut Avenue in the 1870s made the square accessible to large numbers of people. This raised the real estate prices, making the area amenable to redevelopment. At the same time, prominent residents were relocating to higher ground in the uncongested northwest quadrant of the city. Row houses on the north side were converted to offices, and the Army Navy Club purchased and demolished the Riggs House in 1911 in order to construct a much larger building.[12]

By midcentury many new office buildings faced Farragut Square, built to the maximum allowable size to fulfill their economic potential. On the west side was the eleven-story Barr Building, next to the Farragut Medical Building, which was next to the Commerce Building, with the Hill Building on the south side. The YWCA, on the northeast corner, and the Army and Navy Club, on the southeast corner, were the only institutions.

After midcentury, reconstruction of the Farragut Square area into a high-density commercial area progressed rapidly. Approximately thirty new modern office structures were built in this area between 1955 and 1960, replacing small nineteenth-century buildings such as Shepherd's Row (1952), the old Army Navy Club (1962), and the Sargent House (1966).[13] The area became a center for the legal and medical professions, which occupied the high-rent office space.

The park itself retained its 1880s design until the 1960s, when it was refurbished as part of Ladybird Johnson's city beautification program. Perennial azalea and tulip beds were planted around the statue and at the Connecticut Avenue corners.

In 1960 the District Motor Vehicle Parking Agency initiated plans to construct a two-level, 375-car parking garage underneath Farragut Square.[14] The Committee of 100 on the Federal City and the National Park Service resisted this as an attempt to sully a public reservation. The agency subsequently decided that it would be too costly to build the garage in part because of ground-water problems. This established a precedent and led to a National Park Service resolution that in the future

L'ENFANT'S LEGACY

none of the park areas included in the original L'Enfant Plan would be considered for parking facilities.[15] As a result, unlike in most other cities, there are no underground garages beneath the public open spaces in Washington. Zoning regulations now require developers to provide parking facilities for their commercial buildings.

To alleviate traffic congestion, Washington, D.C., built its subway system beginning in the 1970s. Two stations serving three different lines are located at Farragut Square: Farragut North and Farragut West. An underground pedestrian walkway is slated to link them. A small, four-story shopping mall called the Connecticut Connection was built at the entrance to the Farragut North station. The Farragut West station is under the Hill Building, on the southwest corner of the square. The north side of the square is also an active bus waiting and transfer area, although poorly accommodated.

The architecturally most interesting building on Farragut Square is the Army Navy Club, on the east side, designed by Hornblower and Marshall in 1911 as a Renaissance palazzo with a two-story ballroom facing the park at the top. In the 1950s it was expanded with an additional story and another bay. Finally, in 1987 Shalom Baranes Associates designed a four-story addition on top to fill the allowable zoning envelope with rental offices.[16] In spite of design elements intended to integrate old and new, the composition still looks like a new building sitting on top of an old one (fig. 7.3).

Fig. 7.3. Army Navy Club, east side of Farragut Square

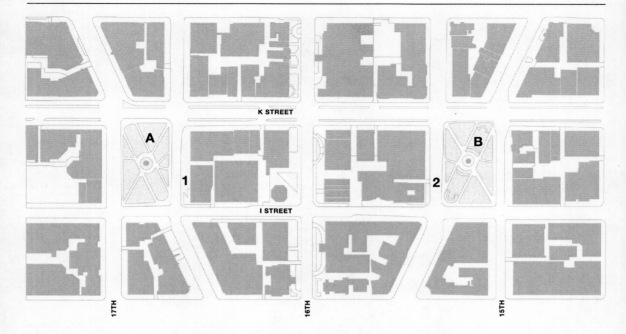

In 1999 Farragut Square was completely defined by eleven-story of-fice buildings with ground-floor commercial space (fig. 7.4). None of the buildings surrounding the park are obtrusive. Most have straight street facades that express the repetitive grid of office spaces with storefronts at street level. They all meet the allowable height limit, creating an almost uniform cornice height around the entire square. These dominant street walls create a strong architectural frame that clearly defines the park; however, this definition is weakened at the corners by the wide angular slash of Connecticut Avenue.

Commentary

In the 1970s the area around Connecticut Avenue and K Street was the crossroads of the legal community in Washington, with nine of the ten largest law firms located there. By the 1980s most had moved to the newly favored location along Pennsylvania Avenue.[17] Many law firms sought to consolidate space in one prestigious location with nearby amenities. They were replaced by smaller law firms, trade associations, consultants, and financial institutions.

Farragut Park has a large number and variety of users, including busi-ness people, vendors, couriers, homeless people, and tourists. Some spend time there on the park benches or grass to enjoy the greenery. Others use it as a pedestrian passage. A business improvement district formed by property owners helps maintain the park and cosponsors events with the National Park Service, such as a summer concert series. On the weekend and at night, however, the daytime users leave, except for the homeless; few people live in the area, and the commercial establishments are closed. For decades city officials have been encouraging, if not enticing, develop-ers to provide downtown housing, but it generally is not profitable for them to do so. If the economics could be changed through tax incentives

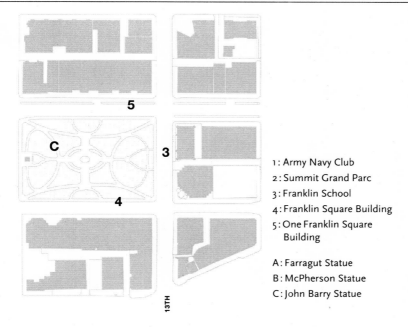

1 : Army Navy Club
2 : Summit Grand Parc
3 : Franklin School
4 : Franklin Square Building
5 : One Franklin Square
   Building

A : Farragut Statue
B : McPherson Statue
C : John Barry Statue

Fig. 7.4. Farragut, McPherson, and Franklin squares in 1999

or zoning bonuses, Farragut, McPherson, and Franklin squares would not be such lonely places at night and on the weekends.

Farragut Square functions well as a democratic place preserving L'Enfant's legacy of public spaces. It is an intermodal transit center for transferring between cars, taxis, buses, and the subway. This activity and the large employment base generate extensive pedestrian traffic that supports the ground-floor establishments. The public space also functions as a passive social center, primarily during business hours. The Army Navy Club adds to this social purpose, giving the square an identity in conjunction with the memorial function of the Farragut statue.

McPherson Square

McPherson Square (1.7 acres) is the eastern twin to Farragut Square, also located two blocks north of the White House. It is located between I and K streets and is intercepted by Vermont Avenue. Fifteenth Street is divided by the park, forming block-long east and west segments. There are southern vistas to Lafayette Square, the White House, and the Washington Monument.

The Nineteenth Century

McPherson Square is included on both the L'Enfant and Ellicott plans of the city. It was not improved until after the Civil War, at which time there was vacillation regarding whether it should take the form of a rectangular space or two triangular spaces. Initially it was two triangles, but in 1867 it was formed into a rectangular space. A year later Congress named it Scott Square to honor Lieutenant General Winfield Scott. This scheme changed in 1872, and the Scott statue was located in the circle at the intersection of Massachusetts and Rhode Island avenues.

During the era of territorial government the square was again divided

Office Squares

Fig. 7.5. Statue of General
James B. McPherson,
McPherson Square

into two triangles by extending Vermont Avenue as a wide roadway lined by silver maple trees. The two triangular spaces were graded, sodded, fitted with gas and water lines, and surrounded by an iron post-and-chain fence. Concrete walkways were installed along the diagonals and the perimeter.[18]

Congress renamed this square after Brigadier General James B. McPherson in 1876, erecting his statue there. The Vermont Avenue pavement was again torn up, and the area sodded. An earthen mound and granite base were placed in the center for the tall equestrian statue by Louis Rebisso, which faces southwest (fig. 7.5). It was cast in bronze from the metal of a Confederate cannon captured in the battle of Atlanta, where McPherson died.[19] McPherson had led the Army of the Tennessee during General Sherman's Civil War march to the sea. The statue was sponsored by his comrades in the Society of the Army of the Tennessee, who had tried unsuccessfully to have his body interred in the pedestal. The statue was dedicated in 1876 in a ceremony led by Generals Sherman and Logan. The latter, who would soon be honored with his own statue in Logan Circle, gave the oration.

The area around McPherson Square developed with prestigious residences and hotels a little earlier than that around Farragut Square. By 1861 half the lots were occupied by buildings, including a Colored Presbyterian Church on the east side, an unlikely structure in this prestigious neighborhood during the Civil War.[20] A house built in 1860 on the south side by Jonah Hoover, the District of Columbia marshal, was later occupied by Hamilton Fish, President Grant's secretary of state.[21] The Arlington Hotel was built by W. W. Corcoran on the southwest corner of the square in 1868, replacing several row houses. On the north side, the real estate developer Archibald Lowery built a grand Second Empire house in 1875. A map showing McPherson Square in 1888 shows all of these struc-

tures, plus a small McPherson Hotel on the southeast corner. Formerly the Senator Palmer House, built in 1884, it had been converted into a hotel in 1887 (see fig. 7.2).

The area around the square continued to attract notable and wealthy residents, such as Cornelius Vanderbilt from New York and Mrs. Phoebe Hearst, who rented the Lowery House.[22] In 1890 John McLean and his wife moved into the original Hoover House and enlarged it to fill the entire south side of the square. This shrewd businessman, after whom the city of McLean, Virginia, is named, was involved in banking, utilities, railroads, and publishing.[23] The house was designed by John Russell Pope in 1907 as a great two-story brick palazzo with a third floor for servants within the frieze. The entire thirty-foot-high first floor, with magnificent rooms facing the park, was for entertaining (fig. 7.6).

The Army Corps of Engineers Office of Public Buildings and Grounds completely redesigned the park in 1892. The symmetrical, picturesque scheme had curving paths from each corner focusing on an elliptical center with a circular mound for the statue. The iron fence was removed, the entire grade was elevated, and many trees and shrubs were removed.[24]

The Twentieth Century

As the century turned, the wealthy residents began to move from this neighborhood to larger, less congested areas north and west of the city center. The area around McPherson Square was converted to offices for banks and organizations since its proximity to Lafayette Square and the White House attracted prestigious tenants. The Southern Railway Building (1923) occupied the northwest corner of the square, and the Investment Building, of the same year, occupied the north side of K Street. In 1925 the original Palmer House was demolished and replaced by the Rust Office Building, and the Lowery House was converted to offices for the Justice Department. The Veterans Administration built a block-long building along Vermont Avenue to replace the Arlington Hotel in 1921. On the southwest corner, the University Club built a handsome five-story Renaissance Revival building designed by the Washington architect

George Oakley Totten Jr. in 1911.[25] Later it was occupied by the United Mine Workers' Union, which added another floor of grand offices for President John L. Lewis. Commercial growth continued to expand when the McLean House was demolished in 1939 and replaced by the Export Import Bank of the United States. In 1920 the park's design was returned back to diagonal paths with a landscaped panel aligning with Vermont Avenue to suit the needs of business people seeking a more amenable pedestrian shortcut.[26]

In the second half of the twentieth century additional, modern highrise office buildings were built to accommodate the legal profession and the trade associations. This additional office space was necessary because of improved access to the area via a Metro station serving two lines built beneath the park in the 1970s, accessed at the corner of the Veterans Administration Building. Among the new buildings was the twelve-story McPherson Building in the southeast corner, completed in 1987.[27] The park is now completely surrounded and defined by large office buildings that create a strong architectural frame (see fig. 7.4).

Commentary

McPherson Square has recently burgeoned as a place of redevelopment, and there have been several large building projects. The location is attractive because of its position in the office district, the amenity of the park, and the subway access. On the west side, the United Mine Workers Building was renovated in 2002 as the Summit Grand Parc, with twenty apartments and offices attached to a new fourteen-story building on I Street with 85 luxurious apartments and an automated four-story underground parking garage (fig. 7.7).[28] The Investment Building was renovated, featuring a modern circular atrium, and a large new office building called the Flagship of McPherson Square was completed on the northeast corner. Finally, on the southeast corner the Bowen Building has been rebuilt, saving only the facades. Some of the boom in office redevelopment is being driven by prestigious law firms who demand at least twice as much high-quality space per employee as other tenants.

The park itself is a weekday refuge for the thousands of office workers in the area. To protect this asset, businesses in the area have formed the Downtown DC Business Improvement District to maintain and improve the park and host noontime concerts. The diagonal landscape panel has been planted with azalea beds bordered by a hedge at either end and around the statue. Shrubs, trees, and benches along the walkways guide pedestrian movement. In the evening the park is a place for homeless people to gather and receive a variety of food, medical services, and clothing.[29] This is conducted with orderly decorum so as not to disturb patrons of the park or surrounding restaurants.

There is nothing remarkable or noteworthy about McPherson Square. Its architectural frame has no exemplary architecture. Most of the buildings have facades of grid or strip windows expressing their office function. All reach the allowable height limit except for the old University Club and the older midblock buildings on the east side, which are lower. The landscape design is appropriate but not noteworthy. Except for the statue, there is no tourist attraction. It is a space for office workers and residents living in the new Summit condominiums. Yet it is a pleasant

and useful place clearly appreciated by the many people who use it for strolling, sitting, reading, eating, drinking, and relaxing on a daily basis.

The urban-space legacy is honored in this democratic place. It functions as a transportation node, albeit to a lesser extent than Farragut Square. It is also a thriving activity node with active street-level commerce and upper-level business. The park functions as a social center for spontaneous meeting and greeting, while the equestrian statue represents the memorial function. If other apartments or condominiums are added, the park will also once again become a neighborhood center.

Franklin Square

During the Civil War Franklin Square was a campground for Union troops under the command of General Joe Hooker. Women who offered soldiers their favors there gained the nickname "hookers," a term still in use today.[30] During the 1960s and 1970s prostitutes and others associated with sexually oriented businesses returned to control the west side of the square. After city officials and developers managed to purge this Fourteenth Street zone the square enjoyed a great resurgence. It is today a green oasis surrounded by midrise office buildings.

Franklin Square is a true green park, almost entirely forested and planted, with a central fountain. It is sometimes even called Franklin Square Park. It is not heavily used since it is large—about 4.8 acres in area and measuring 600 feet by 390 feet, sloping down to the south approximately twenty feet—and there are three other green public spaces nearby.

Franklin Square lies within the heart of the business district of Washington, D.C., just two blocks northeast of the White House. It is bounded by K Street to the north, I Street to the south, Fourteenth Street to the west, and Thirteenth Street to the east. K Street is the principal street in the office district, linking with the Whitehurst Freeway and the Key Bridge to Virginia. Fourteenth Street is also an important egress street, cutting across the Mall and leading to two bridges that access freeways in Virginia. I and Thirteenth streets are typical business district streets, part

Fig. 7.7. McPherson Square, west side

of the original grid system. Franklin Square differs from most urban open spaces in Washington in that it is not connected to a diagonal avenue.

The Nineteenth Century

Franklin Square does not appear on either L'Enfant's or Ellicott's plan of the federal city. It was originally divided into lots, but when several large natural springs were discovered it became known as Fountain Square. About 1830 the U.S. government purchased the urban block to provide water through wooden pipes for the executive offices on Pennsylvania Avenue and the White House.[31]

In 1856 L. S. Lindsay, a merchant, built one of the square's earliest houses on the northeast corner; it served as the Mexican Legation during the Civil War.[32] Other important government officials and politicians lived along K Street.[33] In 1853 the park was first filled and graded. Improvement funds were appropriated in 1865, and the park was laid out in a picturesque, asymmetrical design in keeping with Andrew Jackson Downing's design for the Mall.[34] Walks, planting beds, and lawns created a handsome open space. The park was later enclosed by a high iron fence with four gates.

Franklin School, occupying half of the eastern block frontage, was designed in 1869 by Adolph Cluss to accommodate nine hundred pupils. A prominent architect in Washington after the Civil War, Cluss went on to design six city schools and the Smithsonian Arts and Industries Building.[35] The school, which closed in 1925, is an important part of local history and civic pride for Washington. Franklin School was a strong symbol of the city's rebirth after the Civil War and its dedication to public education. One can imagine the power of this building in the residential neighborhood of that era, with its entrance stairs leading to the adjacent park as the school's playground. An 1886 etching shows the school as viewed from the fountain area of the park.[36]

The multistory urban school was a new building type after the Civil War, with spacious, well-lit, and well-ventilated classrooms. The massing of Franklin School is functionally direct, with symmetrical, three-story wings for boys and girls and a higher central volume for common spaces. The first and second floors each had six large classrooms, and the third floor had two classrooms in each wing with a large hall in the center used as a gymnasium and auditorium. The bell towers served as ventilation shafts. Franklin School achieved great renown; a model of it was exhibited in Philadelphia and won honors in Vienna and Paris.[37]

After decades of neglect the exterior of Franklin School was restored in 1982 based on vintage photographs and original Cluss sketches. Coverage of the restoration cost was part of a zoning bonus for the developer of an office building on the remainder of the block east of the school. The restoration brought back the school's architectural glory—twin bell towers, a central dormer, chimney caps, and gold finials. It is the corner towers, the elaborate brickwork, and the roofline embellishments that make this building a highly visible civic landmark. The intention was also to restore the interior to serve as administrative headquarters for the city school system. After a dozen years this has not been realized, and the city government now intends to sell or lease the site for commercial development (fig. 7.8).

During the three-year territorial government in Washington, water

Fig. 7.8. Franklin School, west elevation

and sewer lines were placed around the park, streets were paved, and thousands of street trees were planted. Pipes were extended to the Potomac River to supply water for a large granite fountain bowl with jets. As the park developed with seasonal displays of plants and flowers, the number of visitors increased, necessitating a full-time watchman during the day. A watchman's lodge with toilets was built west of the fountain.[38] In 1874 President Grant gave the Office of Public Buildings and Grounds an American eagle, which was displayed in a cage in Franklin Square. Two additional eagles were added in 1876. In 1877 Chief of Engineers Thomas Lincoln Casey stated, "This park has been very much improved, and, as a popular place of resort, is probably only second to Lafayette Square."[39]

Gas lamps were installed in the 1880s, allowing the park to be open all night during the hot summer months.[40] The restrictions of fences and gates frustrated visitors, and citizens lobbied for their removal in 1889.

This public space became known as Franklin Square because of a group of Victorian row houses along K Street called Franklin Terrace.[41] The area became a prosperous residential community surrounded by elegant town houses. A map showing the square in 1888 shows the design of the park, as well as the almost continuous walls of row houses defining it on all sides (see fig. 7.2). On the northeast corner is Franklin School, next to a smaller school.

The Twentieth Century

George Burnap, a landscape architect for the Army Corps of Engineers, oversaw the redesign of Franklin Square in the second decade of the twentieth century. He wrote a book on park design in which he criticized the "plethora of petrified generals" in Washington's parks and recommended in their place memorial fountains or allegorical sculpture. "In America, we have the horrid habit of placing an equestrian statue to some war hero or other in the exact centre of every park . . . A park is a park and should not be made into a setting for a statue."[42] As a result, in 1914 the statue honoring Revolutionary War naval hero John Barry,

a bronze portrait statue by John J. Boyle, sponsored by Irish American groups,[43] was placed on the west side of the park, facing Fourteenth Street. A new watchman's lodge was built on the east side of the park, near Fifteenth Street.[44] During this period the neighborhood surrounding the park became a popular entertainment district with many restaurants, hotels, and nightclubs. There was also entertainment in the park: military band concerts on summer evenings (fig. 7.9).

In the 1930s the Works Progress Administration installed a new, symmetrical park design in Franklin Park. The statue and lodge were left in place, but a new, quatrefoil-shaped fountain was installed in the center, surrounded by a flagstone patio. New wide, curving walks linked these elements and allowed existing trees to remain. Nine new willow oaks and more than three thousand shrubs were planted.[45]

The uses of the buildings defining the square gradually changed during the first half of the twentieth century. Real estate values increased owing to development of the business district, encouraging residents to sell and move to newer neighborhoods. Initially row houses were purchased and converted to commercial or institutional uses. Later they were demolished and replaced with larger buildings.

After midcentury, businesses began to move away from Franklin Square to newer buildings and more prestigious locations. The hotels around the square declined in quality. The Fourteenth Street corridor, with easy access from northern neighborhoods and southern tourist features, became a sleazy district oriented to sexual entertainment. Drug dealers and prostitutes used the park for their illegal activities, frightening away businesses and pedestrians. The park fell into disrepair, and the fountain at its center ceased to work.

The Franklin Square Association was formed in 1983 by building owners and managers to redevelop the area. Through legal enforcement it succeeded in discouraging adult video and bookstores owners, causing them all to close by 1991. Since then almost the entire perimeter of the square has been rebuilt with new office buildings. More than 7 million square feet of office space in the area has been leased to eight hundred new firms with twenty-three thousand office workers.[46]

The Franklin Square Association also organized and funded a major facelift for the park. In 1990 the National Park Service replaced the lampposts with Victorian-style fixtures; the city paid for replacing and widening the perimeter sidewalks. New flower beds were planted, and the fountain in what was once Fountain Square was repaired to flow again.[47]

Although the park has a formal design, it is mostly two-dimensional and related to the curving pattern of walkways that outline three elliptical spaces. The trees were originally planted based on a different design, so they bear little relationship to the current path scheme. The trees have also grown at different rates or died, resulting in an erratic pattern. Since they are mostly deciduous trees, the park goes through a metamorphosis from winter to summer. The twenty-foot drop in elevation from H Street to I Street is barely noticeable except along the cross-axis path, which employs steps.

Except for the Franklin School and the Almas Temple, twelve-story buildings surround the square (see fig. 7.4). All except two are architecturally undistinguished, but they are effective in defining the open space with their straight, tall facades.

Half of the long south side of the square is defined by a speculative office building named Franklin Square (1989) designed by Philip Johnson and John Burgee, of New York City. This symmetrical, classically inspired, postmodern-style building clad in stone has columns eleven stories tall defining twelve bays. The twelfth story, which serves as a cornice, is topped by a metal mansard roof. The building's ground-level commercial spaces and its office population, who overlook the park and use it at lunchtime, contribute to the pedestrian activity in the park.

Most of the north face of the square is defined by one very large (1.1 million square feet) office building named One Franklin Square, completed in 1990. It was designed by Hartman-Cox in a manner that is contextual yet distinctive. To create a site for this large building, Prentiss Properties, the developer, agreed to preserve and move the jewel-like Shriner's Almas Temple (1926) further west in the same block. This restored temple helps to activate this block of K Street during nonbusiness hours with its bar, restaurant, and banquet hall. On the corner is the 1922 Beaux-Arts Hamilton Hotel, now remodeled as a Crowne Plaza Hotel with two additional, awkward stories.[48]

The long, horizontal form of One Franklin Square is visually activated by two building entrances through pinnacled towers that extend from the ground to 90 feet beyond the permitted 120-foot height limit. The towers were exempted from the height limitation since they are unoccupied. Yet these towers are the primary architectural features as articulated at street level and as distinctive profiles against the sky. Two additional setbacks at the top of the building, each two stories high, help to further articulate the massing and break down the scale. The light pink, unpolished granite facade is beautifully composed and proportioned with paired windows. The detailing achieves depth and shadow, visually enlivening the repetitive composition (fig. 7.10). One Franklin Square serves its urban design role in defining the square, with the extra benefit of enhancing the skyline through its pyramid-topped towers, which can be seen above the trees.

More than any other building on the square, One Franklin Square, because of its size and presence, engages this public space in a spatial and

Fig. 7.10. Franklin Square, north side

contextual dialogue. Although it is a symmetrical building, it does not have a central entrance like its counterpart across the square. The west tower is on axis with the center of the park, a strong formal relationship. The scale of the bays has been adapted from that of the bays of the Hamilton Hotel to the west, and the entrances are related to that of the Moorish Almas Temple.[49] It is not neoclassical in any way, a welcome respite from this style in the federal city. In fact it is hard to label the style of this building, for it is eclectic in the best sense of the term.

Franklin Square is an interesting case study in late-twentieth-century contextual office building design in Washington. Each building relates to the park somewhat differently, deferring to the larger purpose of providing an architectural frame for the open space. All of these office buildings accommodate the same uses, follow the same zoning code, and abide by the same development economics, but they also compete with one another for tenants, and one aspect of this competition is image or appearance. They differ in design, a form of symbolic free speech guaranteed by the First Amendment of the U.S. Constitution.

Commentary

Franklin Square is now a haven for workers from this precinct of the city. During working hours many can view the park from offices surrounding it. At lunchtime they use the green oasis for strolling, reading, talking, eating, or simply sitting on the grass. With the large number of trees closely planted, the park seems like a shady urban forest. In summer there is a noontime concert series. In addition to the city police and U.S. Park Police, the Franklin Square Association funds a security patrol from late morning to early evening on weekdays. Traffic will continue to be a problem for pedestrians, but the subway station across from the southwest corner alleviates a considerable amount of it.

It is unusual to find such a large, lush green space in the business district of any American city. It was a residential square (Franklin School serves as a reminder), but no one envisioned twelve-story office buildings. In fact, the density of trees and foliage keep it from being visually overwhelmed by its built context. As such, it is a welcome respite from its hard-edged milieu and a contrast to the nearby parks that are much more visually open. It is a soft space of grass and flowers with old-fashioned park benches and a low-profile fountain conducive to its present use and purpose.

Pierre L'Enfant would probably be displeased with Franklin Square because of its odd location, unrelated to a diagonal avenue. He would be pleased with the extant public school, which symbolizes a precept of democracy requiring an educated citizenry. He would also be pleased that the park exemplifies an egalitarian democratic ideal. It is a highly accessible public open space available for free use by all. Unlike in most other parks in Washington, the memorial role does not compete with the primary purpose of affording spatial rights for residents and visitors.

Rawlins Park

Rawlins Park does not appear as an articulated open space on L'Enfant's plan for the city. It does appear on Ellicott's 1792 plan and has been an open space ever since. It is located at the intersection of E Street and New York Avenue, which has been reconfigured to form a rectangular open space. This situation occurs again east of the White House, at the intersection of E Street and Pennsylvania Avenue, resulting in Freedom Plaza.

Rawlins Park is bounded by a divided E Street to the north and south and by Eighteenth and Nineteenth streets to the east and west. New York Avenue terminates at this park, which is an area of about 1.5 acres. Rawlins Park is two blocks west of the White House and two blocks north of the Mall; however, these vistas are now blocked by buildings.

The Nineteenth Century

When the city was first laid out, the west side of Rawlins Park was in a town on the Potomac River called Hamburgh, platted by Jacob Funk in 1772. There were commanding views of the Potomac River to the south before it was filled to create West Potomac Park. The area was low and swampy, a reason for its slow development.

The first significant structure in this area was the Octagon House, built by John Tayloe in 1800 on the northeast corner of the intersection of Eighteenth Street and New York Avenue. Designed by William Thornton, the architect of the Capitol, this three-story Federal house was one of the first grand houses in the new city. The unusual floor plan is actually a hexagon with a semicircular tower fitting the corner of the angled site. All of the ancillary service buildings are gone, and the gardens are much reduced in size. The beautifully detailed red brick edifice served as the temporary presidential residence in 1814 when the British burned the city. The American Institute of Architects occupied the house when this organization moved from New York City at the end of the nineteenth century.[50] After extensive restoration it is presently a historic house museum.

Fig. 7.11. Statue of Major
General John A. Rawlins, east
end of Rawlins Park

The American Institute of Architects built its new headquarters behind the house in 1972, creating a courtyard in between.

Rawlins Park was first improved during the territorial government. Roadways around the park were paved after sewers and gas lines were placed. The park itself required extensive filling and terracing before a variety of trees and bushes were planted.[51] It was enclosed with an iron post-and-chain fence, and gas lamps were installed.

In 1872 Congress appropriated funds for a statue honoring Major General John A. Rawlins to be located in the park. The bronze portrait statue sculpted by Joseph A. Bailey was placed on a granite pedestal on the east side of the park two years later.[52] General Rawlins was a lawyer, not a war hero, but he was General Ulysses Grant's aide-de-camp, President Grant's secretary of war, and Grant's close personal friend. Upon seeing the poor condition of the park in 1880, Union Army veterans had the statue moved to a reservation at Tenth and D streets, NW. Soon the statue was moved again, to a reservation at Seventh Street and Pennsylvania Avenue, and yet again, across the avenue, where it remained until the National Archives was erected. Finally, in 1931 the statue returned to Rawlins Park (fig. 7.11).[53]

The 1903 Sanborn maps show several row houses south and west of the square but few buildings on the large lots north of the square. The park design consisted of curved pathways from the street corners and the E Street sides to a circular fountain in the center.

L'ENFANT'S LEGACY

The Twentieth Century

The 1902 McMillan Plan for the design of the federal core of the city eliminated Rawlins Park and proposed a new circle at the intersection of New York and Virginia avenues. Decisions regarding new federal buildings were made ad hoc until the Public Buildings Act of 1926. The location of the first Department of the Interior building on the north side of Rawlins Park in 1915 was considered a possible threat to the McMillan Plan.[54] The apprehension of the Commission of Fine Arts was correct, for in 1931 the National Capital Park and Planning Commission developed a scheme for the Northwest Rectangle around a reshaped Rawlins Park. This group of federal buildings would be similar in concept to the Federal Triangle but would have self-contained parking.[55] This was a change to the McMillan Plan but not a threat to its overall significance.

The Department of the Interior building was built on the north side of the square in 1915 as designed by Charles Butler with the Office of the Supervising Architect of the Treasury Department. This seven-story building occupied the entire block, with entrances on E and F streets. The E-shaped floor plan with its back on F Street created two large, light courts open to the park. Although it was intended to be only a functional office building, it was monumental, with a limestone facade and classical details.[56] The General Services Administration has occupied this building since 1949.

In response to this new federal building, the park was redesigned in 1916 to accommodate office workers rather than residents. The design trend for laying out paths in business areas was to create direct lines of movement for efficiency.[57] Two concrete paths were placed from corner to corner, meeting in the center around a marble fountain dedicated to the civil engineer Alfred Noble. When the statue of General Rawlins was returned, it was placed at the east end, and access paths were added.

In 1935 the Department of the Interior built another enormous new building on the two city blocks south of the park, thereby closing D Street. A pedestrian tunnel under the park connected the two buildings. The style of this vast building by the well-known Washington architect Waddy B. Wood is reserved neoclassical. Its plan has a central north-south spine with six projecting wings to either side separated by light courts. The seven-story building has a two-story pink granite base, a three-story colonnaded limestone facade, and a two-story recessed attic with a monumental frieze featuring the seals of the original thirteen states.[58] Although intended as a utilitarian building, it has many classical elements and ornaments.

The new building prompted another redesign of the park in 1935, which remains to the present.[59] To provide for increased traffic, all the roadways were widened. The formal design has three flagstone terraces to accommodate the sloping site, with two reflecting pools on either side of the central fountain. Landscape panels in the perimeter zone have dense shrubs with sycamore trees, while those in the interior zone have grass with saucer magnolia trees. Lamps of two different shapes light this park, Washington globe lamps around the perimeter and Saratoga lamps in the interior.

In the cause of traffic improvement the west side of Rawlins Park was

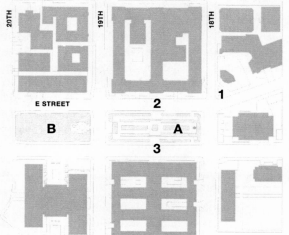

1 : Octagon House

2 : General Services
Administration

3 : Interior Department

A : John Rawlins Statue in
Rawlins Park

B : Walt Whitman Park

**Fig. 7.12. Rawlins Park in
1999**

changed in the 1960s. E Street became a sunken expressway beginning at
Twentieth Street, leading to the Whitehurst Freeway. New York Avenue
southwest of the park was eliminated when a huge Department of State
building was constructed in its path.

Along with the street changes, another park, Walt Whitman Park, was
created on the block west of Rawlins Park. The Washington Auditorium,
built in the 1920s, was demolished for this purpose. The eastern side of
the park has a fenced playground for children, and open playing fields
make up the remaining area.

A map of Rawlins Park in 1999 shows additional new buildings (fig.
7.12). To the south of Walt Whitman Park is the Theodore Roosevelt
Building for the Office of Personnel Management, to the north is the
new George Washington University School of International Affairs, and
to the east is the United Unions Building, headquarters for several trade
unions.

Commentary

Rawlins Park is a handsome urban space, a formal place with abundant paving appropriate for its dense context. During lunchtime on nice
days it is full of workers from the adjacent buildings, who use it and enjoy
it in many ways. The fountain and reflecting pools with aquatic plants
and ducks are refreshing. The large buildings define the park well, and
the rows of trees clearly define zones within the park.

Rawlins Park is a good example of a compatible design relationship
between a memorial purpose and the communal function. The statue
at one end does not inhibit social uses. The centrally located reflecting
pools push social activity to the perimeter zones. Social encounters can
be private but within the public context, with mutual visibility across the
water. The park is a place for both arranged and chance social encounters
within the context of a dense bureaucratic setting.

Walt Whitman Park lacks quality design development, so that its arrangement appears temporary. A recreational park within a zone of federal office buildings may be unwarranted. If the playground is a good use,
it needs to be designed to fit this highly visible urban context and sheltered

L'ENFANT'S LEGACY

from the streets and traffic. If the playing field is an appropriate use, it also needs to be screened from the high volume of traffic surrounding it.

Gompers-Burke Park

Throughout the L'Enfant Plan and subsequent plans there are almost three hundred small reservations, mostly located at the intersections of the grid streets with the diagonal avenues. Some of these have been developed; others have not. Some are designated as future memorial sites in the Memorials and Museums Master Plan.[60] Some of these sites are leased to adjacent property owners; others are within the purview of the District of Columbia parks or street department. Because they are distributed throughout the city, they offer a significant opportunity to enlarge and diffuse the extent of democratic public space. Gompers-Burke Park is representative of the small reservations.

In several locations east-west grid streets jog when they intersect avenues, resulting in small triangular open spaces. This occurs twice on Pennsylvania Avenue, NW—at I Street and again at H Street. At the latter intersection is the Edward R. Murrow Park, with a memorial dedicated to the journalist. Along Massachusetts Avenue, NW, L Street jogs between Tenth and Twelfth streets, resulting in a rectangular place with two triangular parks, named after Edmund Burke and Samuel Gompers. Vistas are available along Massachusetts Avenue northwest to Thomas Circle and southeast to Mount Vernon Square.

The Nineteenth Century

The jog in L Street appears on L'Enfant's 1791 plan but not on Ellicott's 1792 plan. However, it subsequently reappears and is evident on Boschke's 1861 plan.[61] This map shows a great deal of development around this square since it was part of the Northern Liberties neighborhood, an area of early urban growth around the market located at Mount Vernon Square, one block to the southeast. The Federal-style Nourse House, at 1107 Massachusetts Avenue (1840), with its unique ogee front facade, is an early antebellum structure facing this park. The adjacent Greek Revival house (1863), known as the "Wisteria House," was razed to make way for an apartment building in 1924.[62]

During the era of territorial government there were improvements to roads and utilities throughout the city. The Office of Public Buildings and Grounds subsequently created parks on many of the federal reservations. These two triangular open spaces were enclosed with picket fences, and in 1875 they were graded and seeded. Post-and-chain fences were added, along with lampposts, along the asphalt paths. Two drinking fountains were relocated from the Capitol grounds.[63]

As the parks were improved, additional structures were built in the neighborhood to take advantage of them. Two merchants named David L. Morrison and Reuben B. Clark built a duplex on the northeast corner of Eleventh and L streets in 1865, and the Episcopalian Church of the Ascension was built on the northwest corner.[64] Subsequent improvements to these parks included evergreens, deciduous trees, dwarf shrubs, and large flower vases on each parcel.[65] The original fences were replaced with quarter-round concrete copings.[66] By the end of the century this open space was surrounded by fashionable town houses.

The Twentieth Century

The land for most of Washington's federal reservations is within the right of way of city streets. Thus they can be reshaped by the city streets department to serve the needs of traffic. In 1921 two small triangular traffic islands were created to better define Eleventh Street. They were paved with brick, and one tree was planted on each island.[67]

In 1922 the Sulgrave Institution donated a memorial intended to promote better relations between America and Britain. The statue of the British orator Edmund Burke, located on the western triangle, now called Burke Park, is a copy of the one in Bristol, England. Burke championed the cause of the American colonies in the British Parliament, of which he was a member. The bronze portrait statue, sculpted by J. Harvard Thomas, sits on a granite base designed by Horace W. Peaslee (fig. 7.13).[68]

During the 1920s, as Massachusetts Avenue developed into an important thoroughfare, several high-rise apartment buildings were built in this area. The Women's Army and Navy League bought the Morrison House in 1923 and the Clark House in 1930, connecting them together to board transient servicemen. The league converted the stable to dormitories during the war and added a dormitory wing in 1962.[69]

Fig. 7.14. Samuel Gompers
Memorial, Gompers-Burke
Park

In 1933 the eastern triangle became the site of a memorial to the labor leader Samuel Gompers, a bronze sculptural group created by Robert I. Aitken. It features a seated Gompers and six allegorical figures representing the American labor movement, placed on a granite base. The American Federation of Labor, the labor union Gompers founded, donated the memorial.[70] In 1955 this reservation was named the Samuel Gompers Memorial Park (fig. 7.14).

During the 1950s and 1960s many prosperous residents left this neighborhood. This migration continued following the assassination of Martin Luther King Jr., when riots destroyed many buildings in the area. As conditions improved, town houses were converted to businesses or demolished to make way for the construction of large office and apartment buildings.

The dominant building defining Burke Park, a twelve-story office building occupying the entire block, is on the south side, forming a strong background. On the north side of Burke Park high-rise apartment buildings on Eleventh and Twelfth streets define the corners well, with lower, older apartments in between. On the west side are two four-story office buildings. The Strong John Thompson School, an interesting nineteenth-century building on the southwest corner, has been closed, and the building awaits conversion to another use.

The primary feature defining Gompers Park is the historic Morrison-Clark House, on the north side, now an elegant inn with a cantilevered Chinese porch. Next door is the Chinese Community Church. On the south side are the multistory American Road and Transportation Building Association headquarters and a new multistory apartment building; on the east side is a banal utility building.

Commentary
The architectural frame defining this urban space is incoherent in all regards—building height, style, use, age, and massing. The changing uses

A : Edmund Burke Statue in
    Burke Park
B : Samuel Gompers
    Memorial in Gompers Park

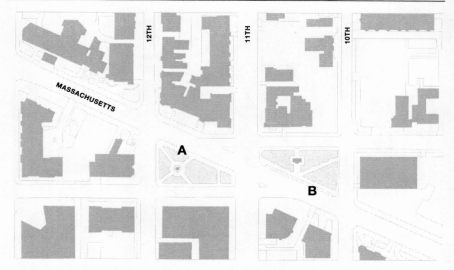

**Fig. 7.15. Gompers-Burke
Park in 1999**

and economics associated with urban development created this situation
(fig. 7.15).

Burke Park has a circular mound defined by paths and shrubs connected to the perimeter sidewalks. Unfortunately, the small statue of
Burke is located in the grass instead of on the mound, which can easily
be corrected. The landscaping here is sporadic, although there are street
trees along the avenue.

The Gompers Memorial is an impressive piece, well situated on a
slightly elevated black aggregate terrace connected to the perimeter sidewalks. The landscaping of Gompers Park is much better than that of
Burke Park, with a low hedge running along L Street, a group of large
holly trees, and several other deciduous trees.

These two triangular parks are handsome additions to the city's public spaces but are not well maintained. The memorials give each park an
identity and a focus. They provide the amenity of open space in a high-
density residential and business zone. As such, they should be better appointed with street furniture to encourage use. The memorials and parks
represent two fundamental democratic freedoms, freedom of speech and
freedom of assembly.

CHAPTER EIGHT

CONSTITUENT CITY

Scott Circle, Thomas Circle, Logan Circle, Dupont Circle,
Washington Circle

JON'S THEORY that Dupont Circle is a paradise in the heart of the city and the nation goes this way: In Dupont Circle poor meets rich, old meets young, gay meets straight, native meets new arrival, and the people, styles and languages all squish together to form America. Love begins here during morning rush hour with a glance. At midday, political and religious evangelists stop passersby with a few words, a petition, a holy book. In the afternoon, solo figures pursue venture capital and real estate deals using tiny phones. People find good food nearby, designer and regular ice cream, coffee simple or embellished, newsstands, movie theaters with smallish screens. All of this in Jon's eyes is persuasive.

PAUL KAFKA-GIBBONS, *Dupont Circle*

All of the spaces discussed in this chapter—Scott, Thomas, Logan, Dupont, and Washington circles—were originally residential in nature, located in the zone of development just north and west of the office squares. These parks were surrounded by urban mansions and town houses, which considered these open spaces at their front door as recreational gardens.

Although the houses were of different architectural styles that might not relate well to one another, they all related directly to the public space, usually through their primary entrance facade. Each of the park spaces also assumed a somewhat different character depending on its urban context and local history. The scale of the residential architecture relative to the public landscape became antithetical as each open space acquired a large memorial. This changed the social configuration of the space from centripetal, focused on an occupiable center, to centrifugal, focused on the perimeter zone.

The five public places discussed here, imbued with layers of history, being part of L'Enfant's original plan, play an important role in the life and purpose of Washington, D.C. Their character has suffered as the surrounding streets have been enlarged to accommodate increasing traffic. Yet these places maintain their presence as nodes of identity within the ever-changing urban matrix. They serve dual roles as monumental settings for the larger city and recreational spaces for their neighborhoods.

Whereas these five urban places had similar origins as residential focal points, they evolved quite differently. Scott, Thomas, and Dupont circles are located within the Massachusetts Avenue institutional corridor, whereas Washington Circle is dominated by George Washington University; only Logan Circle remains a true residential enclave. Although they all feature memorials dedicated to war heroes, their true unifying characteristic is their continuing presence within residential neighborhoods. Logan Circle is defined by its neighborhood, and all but Dupont Circle have some residences facing them. Moreover, they also have uses around them that support those neighborhoods, making them an integral part of the constituent city where residents go to shop, bank, worship, dine, or seek medical services.

These public spaces exemplify a variety of democratic ideals. Each one has a public memorial function, an example of freedom of speech. Dupont Circle is both a vibrant heterogeneous social setting (freedom of assembly) and the locus for many political protests (freedom of speech). Logan Circle is an egalitarian place where diverse residents can develop a genuine sense of community through freedom of assembly. Washington Circle satisfies the democratic requisite for education as part of a university setting. Unfortunately, the social purposes of Thomas and Scott circles have been eroded, so that they now retain only their memorial function.

Scott Circle

Scott Circle lies at the symmetrical intersection of Massachusetts Avenue, Rhode Island Avenue, and Sixteenth Street, the north-south axis of the White House and the formal northern approach to the federal city. L'Enfant's concept of reciprocal views between the open spaces works well here since there are clear vistas from Scott Circle south to Lafayette Square, east to Thomas Circle, west to Dupont Circle, and northeast to Logan Circle.

Scott Circle appears on L'Enfant's plan as a rectangular space, not a numbered appropriated square. It was enlarged on Ellicott's 1792 plan to extend from Seventeenth Street to Fifteenth Street. Today the buildings surrounding it define a rectangular space as shown on L'Enfant's plan, although the road pattern defines a bow-tie-shaped space. It has never been circular. It is now actually three public reservations related to Sixteenth Street: a triangle on the west side, an ellipse in the center, and a triangle on the east.

The Nineteenth Century

The Scott Circle area, on a tract known as Jamaica, was undeveloped until the 1870s. To the west was a tributary of Rock Creek known as Slash Run. During the brief territorial government the surrounding streets were graded and paved, and the parks landscaped. The reservations were formed as a small circle flanked by two isosceles triangles. The Board of Public Works paved Massachusetts Avenue with concrete and Rhode Island Avenue and Sixteenth Street with wood.[1] Water, gas, and sewer lines were laid, and Slash Run was enclosed in a sewer.

Scott Circle got its name and statue inadvertently in 1874 when plans changed regarding the statue's proposed location at McPherson Square.[2] General Winfield Scott was a military hero of three wars who served in the army under every president from Jefferson to Lincoln. The fifteen-foot-tall bronze equestrian statue, which faces south toward the White House, was sculpted by Henry Kirke Brown. It rests on a pedestal formed

from a single piece of granite. General Scott, who weighed more than
three hundred pounds, rode a mare that is depicted in the memorial as
a small stallion.[3] The memorial, sponsored by the federal government,
was placed on a grassy mound surrounded by granite curbing, a circular
flagstone walkway, and four ornamental lampposts (fig. 8.1).

As the park was being formed the neighborhood was developing with
elegant houses built by powerful politicians and rich businessmen. An
elaborate Victorian mansion was built east of the circle by John and Jessie
Brodhead in 1879.[4] The Brodheads sold the house to Gardiner Hubbard,
whose daughter Mabel and her husband, the inventor Alexander Graham
Bell, lived there from 1882 to 1889. Bell ran an experimental school for
both young deaf and normal hearing children in a small rented house on
the south side of the circle. The house was then sold to Levi P. Morton,
the newly elected vice president.

Northeast of the park were a mansion built by Pennsylvania Senator
Donald Cameron and a large house built by Ohio Senator George H.
Pendleton, both constructed in the 1880s.[5] The latter house was occupied
by President Cleveland's secretary of war, William C. Endicott, from 1885
to 1889. On the northwest side, President Chester Arthur's secretary of
the treasury, William Windom, erected a large brick house in 1881.[6] On
Massachusetts Avenue east of the circle Washington's great philanthropist W. W. Corcoran established the Louise Home in 1871 as an opulent
refuge for Southern ladies impoverished by the Civil War.[7]

In 1900 the two triangular reservations on opposite sides of the circular park were dedicated to a statesman and a physician. The western triangle was dedicated to New Hampshire Senator Daniel Webster, who had
lived nearby at 1603 Massachusetts Avenue. The twelve-foot-tall bronze
portrait statue, sculpted by Gaetano Trentanove, sits on an eighteen-foot
granite pedestal that features front and back bronze panels illustrating
two significant events in Webster's life.[8] The statue was a gift of Stilson
Hutchins, founder of the *Washington Post* and an admirer of Webster's.

Constituent City

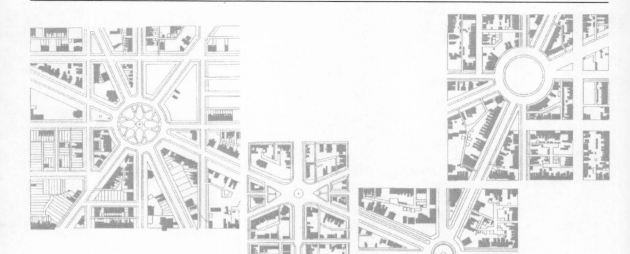

Fig. 8.2. Scott, Thomas,
Logan, and Dupont circles
in 1888

The eastern triangle was dedicated to Dr. Samuel Hahnemann, a German doctor and founder of homeopathy, a still-controversial alternative to conventional medicine. The memorial, sponsored by the American Institute of Homeopathy, was designed by the sculptor Charles Henry Niehaus and the architect Julius F. Harden. The bronze seated figure rests on a plinth within a granite exedra decorated with four bronze relief panels depicting Hahnemann's life.[9] Both memorials are placed within landscaped plots with low hedges, grass, shade trees, and walkways. A map showing Scott Circle in 1888 shows these memorials and the large residences (fig. 8.2). The avenues are lined with almost continuous blocks of row houses except on the northwest side of the circle, where several large parcels are vacant along Massachusetts Avenue.

The Twentieth Century

The neoclassical design approach of the Senate Park Commission influenced the design of federal reservations throughout the city. Regarding minor reservations the final report says, "Unfortunately for the general effect, the sculptural decorations have seldom been treated as a part of the design, but have been inserted as independent objects valued for their historic or memorial qualities or sometimes for their individual beauty, regardless of the effect on their surroundings."[10]

In response to this critique the Office of Public Buildings and Grounds in 1911–12 redesigned the three reservations around Scott Circle to form a more coherent ensemble, sodding and enclosing them with a wide border of English ivy. The Webster statue was accentuated with an evergreen hemlock background, whereas the Hahnemann memorial was enhanced with three flowering peach trees. The paths, lined with rhododendrons, were redone to focus on the memorials, and flower beds were placed in the foreground.[11]

L'ENFANT'S LEGACY

In the new century, living near Scott Circle continued to be desirable for a couple of decades. In 1906 Simon Guggenheim built a massive, Georgian Revival mansion at the northeast corner of Sixteenth and M streets, and in 1907 Carolina Caton Williams built a Beaux-Arts house at 1227 Sixteenth Street.[12] In 1912 the architect John Russell Pope redesigned the Bell House, then owned by Levi Morton, in the neoclassical style.[13]

In subsequent decades prosperous residents moved to less congested locations in the northwest quadrant of the city. The elegant residences surrounding Scott Circle housed private organizations and embassies. The Bell House became home to the National Democratic Club in 1930, then the National Paint and Coatings Association. On the lot south of it the American Association for the Advancement of Science removed the existing houses to construct its headquarters. The William Windom House became the Peruvian Embassy, and the Chinese Legation occupied a house on the northeast side of the circle.[14] Gradually the residences were replaced with large buildings. In 1940 the Pendleton and Cameron houses were replaced by the General Scott Apartments, the first of many such buildings in the area.[15]

With this changeover from residential to institutional uses traffic around Scott Circle increased dramatically. In 1941 a four-lane tunnel was built underneath the park for through traffic on Sixteenth Street, with double-lane slip ramps for access. The traffic lanes around the space were widened, and four triangular sodded islands were placed to direct traffic on the avenues around the elliptical island.

During the next half-century the area around Scott Circle along the Sixteenth Street corridor became especially attractive to organizations seeking political influence in the nation's capital. Massachusetts Avenue from Scott Circle west to Kalorama became known as Embassy Row. The Windom House was demolished to make way for the modern concrete Australian Embassy (1964). The Williams and Guggenheim houses and the Hotel Martinique on Sixteenth Street were razed to make way for the National Education Association (1968) office complex (fig. 8.3).

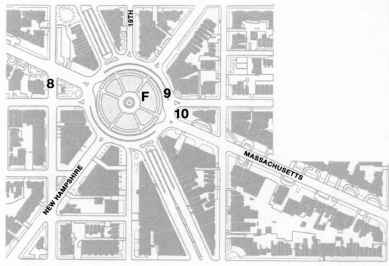

1 : Alexander Graham Bell House
2 : Australian Embassy
3 : Philippine Embassy
4 : Tunisian Embassy
5 : Luther Place Memorial Church
6 : National City Christian Church
7 : No. 1 and No. 2 Logan Circle
8 : James Blaine House
9 : Robert Patterson House (Washington Club)
10 : Wadsworth House (Sulgrave Club)

A : Scott Statue
B : Daniel Webster Memorial
C : Hahnemann Memorial
D : Thomas Statue
E : John Logan Statue
F : Dupont Circle Fountain

A 1999 map shows a completely built up area (fig. 8.4). Embassy Row now extends around Scott Circle since the Philippines built a handsome, classically inspired embassy behind the Webster memorial in 1993. It joins the Australian Embassy on the north side and the Embassy of Tunisia, which occupies the old American Association for the Advancement of Science building behind the Hahnemann memorial. The area has also attracted hotels, including the Governor's Inn, the Wyndham Hotel, and the Marriott Courtyard.

The present-day ellipse featuring the General Scott statue is not intended for pedestrian use; there are no pathways to it or around it. The statue sits on a turf mound with elongated shrub beds to the north and south. The other two reservations are intended for pedestrian use, with concrete perimeter and interior walkways, benches, shade trees, and landscaping.

Commentary

From an urban design perspective, the buildings surrounding Scott Circle generally define a rectangular space. Those on the north and south sides are large enough (about nine stories) to shape the space. Much lower buildings on the east and west sides cause the space to lose its definition. The wide, intersecting diagonal avenues fragment the urban space at its crucial corners. Spatial definition is also lost at Sixteenth Street, which has been widened to accommodate the traffic tunnel and slip ramps. Un-

L'ENFANT'S LEGACY

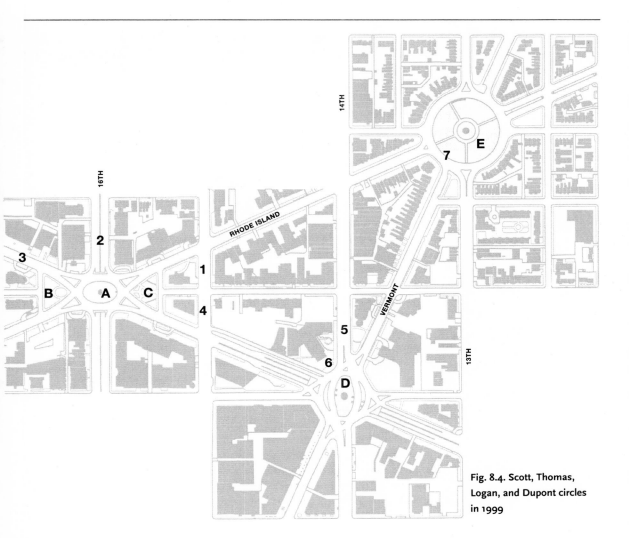

Fig. 8.4. Scott, Thomas, Logan, and Dupont circles in 1999

less the roadways are visually narrowed with a stronger composition of trees and plants, this design situation cannot improve.

This central elliptical park may never return to being a pedestrian amenity since it is locked within a zone of swirling traffic. As an important monumental public space, it should be visually enhanced to give it prominence. The triangular reservations are underutilized, with only the front parts occupied by the two memorials. The area behind the Webster Memorial is almost completely planted with low hedges; the area behind the Hahnemann Memorial has a few benches. Each should be made more amenable for use by the many residents in the vicinity to compensate for the inaccessibility of the central space.

Thomas Circle

Thomas Circle lies east of Scott Circle along Massachusetts Avenue. They are the most proximate of the original appropriated squares. It is only an intersection labeled number 9 on L'Enfant's plan but appears as a fully formed circle on Ellicott's plan. The circle is located at the intersections of Massachusetts and Vermont avenues and Fourteenth and M streets. Since it occupies a topographic high point, there are good vistas northwest to Scott Circle and southeast to Mount Vernon Square. To the southwest one can see McPherson Square, and to the northeast is Logan Circle. From this location L'Enfant's design concept of reciprocal views between public spaces is very evident, especially in the winter, when trees overhanging the streets shed their leaves.

The Nineteenth Century

There was little development in this area of the city before the Civil War. It was considered countryside in 1820, when Secretary of the Treasury William H. Crawford built his house surrounded by spacious grounds in the northwest quadrant of the circle.[16] The next prominent house was built by Thomas Coltman in the northeast quadrant of the circle in 1843.[17] This classically proportioned, three-story brick mansion was later occupied by Andrew Wylie, a District of Columbia judge.[18] The axis through the center hall of this stately Federal residence originated in the center of the circle.

Only four blocks north of Lafayette Square along Vermont Avenue, Thomas Circle became an attractive location for grand residences and apartments after the Civil War. This was abetted by a street railway installed along Fourteenth Street in the 1860s, making this area and the area to the north readily accessible.[19] Highland Terrace, along Massachusetts Avenue west of the circle, became a refined neighborhood of prominent residents.[20]

To mark the return to peace after the Civil War, the Lutheran community decided to erect a memorial church on the north side of Thomas Circle, on the narrow triangle of land between Vermont Avenue and Fourteenth Street. Designed by Judson York in 1870 in a High Victorian Gothic style, the Luther Place Memorial Church was built of red sandstone with a prominent tapered entry tower facing the circle.[21]

Under the territorial government Massachusetts Avenue around the circle was paved with concrete. Other streets were graded, and gas and sewer lines placed. The first true improvement of this open space was made in 1871 by the Office of Public Buildings and Grounds. It was called Memorial Circle because several residents planted memorial trees there to honor their home states: buckeye from Ohio, hemlock from Vermont, white pine from New Hampshire.[22] A sandstone walk was installed around the circular park, and flagstone walks crossing the streets provided pedestrian access. Near the center were four handsome, candelabra-style, cast-iron gas lamps.

Unfortunately, the entire park had to be redone the following year because the vegetation died as a result of poor soil preparation.[23] An antique terra cotta fountain was installed in the center. Rustic stone furniture and wooden chairs were placed, along with evergreens, trees, shrubs, and flowers. A day watchman maintained the seasonal plants and flower beds.

In 1879 one of the city's first apartment buildings was built on the south side of the circle, on the narrow triangle of land opposite the Luther Place Memorial Church. The six-story Portland Flats was designed by the prominent Washington architect Adolph Cluss with an octagonal,

balconied tower facing the circle.[24] The strongly articulated bays of this Renaissance Revival building greatly enhanced the streetscape along Vermont Avenue and Fourteenth Street. These were the city's first luxury apartments, each having seven rooms and twelve-foot ceilings (fig. 8.6).

Also in 1879, the public space was named after the Civil War hero Major General George H. Thomas, and his statue was erected in the center. John Quincy Adams Ward sculpted the sixteen-foot-high bronze equestrian monument that stands on a granite pedestal with a stepped, circular granite base. The statue depicts the general surveying the battle from the top of a hill. Many art critics consider it among the best equestrian statues in the city.[25] The statue, donated by the Society of the Army of the Cumberland, faces southwest toward the White House (fig. 8.5).

Surrounding Thomas Circle are four small, triangular public reservations. By 1894 all had been planted with grass and enclosed with iron railings. In 1884 the Lutheran church erected a bronze statue of Martin Luther on a high granite base (a copy of one in Worms, Germany) just behind one of the federal reservations.[26] On the west side of the circle, Annie Cole bought an 1874 house and proposed an addition on the adjacent triangular reservation. Her architect designed and built a sympathetic addition, but the bays were too large and encroached upon the public space. Mrs. Cole lost a suit to the federal government but was not required to revise the building since there were many similar violations in the neighborhood, including by the Portland Flats.[27] Since the Office of Public Buildings and Grounds was unable to maintain all public reservations, they were often leased to adjacent property owners throughout the city.

Fig. 8.5. National City Christian Church with General Thomas statue from Thomas Circle, view to north

Fig. 8.6. Portland Flats from Thomas Circle, 1900. Photo by Wm. Edmund Barrett, The Historical Society of Washington, D.C./City Museum

A map of the area in 1888 shows the Wylie House, the Luther Place Memorial Church, and the Thomas Building; the latter does not relate to the circle. Other quadrants contain additional townhouses, Portland Flats, and Annie Cole's house without the addition (see fig. 8.2).

The Twentieth Century

An aerial view of the north side of Thomas Circle about 1900 shows a tranquil pedestrian setting (fig. 8.7). A broad walkway encircles a well-maintained lawn with circular flower beds. Four gas street lamps with elaborate cast-iron supports are located at the perimeter so as not to obstruct views of the statue with its light-colored granite base. Four Camperdown elms and additional shrubs surround the statue. Many pedestrians can be seen strolling on the walkways, and there are horse-drawn carriages in the wide, paved, tree-lined roadways. Trolley tracks and an electric streetcar are visible. Flanking the Luther Place Memorial Church are the Thomas Building on the left and the Wylie House on the right.

As the century progressed, Thomas Circle deteriorated as a public space. Park maintenance became a problem, and all the trees except the elms and all the flower beds were removed. The ornate gas lamps were replaced by simple electric ones. In 1930 a grand new structure, the National City Christian Church, was built on the north side between Fourteenth Street and Massachusetts Avenue. Designed by John Russell Pope for the Church of the Disciples of Christ headquarters, this neoclassical limestone edifice with its elaborate tiered steeple is entered from the circle via a grand set of stairs leading to a portico (see fig. 8.5).[28]

The streetcar line, installed in the 1890s, steadily brought more commerce to the Thomas Circle area. One by one, residences were demolished and replaced by commercial buildings or converted to other uses. The Wylie House, for example, was demolished in 1947 and replaced by the 340-room, nine-story Washington Plaza Hotel, designed by Morris Lapidus, the famed designer of flamboyant Florida hotels. The hotel's design, with a glass-domed swimming pool in front of a concave facade,

L'ENFANT'S LEGACY

detracted from the circular form of the open space. The pool has now been removed, and the forecourt landscaped. A proposal to demolish the hotel in order to construct a larger office-and-apartment complex was denied by the District of Columbia Zoning Commission in 1990.[29]

Fig. 8.7. Aerial view to north of Thomas Circle, 1900. Washingtoniana Division, DC Public Library

Auto traffic continued to increase around Thomas Circle before and after World War II because two major routes intersected there. Fourteenth Street was a major north-south route leading to Memorial Bridge and across the Potomac River into Virginia. Massachusetts Avenue was a major east-west route leading to the northwest suburbs. In 1941 a four-lane tunnel with slip ramps was constructed to take this avenue under the park. In 1952 Fourteenth Street traffic was routed through the circular park by reforming it as an ellipse with through-traffic lanes on both sides of the statue. Crescent-shaped planting beds separated the through lanes from the local traffic routed around the perimeter. The remaining green space was less than half the area of the original circle; the Camperdown elms did not survive the construction.

During the latter half of the twentieth century dramatic physical changes around Thomas Circle continued. The access to this location caused real estate prices to escalate, fostering dense commercial development. Portland Flats was demolished in 1962 to enable construction of an anonymous eleven-story office building. Likewise, Annie Cole's house was demolished in 1974 to make way for the National Association of Homebuilders headquarters. One Thomas Circle, another mundane twelve-story office building, was built on the south side between Vermont Avenue and M Street, and a twelve-story Holiday Inn was built between Fourteenth Street and Massachusetts Avenue. The National City Christian Church built wings on either side of the original structure.

The 1999 map shows the irregular geometry of this area. Definition of the space must rely on the buildings occupying the four larger blocks in each quadrant, and yet the two on the north side do not support this purpose. Large residual spaces in front of the National City Christian Church and the Washington Plaza Hotel do not contribute to definition of this public space. On the south side, One Thomas Circle and the Holiday Inn contribute to the definition of the circular space. The seven-story office building on the east side, now home to the National Air Traffic Controller's Association, recedes from the park, as does the Residence Inn on the south side. On the west side, the National Association of Homebuilders has a new building with a prominent curved end closer to the park (see fig. 8.4).

Commentary

By 1871 Thomas Circle had become one of the most prestigious neighborhoods in Washington. The public space was well appointed with amenities, landscaping, and a beautiful fountain. It was a wonderful democratic place where women and children spent the day and residents strolled in the evening. Then the equestrian statue replaced the fountain, imposing its presence upon the space and changing its scale; its social character as a centripetal space around the fountain shifted to being that of a centrifugal space around the perimeter.

The most serious damage to the integrity of the circular park resulted from reforming it as an ellipse with two crescents to enable through traffic on Fourteenth Street. Thomas Circle has the worst traffic configuration of any circle in Washington because it has both an underpass and through-traffic lanes. This results in an enormous area of asphalt paving and very confusing traffic patterns. Other changes have removed all pedestrian pathways, lights, and landscaping, resulting in a forlorn urban place. For more than one hundred years physical changes have caused Thomas Circle to deteriorate as a viable public space. At present it does not serve the city as a monumental place, nor does it serve the residents as an amenity.

As an urban space Thomas Circle is fragmented in both form and image. Because of their varied setbacks and disparate architecture, most of the buildings do not help to define the circular space. Thus the park itself must be strong in form in order to create a memorable place. This public space needs to be reformed as a monumental circular space by removing the Fourteenth Street through-traffic lanes. Dupont and Washington circles have traffic similar to that of Thomas Circle, each with one underpass, and they have not been subdivided or reduced in area. The setting for the equestrian statue should be dignified, with supporting landscaping and lighting. There could be pathways leading to the statue for those who want to view it up close. Thomas Circle could be redesigned with a character similar to that which it had in 1900. Preservationists in Washington should pursue redesign of the circle as a preservation action since the L'Enfant Plan is on the National Register of Historic Places.

Massachusetts Avenue is the dividing line between a redeveloped residential neighborhood to the north and a burgeoning commercial area to the south. This division has been supported by the District of Columbia Zoning Commission, which downzoned the Fourteenth Street corridor north of Thomas Circle to limit the building height to sixty-five feet and encourage investment in street-level shops and restaurants.[30] The constant presence of residents on the north side has the potential to infuse Thomas Circle with pedestrian activity like that at nearby Logan Circle.

The two churches give this urban place a strong institutional presence. The residents and churches can work to limit the prostitution and drug sales surrounding the hotels.

The four triangular federal reservations around Thomas Circle are currently leased to adjacent property owners. Each of these miniparks should be available to the public rather than used exclusively by adjacent landowners. Each minipark could be developed as a pedestrian setting related to its immediate context, forming a series of useful and enjoyable pedestrian spaces. Residents of the neighborhood and the two churches facing the circle should work to have the four reservations redesigned as miniparks.

Logan Circle

Logan Circle has the distinction of being the last remaining residential circle as defined by land use. This circular park, 360 feet in diameter, is at the intersection of P and Thirteenth streets and Rhode Island and Vermont avenues. South on Rhode Island Avenue there is a vista to Scott Circle, and south on Vermont Avenue there is a vista to Thomas Circle. Dupont Circle lies five blocks west on P Street, too far for a clear vista. The geometry of the eight-street intersections results in two large quadrants northwest and southeast of the circle and six narrow frontages. This creates four small public reservations; two have been developed as small triangular parks, and two are leased to the adjacent property owners.

The Historical Evolution

Logan Circle appeared on the 1791 L'Enfant Plan as a two-block-long, triangular open space, not one of the numbered squares designated for memorials. It was called Iowa Circle from 1879 to 1930, although it was never appropriated by that state. Logan Circle was defined as a circular space by Andrew Ellicott on his 1792 plan. Since it was so far removed from the city center, it remained mostly rural, except for a scattering of small wooden dwellings, for three-quarters of the nineteenth century. During the Civil War it was used as a camp and a location for hanging Northern deserters.[31] In October 1862 it was the scene of a dramatic event, the hanging of Private Michael Lanahan, convicted of killing his superior officer.[32] After the Civil War the area was inhabited by freed slaves.[33]

Logan Circle developed after the territorial government made infrastructural improvements. During this period Thirteenth Street was paved with concrete, and Rhode Island Avenue and the street around the circle were surfaced with wood. The circular park was laid out in a flower pattern formed by curved asphalt paths leading from the perimeter walk to the central fountain, which was thirty feet in diameter and five feet deep with a water jet. The depth was later reduced to eighteen inches because a water depth of five feet was dangerous to children. A row of horse chestnut trees defined the perimeter; the paths were lined with other trees and shrubs, along with lampposts.[34] By 1877 there were four ornamental iron vases, ornamental settees along the graveled paths, and a post-and-chain fence.[35] The two triangular parks were also improved with plantings and enclosed with cast-iron post-and-chain fences.

Following this improvement of the park, real estate speculators began to build grand town houses around the circle. A gas line to the circle spurred this growth, as did a trolley line on Fourteenth Street. High Victorian–style and Richardsonian-style houses of stone and brick boasted elaborate architectural features. Most of the extant buildings around the circle date from this 1875–90 era. A map showing the circle in 1888 shows most lots in the two large quadrants occupied by town houses and one apartment building. Larger, specially shaped houses occupy three of the narrower block faces (see fig. 8.2). The neighborhood is also the locus of several churches.

Iowa Circle became a fashionable and prosperous neighborhood but also one with economic and racial diversity. A full-time watchman provided security and maintenance. In 1904 a frame lodge was moved from the White House grounds to the triangular park north of the main park for the watchman's use.[36] There were military band concerts in summer and cycling races on the street circling the park.

In 1889 the circular park was selected for a statue honoring Civil War General John A. Logan, and it was redesigned for this purpose. The new pattern of asphalt paths continued the lines of Thirteenth and P streets, dividing the park into four quadrants. The central fountain was removed, and two drinking fountains were relocated.[37]

General Logan, who had been involved in the capture of Vicksburg, had commanded the Army of the Tennessee, whose veteran organization sponsored the memorial. The twelve-foot-high equestrian statue stands atop an even higher bronze pedestal atop a shallow pink granite base. The classically inspired pedestal, designed by the noted architect Richard Morris Hunt, is unusual for an equestrian statue. Two sides of the bronze base have allegorical figures representing war and peace, whereas the other two sides depict scenes from Logan's life.[38] Sculpted by Franklin Simmons and dedicated in 1901, the statue faces south toward the White House along Vermont Avenue (fig. 8.8). Interestingly, Logan lived at 4 Logan Circle for a brief time in 1885.[39]

The city expanded to the northwest at the turn of the century, when elite white residents moved to new homes around Dupont Circle and beyond. Logan Circle retained its integrity as a middle-class neighborhood until the 1940s. Along with the Shaw and LeDroit Park neighborhoods, this area of the city became an African American social and intellectual center that was home to professionals and government officials. The churches were community gathering places for civil rights meetings and musical performances. Several civil rights leaders lived here, including Mary McLeod Bethune, who was later memorialized with a statue in Lincoln Square. Bishop Charles M. Grace lived in the mansion at 11 Logan Circle and founded the United House of Prayer for All People, and the first African American architect in Washington, John A. Lankford, had his office and home at 1448 Q Street.[40]

In the 1950s, large houses were converted to boarding houses, and prostitutes began to live in the area. This was followed by drugs and street crime and a steep decline in the quality of the neighborhood. This decline was exacerbated by street-widening projects, which exposed the precinct to more through traffic. Rhode Island Avenue was widened, and the circular park was reduced in size by subtracting ten feet from the fifteen-foot width of the perimeter walk. Then Thirteenth Street was carried through the park in 1950, reducing its size and changing its shape to

Fig. 8.8. Statue of General
John A. Logan, Logan Circle

that of a lemon. The surrounding blocks remained exclusively residential, with some small in-home shops and offices. The eight-story Iowa Apartment Building, just south of the circle on Thirteenth Street, was built by the prolific local architect Thomas Franklin Schneider in 1900.[41]

Racial riots after the assassination of Martin Luther King Jr. devastated the area northwest of Logan Circle but did not impact the circle itself. In the aftermath, the circular park and two small public reservations were refurbished in 1968 as part of Ladybird Johnson's city beautification program. The park received new plantings and an irrigation system, and the triangles were paved and furnished with planters and benches.[42]

The final blow to Logan Circle appeared to be urban renewal, the mass clearing of entire blocks to prepare for redevelopment. The park was designated as the southwest corner of the Shaw School Urban Renewal Area, but historic preservationists recognized the high quality of its architecture and organized to save it from demolition. The area was designated as an oddly configured historic district in 1972, offering protection for the structures.[43] Houses were sold at a discount to those who would restore them, and all but three of the original homes facing the park were saved. The district was expanded in 1994 as the Greater Fourteenth Street Historic District, an area comprising seven hundred structures.[44]

The best part of the story is that the neighbors convinced the District of Columbia and the National Park Service to return Logan Circle to its original circular form. The neighborhood could not be rejuvenated if through traffic threatened pedestrians. In 1981 the Thirteenth Street through-traffic lanes were removed; now there are three lanes of counterclockwise traffic with traffic islands and two stoplights.[45]

The park has recently been refurbished with new plantings and historic-reproduction lampposts. The present circular park has four straight concrete walks leading to a central circular concrete walk; there is no perimeter walk. A low iron fence lines these paths. Three of the four straight walks align with streets. There are long, curved wood-slat benches around the central circular walk.

The Architectural Context

Logan Circle was designated a historic district because of the many intact blocks of high-quality, High Victorian and Richardsonian architecture. The three- to four-story town houses with partially exposed basements share party walls, resulting in continuous street facades. They occupy irregularly shaped lots with curving fronts, resulting in many design variations. Although most houses have been divided into apartments or condominiums, few exterior changes have resulted. Moreover, landscape details such as fences, walls, and stairs in the small front gardens are also mostly intact. Only three residences were demolished in the southeast quadrant during the twentieth century.

There is considerable stylistic variation in the architectural elements of these houses but also unity in their materials and scale, resulting in one of Washington's distinctive historic districts. Exteriors vary in color or tone, but the materials are mostly brick with stone trim. The large wooden windows are often composed in pairs or triples, and many houses have round or angled bays, with turrets at the corners. The high roofs are mansard or gable in form with large dormers of slate or metal. Additional features include prominent recessed entrances and balconies.

Numbers 4 to 14, between P and Thirteenth streets in the northwest quadrant of Logan Circle, make up the most intact block of preserved residences. This series of three- to five-story town houses represent the exceptional architecture that has made Logan Circle noteworthy. They were built by prominent architects and builders, including Henry R. Searle (no. 6) and Thomas Franklin Schneider (no. 12).[46] Number 4, at the corner of P Street, features delicate iron porches; number 14, at the Thirteenth Street corner, has ornamental iron work and cast-metal porches. Number 6 is an elaborate, stone-faced Victorian, and number 8 is an elegant house with classical motifs. Number 10 has a large turret facing its side garden. This entire group of houses has been restored and preserved with quality craftsmanship (fig. 8.9).

In the southeast quadrant only five of the original ten houses remain. They are handsome brick, three-story town houses, but they do not have the same degree of architectural invention as their counterparts across the circle. The developer P. N. Hoffman is responsible for the fourteen new condominiums built on the vacant site in the southeast quadrant of the circle where a hotel once stood. The level of architectural quality is not commensurate with the historical context.

At numbers 1 and 2 Logan Circle is a freestanding double house constructed between Rhode Island and Vermont avenues southwest of the park in 1877. The builder may have been the son of President Ulysses Grant, and it later served as the Venezuelan Legation and a sanitarium. It is a painted brick, Second Empire building, three stories on a raised basement, with a mansard roof and elaborate metal dormers. The four-story entrance tower facing the park unites the two houses in spite of the double stair and separate entrances. The structure was recently rebuilt as eight luxurious condominiums.[47]

Fig. 8.9. Logan Circle houses in the northwest quadrant. Library of Congress, Prints and Photographs Division, HABS No. DC 464-4, photo by Ronald Covedy, 1970

Commentary

The Logan Circle neighborhood is a textbook case of a once prosperous area declining and being revitalized. In this instance the decline occurred early in the century as a result of population migration within the city. Large, beautiful homes were converted to apartments and rooming houses before deteriorating and being abandoned. At a time when the community was weak the city enabled through traffic to increase in the neighborhood. Easy and quick access turned the streets into open markets for criminal activity. After other neighborhoods in the city were rehabilitated, new urbanites seeking real estate bargains began to invest in the Logan Circle area and to rehabilitate the once-glamorous structures. This in turn strengthened the community, putting pressure on the police to clean up the streets. Two blocks south of the circle are three historic churches that have actively pursued social ministry for the poor and the homeless. Now the area is threatened by developers who want to redevelop the Fourteenth Street commercial corridor.

Before the Logan Circle neighborhood could be revitalized, the crime problem needed to be controlled to make the area safe for residents to inhabit. This has been an ongoing process, now vigilance rather than active campaign. The effort was fostered by a strong Logan Circle Community Association, which aided police in their prosecution of prostitution and the street sale of drugs.

Logan Circle as a park is currently designed for passive recreation. Its grass, large deciduous trees, and curved park benches make it conducive to strolling, sitting, gathering, and chatting. It is a favorite place for walking dogs, although this activity may need to be localized in the future so that children and others can also use the lawn areas. A contingent of elderly men, perhaps some vagrants, who tend to occupy the central area during the day may pose a threat to other users. The traffic is still a hazard for pedestrians, especially at rush hour, making it difficult to cross the street to the park. It also generates noise, disturbing the tranquility of the place.

In spite of a long history of travails, the park at Logan Circle retains its purpose as a democratic and egalitarian public space. It was better suited for this purpose when it had a fountain in the center rather than a large equestrian statue on a pedestal. But since it has a large diameter, the remaining peripheral space is generous in size and open in character. The constant presence of residents forming an enclosing circle around this place profoundly proclaims its nature as a social place for the gathering of equal citizens. At one time all of the circles in Washington had a similar character. Logan Circle clearly shows what has been lost.

Dupont Circle

Dupont Circle is certainly Washington's most socially thriving and vitally active public space, as depicted in a recent novel entitled *Dupont Circle*.[48] Presently its design character and its social diversity are reciprocal. The area is an eclectic juxtaposition of middle-class row houses, converted old mansions, apartment buildings, hotels, and modern office buildings all held together in centripetal tension by the powerful circular place.

Dupont Circle was not among the fifteen numbered appropriated spaces on L'Enfant's plan; it was shown only as an open area. When Andrew Ellicott redrew the map in 1792, it was clearly shown as a circular open space. Its significant role in contemporary Washington was ensured by the geographic circumstance of five intersecting streets and avenues, resulting in ten points of land facing the circular space, the only such circle in the City of Washington. Its position at the intersection of three prominent avenues, Massachusetts, Connecticut and New Hampshire, assured its future role as a transit hub and commercial center. It is now a 360-foot-diameter circular park with two small triangular reservations, on the east and west sides.

The Nineteenth Century

The area around this circle that was included in the original city plan was among the last to develop because of its distance from the government and business center. Before the Civil War the area consisted of scattered shacks and frame dwellings. The installation of trolley tracks along P Street from Georgetown to the circle in 1868, then along Connecticut Avenue to the White House, prompted development of the area. These tracks were soon extended north along Connecticut Avenue to Florida Avenue.[49]

Dupont Circle was first improved during the era of citywide public works improvements directed by the legendary Alexander "Boss" Shepherd. By 1873 it had water and gas lines, walks paved with gravel, twelve lampposts, and an iron post-and-chain fence.[50] The paths were configured as a series of rotating curvilinear figures. In his 1877 annual report the chief of engineers suggested, "From the commanding position of this reservation a fountain of sufficient size, provided with suitable jets, would be very conspicuous from the surrounding avenues, and would prove a most attractive feature in the general ornamentation of the park."[51]

In 1884 a bronze statue by Launt Thompson of Rear Admiral Samuel Francis Dupont on a granite pedestal, sponsored by the federal government, was dedicated in the center of the park.[52] Dupont achieved success during the Mexican War but failed to hold off the Confederate attack

Fig. 8.10. Statue of Rear Admiral Samuel Francis Dupont, Dupont Circle, 1880–90. The Historical Society of Washington, D.C./City Museum

on Charleston in 1863 and was relieved of his command (fig. 8.10).[53] The park was named Dupont Circle and improved for this dedication with new walks, lawns, and 850 ornamental trees and flowering shrubs.[54] The park design was based on a series of flower petals radiating from the center.

Concurrent with improvements to the park was the construction of large mansions on the surrounding tracts. Prosperous residents sought larger sites removed from the congestion of the city center. In the 1870s the urban space was known as Pacific Circle, possibly because a group of real estate speculators known as the California Syndicate had purchased a large tract of land around the circle and built opulent homes in the vicinity.[55] The first of these homes to face the circular park, designed by Adolf Cluss, was built by Senator William Morris Stewart, of Nevada, in 1873. Located to the northwest between Connecticut and Massachusetts avenues, the five-story, red stone "Stewart's Castle" also became known as "Stewart's Folly" because it stood alone in what was then a remote part of the city.

Starting in 1880 a prestigious neighborhood began to take shape with the building of other grand houses around the circle. In that year a duplex for two sisters, known as the Hopkins-Miller House, was built to the southeast between Massachusetts and Connecticut avenues. In 1885 Senator James G. Blaine, of Maine, built an expansive brick Queen Anne home with a massive tower and elaborate mansard roof, designed by John Fraser, west of the park between Massachusetts Avenue and P Street. Owned by George Westinghouse from 1901 to 1914, the home still stands today.[56]

In the next decade, new homes built facing the park were neoclassical in design, following the architectural style espoused by the influential Senate Park Commission. In 1891 Levi Leiter, a department-store magnate, built his large neoclassical home, designed by the Philadelphia architect Theophilus Chandler, to the north, between Nineteenth Street and New Hampshire Avenue.[57] Senator William Clark, of Montana, purchased Stewart's Castle in 1899 and demolished it in 1901, hoping to build a grand house on the site. The lot remained vacant, however, until 1923, when the Riggs Bank was constructed there. The circular open space itself became somewhat of a private park for those dwelling around it since they were few in number.

A map showing the circle in 1888 reveals the locations of these mansions and other structures (see fig. 8.2). To the east an Episcopal church stands on the triangle of land that is a government reservation. On the streets surrounding the circle are small groups of townhouses and row houses.

At the turn of the century the area was composed of mansions on large, landscaped lots along the tree-lined diagonal avenues and row houses lining the streets of the grid pattern. This juxtaposition of sculptural mansions in open space with the tightly defined repetitive rows created an unusually rich architectural setting. The use of eclectic design was often necessary because of the oddly shaped lots, resulting in asymmetrical facades and massing. The mostly brick row houses were also eclectic in design, employing steeply pitched roofs, turrets, bay windows, and fanciful chimneys. Some were designed and built as individual houses, but most were built in multiples to form long rows with distinctive corner houses. The variety of styles and details provided a visually engaging urban architecture forming well-defined streetscapes.

The Twentieth Century

Grand houses continued to be built around the circle in the twentieth century. The Robert Patterson House, designed by the famed New York firm of McKim, Mead and White in 1901, was located between New Hampshire Avenue and P Street. In form it is a highly ornate Renaissance palazzo with white marble facades and an entrance that diagonally faces the street corner. It remains in restored glory as the Washington Club (fig. 8.11).[58] The widow of Ohio Congressman Robert Hitt retained John Russell Pope in 1908 to design her elegant limestone-faced house adjacent to the Patterson House.

In 1917 the family of Admiral Dupont petitioned the city to relocate his statue to their hometown of Wilmington, Delaware, and to replace it with a fountain. The white marble fountain was designed by the architect Henry Bacon and sculpted by Daniel Chester French, the team that had just completed the Lincoln Memorial on the Mall. Completed and installed in the center of the park in 1922, utilizing piping placed forty-five years earlier, it remains the compelling centerpiece of this urban space to the present day (fig. 8.12).[59] The pathway design was also changed at this time to a configuration of six straight radial paths, aligned with the center lines of the intersecting avenues, leading to a flagstone circle around the fountain.

In the 1920s Dupont Circle was the center of a fashionable neighborhood. Residents came to hear military band concerts and stroll in the park. Children came with nannies to play in the sandboxes and fountain (fig. 8.13). The public restroom constructed on the small reservation to the west portended impending social changes. People from outside the neighborhood began to use the park, causing social tensions, and some wealthy residents moved to more tranquil areas to the north and west. Others stayed to form the Dupont Circle Citizens Association and to work to maintain the high standard of residential quality.[60]

In 1933 the National Park Service assumed management and maintenance of Dupont Circle. At first it installed sandboxes for the neighborhood children, but it removed them six years later because dogs and vagrants were using them as toilets, foreshadowing the tensions and struggles between the users of the park and its federal overseer ever since. In a positive effort to provide for increased use, the National Park Service installed long, curved benches in 1964 and removed the iron fence around the fountain in order to provide direct access to it.[61]

In the period 1910–30 the neighborhood was home to six incoming or departing presidents of the United States, indicative of its prestigious status. Woodrow Wilson lived here in 1915, Franklin Roosevelt from 1917 to 1920, Warren Harding from 1917 to 1921, Herbert Hoover from 1921 to 1929, and William Howard Taft from 1921 to 1930;[62] and in 1927 the Patterson House was the official residence of President Calvin Coolidge while the White House was undergoing renovation.[63]

In the early decades of the twentieth century commercial corridors developed along Connecticut Avenue and P Street on both sides of Dupont Circle. Initially, converted residences were used for offices and stores. After midcentury new, larger office buildings with commercial space at street level were built.

Increased traffic led to the widening of Connecticut Avenue in the 1920s. Despite this improvement, congestion continued to increase and exacerbated conflicts with pedestrians crossing the streets to the park. This resulted in the 1948 placement of medians, which diverted through traffic on Massachusetts Avenue to the inner lanes, leaving the outer lanes for local traffic.[64] Eventually, traffic signals and crosswalks were added around the circular park to aid pedestrians, but the conflicts remain. To improve traffic circulation Connecticut Avenue was placed in a tunnel, completed in 1950. The underpass also served streetcars, with platforms under the park accessed by four sets of stairs.

Streetcar service was discontinued in Washington in 1964, and the

Fig. 8.11. Robert Patterson House, view to north at P Street

Top: Fig. 8.12. Dupont Circle fountain

Bottom: Fig. 8.13. Dupont Circle gathering of women and children, 1900. Photo by L. C. Handy, Washingtoniana Division, DC Public Library

tracks were replaced with landscaped medians. For a time the Connecticut Avenue underpass was sealed to create a civil-defense shelter if needed. In 1993 the developer Geary Simon leased the two streetcar stations from the city to create a neighborhood market and food court in the west station based on a streetcar design theme. The east station was to be a health club. The original stair and tunnel accesses would be opened up to provide a pedestrian route under the park. Two of them were cov-

L'ENFANT'S LEGACY

ered with large steel and glass canopies. The food court opened in 1994 and endured for two years, but Geary Simon had financial problems and never finished the project.[65] Dupont Down Under was an appropriate use for these high-ceiling, tiled spaces, and completion of this project should be seriously considered in the future. It would also provide a safe and convenient pedestrian passage under the park.

Just before midcentury several of the grand residences on the circle were either demolished and replaced by commercial buildings or converted to embassies, clubs, or apartments. The Leiter House was razed in 1947 to make way for construction of the Hotel Dupont Plaza. The remaining half of the Hopkins-Miller House met the same fate in 1948 (half of it had been demolished in 1912 to make way for a bank).[66] A Riggs Bank was constructed on the site of the former Stewart's Castle in 1923. In 1931 the architect Mihran Mesrobian designed the Dupont Circle Building, a twelve-story office building with handsome limestone-and-brick articulated facades, to replace the row houses on the wedge-shaped site at Connecticut Avenue and Nineteenth Street.[67] The Wadsworth House, which replaced the Episcopal church at Massachusetts Avenue and Eighteenth Street, was converted to the Sulgrave Club. The scale of buildings around Dupont Circle and their uses were rapidly changing.

During the second half of the century the immediate area around Dupont Circle was transformed into a thriving commercial district. At One Dupont Circle, between New Hampshire Avenue and P Street, a mundane, multistory office building replaced a handsome group of townhouses. The Hitt House was demolished and replaced by another drab office building. In 1971 Hartman-Cox Architects designed a handsome contemporary building to the south between Nineteenth Street and Massachusetts Avenue. The eight-story, brick-and-concrete Euram Building addresses the circular park directly with a recessed entrance that leads to a small courtyard, both on a radial line of Dupont Circle. It recalls the similar entrance treatment of the Patterson House across the circle.

In 1952 the city planning commission proposed an inner-loop highway that would have passed just north of Dupont Circle. This would have greatly increased traffic congestion by bringing more automobiles to and through this district. The strong protest of citizen groups prevailed to stop it. The best form of traffic alleviation was the construction of the Metro system in the 1970s. The red line was placed beneath Connecticut Avenue, and a station was located beneath the park with entrances at the corner of Twentieth and Q streets and at the Dupont Circle Building. The result was considerable traffic reduction and greatly improved access to this neighborhood.

In an effort to protect the remaining historic architecture in the area, the Dupont Circle Historic District was created in 1978 and listed on the National Register of Historic Places. Although the district has a great deal of architectural integrity, there are some large, mid-twentieth-century office buildings south of the park. The Dupont Circle Citizens Association, formed in 1922 and the North Dupont Community Association, along with the Advisory Neighborhood Commission, constantly monitor proposed intrusions in the form of either overscaled new development or demolition of historic architecture. There has already been extensive renovation and preservation in the historic district by private individuals and businesses or by the many embassies and clubs that make effective use of the remaining mansions.

The division between the areas north and south of Dupont Circle is a by-product of both history and zoning. The south side is a continuation of the high-density "downtown" office-building district. The north side is a neighborhood with various housing types, making it a desirable location for a wide variety of residents. The dividing line is Massachusetts Avenue, where many of the old mansions have been preserved as homes of clubs, organizations, and embassies. The diversity of activity in the circular open space is a reflection of the diversity of tenants surrounding the circle—offices, banks, organizations, stores, a hotel, and a club.

The greatest force for change in this district is the burgeoning real estate development. This has been the trend during most of the twentieth century. After World War II undistinguished office buildings built to the maximum size allowed by zoning regulations were constructed south of the circle and on the surrounding blocks. This is soon likely to occur at One Dupont Circle because of this site's underutilized economic potential. The Riggs Bank site is also vulnerable to increased development, as proposed in 1990, with a seven-story office building covering the entire block (including the Metro entrance).[68] Efforts by neighborhood groups have thus far blocked this project.

The District of Columbia zoning code limits the height of buildings facing a public reservation to the width of the widest street, which here is Massachusetts Avenue, with a width of 160 feet. These are maximum height limits, which can only be obtained through a system of bonus amenities provided by developers. Realizing the negative potential of this height for this area, in 1991 the District of Columbia Zoning Commission established the Dupont Circle Overlay District to limit building height and bulk to a smaller scale that is compatible with the character of the neighborhood.[69]

Another force for change is the increasing commercialism induced by the popularity of the park. Heavy pedestrian traffic to and from the Metro entrances makes them a desirable location for bookstores, cafes, coffee shops, bars, art galleries, and restaurants. Indeed, they are now located up and down Connecticut Avenue and along the side streets.

The open space itself is in constant need of maintenance and replacement because of the heavy pedestrian use. The fountain was completely renovated in 2001. The design of the park seems to be adequate for the time being, although additional trees need to be planted to replace those that have disappeared. The public restroom building should either be demolished or converted to an amenable use.

In terms of urban design, it is very difficult to define an urban open space that is fragmented by ten wide, intersecting streets. The difficulty is exacerbated by the two small, triangular reservations, which create gaps in the circular form. On the 1999 map these conditions are delineated by the building footprints (see fig. 8.4). The many eight-story building facades help to define the space, although they have narrow fronts addressing the circular park.

The Democratic Milieu

In the early 1960s Dupont Circle became a gathering place for a large number of people from all walks of life. An article in the *Washington Post Potomac* referred to it as "a simmering bouillabaisse of classes, colors, and types; a ferment of beatniks, genteel matrons, foreign students, thrill-seekers and curiosity-hunters."[70]

During the 1960s and 1970s Dupont Circle was second only to the Mall as a location for civil rights and Vietnam War demonstrations. This was due to its high accessibility and the variety of people who lived in the surrounding neighborhood. In addition to the protesters, Dupont Circle also attracted hundreds of homeless people, hippies, and tourists. All of this activity and all of these people resulted in wear and tear on the landscape and continuous problems with trash and debris.

Dupont Circle also became a gathering place for the gay community of Washington, supported by the nearby location of Lamda Rising, a gay-oriented bookstore, and several gay bars. This caused tensions between gays, the police, and local residents. In 1975 Gay Pride Day became a peaceful celebration of both gay militancy and the community's acceptance of gays.

Dupont Circle is presently Washington's most socially vibrant open space. It supports a wide variety of users in great numbers, who populate the space almost twenty-four hours a day, seven days a week, fifty-two weeks a year. For example, an entire subculture has developed on the east side around the eight remaining concrete chess tables. The chess scene involves players from all walks of life, including homeless men, business men, and everyone in between. They have created their own competitive sport, "park chess," which has been played for wagers for twenty-five years.[71]

Dupont Circle is an excellent example of a democratic milieu of free public assembly where all kinds of people can peacefully enjoy the park and one another's presence. This social interaction is aided by the landscape design, with long, curving benches, the attractive fountain, and many places to view or become part of the passing scene. It is the model of a thriving urban social space generated by a diversity of uses and a diversity of inhabitants. This melting pot has made it a supportive location for social and political protests, demonstrating the American freedom to criticize the government. In 2003 an "open-mic" forum developed: anyone can get on a platform with a microphone to announce his or her political views, as on the well-known speakers' corner in London's Hyde Park.[72]

Dupont Circle has had a long and interesting history that will continue to evolve because of its geographic location as a transit hub and as an amalgam of urban uses. As in most urban neighborhoods, there are problems with assaults and burglaries. Yet Dupont Circle exemplifies the value of public space in America, where people can exercise their constitutional freedoms and personal rights.

Washington Circle

Washington Circle is located along Pennsylvania Avenue less than one mile west of the White House. It is also near the western end of the city's busiest thoroughfare, K Street. These two facts alone assure its prominence within the city as an important activity node. In addition to Pennsylvania Avenue and K Street, New Hampshire Avenue intersects the circle, providing distant vistas southwest to the Kennedy Center for the Performing Arts and northeast to Dupont Circle. A vista south to the Lincoln Memorial is provided along Twenty-third Street. The circular park is 350 feet in diameter, and there are two smaller, triangular public reservations to the east and west.

When first developed, this was a residential neighborhood with some local institutions, all focusing on the park. When George Washington University (GWU) decided to relocate there early in the twentieth century, the character of the area changed dramatically. George Washington University Hospital later located on the southeast side of the park, creating a strong institutional presence. More recently, the area along Pennsylvania Avenue east to the White House has developed a financial focus, culminating with the International Finance Corporation building, facing Washington Circle. The north side has retained some of its nineteenth-century residential tradition.

The Nineteenth Century

Washington Circle is clearly delineated on L'Enfant's plan, although it is not one of the numbered appropriated open spaces. It also appears on Ellicott's 1792 plan. Logan, Dupont, and Washington circles are equidistant from the White House, yet the area around Washington Circle developed first because of its location on Pennsylvania Avenue leading to prosperous Georgetown.

Washington Circle is located within a formerly swampy, disease-prone area known as Foggy Bottom because of the mist generated by the still water. It was first an industrial area including a gasworks, a glass factory, and a brewery. Workers' housing south of the circle was very modest in size and style.

The Pennsylvania Avenue corridor between Washington Circle and the White House developed before the area around the circle itself. The 1861 Boschke map of Washington depicts almost continuous rows of buildings along this part of the avenue (see fig. 1.3).[73] The first significant building on the circle, on the triangle between K Street and New Hampshire Avenue southwest of the park, was built in the 1820s and occupied by the British Legation from 1836 to 1844.[74] From 1860 to the 1940s it housed the St. Ann's Infant Asylum. In 1867 St. Paul's Episcopal Church was built nearby at the corner of 23rd Street.

Washington Circle was the first circular reservation developed as a park, in 1856, when it was landscaped with trees and shrubs and enclosed with a wooden fence.[75] In 1853 Congress appropriated funds for a statue to honor George Washington, but it was not installed until 1860. The bronze equestrian statue of the Revolutionary War general by sculptor Clark Mills stands on a marble base facing east toward the White House; it was first intended to be placed east of the Washington monument. The statue is incongruous in that it depicts a composed general on the field of battle astride a terrified stallion.[76]

During the Civil War this and many other areas in the city were used for Union army encampments. An 1865 print shows the Camp Fry army barracks in rows south along Twenty-third Street. The print also shows

a handsomely landscaped park, enclosed by a fence, dominated by the equestrian statue (fig. 8.14). Many shade trees provide comfort for the well-dressed strollers. During the Civil War the first tracks for horse-drawn streetcars were laid along Pennsylvania Avenue and around Washington Circle.[77]

Fig. 8.14. Washington Circle, view south to Camp Fry, 1865. The Historical Society of Washington, D.C./City Museum

After the Civil War, Washington Circle did not require the degree of improvement required by other parks. The paths were re-laid, and an iron perimeter fence was installed. The chief of engineers requested funds for a watchman because the circle was "filled with cattle and horses and with gangs of boys who make all sorts of depredations within the enclosure." He received numerous complaints from citizens about the desecration, but the residents would not control the gates when asked to do so.[78]

In the 1880s the surrounding streets were regraded, as was the park. The original pattern of paths following the axes of the two intersecting avenues was retained, and curved paths were added in between, forming four oval areas. The tall iron fence was removed to provide free access to the park. A watchman was hired to perform park maintenance, and a small shelter was built for his use. The two small, triangular reservations east and west of the circular park were also landscaped at this time.[79] The chief of engineers reported, "The improvement of this handsome reservation has been continued, and it is now an ornament to the section of the city in which it is situated, and is frequented by residents in the vicinity; the removal of the iron fence, the construction of walks and the improvements generally have caused favorable comments."[80]

A map of the circle in 1888 shows the highest density of buildings east of the circle, but the circular park itself is not well defined by buildings (fig. 8.15). The infant asylum and St. Paul's Church are shown, along with

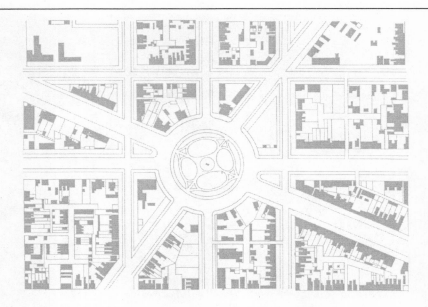

St. Stephen's Catholic Church west of the park. On a large block facing L Street are the initial buildings of Columbia Hospital, a medical center for destitute women and children. The corner building is the expanded Ringgold House, built in 1812.[81]

The handsomest town houses built in this popular neighborhood were called Schneider Triangle. Located on the entire small block northeast of Washington Circle bounded by New Hampshire Avenue and Twenty-second and K streets, they were built for John W. Paine in 1889 by Thomas Franklin Schneider to house professionals and civil servants.[82] This incomparable group of twenty-two row houses (twenty-one remain) epitomizes the adaptation of Victorian architectural styles—Queen Anne and Richardsonian Romanesque—to a unique, sloping triangular site. Every row house was designed to be individual, yet they are composed as a total entity. The houses that face the circle and New Hampshire Avenue, with turrets and bays, are more elaborate than those facing Twenty-second Street, which are simpler in appearance. Most of them were renovated in the 1970s as luxury single-family dwellings with preserved exteriors and modernized interiors (fig. 8.16). The missing house on K Street was destroyed by fire and replaced by a house of somewhat incongruous design.

The Twentieth Century

After the turn of the century most of the industries south of the circle closed, and residents started to move away from the area because of the increasing traffic. The character of the area was forever changed when GWU relocated to the southeast quadrant in 1912.

After World War II automobile traffic around the circular park increased dramatically, and the trolley tracks were removed in the 1950s to make room for more cars. The park itself became an island within clogged roadways, difficult for a pedestrian to reach and inhospitable to occupy. It had been redesigned during the Depression years, when the paths were once again re-laid and simplified to their earlier axial pattern. In order to reduce the traffic around the circular park there was

Fig. 8.16. Schneider Triangle, view to northeast

a plan to run Pennsylvania Avenue through it, slicing it in two.[83] The plan was vetoed, and K Street was placed in an underpass leading to the Whitehurst Freeway along the Potomac River. The four-lane, four-block underpass with service ramps was constructed in the 1960s. Fortunately, the geometric integrity of the open space was retained because through lanes for Twenty-third Street were not created, unlike at Thomas Circle.

In 1944 GWU decided to build its new hospital southeast of the park on the site of the Episcopal church. This was the beginning of the consolidation of all GWU's facilities related to medicine. The new, five-hundred-bed hospital was designed and built by the Public Buildings Administration of the Federal Works Agency in 1948.[84] It was divorced from its context as a freestanding, six-story structure with a highly articulated footprint. The main entrance and facade faced Twenty-third Street. An emergency entrance was later added to the facade facing the circle. President Ronald Reagan was brought here for emergency surgery after the failed assassination attempt against him in 1981.

In the 1960s and 1970s residential densification continued north of the circle owing to the area's easy access to Georgetown, GWU, and the office district to the east. Town houses were destroyed to build an eight-story apartment building west of Schneider Triangle that later became the luxury hotel suites of Washington Circle Inn. In 1979 a developer saved only the town house facades on the large site in the northwest quadrant, destroying the remainder of the block and the Lewis School. Here he built an innocuous brick apartment building stepping up to a height of ninety feet.[85] Adjacent to this complex on the west the town houses have been saved, but a highly noncontextual building of dark glass has been inserted behind them.

In 1970 the Foggy Bottom Metro station opened on Twenty-third Street south of the circle; it is heavily used by students and employees of GWU. The area around the station entrance has become an active gathering place full of vendors and kiosks. The Metro alleviated automobile traffic and parking in the university precinct but not through traffic

Fig. 8.17. The new George
Washington University Hos-
pital with statue of George
Washington in Washington
Circle

around the circular park. Row houses on the large triangular site northwest of the station were removed to create a hospital parking lot.

The International Finance Corporation, part of the World Bank
group, completed its eleven-story building on the triangle between K
Street and Pennsylvania Avenue east of the park in 1997. The handsome
building by the architect Michael Graves has an elegant rounded bay facing the circular park. The six-hundred-foot-long facade along the avenue
has articulated projecting bays of limestone and brick classically composed as base, middle, and top.[86] Due to security concerns, the facade
at the street level, with concrete planters and small windows, is not pedestrian friendly. The two entrances are highly controlled, and the main
public space, a rotunda 150 feet high, is inaccessible to the public.

The most dramatic change at the end of this era was the construction
of a replacement hospital for the GWU medical center on the parking lot
south of the park. The main entry is adjacent to the Metro station, and
there is a new emergency entry on I Street. The new building opened in
the summer of 2002 with 371 hospital beds, primarily in single rooms.
The exterior of the six-story building is brick and cast stone with large
expanses of glass and a rounded corner facing the park, similar to the
International Finance Corporation building (fig. 8.17). Designed by HKS,
the hospital is now jointly owned by GWU and Universal Health Systems,
Inc. The old hospital has been demolished and will be replaced with a
multiuse structure.

A 1999 map shows a partially formed circular place (fig. 8.18). The
buildings to the north contribute to this definition, whereas the Warwick
Building (formerly an infant asylum, now a GWU office building) does
not. Since the Warwick Building is an underutilized site, a new building
there could contribute to defining the circular space. The design of an
architecturally compatible multiuse building on the old GWU Hospital
site is crucial to completing the redevelopment of Washington Circle.

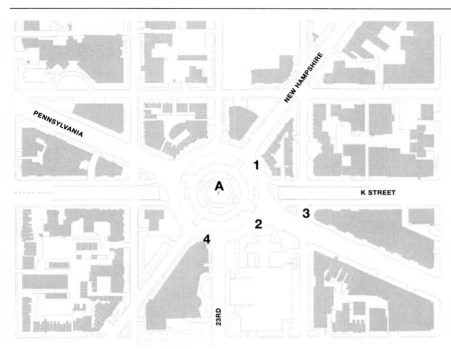

1: Schneider Triangle
2: Old George Washington
   University Hospital
3: International Finance
   Corporation
4: New George Washington
   University Hospital

A: George Washington Statue

Fig. 8.18. Washington Circle in 1999

Commentary

Both commercial and institutional development pressures have destroyed large parts of thriving neighborhoods, including Foggy Bottom, southwest of the circle, and the West End, northwest of the circle. The historically African American West End was destroyed to make way for a series of office buildings, hotels, and high-rise apartments in the late 1970s. The Foggy Bottom neighborhood has been taken over by George Washington University, resulting in a reduced number of residents: 10,000 in 1990 compared with 14,500 in 1970.[87]

GWU has a contentious relationship with the Foggy Bottom neighborhood because of expanding campus boundaries, increasing parking problems, and negative student behavior. The new hospital brings increasing numbers of patients and medical staff to the area via various modes of transit. New academic and research programs at GWU have resulted in the construction of many new buildings, not all contiguous with the forty-five-acre campus. The university student body has grown rapidly in recent years—it now exceeds sixteen thousand—necessitating the construction of new dormitories and/or utilization of existing buildings for student housing.[88] The city has entered the fray by not allowing the rezoning of additional residential land and requiring the university to house all first- and second-year students on campus. But as the city's largest private employer, the university is a strong political force.[89]

The existing Washington Circle has two concentric circular paths intersecting the pathways on axis with the two avenues and no perimeter walkway. The narrow inner path is of concrete, and the wide outer one is of flagstone. Along the outer pathway is a low hedge with interspersed benches and lights. The monumental statue is on a grass mound surrounded by a post-and-chain fence. There are shade trees of varying sizes around the perimeter zone and floral planting beds on the east and west sides. Ventilation grates for the subway are located in the northwest quadrant.

Traffic around the circular park continues to increase, making the open space an island that is difficult for the pedestrian to reach rather than an oasis to enjoy. Traffic lights have been provided to allow pedestrians to cross safely. Very few pedestrians use the open space for recreation in spite of the plethora of students and residents in the area, probably because of traffic noise and pollution. Few people even venture over to view the magnificent statue or long vistas. Yet it is a handsome space, with maintained landscaping and a broad flagstone promenade. Perhaps nothing can be done to improve this situation. Placing additional barriers of trees or landscaping around the periphery would shield the park. These barriers would have to be designed so as to preserve public safety.

Washington Circle has the great potential to be an ideal democratic place where neighbors interact with students, where town meets gown. There is no other neighborhood open space, and the university has only a couple of small plazas. Making design improvements would promote the creation of an idealized public space like a Greek agora or a Roman forum, where scholars and citizens could encounter each other for intellectual discussion.

CHAPTER NINE

CAPITOL HILL

Capitol Hill, Lincoln Square, Stanton Square, Seward Square, Eastern
Market Square, Folger Park, Marion Park, Garfield Park

HAD I BUT PLENTY of money, money enough and to spare,
The house for me, no doubt, were a house in the city-square.
Ah, such a life, such a life, as one leads at the window there!

ROBERT BROWNING, "Up at a Villa—Down in the City"

Capitol Hill

The four-square-mile plateau east of the Capitol defined by the curving Anacostia River on the east and south sides is known as Capitol Hill.
It encompasses the entire southeast quadrant of the city and the northeast quadrant up to Florida Avenue, the historic boundary of the L'Enfant
Plan. The street system of Capitol Hill remains true to L'Enfant's 1791
plan. The gracious urban design is achieved by the wide, public rights
of way, from building face to building face, with only the central portion
paved as the street. The resulting front yards are publicly owned green
space that is privately maintained, giving the area its verdant quality.

Capitol Hill developed slowly for most of the nineteenth century owing in large part to the lack of a reliable water source. The Potomac River
was the city's primary source, with water mains first serving the northwest
quadrant, the area closest to the source. The water supply was temporarily
improved in 1890 with a water main along East Capitol Street. A permanent water supply for Capitol Hill arrived in 1903 with a water main supplied from the Howard University Reservoir, which in turn was supplied
from the Potomac River above Great Falls.[1] The Anacostia River evidently
never had sufficient flow to serve as a water source for Capitol Hill.

After the Civil War the federal bureaucracy grew substantially. The
heyday for construction of housing on Capitol Hill to accommodate new
civil servants was 1870–90. Frame houses, which were outlawed in 1877
for fire safety, were replaced with two- and three-story brick row houses
in a variety of architectural styles, including Queen Anne, Richardsonian
Romanesque, and Eastlake. The design quality changed as a result of an
1871 city law that permitted bay windows, towers, and projecting cornices
to extend over the front setback line.[2] Many row houses featured fine
decorative brickwork, turrets, three-story bays, and handsome porches
or wrought-iron balconies.

After a slowdown during the 1890s, inexpensive housing development
during World War I expanded into the undeveloped areas east of Lincoln

Square. The primary construction material continued to be brick, combined with other, less costly materials. The front facades often were flat and lacking in ornamentation, with a roofed front porch.

By the twentieth century Capitol Hill was an extensive middle-class community for employees of Congress, the U.S. Government Printing Office, and the Navy Yard. Steady government employment extended this prosperity through the economic depression of the 1930s. Another great population influx occurred during World War II, when single-family residences became rooming houses or apartments. After this war much of the population migrated to the suburbs, abandoning many blocks of solidly constructed housing stock.

In the last decades of the twentieth century young professionals began to return to this area to purchase and restore houses, their efforts aided by the Capitol Hill Restoration Society. A strong architectural review board managed to retain the historic integrity of the Capitol Hill Historic District, established in 1976, during these preservation projects. In many cases they prevented wholesale demolition for large-scale development. The 150-block historic district lies essentially between the Capitol, Lincoln Square, the Southwest/Southeast Freeway, and E Street, NE. Commercial and institutional buildings were converted to housing and other uses, but overall the largest historic district in the city retained its ambiance of avenues and streets lined with rows of handsome dwellings and trees. In 1985 the Architect of the Capitol created the U.S. Capitol Interest District to protect a five-square-mile area around the Capitol from unwanted intrusions or changes.[3]

The major neighborhoods of Capitol Hill have been through at least one redevelopment cycle. Yet it remains both the largest and the most cohesive residential area in Washington, unspoiled by commercial or federal intrusions. According to the longtime resident and late historian Ruth Ann Overbeck, "Although federal activities on the Hill have expanded to claim some of its oldest buildings, the neighborhood has survived its proximity to power. Its largely nineteenth-century buildings remain intact to house a varied population in a comfortable residential neighborhood just steps from the Capitol of the nation."[4] But the potential for significant commercial or federal intrusions continues to exist because of the neighborhood's proximity and accessibility to the Capitol. The delicate balance that currently exists between historical and new, black and white, rich and poor, residential and commercial, must be continually monitored and adjusted.

Capitol Hill is in many ways the ideal democratic precinct, a socially vital series of neighborhoods dedicated to urban living and community participation. Its many active neighborhood organizations have rallied to stop additional freeway construction and keep East Capitol Street from becoming a boulevard of federal office buildings. They are very active in historic preservation and restoration, sponsoring house tours and workshops. These neighborhoods are focused on green open spaces that provide their spatial center.

Lincoln Square

Lincoln Square has a prominent location on East Capitol Street, halfway between the Anacostia River and Capitol Square. It has the highest topographic elevation on Capitol Hill, higher than that of the Capitol itself. It is also the largest residential park in the city, encompassing two large blocks between Eleventh and Thirteenth streets, an area of 6.5 acres. East Capitol Street divides as it goes around the park, with two lanes of traffic moving in a counterclockwise direction. The park on the hill has grand vistas east to Robert F. Kennedy Stadium and west to the Capitol and to the Washington Monument beyond. Four diagonal avenues, Massachusetts, North Carolina, Kentucky, and Tennessee, intercept this park.

The Nineteenth Century

In his 1791 plan for the city L'Enfant established Lincoln Square as a prominent open space. It was designated as location B on this plan, "an historic column also intended for a mile or itinerary column from whose station, (a mile from the Federal house) all distances of places through the continent, are to be calculated."[5] The square was located along East Capitol Street, which is on axis with the Capitol dome. L'Enfant also intended Lincoln Square to be part of the business district of the city since his plan proposed arcaded shops along East Capitol Street leading to Capitol Square.

During the Civil War the park was the site of the Union's Lincoln Hospital.[6] The park's location north of the Navy Yard brought military activity to the surrounding area. In 1865 people owning property around the square appealed to Congress to have it improved.[7]

Following President Abraham Lincoln's assassination in 1865 Congress authorized naming the park Lincoln Square as a memorial tribute. Since Lincoln had freed the slaves with his Emancipation Proclamation of 1863, African Americans wanted to create a memorial to him. Charlotte Scott, a freed black woman from Virginia, donated the first five dollars she earned to the Western Sanitary Commission in St. Louis, which agreed to collect the memorial funds.[8] The memorial was sponsored by a multitude of freed slaves who donated funds for its creation.

The sculptural memorial, *Emancipation,* was cast in bronze in Germany by the American sculptor Thomas Ball. It shows a life-size Lincoln on a granite pedestal with a kneeling freed slave amid shackles, chains, and a whipping post.[9] The memorial was dedicated on 14 April 1876, the eleventh anniversary of Lincoln's assassination, in a ceremony attended by President Ulysses S. Grant and his cabinet.[10] The abolitionist Frederick Douglass was the principal speaker.

Prior to the memorial installation the park and the surrounding streets were improved. During the era of territorial government East Capitol Street from Capitol Square to Lincoln Square was paved with wooden blocks. Chief of Engineers O. E. Babcock requested funds in 1872 for the purpose of "embellishing it in a manner commensurate with its name, and to compare favorably in beauty and attractiveness with any of the public squares in the city. This should be done in honor of the illustrious and lamented Lincoln, after whom the square was named."[11]

In 1874 the Office of Public Buildings and Grounds erected a lodge southwest of the park's center with toilets for visitors and storage for the watchman. Two brick fountain bowls thirty feet in diameter were located at the north and south entrances, and there was a mound in the center for a statue.[12] The following year an organic design was implemented that

reflected Andrew Jackson Downing's plan for the Mall. It had curvilinear gravel paths forming oval panels of grass and flowers. An iron post-and-chain fence enclosed the entire park, which was illuminated at night by gas lamps. *Emancipation* was located on the west side of the park facing the Capitol, with a short mall connecting it to Eleventh Street (fig. 9.1).[13] Improvements to the park and the memorial statue made Lincoln Square a popular attraction for residents and visitors.

The design and construction of houses in the Lincoln Square neighborhood included single town houses and groups of row houses on scattered lots, with eventual infill to form integrated street fronts. Architects usually designed the single houses, whereas builders created the blocks of standardized row houses. These two- and three-story brick dwellings have high basements with recessed entrances between projecting bays. By 1904 almost all lots around the square west of Thirteenth Street contained town houses. Those on the oddly shaped corners were usually larger and more elaborate in configuration (fig. 9.2).

The Twentieth Century

In 1902 the Senate Park Commission completed its grand plan for the monumental core of the city, and in subsequent decades much of it was implemented. But as the federal government grew, so did its need for buildings to house its many departments and bureaus. The area along East Capitol Street was viewed as a logical place for federal expansion after the Federal Triangle along Pennsylvania Avenue was completed. In relationship to the Capitol it is the eastern equivalent of L'Enfant's Grand Avenue (the current Mall) as a location for monumental buildings. President William Howard Taft even suggested that the new Supreme Court building be built facing Lincoln Square.[14] The Beaux Arts Institute sponsored a competition for Independence Square, honoring the original colonies, in this location.[15] But the neighborhood rejected these proposals

L'ENFANT'S LEGACY

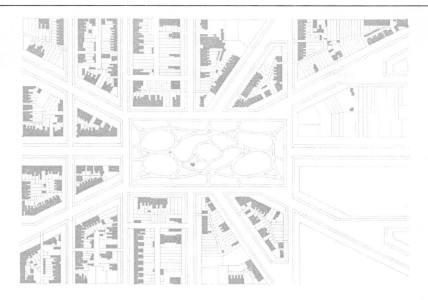

and others that followed to preserve the residential quality of the area around the park.

Fig. 9.2. Lincoln Square in 1904

In 1929 the National Capital Park and Planning Commission proposed an "Avenue of the States" lined with exhibition pavilions that extended the axis of the Mall east to an enormous amphitheater on the Anacostia River. Lincoln Square would be reconfigured to become "Colonial Square," surrounded by buildings honoring the original thirteen colonies.[16] Another version of this scheme, with public and semipublic buildings lining East Capitol Street and federal buildings around a smaller park, was put forth in 1941.[17] The development terminated on the west side of the Anacostia River with a stadium and recreation area. The construction of the Robert Kennedy Stadium in this location in 1965 was the only part of this plan that was implemented.

The park at Lincoln Square has often been the setting for programmed events such as band concerts, freedom rallies, and religious services. After electric lights were installed local military bands gave evening concerts on portable bandstands. This continued until the Lincoln Memorial was completed at the western end of the Mall in 1922. The park then became an informal neighborhood green space serving the residents who lived around it. In keeping with the humble spirit of Lincoln, the residents wanted to keep the park as a quiet place for rest and contemplation. In 1942 twenty-three churches held religious services and Bible classes in the park.[18] It was continually beautified with large areas of shrubs, numerous trees, and seasonal flowers.

During the 1930s the Works Progress Administration implemented a new park design influenced by the work of Frederick Law Olmsted Jr. on the Mall. Straight concrete walks paralleled East Capitol Street, and diagonal paths joined the corners to a mall-like area along the east-west axis. The central mound was shifted west to line up with Twelfth Street. New fountains were installed, along with new sandboxes, and the lodge was relocated on the east side.

Fig. 9.3. Mary McLeod
Bethune Memorial, Lincoln
Square, with *Emancipation*
statue in the distance

Lincoln Square became a rallying place for the city's African American community during the civil rights era of the 1960s. Numerous freedom rallies and peaceful demonstrations were held there, although they did not receive as much publicity as those at Dupont Circle or Lafayette Square. All the while, the neighbors continued to use the open space for many forms of recreation.

The most recent large-scale improvement to the park took place in 1973 to accommodate a new sculpture group. The Mary McLeod Bethune Memorial shows the elderly African American educator handing her legacy to two black children (fig. 9.3). Sculpted in bronze by Robert Berks and placed on a six-sided pedestal with an inscription,[19] the memorial was sponsored by the National Council of Negro Women, which Bethune had founded in 1935 to improve the living and working conditions of African American families. Insistence on including a meeting room beneath the sculpture delayed construction of the memorial past the hundredth anniversary of the Emancipation Proclamation. The meeting room was eventually rejected by the National Park Service as inappropriate for a public park.[20]

To accommodate this new memorial, the park was redesigned by the local architect Hilyard R. Robinson. The Bethune Memorial was placed on the east side, displacing the lodge, and *Emancipation* was rotated to face it. The latter was also moved to line up with Twelfth Street, eliminating the short pedestrian mall aligned with East Capitol Street. *Emancipation* is now located on a square plaza lined with magnolia trees, whereas the Bethune statue is on a semicircular plaza surrounded by white oaks and lindens. Together, with a sunken gathering area between them, they create a formal central space defined by trees, benches, and planters. Straight orthogonal paths connect this central area to the adjacent streets, and there are two small, circular playgrounds north and south of the Bethune Memorial. The park perimeter has a dirt jogging path and a brick sidewalk. A map showing Lincoln Square in 1999 (fig. 9.4), which shows the continuous row houses and apartment buildings that surround the

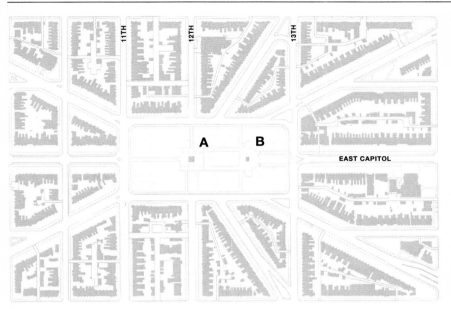

A: *Emancipation* Statue
B: Mary McLeod Bethune Memorial

Fig. 9.4. Lincoln Square in 1999

park, along with some neighborhood services and the United Methodist Church at the northeast corner, is similar to a map showing the square in 1904 (see fig. 9.2). Serving the lots are numerous alleys, where garages are located.

The population of the Lincoln Square neighborhood remained stable during the Depression and World War II. In recent decades there has been considerable residential preservation and gentrification. Some homes have been rehabilitated by new, white residents, but many older black residents have continued to live in the same homes; the neighborhood has long been known for its successful racial integration.

Commentary

Lincoln Square is a place of both commemoration and community. The two symbolic memorials are easily accessible to visitors without infringing upon community tranquility. During the active civil rights era the community was probably less tolerant of large crowds invading the neighborhood for parades and rallies. Otherwise, the community has welcomed the presence of the two national memorials and gained its identity from them.

Until 1900 the park at Lincoln Square was the setting for an annual Emancipation Day celebration commemorating the signing of the Emancipation Proclamation. It was the biggest African American event in the city, and black schools were closed for the long parade featuring many brass bands.[21] Revived in 1994, the celebration takes place annually in April, with growing participation from the African American community.[22] With its large, paved central area, the park is ideally suited for large gatherings.

Now that the *Emancipation* statue has been relocated away from the Capitol and moved near the center of the park, there is room for another large-scale element. Perhaps L'Enfant's original proposal for a large column should be reconsidered. It could become a memorial related to civil rights, the present theme of the two existing memorials. A vertical element would give visibility to Lincoln Square on the skyline, directly related to the axis of the Washington Monument.

In terms of community the park has always been regarded by the neighborhood as a place of recreation, including sunbathing, picnicking, and strolling, along with some active pursuits such as jogging. Attempts to improve the park for active recreation such as basketball or bicycling have met with resistance. Even a proposal for chess tables was resisted as an infringement upon the tranquil setting. The large area of the park relative to the number of users allows multiple activities to occur simultaneously without conflict. Moreover, the various areas of the park have excellent visibility from the streets.

Lincoln Square is definitely a neighborhood for dog owners, with walking dogs to and from the park as well as around it one of the primary recreational activities. Occasionally there are festivals featuring music, painting, photography, and pottery that include exhibits and tables for community information. Annually the circus parade from Union Station to the D.C. Armory, with elephants and horses, has passed by the park. Other annual events include a Halloween costume party and a house tour.[23] All of these events are organized by an active neighborhood association.

The park at Lincoln Square had a very different appearance in the past than it does today. It was essentially a forest with paths cut through it and a clearing for the *Emancipation* statue. A blizzard in 1888 and a hurricane in 1896 damaged many of the old trees, necessitating their removal.[24] Enough of these oaks, maples, elms, hollys, and junipers remained to form a dense and mature tree cover, creating an ambiance of tranquility similar to that of Franklin Square. The trees in the park today are neither mature nor dense, nor are they planted in a particular pattern. In the interest of visibility for safety, the trees are pruned high and the plantings are intermittent.

Hilyard R. Robinson's 1962 design scheme for the park proposed large, closely spaced trees at the west end, and formalized shrub masses around both the central space and the Bethune Memorial at the east end.[25] The intent of this scheme was to form strongly defined outdoor spaces that featured the two memorials and enabled programmed gatherings to take place.

The present-day park lacks a sense of defined open spaces to form activity areas. Only the separation of distance keeps the various activities from conflicting with one another. The park has a large scale and therefore large-scaled, bold gestures are required to create a significant visual and spatial impact. The National Park Service should consider a landscape design direction that is similar in intent to Robinson's 1962 scheme, while maintaining a reasonable measure of visibility for safety and security.

In many ways Lincoln Square is a model democratic space where commemoration and community reinforce each other. The two memorials give this place a symbolic identity within the city as a place for civil rights rallies. The continuous architectural frame of residences symbolizes the bonds of the community in shaping and using this space as equal citizens regardless of race. That this should occur on axis with the Capitol

L'ENFANT'S LEGACY

a mile away is testimony to the enduring power of the nation's democratic ideals.

Stanton Square

Stanton Square is located in the northeast quadrant of the city at the intersection of Massachusetts and Maryland avenues. This 4.5-acre rectangular space between Fourth and Sixth streets straddles a split C Street, which defines it on the north and south sides. From this elevated location there is a vista northwest to Union Station Plaza. There is also a vista southwest to the Capitol, especially in the winter, when the trees are bare. Lincoln Square, along Massachusetts Avenue to the southeast, is not visible because of the five-block distance.

The Nineteenth Century

Stanton Square was one of the original yellow appropriated squares on L'Enfant's 1791 plan, designated number 5 and shown as an oval in a rectangular area. It appears on Ellicott's plan as a rectangular open space. There was little development in this area before the Civil War, with only a few buildings facing the park.

In 1867 Chief of Engineers Nathaniel Michler recommended improvements to this park because of improvements to the surrounding street system and the construction of new houses.[26] However, funding for improvements was not forthcoming until 1871–74. Chief of Engineers Orville E. Babcock first referred to the park as Stanton Place in his 1872 annual report.[27] Thus it was named after President Lincoln's secretary of war, Edwin Stanton. Its twin square to the south was subsequently named Seward Place, after Lincoln's secretary of state, William Seward. Many people visiting Lincoln Square to the east would first pass by one of these public parks.

In 1874 Congress funded a memorial at Stanton Square dedicated to Major General Nathaniel Greene, a Revolutionary War hero from Rhode Island, whose greatest success was engaging the British commander Charles Cornwallis. His bronze equestrian statue, erected in 1877, was sculpted by Henry Kirke Brown and placed on a high limestone pedestal.[28] It is considered one of the best equestrian statues in the city. The pedestal and horse are oriented diagonally along the Maryland Avenue axis toward the Capitol, whereas Greene himself faces south (fig. 9.5).

In 1879 the park was formed into a coherent rectangular open space with rounded corners. It was graded, and paths were placed around the statue. Prior to this the two avenues divided the area into four triangles around a small traffic circle. Improvements included water pipes, gas pipes, lampposts, and two rock fountains, all enclosed with an iron post-and-chain fence.[29] There was an entrance to the park from each intercepting street, and a symmetrical system of curvilinear paths led to a central circle (see fig. 9.7).

While the park was being improved and the statue placed, the largest elementary school in the city for white children was being built on the south side of the square, at the corner of C and Fifth streets. The George Peabody School was designed in 1879 by the Office of the Building Inspector of the Army Corps of Engineers.[30] Its frugal appearance is a reaction against the excessive spending on public works during the territorial

Fig. 9.5. Statue of General
Nathaniel Greene, Stanton
Square

government. Nevertheless, it is a handsome, three-and-one-half-story structure with high-quality brickwork, projecting bays on the cross-axes, and an unusual fourth-story penthouse of wood (fig. 9.6). Its location formed a synergetic relationship: the large public building engaged the park with its dominant facade, while the children utilized the open space as their playground. It is currently the Peabody Early Childhood Campus.

During the 1880s the park was maintained and guarded by a watchman who planted flowers around the fountains and the statue. Water was scarce, so the fountains operated only one hour per day. A lodge for the watchman was not provided until 1905, when it was moved from Garfield Park to a location on the north side.[31]

In his 1887 annual report Chief of Engineers John M. Wilson denounced the recurring vandalism: "Unfortunately we have had much trouble in protecting our flower beds in these parks. Plants and bulbs were frequently pulled up by the roots at night after the watchman had gone home. On one occasion forty hyacinths were plucked from a bed in Stanton Square. Much annoyance has been caused by chickens running at large and destroying the lawns and flower-beds. The law appears to grant no protection in the latter case."[32] Complaints about vandalism continued in 1890, with the vandals claiming that they could go anywhere on public ground.[33]

By 1904 there were few vacant lots facing the park. The Eastern Presbyterian Church was on the northeast corner, and there was a coal and wood yard on the north side. The dominant structure was the Peabody School (fig. 9.7).

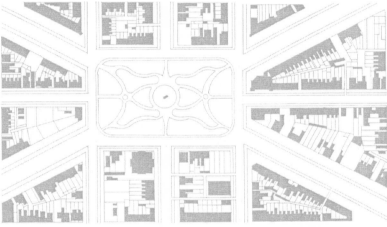

Top: Fig. 9.6. Peabody School, south side of Stanton Square

Bottom: Fig. 9.7. Stanton Square in 1904

The Twentieth Century

Following the lead of the Senate Park Commission Plan of 1902, parks in the city were redesigned with simplified formal schemes. Stanton Square was not redesigned until 1921, with a large oval path between the perimeter walk and the central circle with its statue. Diagonal paths on axis with the avenues led to the central circle, along with a pair of paths aligned with the sidewalks of Fifth Street. Along the C Street axis the entrance paths stopped at the oval path. This is essentially the present path system. A new, modern lodge was erected on the north side of Stanton Park identical to the ones at Lincoln, Judiciary, and Lafayette parks.[34]

White flight to the suburbs after World War II resulted in neighborhood deterioration and the city's decision to consider the neighborhood for urban renewal. This was resisted, and the National Park Service re-furbished the park according to Ladybird Johnson's city beautification program. A playground with equipment added on the west side at this time helped foster redevelopment and gentrification by young professionals, who bought and restored many of the Victorian row houses. Because of the quality and integrity of the architecture in the neighborhood surrounding Stanton Square the area was included in the Capitol Hill Historic District, National Register of Historic Places, in 1976. The recent restoration of Union Station and the addition of a shopping center have fostered a resurgence on Massachusetts Avenue leading to Stanton Square.

The area developed into a desirable residential neighborhood with excellent access to the Capitol and other federal buildings along the Massachusetts Avenue corridor. The architectural frame consists mostly of two- and three-story brick row houses with projecting bays, raised entrances, and fenced front gardens. During the 1930s a service station (now gone) was built on the north side of the square, and a neoclassical funeral home was built on the west side. The funeral home is now the Daniel Webster Senate Page Hall. The Richardsonian church at the corner of Maryland Avenue and 6th Street, with its prominent round steeple, became the Imani Temple.

Because of this square's proximity to the Capitol, some of the row houses have been converted to office use, and some new office buildings have been built on the north side as permitted by zoning. In the 1980s zoning amendments eliminated commercial uses from the east and south sides of the square.[35] The most interesting new building is on the northeast corner, designed by the architect Amy Weinstein in 1991.[36] This office building relates well to its context by utilizing interpretations of contextual motifs: a brick-patterned facade, gabled forms, and projecting bays. The most forceful element is the corner tower, a cylinder encased in a square brick screen, which relates to the church steeple across the intersection.

The present-day Stanton Square is an excellent example of a residential park with an appropriate balance of formal and informal areas. A wide concrete path circles the statue on a mound defined by low hedges and a continuous curved bench. Low hedges also define the playground area on the west side and a dog-walking area on the east side. Areas between the paths are landscaped with grass, shade and flowering trees, and large flower beds. Throughout the park there are additional benches, drinking fountains, and lampposts along the paths. Two lanes of traffic move around the park in a counterclockwise direction; raised concrete islands at the corners of the park define traffic lanes (fig. 9.8).

Commentary

The Stanton Square neighborhood extends from East Capitol Street north to H Street and from Second Street east to Tenth Street in the northeast quadrant. It is a close-knit neighborhood of five thousand residents with much socialization and mutual support.[37] The residents are congressional staffers, college students, and young professionals working at the Capitol or elsewhere in the city.

Stanton Square is thriving as a residential neighborhood with the gen-

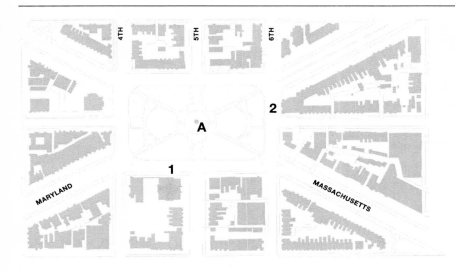

Fig. 9.8. Stanton Square in 1999

erous green space as its spatial focus. The area has a diversity of residents: black and white, old and young, renters and owners, singles and families with children. There is also a diversity of use: row houses and apartments, small neighborhood services, offices, a preschool, and a church. These diversities support each other in a synergetic relationship.

Nothing significant really needs to be done to improve this neighborhood or its park, but the existing balance takes effort to maintain. Increases in crime, drug sales, and the presence of homeless persons could disrupt it. So could escalating real estate prices, which would make it an exclusive enclave. Conversions of residences to offices or new commercial development could also change the balance and bring in people who do not have the same vested interest as residents and property owners. Thus, the Stanton Park Neighborhood Association must remain vigilant in monitoring impending changes while working with the city to maintain this ideal urban residential setting. This includes working with the National Park Service to maintain and/or improve the quality of the park.

Stanton Square is one of the best examples in the city of the kind of democratic public place L'Enfant intended as the center of a neighborhood. The prominent church is an expression of the nation's religious freedom, and the prominent school is an expression of its public education system. Although universal education was not a constitutional right, it was deemed a necessity for a democratic society by the nation's founders, especially Thomas Jefferson. The rows of residences with architectural and scalar variation are expressive of the diverse citizens who constitute the democratic community with freedom to engage in public activity in the common open space.

Seward Square

Stanton Square's twin to the south is Seward Square, which is aligned in the same position relative to the Capitol and Lincoln Square, forming a symmetrical plan composition. Seward Square is located at the intersection of Pennsylvania Avenue, SE, and North Carolina Avenue. All street traffic is two-way, and C Street splits into north and south sections. The biggest difference in comparison with Stanton Square is that in the case

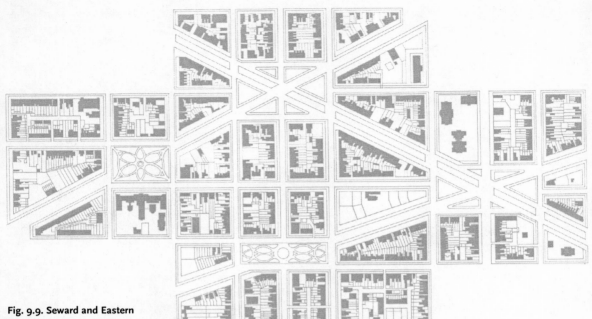

Fig. 9.9. Seward and Eastern Market squares and Folger and Marion parks in 1904

of Seward Square the two avenues go through the park, dividing it into triangular areas, a net area of about 2.5 acres. The vista to the Capitol is blocked by the inadvertent position of the Library of Congress; in the opposite direction there is a vista to Eastern Market Square. To the south-west is a vista to Folger Park, whereas Lincoln Square to the northeast is barely visible because of the five-block distance.

The Nineteenth Century

Seward Square was one of the appropriated squares, labeled number 14, on L'Enfant's plan and was shown as a large rectangular open space on Ellicott's plan. On the former, North Carolina Avenue ended after crossing the square, whereas on the latter plan it was extended southwest to Folger Park. Seward Square is sited along Pennsylvania Avenue, SE, a major gateway to the Capitol from the southeast. It was acquired by the federal government as part of the rights of way for streets.

In spite of its proximity to the Capitol and its location directly north of the Navy Yard, the area around the square developed slowly until after the Civil War. During the territorial government Pennsylvania Avenue, SE, was paved with wooden blocks southeast to Eighth Street, and trolley tracks ran down the center of the roadway.[38] In 1881 it was repaved with asphalt and lined with a double row of maple trees, whereas North Carolina Avenue was paved with gravel. A map of the square in 1904 shows it almost completely defined by large town houses, except for the Trinity Methodist Episcopal Church on the south side (fig. 9.9).

Seward and Eastern Market squares are the only two open spaces in the city intersected by roadways. Chief of Engineers Thomas Lincoln Casey, referring to this square as "Seward Place," recognized the difficulty of creating a park under these circumstances. In 1880 he recommended removing the roadways and the rail tracks; this did not occur, and the triangular parcels were improved with grass, flower beds, and fences.[39]

The Twentieth Century

In 1903 Congress officially named the public space Seward Square in honor of William Seward, President Lincoln's secretary of state. The same year, a wide grass median was formed in the middle of Pennsylvania Avenue, SE, and lined with a double row of trees. It was intended to separate the streetcars from the other traffic and to visually screen their presence. The streetcars were discontinued in the 1950s, but the grass median lined with trees remains. It was not until 1963 that Fifth Street was removed, consolidating the park by reducing the number of triangular parcels from six to four.[40]

The area surrounding Seward Square continued to develop with residences and small commercial buildings during the twentieth century, fostered in part by the streetcar lines. As auto transit became popular after World War II, the area was bypassed for redevelopment. In some ways this is a blessing, for many of the original nineteenth-century structures survive. Now, with a subway station nearby, Seward Square has the potential to be redeveloped. This has already begun with the recent five-story bank building along Pennsylvania Avenue, SE, at 6th Street, whose design unfortunately does not help to define the park.

In the 1970s part of the Metro system was built beneath the south side of Seward Square, which was entirely excavated for the construction. Ventilation grates were installed in this part of the park, which was landscaped with a circular seating area paved with Belgian blocks and defined by hedges and holly trees. The subway station itself is located two blocks southeast at Eastern Market Square.

Seward Square today, as depicted on a 1999 map, is surrounded by a wide variety of building types and uses (fig. 9.10). In addition to the above-mentioned bank, there are a gas station, a modern church, several apartment buildings, and a multitude of row houses. The circular landscaped setting on the south side forms an appropriate forecourt for the Capitol Hill United Methodist Church (fig. 9.11). The gas station on the west side is a noxious use and should be replaced. As part of the Capitol Hill Historic District, Seward Square should continue its preservation and rehabilitation of nineteenth-century row houses and apartment buildings. There has also been a recent trend to convert row houses from rental units to owner-occupied homes, which contributes to the stability of the neighborhood.[41]

Commentary

Some efforts have been made to improve the park, but more are needed. Modern light standards have been replaced with historical replicas, and concrete sidewalks along Pennsylvania Avenue, SE, have been replaced with brick. These efforts should continue around the entire park, and there should be an intensive landscaping program of trees and shrubs to separate the park areas from traffic. For example, most of the perimeter walkways have openings for shade trees, but shade trees are not consistently planted there. New trees have recently been planted in the median along the entire length of Pennsylvania Avenue,

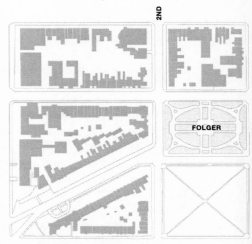

1: Capitol Hill United Methodist Church
2: South Eastern Branch Public Library
3: Hines Junior High School
4: Eastern Market Metro Station

5: Brent Elementary School
6: St. Peter's School
7: Police Substation
8: Pleasant Lane Baptist Church

SE. The shrub beds at the corners are too small to have a visual impact. The park is used little by the residents because of its shabby condition and lack of amenities. The most frequent use is by homeless people and church volunteers distributing food to them.

As the primary approach to the Capitol from the southeast, Pennsylvania Avenue, SE, will continue to cross Seward Square in the future. There are several existing precedents in the city for tunneling an avenue under a circular open space but none for tunneling under a rectangular open space, especially on the diagonal.

North Carolina Avenue should be removed from Seward Square just as South Carolina Avenue was removed from Eastern Market Square in 1969. Maryland Avenue does not traverse its Capitol Hill counterpart Stanton Square, and there is insufficient traffic on this portion of North Carolina Avenue to justify its intrusion into this park. Seward Square would then be consolidated into two large triangular areas to create a more viable public open space for the neighborhood; it could then be redesigned with new pathways and landscaping.

Seward Square has the potential to be a much more significant neighborhood public space. The church and its landscaped forecourt on the south side demonstrate its potential as a civic space. Another public use on the north side would contribute to this role. The park lacks identity and a positive image, which could be provided by memorials, perhaps dedicated to civic leaders as L'Enfant originally intended.

L'ENFANT'S LEGACY

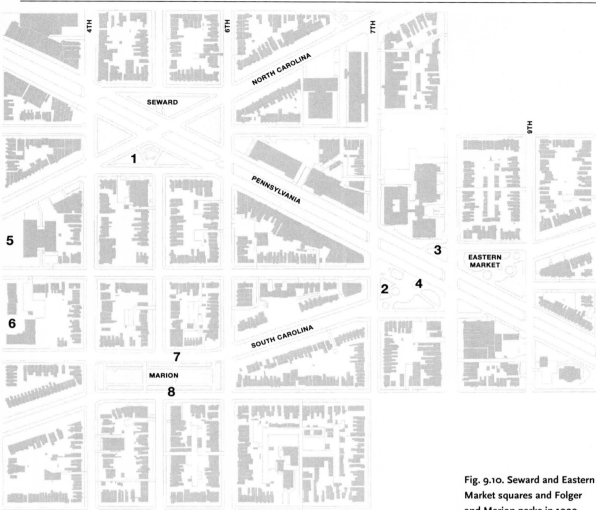

SEWARD

NORTH CAROLINA

PENNSYLVANIA

SOUTH CAROLINA

MARION

EASTERN MARKET

Fig. 9.10. Seward and Eastern
Market squares and Folger
and Marion parks in 1999

Eastern Market Square

Eastern Market Square is located at the intersection of Pennsylvania Avenue, SE, and South Carolina Avenue. It is bounded by Seventh, Ninth, and D streets. This square never had a name associated with it. When the subway was constructed, the station at the square was named after the nineteenth-century market one block to the north at Seventh and C streets; the square has since been known as Eastern Market Square. There are vistas up Pennsylvania Avenue, SE, to the Capitol and southwest to Marion Park.

The Nineteenth Century

This open space appears on L'Enfant's 1791 plan and Ellicott's 1792 plan as a large rectangular place. It was acquired by the federal government in 1791 as part of the right of way for streets and avenues. The Marine Barracks located two blocks to the south fostered early development in their vicinity but not as far as this square.

The area around Eastern Market Square developed slowly in spite of its location along Pennsylvania Avenue, SE, which led to a ferry crossing the Anacostia River to Maryland. One of the earliest hotels in the city, Tunnicliff's Tavern (1795), faced the park on the south side. Subsequently known as the Eastern Branch Hotel, it later became a spacious residence, with the park serving as its rose garden. After the Civil War the structure became a beer garden, then a storage building, and finally a gas station before being razed in 1931.[42]

During the Civil War the population of the city increased, and the north side of Eastern Market Square became the location of the first modern public school, named after Mayor Richard Wallach Jr. Designed by the architecture firm of Cluss and Kammerheuber in 1864, the school had a prominent central bay and separate wings for boys and girls with brick corner chimneys for ventilation.[43] The innovative design accommodated ten classrooms for six hundred pupils; unfortunately, it was razed in 1950 to construct Hines Junior High School in 1966.

Eastern Market Square was unrecognized as a federal reservation by the Office of Public Buildings and Grounds until 1872. By then streetcar tracks crossed it along Pennsylvania Avenue, SE, turning south along Eighth Street to the Marine Barracks and the Navy Yard. This prevented it from becoming a coherent rectangular space. Instead, it was graded and planted with grass and flowers as six triangular parcels in 1886.[44] These parcels were further improved in 1894 with additional trees, shrubs, and fencing.

A map showing the square in 1904 shows a fragmented space of six triangular parklets of different sizes (see fig. 9.9). The architectural frame consisted mostly of row houses. The Henry Rabe House (1891), at 820 D Street, is one of the most notable single houses, with Richardsonian Romanesque and Queen Anne styles combined.[45] Also on D Street, on the north side of the square, is the Charles Gessford Row (1892), five contiguous three-story houses on high basements featuring bays with high roofs and a variety of brick patterns and details. Additional buildings facing the park are the freestanding Wallach School on the north side, Grace Baptist Church on the east side, and Haines Department Store on the south side.

The Twentieth Century

There was considerable change to the area around Eastern Market Square in the first half of the twentieth century. Pennsylvania Avenue, SE, became more of a commercial corridor with increased traffic. Haines Department Store became a furniture store, and a gas station was built on the adjacent parcel. Grace Baptist Church remained, but Tunnicliff Tavern and the Wallach School were razed. The South Eastern Branch Public Library was built on the west side of the square in 1922, funded by Andrew Carnegie and designed by the noted library architect Edward L. Tilton in a neoclassical style. It provides a range of services, including an actively utilized community meeting room.

In the late 1950s the trolley tracks were removed as buses provided public transit. Twenty years later part of the Metro system was constructed under Pennsylvania Avenue, SE. A station was located at Eastern Market Square on the south side. Eighth Street was left intact, crossing the square, but the portion of South Carolina Avenue through the square was closed at this time, with the parcels on either side consolidated into large trapezoidal areas. These areas were improved with new landscape designs based on curvilinear patterns. There are large central areas paved in brick featuring circular flower beds flanked by areas of grass, trees, and shrubs. Other areas of this park have a similar appearance, defined by brick or concrete perimeter walks with sporadic street trees. There are numerous concrete benches, streetlights, and two bus stops. However, these parks have not been well maintained, and many of the plants and trees have died or grown poorly, resulting in an unkempt appearance. The medians of Pennsylvania Avenue, SE, have a recently planted double row of trees (see fig. 9.10).

Commentary

Eastern Market Square has the constant flow of vehicular traffic along Pennsylvania Avenue, SE, which creates conditions for viable commerce. The park will always remain divided by the avenue, as is Seward Square to the west. The library, the junior high school, and the market are public uses that assure steady pedestrian traffic. There is a great potential for vitality here engendered by the variety of uses, including many residences.

The subway stop is a catalyst for change at Eastern Market Square. The area around the subway entrance at Pennsylvania Avenue and Seventh Street is constantly active with pedestrian movement (fig. 9.12). There is a wall around the escalators descending to the station and an enclosure for the elevator. The Metro system is planning to install large canopies over city subway entrances to protect the escalators and passengers from precipitation. The proposed design is a curved roof of glass and steel, which will provide an attractive feature to enhance the image of this public space.

Eastern Market Square is a relatively large space, currently surrounded

Fig. 9.12. Eastern Market
Square at Metro station with
South Eastern Branch Public
Library

by two- to four-story buildings that are too low to effectively define it.
The architectural frame is composed of an unrelated series of buildings
that do not provide a coherent perimeter. A large commercial building
anchors the southeast corner, but the northwest corner is poorly defined
by the junior high school. The block adjacent to the school on the east, a
preserved group of nineteenth-century row houses, is the most coherent.
There is a similar group of nineteenth-century buildings south of the
subway stop. Facing the park on Seventh Street is a branch public library,
and on the opposite side, on Ninth Street, is the handsome Richardsonian church converted to condominiums in 1991. None of these buildings
are visually obtrusive; they just do not relate well to one another.

Since the architectural frame is so incoherent, the landscape design
needs to be strong in order to shape this urban space. But it is primarily
two-dimensional in form, without elements to form spaces. The subway
canopy on the south side will provide a prominent feature there. A similar element or memorial on the north side would help to provide identity
for that part of the park.

Eastern Market Square should become a much more significant public space. The junior high school and the public library are traditional
civic uses that bring constant vitality to this location. The subway station
is a contemporary civic use and source of a steady flow of pedestrians.
The park has been recommended as a location for future memorials in
the National Capital Planning Commission master plan. All of the elements are there; what is lacking is the vision to make this square an important civic place.

Folger Park

Folger Park is one of several open spaces on Capitol Hill that serves
its constituent neighborhood. It is a residential square of about two acres
with an elementary school on its east side. The adjacent block to the south

was cleared in 1964, but it remains largely undeveloped as a green open space. The Capitol South Metro station is located at First and D streets, one block west of the park.

The Nineteenth Century

Folger Park was not part of L'Enfant's formal plan for the city. It first appears on Ellicott's plan as a rectangular area between Second and Third streets created by the jog of D Street. North Carolina Avenue intercepts the park on the diagonal. Although the park is only three blocks from Capitol Square, large buildings block vistas to the Capitol; the only vista is northeast to Seward Square.

The area remained largely undeveloped until after the Civil War, when modest two- and three-story row houses were built on the north and west sides. A map showing the park in 1904 shows a large livery on the north side, a hospital on the south side, and Brent School on the east side (see fig. 9.9).

The massive, five-story Providence Hospital, built in 1866, occupied the entire south side of Folger Park. It was founded by the Sisters of Charity in 1861 when a group of physicians asked them to open a civilian hospital to replace the Washington Infirmary on Judiciary Square, which had been confiscated by the Union Army.[46] They first rented a large frame house at the corner of Second and D streets and eventually acquired the entire block. The hospital, mostly a series of tents, served both military and civilians during the Civil War. Congress appropriated funds in 1866 and 1868 to construct a five-story brick Second Empire–style hospital with Italianate features. With three pavilions and wings extending south, the structure had a formal institutional presence on the park. By the end of the century it was the largest hospital in the city, a center for training doctors and nurses, and the locus of many innovations in health and social care. In 1904 the building was enlarged to four times its original capacity according to a design by the local architect Waddy B. Wood. The original building was remodeled in the unlikely Mission style, with stucco covering the brick facades and an incongruous 175-foot bell tower (fig. 9.13).

Folger Park was so heavily utilized by patients, staff, and visitors to the hospital that it was referred to as Providence Hospital Square.[47] The presence of the hospital certainly contributed to development of the area, but the Office of Public Buildings and Grounds had difficulty securing funds for park improvements. Finally, in 1884 it was improved with grading, gravel walks, grass, lampposts, and a row of shade trees inside a post-and-chain perimeter fence.[48]

The following year, President Chester Arthur named the park after the late secretary of the treasury Charles J. Folger.[49] This fostered additional improvements, including extensive planting of evergreens and shade trees. A drawing in the 1886 annual report of the Office of Public Buildings and Grounds shows the park design as a floral pattern of curved paths forming four ovals and two teardrops around a central fountain.[50] In spite of the elegant design, Chiefs of Engineers John M. Wilson and Oswald H. Ernst complained: "In Folger and Stanton parks the flower-beds are still subject to the ravages of dogs, while fowls, which are permitted to run at large in the vicinity, do considerable damage to the lawns."[51]

The Twentieth Century

Under the auspices of the Works Progress Administration in 1936, the park was redesigned to conform to the simpler formal style introduced by the Senate Park Commission for the Mall. The new scheme featured a cross-axis of flower beds surrounded by an oval path. The central focus was a square flagstone plaza with an octagonal pool. On the east and west sides were large bench and fountain structures of cast concrete with a mosaic depicting the park plan (fig. 9.14).

Providence Hospital had deteriorated by 1947, and the trustees abandoned the site, selling it to the federal government for use by the Commerce Department. The entire structure was demolished in 1964, and the site was placed under the jurisdiction of the Architect of the Capitol. Proposals in 1965 and 1977 to convert it to a congressional parking lot were thwarted by neighborhood opposition.[52]

The present-day Folger Park is a handsome landscaped setting, albeit somewhat poorly maintained. It retains the flanking east and west fountains with rose beds on the cross-axis around a central octagonal flower bed. The perimeter sidewalks are brick, while the internal paths are asphalt. There are evergreen hedges around the perimeter and lampposts along the internal pathways. There are shade trees around the perimeter and in the center and dense foliage behind the concrete fountains. Since the subway runs under the square, there are large, steel ventilation grates in the northwest corner.

The most dramatic change to the architectural frame of the square in the last fifty years was the removal of the dominant hospital structure along the south side. The original Brent School on the east side was replaced in 1968 by a two-story, modern, concrete elementary school. Because it is set back from Third Street behind a parking lot, it does not contribute to the definition of the park space. The nineteenth-century row houses remain on the west side (see fig. 9.10). On the north side, three new town houses are being added next to the Washington Sports Club.

L'ENFANT'S LEGACY

Commentary

Pressures to redevelop the Folger Park area will persist because of its proximity to Capitol Square and the nearby Metro station. The most vulnerable space is the open urban block south of the park (which needs a name like Providence Park), under the jurisdiction of the Architect of the Capitol. It is a very large, open space that is inadequately utilized by the community, although both Brent Elementary School and St. Peter's School on the east side utilize it for physical education and recess. It would certainly be feasible to build an underground parking garage there without seriously compromising the block's recreational amenity. Part of it could also be occupied by a small institution or a medium-density residential development. The neighborhood and the schools will continue to have difficulty justifying the need for such a large open space when there is a handsome park on the adjacent urban block. But many more deleterious scenarios are possible, such as the construction of a large federal office building.

Folger Park and its counterpart are ideal residential parks in very proximate location to Capitol Square. The two schools are civic buildings that give these parks an identity and a functional purpose, as at Stanton Square and Garfield Park. The sports club and lodge afford semipublic uses. Both of these green places are surrounded by a variety of residences. Together, these uses contribute to the formation of an active democratic place with a vital civic role.

Marion Park

Marion Park is located on Capitol Hill between Fourth and Sixth streets, which also define the eastern and western edges of Seward and Stanton squares to the north. South Carolina Avenue intercepts the park at the southwest and northeast corners, whereas E Street divides and jogs around the park to define its north and south sides. The long, narrow park has an area of about 1.5 acres. There are vistas along South Caro-

Fig. 9.14. Folger Park, view to west

lina Avenue southwest to Garfield Park and northeast to Eastern Market Square.

The Nineteenth Century

Marion Park is not indicated as an open space on L'Enfant's plan, and it is difficult to identify on Ellicott's plan. It is clearly shown on Boschke's 1861 survey map as a two-block-long open space surrounded by several houses.[53] It was acquired by the federal government in 1791 as part of the street rights of way. The neighborhood around this square developed somewhat earlier than other parts of Capitol Hill owing to its proximity to the Marine Barracks and the Navy Yard.

In the 1872 survey of federal properties Marion Park was listed as two triangles bisected by South Carolina Avenue.[54] Four years later it was identified as a rectangle bisected by Fifth Street and called Long Square. In 1885 and 1886 the reservation was improved with trees, shrubs, gas lamps, and gravel or brick paths. The 1886 annual report of the Office of Public Buildings and Grounds states, "The reservation is now quite ornamental to this section of the city, which private enterprise is rapidly improving."[55]

In 1887 the park began to assume memorial status when it was named Marion Park in honor of the Revolutionary War hero Francis Marion, nicknamed the "Swamp Fox."[56] It is appropriate that this South Carolina soldier would be honored by a park located on South Carolina Avenue. The same year, a large iron vase from Rawlins Park was located in the middle of a small traffic circle along Fifth Street; in the ensuing decades it was filled with tropical and flowering plants.

In the 1880s and 1890s the Marion Park neighborhood developed rapidly with three-story row houses, many extant. A map showing the park in 1904 also shows a police station on the north side, built in 1851. The park design was a series of curvilinear paths running between Fourth and Sixth streets around the traffic circle at Fifth Street (see fig. 9.9).

The Twentieth Century

The park and neighborhood remained largely unchanged until the 1960s, when the green space was slightly narrowed on the north side to widen E Street. When Fifth Street, the traffic circle, and the vase were removed in 1963, the park was redesigned.[57] Straight new brick paths were installed, defining large grass panels and a playground at the west end.

A 1999 map shows a Metropolitan Police First District substation on the north side and the Pleasant Lane Baptist Church opposite it on the south side (see fig. 9.10). A group of row houses on the south side, across Fifth Street from the church, has been replaced by a three-story apartment building. There is a continuous hedge along the north side and a low metal picket fence around the east end, with a separate, taller metal picket fence around the playground. There are lampposts along the paths, two drinking fountains, wood-slat benches, and assorted small trees.

Commentary

Marion Park is reasonably well defined by the surrounding buildings. However, the park design has little landscape character and lacks focus (fig. 9.15). The design was better before the circle and vase were removed.

Perhaps this central feature should be reinstituted, with a fountain dedicated to Francis Marion, which would provide both a park amenity and an identifying feature.

Marion Park today is a quiet neighborhood open space used moderately by the surrounding residents. The century-old church offers an expression of religious freedom, whereas the century-old police substation is a continuing benign presence that gives the community assurances of safety and security. The well-appointed and well-used playground is a good indicator of a strong neighborhood. Once again the continuous rows of residences express the abiding presence of citizens in a free society.

Garfield Park

Garfield Park has had a difficult history of fragmentation; it is now but a remnant of the original. It is an oddly shaped open space now essentially defined by Third Street on the east side, F Street on the north, and the Dwight D. Eisenhower Freeway, or Southwest/Southeast Freeway, on the south. The latter is a horrendous elevated intrusion into this neighborhood that seriously compromises the value of this park as a neighborhood open space. One of the original seventeen reservations purchased by the federal government, Garfield Park is now owned and maintained by the District of Columbia.

The Nineteenth Century

On L'Enfant's 1791 plan the location of Garfield Park was prominently featured as a large open space where South Carolina, Virginia, and New Jersey avenues converged. It was designated by the letter E and described as "five grand fountains intended with a constant spout of water."[58] This was possible because of the site's many springs, which drained into the canal along South Capitol Street, defining the western edge of the park. The shape of Garfield Park was regularized on Ellicott's plan with a turning basin added on the canal. His plan also extended North Carolina Avenue to the park.

Some historians have speculated that L'Enfant intended this site for the city's civic center, with the city hall or a cathedral on a great plaza.[59] Both the L'Enfant and Ellicott plans show a large symmetrical building on axis with G Street, with a plaza fronting the canal. Although none of these proposals reached fruition, this site has always attracted the attention of city planners.

The area developed slowly, with only one prominent structure occupying a full urban block on the north side. This was Duddington, the 1793 mansion of Daniel Carroll, one of Capitol Hill's largest early landowners. Duddington was the first important house built in the city after its urban plan was established. Carroll was partially responsible for L'Enfant's dismissal: when he built his first house, in 1791, seven feet over the proposed line of New Jersey Avenue, L'Enfant had the walls razed, which resulted in Carroll's protesting to President Washington. The four-acre grounds of Duddington, along with many outbuildings, were enclosed by a brick wall.[60] The handsome Federal-style house was demolished in 1886 to make way for workmen's row houses.

Before the Civil War, citizens unsuccessfully petitioned Congress for funds to improve Garfield Park. It had been defaced by gravel quarries that left large open pits. Finally, in the 1880s, the Office of Public Buildings and Grounds initiated improvements, with extensive grading and removal of the roadways through the park, principally New Jersey Avenue. In 1884 Chief of Engineers Wilson said that he intended to make this park one of the city's principal resorts.[61]

By 1887 considerable funds had been expended to plant two thousand deciduous and evergreen trees and shrubs in the park.[62] This induced the development of housing in the neighborhood for middle- and working-class residents employed at the Navy Yard, the Marine Barracks, or on the waterfront. In 1901 the Josiah Dent Elementary School was built to serve the children of the neighborhood on the north side of the park, at South Carolina Avenue and Second Street. This handsome brick, two-story, symmetrical building featured stone cornices and a projecting entrance bay.

The Office of Public Buildings and Grounds continued to make significant improvements to Garfield Park, planting thousands of trees, laying extensive pathways, and assigning a day and a night watchman for maintenance and protection. Because of the adjacent railroad tracks along Virginia Avenue, the park was constantly abused by unwarranted activities. In 1892 the Grand Army of the Republic camped there for its reunion, further damaging the landscape.[63]

The Twentieth Century

A series of land transfers commencing in 1903 reduced Garfield Park to about one-quarter of its original twenty-four-acre area. The Pennsylvania Railroad Company was granted the area south of Virginia Avenue, which necessitated regrading the adjacent park land and streets for tracks. The lodge at the intersection of New Jersey and Virginia avenues was demolished, and a new one was built in the northeast corner of the park. At the same time, the District of Columbia government built a large sewer through the middle of the park, causing further disruption.[64] In 1905 Congress allocated six acres of the park between New Jersey Avenue and South Capitol Street for construction of a Capitol power plant.

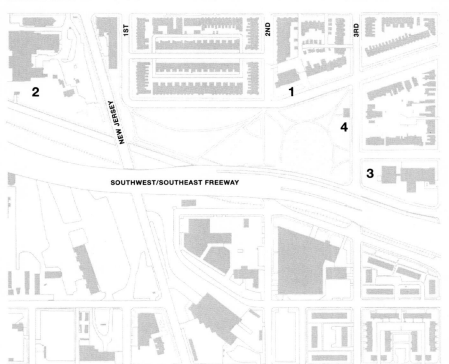

Fig. 9.16. Garfield Park in 1999

In the first decades of the twentieth century Garfield Park and its surroundings prospered as citizens constantly used it for recreation. A large elliptical area was developed on the east side to be used for weekly band concerts during the summer. Additional facilities were provided for tennis, croquet, basketball, quoits, and volleyball. Children played in sandboxes, wading pools, and a playhouse. A large lodge built in 1916 provided toilets for visitors and storage for maintenance equipment.[65]

A 1956 map from Baist's real estate atlas shows Garfield Park with the Potomac, Baltimore and Washington Railroad running south of Virginia Avenue and tunneling underneath it at Second Street.[66] New Jersey Avenue separates the U.S. Capitol Power House from the park. An extensive system of curvilinear paths focuses on an elliptical area at Second Street. The Josiah Dent Elementary School (for white children) is on South Carolina Avenue, and the J. R. Giddings Public School (for black children) is east of the park, on G Street.

By now the park had been reduced to 9.3 acres. One final reduction occurred in 1969, when more than two acres on the south side were allocated to the District of Columbia for construction of the Southwest/Southeast Freeway. Second Street through the park was removed at this time. Although basketball courts were placed beneath the freeway to mitigate the loss of park land, nothing could alleviate the ominous intrusion of this eight-lane, elevated superstructure. The constant noise from cars and trucks destroys any sense of tranquility in the park, and the off ramp at Third Street brings additional traffic to the area (fig. 9.16).

The architectural frame of Garfield Park on the north and east sides is formed by late-nineteenth-century, three-story row houses. The Gid-

**Fig. 9.17. Garfield Park, view
to south with freeway**

dings School is now being used as a large, private fitness center. When the
number of school-age children decreased in the 1940s, the Dent School
was converted to a school maintenance shop. In 1980 it was returned to
its original school use as the private Capitol Hill Day School.[67] The park
is used for physical activity and recess by children from this school.

The area of the present Garfield Park is 7.12 acres, with some sports
facilities and a playground all managed by the District of Columbia Department of Recreation. In the narrow section west of First Street, SE, is
a day-care center for the House of Representatives. Some early features,
including brick pathways, benches, lighting, a lodge, and a large number
of mature shade trees, continue to exist (fig. 9.17).

Commentary

Garfield Park is a place that began with great intentions, which were
eroded by a series of ad hoc decisions that resulted in a compromised
city park. L'Enfant's intentions for the park were ignored despite its
prominent location three blocks south of the Capitol along South Capitol Street. The park was gradually reduced as parcels were appropriated
for other purposes. Now this awkwardly shaped park is bordered by the
intrusive railroad and the elevated expressway. Since the park is not really needed by this neighborhood, which already has Folger and Marion
parks as commodious green open spaces, perhaps it should be used for
the Capitol parking garage once intended for the empty block south of
Folger Park.

Extending the Legacy, the National Capital Planning Commission's
visionary plan for the twenty-first century, outlines an ambitious proposal for South Capitol Street.[68] The Southwest/Southeast Freeway would
be removed and the freight rail lines relocated south of the Anacostia
River. The original city street system would be reconstituted, eliminating
Garfield Park and making new blocks available for redevelopment. The
South Capitol Street corridor would become a new gateway into the city
with a new bridge over the Anacostia River.

In 2004 the city announced its Anacostia Waterfront Initiative, a large-scale plan to redevelop both sides of the Anacostia River in the next twenty-five years. Although Garfield Park is outside the boundary of this plan, it could become one of the focal open spaces of this renewed southeast neighborhood. Redevelopment of the Navy Yard and the Southeast Federal Center, south of M Street, will bring thousands of new jobs, making housing in this area highly desirable. More residents using the park would lead to demands for physical improvements, better maintenance, and additional amenities. Perhaps even L'Enfant's vision of using the springs to create water spouts would eventually come to fruition.

CHAPTER TEN

NEW PUBLIC PLACES

Union Station Plaza, Freedom Plaza and Pershing Park,
Market Square

THE POLIS IS, first of all, the place which a certain group of people recognize that they inhabit in common. Any individual or any group within that place may wish that others did not live there, but they recognize that removing them would, in one way or another, exact too high a price. Given that fact, politics emerges as the set of practices which enable these people to dwell together in this place.

DANIEL KEMMIS, *Community and Politics of Place*

The spaces presented in this chapter are categorized as new spaces. Freedom Plaza and Market Square were shown on L'Enfant's plan but not developed until recently into their present form. Union Station Plaza and Pershing Park are clearly new spaces brought about by the development of the city. Each of the new spaces discussed in this chapter reflects a metamorphosis in the role of urban open spaces in the City of Washington and consequent changes in their design form. Union Station Plaza relates directly to the needs of rail transit and serves as a monumental gateway to the city. Freedom Plaza is a new, highly visible pubic forum for demonstrations and public programs. The adjacent Pershing Park serves as a refuge for the nearby government work force. Market Square is primarily a memorial to the U.S. Navy, although it also serves as a gathering place for visitors.

Additional public open spaces certainly will be created as the city evolves and develops. They may be spaces shown on the L'Enfant or the Ellicott plan that have never reached fruition, or they may be the spatial focus of private or government development projects. Like the public spaces discussed in this chapter, these future places will also have new roles in the city. Their form will respond to current and future realities of their urban context. Their activity programs will reflect an era of widespread electronic communication and computer information networks. They will also address the new urban lifestyles of a vastly multicultural constituency. And one hopes that they will also embody new expressive forms of the democratic ideals manifested by their historic precedents.

Union Station Plaza

During the heyday of rail travel in the 1930s, train stations in the United States were great public meeting places. Rail travel was democratic, enabling all people to freely travel throughout the country in one another's company. The train station symbolized this freedom and gave spatial form to the act of departing and arriving. Union Station served this role in the nation's capital, where the Capitol itself was in full view from the station's plaza.

Union Station Plaza, also known as Columbus Plaza, is the grand forecourt for Union Station, the monumental railroad gateway to the nation's capital. It is a large, semicircular plaza along Massachusetts Avenue at the nexus of Louisiana Avenue, Delaware Avenue, and First Street, NE. In the center is a sculptural fountain dedicated to Christopher Columbus. Vistas are available along Delaware Avenue to the Capitol, along Louisiana Avenue to the Mall, and along Massachusetts Avenue to Stanton Square.

On L'Enfant's plan there is an articulated open space at the intersection of Delaware Avenue, Massachusetts Avenue, and an unnamed avenue extending to the northeast. Ellicott straightened this portion of Massachusetts Avenue, eliminated the unnamed avenue, and changed the open space to a small triangle.

Because of its uneven topography, this tract remained undeveloped until the mid-nineteenth century, when the Baltimore and Ohio Railroad laid its tracks from the north along Delaware Avenue to the station on North Capitol Street. The Baltimore and Potomac Railroad laid its tracks from the south across the Mall and built a grand station at Sixth Street and Constitution Avenue, NW. The railroads and their concomitant noise, dirt, and smoke discouraged further development of this area of the city.

One goal of the Senate Park Commission was to consolidate the railroads at a single location in one station (see chapter 3). This unified station, with the rail yard behind it, would be located north of the Capitol. To reach the station without crossing the Mall, the southern set of tracks would be tunneled underground. Upon arrival, passengers would emerge from the station and view the majestic Capitol to the south. The McMillan Plan showed the location of a new station but not the open-space connections to the Mall that would be developed later.

Daniel Burnham, a member of the Senate Park Commission, was selected as the architect of the new train station. His design inspiration was the imperial baths of Rome, monumental buildings with grand spaces for large crowds. The five-part classical massing of Union Station has a high central pavilion with three arches flanked by smaller pavilions with arches, linked to each other by arcades. The six Ionic columns across the facade support allegorical figures sculpted by Louis Saint-Gaudens. Burnham conceived this railroad station as a gateway to the capital city based on the Roman triumphal arch. It was constructed between 1903 and 1908 of white Vermont granite cladding over a steel and masonry structure.[1]

The articulated facade of Union Station serves well as an introduction to the interior spatial organization. The primary, barrel-vaulted waiting space has a longitudinal axis connected to the flanking ticket lobby and dining hall. Five short barrel vaults perpendicular to the main facade lead to the train concourse, a dramatic skylit shed with thirty-four train platforms. During the peak of rail travel in the 1930s this station annually served 10.9 million passengers arriving on 285 trains daily.[2] This ensemble of spaces with their imperial scale and elegant details continues to be impressive within a city replete with impressive interior places.

New Public Places

Fig. 10.1. Columbus Fountain at Union Station Plaza

As railroad travel waned in the United States after World War II, Union Station deteriorated in use and physical condition. In 1976 it suffered a poorly conceived renovation as a visitor center for the nation's bicentennial celebration. Then in 1988 it was converted to a successful specialty shopping center with more than one hundred stores, restaurants, and cinemas located on three levels.[3] The building continues to function as a multimodal transit center with an Amtrak station and a Metro station. Renovation of the station made the area both a tourist and an employee destination with greatly increased pedestrian traffic.

The attenuated facade provides a magnificent background for the adjacent Union Station Plaza with its semicircular white marble Columbus Fountain, completed in 1912 by Lorado Z. Taft. At the center is a tall shaft supporting a globe and the prow of a ship serving as a pedestal for the heroic figure of Christopher Columbus, facing the Capitol. On the sides are figures representing the Old World and the New World flanked by lions (fig. 10.1). Three tall flagpoles behind the fountain symbolize the explorer's three ships.[4] A replica of the Liberty Bell was added in 1981 in honor of the bicentennial.

Columbus Fountain is at the center of a large plaza designed by Burnham that serves pedestrian traffic and public gatherings related to the train station. It is composed of paving and planting beds of shrubs and seasonal flowers. At both ends are large circular fountain bowls of green granite with handsome stepped bases surrounded by balustrades of white granite.[5] As this is a place of movement, there are no benches. The perimeter of the plaza is illuminated by single and double globe light fixtures (fig. 10.2).

Vehicular traffic surrounds the plaza, with roads radiating outward like spokes in a wheel. Eight oval and circular traffic islands were created around the perimeter of the plaza to separate automobiles on the inside from streetcars on the outside. When trolleys ceased running, the tracks were removed and the islands joined together to separate Massachusetts Avenue traffic from station traffic. A continuous hedge along the inner semicircular driveway defines the plaza.

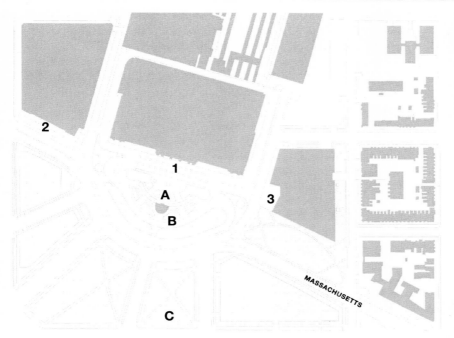

1 : Union Station
2 : U.S. Post Office and Postal Museum
3 : Federal Judiciary Building

A : Union Station Plaza
B : Columbus Fountain
C : Capitol Plaza

Fig. 10.2. Union Station Plaza in 1999

Shortly after the fountain and plaza were completed, the United States entered World War I. To accommodate the large increase in the number of government workers, the Union Plaza Dormitories were built on four blocks opposite Union Station. The complex included rooms for two thousand women workers, a dining hall, an infirmary, a lounge, and a post office. The handsome temporary buildings were not completed until the war was over, when they were used as municipal offices until they were demolished in 1930.[6]

The federal government had acquired twelve urban blocks between Union Station and the Capitol in 1910 for expansion of the Capitol grounds. Louisiana Avenue was added to connect the station to the Mall. Finally, in 1931–32 the area was developed as Capitol Plaza, a series of landscaped blocks with terraces and an underground parking garage for the Senate (see chapter 4). Unfortunately, three of these blocks adjacent to the station continue to be used as surface parking lots, which are visually detrimental to this magnificent setting.

Burnham envisioned neoclassical buildings flanking Union Station to establish a dignified context. The U.S. Post Office Building, erected west of the station, utilizing the same white granite and many of the same architectural features, was designed by his successor firm in 1914. It was converted to the National Postal Museum and city post office in 1992.[7] To the east is the Federal Judiciary Building (1992), designed by Edward Larabee Barnes. It abides by the contextual precedent of the station, albeit in a modified postmodern interpretation. However, the light gray granite used on the facades does not relate well to this context. The building has a stark glass entry wall leading to a large skylit atrium.[8]

Union Station and Union Station Plaza are among Washington's most successful manifestations of the City Beautiful urban design movement. As the first constructed elements of the McMillan Plan, they set the stan-

New Public Places   225

dard for Beaux-Arts architecture that was to follow in this city. Unfortunately, the spaces connecting the plaza to the Mall remain incomplete in their realization, with great future potential for improvement.

Union Station has a prominent location with direct connections to the Capitol and the Mall, a recognition of the power of the railroads at the turn of the century and their role in making America a prosperous country. The grandeur and scale of the station's design symbolized the economic, and therefore political, power of the Baltimore and Ohio Railroad and the Pennsylvania Railroad. This was a place of fervent activity used widely by the traveling public, as well as by dignitaries such as presidents and kings. It is perhaps fitting that this magnificent building has been converted to a specialty shopping center, signifying that commerce is the ruling force in this country's culture at the beginning of the twenty-first century. It is once again a place of fervent activity, albeit mostly focused on entertainment and consumerism rather than the necessary purpose of travel.

Freedom Plaza and Pershing Park

Most American cities have a centrally located civic center, an urban place surrounded by public buildings such as the city hall, the courthouse, the public library, theaters, and museums. This urban design concept derives from European precedents and the New England village green, which included churches and civic buildings. L'Enfant had envisioned Washington's civic center along South Capitol Street, now the location of Garfield Park, although this was not clearly specified on his 1791 plan. Instead, Judiciary Square became the first civic center formed by the city hall and courthouses. In 1908 the city hall moved to what is now Freedom Plaza (formerly Western Plaza), but other municipal buildings remained at Judiciary Square and its extension, John Marshall Park. The public library was located at Mount Vernon Square, and theaters and museums were scattered throughout the city.

In many regards Washington's civic center is now at Freedom Plaza. The city hall, the Willard Hotel, the National Theater, and now the Ronald Reagan Building and International Trade Center all face onto this public place. The McMillan Plan proposed this location as a municipal center with the city hall as the first constructed element. The plaza itself affords a community gathering place for events and demonstrations in a very prominent location on Pennsylvania Avenue near the White House. The eight-lane Pennsylvania Avenue is routed along the south side, with two-lane E Street along the north side.

The primary attraction of Freedom Plaza, in addition to its location, is the vista straight down Pennsylvania Avenue to the Capitol. In the other direction there is a partial vista to the White House, now obscured by the Treasury Building. This plaza was two triangles until 1980, when it was reformed as a rectangle. Thus it is included in this chapter as a new public space.

The adjacent Pershing Park to the west is indeed a new open space. It was a developed urban block until it was cleared of buildings to create a forecourt for the Department of Commerce building in 1926. Both Freedom Plaza and Pershing Park were completely redesigned at the same time as part of the Pennsylvania Avenue Development Plan. Thus they are discussed together in this section.

The Nineteenth Century

L'Enfant included three open spaces along this segment of Pennsylvania Avenue. At the eastern end, where the Washington Canal turned south, there was a square intended for a church. In the middle, opposite the market, there was a square, labeled E, intended to have fountains. At the western end was a long open space straddling Pennsylvania Avenue. It was centered on a wide street to the south lining up with a long vista down the Potomac River. Ellicott moved this square one block to the west on his 1792 plan and eliminated the wide street.

This segment of Pennsylvania Avenue was one of the primary maintained streets during the first half of the nineteenth century because it was a frequently used route between the Capitol and the White House. Thus it developed as a dense commercial route with hotels, dwellings, stores, and taverns. The avenue sliced the future Freedom Plaza into two triangles, which were first improved as open spaces in 1853. Pennsylvania Avenue was destroyed by heavy military traffic throughout the Civil War. Streetcar tracks were installed in 1862 to save the roadbed from uncontrolled streetcar movement. Ten years later the avenue was paved with wooden blocks, which cut down the noise but they soon rotted and had to be replaced with new paving.[9]

The first of six National Theater buildings to face the open space that became Freedom Plaza on the north side was built in 1835, financed by W. W. Corcoran. It burned soon after, along with seven adjacent houses. The second, third, and fourth theater buildings burned after five, eleven, and twelve years, respectively. The fifth building, which lasted from 1885 to 1922, was a grand five-story structure seating nineteen hundred patrons. The present National Theater building followed the design of its predecessor but with a steel structure. Because of turmoil over racial segregation and the decline in the popularity of stage productions, the building was converted to a motion picture theater in 1948.[10] It was restored as a professional theater in the 1970s with a continuing series of high-quality theatrical performances.

The Willard Hotel has always occupied the northwest corner of Fourteenth Street and Pennsylvania Avenue across from what is now Pershing Park. Long associated with famous personages, the hotel originated in 1818 in seven two-and-one-half-story row houses owned by Benjamin Ogle Tayloe. In 1847 Henry Willard assumed management of the hotel, and in 1850 he enlarged it, adding two stories and a uniform Greek Revival facade that gave it the appearance of a single building turning the corner onto Fourteenth Street. The heyday of this hotel was during the Civil War, when it was utilized constantly for meetings between politicians and the military, including Generals Hooker, Grant, McDowell, Pope, Burnside, and Meade.[11] Willard's son inherited the hotel. He demolished it in 1900 and subsequently constructed a grand, twelve-story Beaux-Arts hotel in three sections extending to F Street, designed by Henry Janeway Hardenbergh. The Willard was a prominent hostelry until after World War II, when the entire area deteriorated. After considerable effort by his-

Fig. 10.3. Willard Hotel, view to northwest, 1976. Library of Congress, Prints and Photographs Division, HABS No. DC 542-4

toric preservationists and the Pennsylvania Avenue Development Corporation, the hotel was restored to its original opulent splendor in 1986. A sympathetic office building addition set back from the street on the west side was built at the same time. The Willard Hotel continues to be one of Washington's most elegant hotels, as well as one of the most popular meeting places in the city (fig. 10.3).

All the sites in this area have been rebuilt several times. The original two- and three-story commercial buildings and theaters were replaced by much larger and taller office buildings for newspapers, railroads, and hotels before the turn of the century. The advantage of proximity to the node of political power around the White House induced these changes in building scale and density, as shown on a map of the area in 1903 (fig. 10.4).

When the Office of Public Buildings and Grounds surveyed the public reservations in 1884, the two triangular parks that are now Freedom Plaza were largely unimproved except for large trees and heavy iron-rail fences.[12] Another survey in 1894 revealed complete improvement of the northern triangle, reservation number 33. It was raised several feet above the street, surrounded by a granite curb, and planted with evergreen and deciduous shrubs. A large iron flower vase and a triangular fountain basin were connected to the streets by asphalt pathways. A note in the 1894 annual report of the Office of Public Buildings and Grounds states that this reservation had been selected as the location for a statue

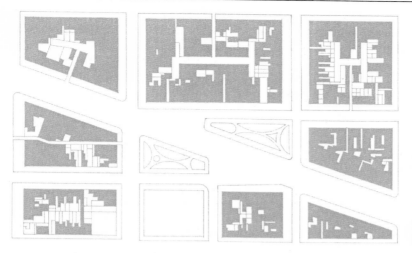

Fig. 10.4. Freedom Plaza and Pershing Park in 1903

of General Philip Sheridan.[13] But the plans were changed, and a bronze equestrian statue of Brigadier General Count Casimir Pulaski, sculpted by Kasimiriez Chodzinski, was installed there on a granite pedestal in 1910.[14] Pulaski was a Polish leader who fought with the Americans in the Revolutionary War. In 1914 the park was redesigned with wide paths lined with benches connecting the ornamental vase in the west corner with the Pulaski statue on the east side.[15]

The Twentieth Century

The McMillan Plan of 1902 proposed that the area bounded by Fifteenth Street, B Street, and Pennsylvania Avenue be devoted to buildings for the city government, including an armory, an auditorium, a new market, and other municipal buildings (see chapter 3).[16] The future Federal Triangle was notorious for its crowded living conditions and criminal population, earning it the nickname "Murder Bay."

The first element of this scheme to be built, in 1908, was the District Building (city hall), at the southeast corner of Fourteenth and E streets, facing north. This five-story, neoclassical structure of white marble on a gray granite base was designed by the Philadelphia firm of Cope and Stewardson in a grand Beaux-Arts style. Originally housing the District of Columbia commissioners, presently it is used by the mayor and the city council. The District Building is now the only municipal element in this location, an out-of-place reminder of the ongoing struggle between the city and federal governments.

The District Building, renamed the John A. Wilson Building in 1994, became the city hall once again in 2001. When it deteriorated in the 1990s, the city turned it over to a developer to renovate, enlarge, and lease to the federal government for twenty years. The city government in the meantime moved to an office building on the east side of Judiciary Square. As the renovation project by the local architects Shalom Baranes Associates was nearing completion, the city council recognized the desirability of being in the original location and negotiated to reoccupy it.[17] It is indeed good and proper that the city hall is once again on the country's main street facing Freedom Plaza.

The southern triangle, reservation number 32, was given to the District of Columbia in 1904 to become a forecourt for the new District Building when a section of E Street was closed. A bronze portrait statue of Alexander "Boss" Shepherd was placed here in 1909, and it became known as Shepherd Park.[18] Later moved to Fourteenth Street and Pennsylvania Avenue and then to a city maintenance facility, the statue is scheduled to be relocated to the front of city hall.[19] This, the first outdoor statue in the city dedicated to a native son, was paid for with funds raised by citizens grateful for his efforts to improve the city's infrastructure when he was director of the Board of Public Works from 1871 to 1874.

The Department of Commerce building as originally designed extended into the urban block to the north; as constructed it stopped at E Street. The urban block to the north became a public reservation cleared of buildings in 1930, including row houses, a hotel, a theater, an armory, and an opera house.[20] The open space was finally landscaped in the 1960s as part of Ladybird Johnson's city beautification program.[21]

Reservation number 33 officially became Pulaski Park in 1954. A new diagonal street was cut through the area from Fourteenth to Thirteenth Street to improve through traffic as the automobile became the primary form of transit. This left a series of traffic islands, which were redesigned in 1960 with new flowering shrubs and ground cover.[22]

President John F. Kennedy noted the tawdry condition of Pennsylvania Avenue during his inaugural parade in January 1961 and vowed to have it redeveloped (see chapter 1). This led to a 1964 master plan by Skidmore, Owings and Merrill proposing a monumental "National Square" at Fifteenth Street to solve two urban design problems, the fragmented series of open spaces in this location along Pennsylvania Avenue and the lack of an arrival space at the White House owing in part to the intervening Treasury Building. The proposed square would be a large paved space with a White House gate, a grand fountain, and a raised belvedere on the north side to expose more of the Treasury Building (fig. 10.5).[23] Measuring 800 feet by 900 feet, it would have an area slightly smaller than that of the Place de la Concorde in Paris. Pennsylvania Avenue would terminate at the plaza, while E and Fourteenth streets would pass underneath, leading to a parking garage. According to the President's Council on Pennsylvania Avenue, this would be "the first truly urban, truly national, square in the United States to serve visitors, shoppers, newspapermen, businessmen and seekers of culture and entertainment."[24]

This important proposal was met with much negative criticism. The plaza was considered to be overscaled and pretentious, and it was later termed "Nixon's Red Square." It was said that the huge paved area would be inhospitable in the summer and would significantly alter traffic patterns. Most important, it would have required the demolition of historic buildings on two urban blocks, including the Willard Hotel, the National Theater, and the National Press Club building. The U.S. Commission of Fine Arts rejected the scheme for these reasons. The dialogue and compromise regarding this plan effectively demonstrated the role of democracy in urban design matters.

The hidden intention behind the "National Square" proposal was to create the American equivalent of Red Square in Moscow or Tiananmen Square in Bejing. These vast paved spaces in Russia and China, without

Fig. 10.5. Rendering of National Square looking south (1964). Courtesy of Skidmore, Owings and Merrill

pedestrian amenities, are utilized to demonstrate to the people and the world the power of those countries. The United States has no need for this kind of space since the ensemble of Capitol Square, the National Mall, and the White House grounds eloquently expresses American democratic ideals.

The Pennsylvania Avenue Development Corporation (PADC) was created in 1972 and charged with overseeing development of the avenue through a combination of public and private initiatives. A 1974 PADC plan proposed retaining the existing configuration of Western Plaza (now Freedom Plaza) but enhancing its landscape quality.[25] Subsequently the two triangular spaces were reformed into a rectangle, much as L'Enfant originally envisioned.

The Philadelphia firm of Venturi and Rauch and the landscape architect George Patton were retained in 1977 to create a bold design for the new Western Plaza. The plaza was to be raised above the street to create a miniature version of L'Enfant's plan. The geometry of streets was depicted in the paving, and there were small replicas of the White House and Capitol. To give the space a monumental vertical emphasis, two towering marble pylons would asymmetrically frame a view to the White House grounds.[26] The pylons were considered bold symbols of federal power in front of the city hall and were rejected by then Mayor Marion Barry Jr. and the PADC board. The public liked the wooden mock-ups of the miniature buildings, but they were rejected by authorities as "toys."[27] When the plaza was constructed in 1980, the only vertical emphasis was two flagpoles. Robert Venturi's intriguing idea of three levels of scale simultaneously perceivable in one place was not completely realized.

The long, narrow rectangle of Western Plaza as completed is raised above the adjacent streets with connecting ramps and stairs. L'Enfant's map of central Washington is depicted with different colors of granite and grass, and there are engraved quotations about the city. At the east end is a street-level circular space landscaped with pin oaks and rose

Fig. 10.6. Freedom Plaza, view east to the Capitol, in the distance

bushes and featuring the Pulaski statue. At the west end is a two-level pool with ornamental grasses. There are few benches or other pedestrian amenities (fig. 10.6).

The architectural frame on the north side of Western Plaza is made up of the J. W. Marriott Hotel, the restored National Theater, and a new office building for the National League of Cities. The hotel, with its mundane facade, is set back from the street to reveal the National Theater. On the east side of the plaza is a thirteen-story 1950s office building with a recent postmodern facade of scored masonry with arches, balconies, and a red tile roof. On the south side are the renovated John A. Wilson Building and the recent Reagan Building, a ten-story structure designed in 1988 by James Freed, of Pei Cobb Freed and Partners. On Pennsylvania Avenue a rotunda signals the pedestrian promenade to the main entrance at a grand circular plaza formed with the existing hemicycle of the Ariel Rios Building.[28]

The trapezoidal open space to the west was redesigned as Pershing Park in 1979 by the New York landscape architects M. Paul Friedberg and Jerome Lindsay. The program included an eating area, a skating rink, restrooms, a maintenance facility, and a memorial honoring World War I veterans and their leader General John A. Pershing. The designers modified the existing terrain, raised the west and south sides, and sunk the central pool and surrounded it with paved terraces. This buffered the park from noise on Fifteenth and E streets and opened it to Pennsylvania Avenue on the north. A grove of honey locusts with underplanting on the south and west reinforces the design concept. A raised pool area on the west side of the main pool houses a Zamboni ice machine and creates a water cascade. The landscaping was later enhanced with wild grasses, bulbs, and water plants. There is a variety of seating options: picnic tables, metal chairs, fiberglass benches around the trees, and the numerous steps and retaining walls (fig. 10.7). Modern lamps and a clear-domed concession stand complete the design elements. A bronze sculpture of a bald eagle perched on a globe atop a tall pedestal, honoring the centennial of the national bird, stands at the northwest corner (fig. 10.8).[29]

Fig. 10.7. Pershing Park
reflecting pool

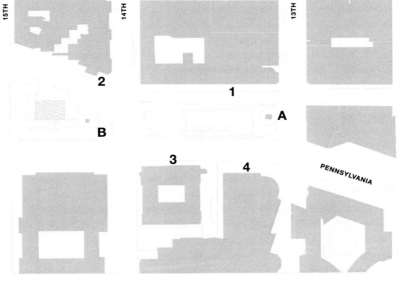

1 : National Theater
2 : Willard Hotel
3 : District Building
4 : Ronald Reagan Building
and International Trade
Center

A : Pulaski Statue in Freedom
Plaza

B : Pershing Memorial in
Pershing Park

Fig. 10.8. Freedom Plaza and
Pershing Park in 1999

The Pershing Memorial is located on its own raised plaza in the southeast corner, above maintenance facilities. On the east and south sides are inscribed high stone walls. The standing bronze portrait statue of General Pershing by Robert White faces west toward a simple marble bench.

Commentary

The combination of adjacent public spaces, one for large organized gatherings and the other for spontaneous social encounters, is an ideal urban arrangement. Both serve their respective purposes well, although the general public prefers Pershing Park to Freedom Plaza. They are designed to be quite different because they serve different purposes.

The architectural frame of Pershing Park retains its historical character, with the Department of Commerce building on the south side and the restored Washington and Willard hotels on the north side. Pershing Park's success is evidenced by the number of workers there at lunchtime on business days. This is the primary clientele, and there are small numbers of tourists seeking refuge at other times. It is a comfortable space for relaxation and rest, with many places to sit and eat. It is also secluded aurally and visually from traffic, with the refreshing sound of flowing water and picturesque seasonal colors provided by the flowering plants. Although this may be a successful new kind of urban park, it is in the wrong location. This is, after all, the entrance to the White House grounds, which requires a design more appropriate in form to the grandeur of this auspicious location.

On the other hand, Freedom Plaza is not considered pedestrian friendly. Some authorities are interested in making it more like Pershing Park, following the design principles advocated by William H. Whyte, such as abundant seating, shade, water features, food service, and visibility from the street.[30] Fred Kent, a consultant hired by the Downtown Business Improvement District, proposes adding carts selling food, books, and flowers or a farmers' market to the sidewalks around the raised plaza.[31] This scheme would not work well during the many large events held at Freedom Plaza.

Freedom Plaza is aptly named, for it has become Washington's primary local civic meeting place for thousands of people. It is used as the beginning or termination of parades from or to other urban public places, and it is the primary space for local cultural festivals, musical performances, and celebrations. The variety of these events is indeed surprising and impressive, including the Freedom Festival (25,000), an annual gay and lesbian pride party and concert; Equality Begins at Home, a 1999 gay rights rally; Justice for Janitors, a 1995 demonstration to organize office cleaners; Worldfest, an annual two-day international street festival; Elderfest (15,000), a celebration and festival for the elderly; Invent America!, an annual teen inventors' national competition; Nelson Mandela Welcome, a 1990 rally for the South African leader; and Colorectal Cancer Awareness, a 2003 colossal colon exhibit (fig. 10.9).[32] These events are in addition to the numerous protests against the war in Afghanistan and Iraq that have occurred since the terrorist attacks on 11 September 2001.

Freedom Plaza has become a very democratic place, the location of choice for local citizens to actively exercise their First Amendment rights of freedom of speech and assembly. Its role as a civic gathering place in the city is comparable to the role of the Mall as a national gathering place. Both are necessary for a well-functioning democratic society.

Market Square

Market Square, a collection of small open spaces and memorials located halfway between the Capitol and the White House, has always been an important location along Pennsylvania Avenue. On both the L'Enfant and Ellicott plans the area between Seventh and Ninth streets is shown as a large rectangular open space. On L'Enfant's plan it is also designated as the location for one of five grand fountains. For more than a century it was home to the primary market in the city.

Fig. 10.9. Colossal colon exhibit in Freedom Plaza, 2003

Market Square has recently been redeveloped with new buildings and
a new plaza. Today it is the site of the Navy Memorial and several smaller
memorials. There are grand vistas up and down Pennsylvania Avenue.
Eighth Street is the axis, with vistas north to the old Patent Office Building, now the National Portrait Gallery, and south to the National Archives
and Records Administration building.

The Nineteenth Century

The two urban blocks designated for the market were located between Market Square and the Washington Canal, which would be utilized for the delivery of goods. But the canal was not extended to this
location until 1815, and the turning basin shown on early plans was never
built. Garbage dumped into the canal became a major noxious, unsani-
tary nuisance. A large eyesore, the stagnant canal was a constant source of
frustration for merchants and politicians. Yet little was done to improve
this situation until after the Civil War.

The first public market in the District of Columbia was built at the
corner of Seventh Street and Pennsylvania Avenue in 1802, designed by
James Hoban and Clotworth Stevens.[33] Over the years it expanded, with
many additions, to fill two urban blocks. Center Market was privately
funded with a congressional charter, allowing its construction on federal
land.

The area became the focus of early commercial activity, with all contiguous urban blocks densely developed, as shown on the Boschke survey map of 1861 (see fig. 1.3). As the canal became dysfunctional, Seventh
Street was opened south to the docks on the Potomac River. It also served
as a primary route north to farms in Maryland. The small triangle of land
on the north side of Pennsylvania Avenue became the first public reservation in this area that was improved as a park, in the 1850s.[34]

During the era of territorial government Pennsylvania Avenue was
paved with wooden blocks around the streetcar tracks after sewer and
gas lines were placed. The decrepit canal was placed in a sewer and cov-

ered with B Street, now known as Constitution Avenue. This eliminated a huge nuisance from this area and enabled vehicular and pedestrian access to all sides of the market.

The market building itself became increasingly dilapidated through decades of use. It was finally demolished and replaced with a new building designed by Adolph Cluss in 1872.[35] The three-hundred-foot-long brick structure was acclaimed as the largest market building in the country. It was added to in the 1880s to accommodate more than one thousand vegetable, meat, and fish stalls. Along B Street, NW, there was space for three hundred farm wagons for deliveries and direct sales. On Pennsylvania Avenue there were two prominent entrances with corner towers and elaborate brick ornamentation (fig. 10.10). The market was razed in 1931 to build the National Archives.

In 1884 two additional, small federal reservations straddling Ninth Street were improved. The trapezoid on the west side was fenced and paved with trees and shrubs planted around a cast-iron basin. The triangle on the east side was fenced and planted with deciduous trees.[36] The statue of General John A. Rawlins was placed here in 1889, its fourth location. The trapezoidal reservation north of Pennsylvania Avenue was subsequently also fenced and planted with deciduous trees. In 1894 it was further improved with paths connecting two large vases, ornamental trees and shrubs, and a low stone plinth.[37] A bronze equestrian statue on a monumental red granite pedestal of General Winfield Scott Hancock, sponsored by the federal government, was placed in the center of the park two years later. General Hancock was a hero of both the Mexican and Civil wars.[38]

East of the Hancock statue, two small parklets were created in the gap between Seventh Street and the bank buildings on the blocks north and south of C Street. The south parklet featured the Temperance Fountain (c. 1880), intended to provide fresh drinking water to quench thirst in lieu of alcoholic drinks. The unusual fountain, donated by Henry Cogswell, a California dentist, is a square temple form with four granite columns that

L'ENFANT'S LEGACY

support a canopy with a bronze water crane on top. The north parklet was a circular planting bed that in 1909 became the site for a memorial honoring Dr. Benjamin F. Stephenson, founder of the Union veterans' organization the Grand Army of the Republic, which sponsored the memorial. The granite base and obelisk have symbolic bronze figures on three sides and a medallion portrait of Dr. Stephenson.[39] Both memorials are poignant examples of symbolic freedom of speech.

The Twentieth Century

The new market reinforced this location on Pennsylvania Avenue as a commercial hub served by city streetcars from all four directions. Several small stores located opposite the market grew to become major department stores. Saks Fifth Avenue was founded in 1867 by Isidore and Andrew Saks as a small store at the corner of Seventh Street. The Boston Dry Goods Shop, founded in 1880, later grew into Woodward and Lothrop, a major Washington, D.C., department store chain. S. Kann and Sons grew into a major store encompassing several large buildings and the entire block between Seventh and Eighth streets.[40]

The 1902 McMillan Plan proposed sweeping changes to the area south of Pennsylvania Avenue now known as the Federal Triangle, constructed throughout the 1930s. The trapezoidal park west of Ninth Street was eliminated when the Justice Department building was constructed. Center Market was demolished to create a site for the National Archives building. The existing triangular park merged with this site, and the Rawlins statue was returned to Rawlins Park, where it belonged. In 1965 the northwest corner of the National Archives site was landscaped as a setting for the simple, inscribed white marble slab dedicated to Franklin Delano Roosevelt. The forecourt of the National Archives has two rectangular pools set in patterned paving.

A second set of sweeping changes occurred in this area in the 1970s as the PADC revitalized the area north of the Federal Triangle. Prior to this, population migration to the suburbs resulted in a commercial decline that caused the large stores to close. The area deteriorated in physical quality and pedestrian activity.

The overall design concept for redeveloping Market Square was to merge all the landscaped islands with their adjacent urban blocks. Construction of the Metro system necessitated closing Market Place between Seventh and Ninth streets and a block of Eighth Street. The triangular park with the Hancock statue merged with the newly configured urban block. The subway station was located there, with escalators north of the statue. The two parklets to the east merged with their adjacent blocks, and C Street was closed to create a pedestrian mall. The resulting new space is full of planters, benches, and trees set within ornamental paving. In the process, the locations of the Temperance Fountain and the Stephenson Memorial were transposed (fig. 10.11).

The oldest buildings on the east side of Market Square represent the nineteenth-century commercial scale of the area. The narrow facade of the so-called Apex Building (now the Sears Company), with two prominent turrets, faces Seventh Street. This rusticated stone building started as the Saint Marc Hotel in the mid-1860s and was then converted to the Central National Bank in 1887, when the turrets were added. On the north

1: National Archives and Records Administrations Building
2: Market Square Building

A: Hancock Statue
B: Stephenson Memorial
C: Temperance Fountain
D: Navy Memorial

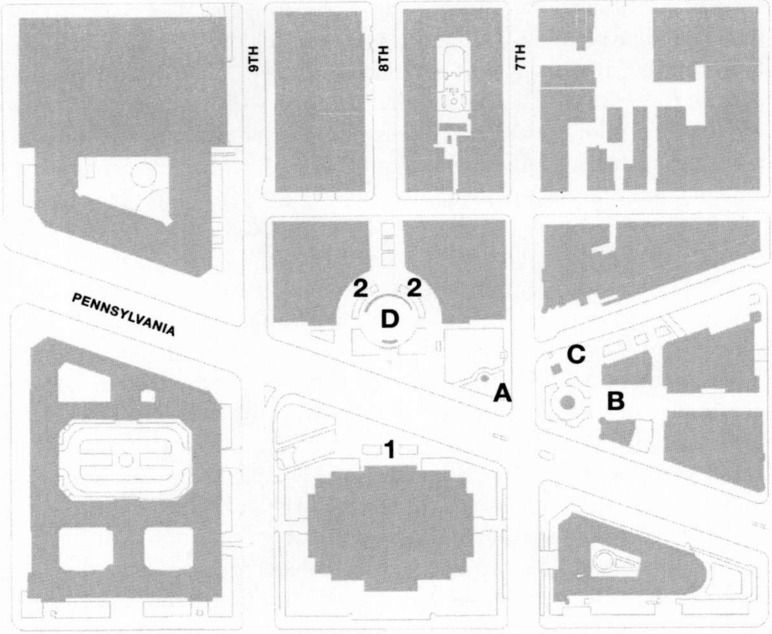

Fig. 10.11. Market Square in 1999

side of C Street is the National Bank of Washington, in continuous use as a bank since 1889.

The Justice Department building (1931–34) is a major element of the Federal Triangle that complies with its Beaux-Arts context but also alludes to modernism. The adjacent National Archives on the Eighth Street axis, designed by John Russell Pope in 1935, is a temple form with different neoclassical facades facing Pennsylvania Avenue and the Mall.[41] Symbolizing its iconic role, the building is taller than the others in the Federal Triangle and has Corinthian porticoes on all four sides. The elevated Constitution Avenue entry leads to a half-domed room in which the primary documents of the nation are displayed. The Pennsylvania Avenue entry leads to vaults and reading rooms holding additional historical records.

The Market Square buildings, completed in 1990, form a new commercial complex providing the context for the Navy Memorial and a small urban park, while shaping the vista north to the old Patent Office Building. The two buildings serve their place-making role well by forming a hemicycle space whose south facade is the National Archives. Thus, the space reaches across the avenue and links the federal precinct to the commercial precinct, the monumental city to downtown. The new buildings are simultaneously a foreground along the avenue and a background for the Navy Memorial (fig. 10.12).

The twin Market Square buildings designed by Hartman-Cox Architects address Pennsylvania Avenue and the Federal Triangle with a monumental curved peristyle of five-story Doric columns of limestone atop a three-story rusticated base supporting a one-story entablature. Eight stories of offices above ground-floor stores are topped by four stories of stepped apartments with balconies and terraces affording splendid views up and down the avenue. The facades transition from the monumental

Fig. 10.12. Market Square
with Navy Memorial, view to
north. Library of Congress,
Prints and Photographs Division, HABS No. DC 617-1,
photo by John McWilliams

to the commercial context on Seventh, Ninth, and D streets with buff-colored brick pilasters between paired windows.[42]

The Navy Memorial, designed by Conklin Rossant Architects of New York and completed in 1987, is a nontraditional memorial—a place for gatherings and personal contemplation. The design features a map of the world's land masses and oceans depicted in the paving of the circular space, with Washington, D.C., at the center. The memorial was funded by the U.S. Navy Memorial Foundation. A bronze statue of a lone sailor is the only vertical element. The circular space is formed by raised fountains along Pennsylvania Avenue with cascades circling the entire space. Two low hemicycle walls hold bronze bas-reliefs depicting naval battles, and two large flagpoles complete the composition. A visitors' center was opened in the east building of Market Square in 1989.

The park on the Seventh Street side, containing the statue of General Hancock, was redesigned to fit into the new context. The subway escalators and elevator are in a lawn area, and a raised planting bed along Pennsylvania Avenue defines a space for the statue.

Commentary

Eighth Street is the only cross-axis intersecting Pennsylvania Avenue between the Mall and the constituent city. On L'Enfant's plan the axis extended between the national church on the north and a naval itinerary column at the Potomac River on the south. Presently this axis extends from Mount Vernon Square on the north, through the National Portrait Gallery and the National Archives, to the Hirshhorn Museum on the south side of the Mall. Urban designers have worked to preserve this axis, as seen in the design for Market Square that engages the axis and forms a new public space along it.

The design of Market Square and the Navy Memorial makes certain allusions to other places in the capital city. The hemicycle form relates to the hemicycle of the Federal Triangle and the new World War II Memorial. The incised map relates directly to Freedom Plaza. Fountains are featured in many memorials and plazas in the city. Lastly, the Navy Memorial follows the design precedent of the Vietnam Memorial, an abstract composition that is open to interpretation.

Market Square is a welcome feature along the grand avenue of bureaucratic buildings. Visitors come to see the Navy Memorial, whereas others enjoy the sound of water and pedestrian amenities. The subway stop and retail stores help generate a constant flow of activity. It is a popular place that begins to emulate the hustle and bustle of the original market square. An important reason for its public success is the many places to sit and rest on benches, lawns, stairs, and low walls. The Navy Memorial is a very urbane place for general public gathering or events such as summer band concerts.

The architecture critic Benjamin Forgey claims that Market Square is a good open space because it is quintessentially urban, has diversity, is purposely inviting, and has human scale. "The daunting challenge is to extend Market Square's influence—the underlying principles, not the forms—to the design of many other major and minor places in the old downtown. If we can do that, we will without question construct one of the great cities on the Earth. If we cannot, well, the existence of this singular place is not small consolation."[43]

The Navy Memorial is dedicated to the thousands of men and women who have served in the U.S. Navy throughout two centuries. The rationale for such a monument in the capital city is self-evident. Indirectly, such a memorial relates to democratic ideals since the navy is one of the protectors of the nation and the ideals it represents. Market Square as an open space also expresses our democratic ideals, for it enables citizens and visitors to freely inhabit a public place along the nation's most symbolic avenue.

CONCLUSION

The Evolution of the Roles of Public Spaces in Washington, D.C., L'Enfant's Legacy

> WITHIN THE DENSE PRESS of the built fabric the greatest luxury of all is empty space. Whether it is used for the spectacle of pomp or for play, the open frame is politically charged; the activities encompassed, freighted with consequence. Only here can a representative proportion of the populace mass to make its mood known at a glance.
>
> SPIRO KOSTOF, *The City Assembled*

The Evolution of the Roles of Public Spaces in Washington, D.C.

Public open spaces in Washington, D.C., have many roles or purposes. First and foremost they express the rights of citizens, enabling them to exercise their political freedom. Public spaces by definition are social spaces where citizens freely associate with one another at formal events or in informal encounters. The functional role or activity program is often strongly influenced by uses in the surrounding buildings that bring people to the area. Part of the functional role is traffic circulation since roads converge at open spaces, requiring orientation for navigation. There is also the design role, to bring formal order to a city plan by creating spatial focal points. Balancing these roles through urban design and planning is the goal. This book analyzes these roles of public space, using the evolution of Washington, D.C., as the case study.

The primary open spaces of the federal precinct symbolize and express the democratic ideals of the nation and the American political process. The Mall in Washington is America's "front lawn," the place where its highest ideals of freedom, equality, and civil rights are daily expressed through many forms of informal public activity and formal events. It is a place of many memorials that commemorate historic events or persons that have significantly contributed to furthering America's democratic ideals. Capitol Square and the federal buildings are the places where public policy is enacted and laws are made, representing the supreme authority of law in a democratic form of government and the role of citizens in shaping legislation through elected representatives. The White House and its grounds are also symbolic, the residence of an elected citizen who is the leader of the country. The adjacent Lafayette Square is a place where citizens meet to express their opinions regarding government policies to the president, utilizing their right to freedom of speech.

The commercial and institutional squares and circles of Washington express democratic ideals in several ways. The churches, clubs, and organizations that face several such public spaces represent our constitutional freedoms of religion and association. Most of these spaces are surrounded by buildings that accommodate a variety of entities, all expressing Americans' freedom to conduct commerce and own private property. In most of these public open spaces are monuments or memorials sponsored by civic associations and supported by the federal government. They often honor individuals who have been instrumental in preserving America's political freedoms through military leadership.

The many residential squares and circles, located primarily on Capitol Hill, also express democratic ideals. Houses standing side by side along the streets bound the open space and represent the common bond of citizenship in a democracy and the common responsibility to ensure its continuity. Often there are churches or schools among these houses, locales where one can worship freely or be educated about democracy. The open space itself provides opportunity for free assembly, to express public opinion or to participate in events. Military memorials in these settings are an infringement upon their domestic tranquility.

The social role is closely related to the political role, for it is through public encounters that we exercise our political and spatial rights. Individuals develop a sense of community in public spaces, recognizing their common human bonds and collective aspirations. Through these engagements they also participate in the evolving physical quality of these spaces, changes in their design. Various groups and authorities compete for control of public spaces as territorial enclaves to serve their intentions. Engaging in political processes enables the community to articulate its intentions and to develop commitment to the longevity of these places. It is in the public spaces that we recognize our role as citizens in a democratic republic and give it free expression.

Frontage on a public open space accords an entity social, political, and economic prestige. It is a privileged location in the city, an easily identifiable spatial locus. Historically, institutions such as churches or clubs seeking to enhance their stature would locate on the square or circle. The same was true of residents, as evidenced in the histories of public spaces in previous chapters noting the important persons who lived there. Now, law firms, lobby groups, restaurants, and stores seek these locations for their economic prestige, a prominent address with high visibility. Real estate developers readily understand that locations on a square or circle have high market potential.

The sociologist Nathan Glazer believes that we are in a state of confusion regarding our purpose for inhabiting the public realm of the city, which necessitates a reconsideration of the role of public space.[1] While the historical role was social and political, the contemporary role is one of commerce and entertainment. How should we use these spaces in the future, and what form should they take?

As a contemporary culture, we still need to have public places where we can develop a sense of community, a relationship to a larger social entity. The city is where we can develop our identity as individuals, where we can establish our social relationships. Now the shared rules of social order have been challenged by greater cultural heterogeneity. Diverse cultures have different notions about public social behavior. This can lead to misunderstanding and confrontation, which in turn can lead to fear and segregation. As Glazer has stated, "There is always a fear of disorder when great crowds gather, but the decline in the power of common rules and in the homogeneity of the population inevitably increases those fears."[2] Now the fear of terrorism adds to the state of confusion.

The functional roles of public space in Washington have evolved for over two centuries. In the early city virtually all of the open spaces, excepting those in the federal precinct, were residential settings. Lack of transportation required people to live near their place of employment, sometimes in the same structure. All the squares on Capitol Hill continue to fulfill this residential role, as does Logan Circle. Farragut, McPherson, Franklin, and Rawlins parks primarily serve office functions for the private sector and the federal government. Judiciary Square, with its courthouses, has a primary governmental role. Mount Vernon Square has a multiuse institutional function dominated by the new convention center. Scott, Thomas, Dupont, and Washington circles are primarily commercial places with some secondary institutional uses in the form of churches, embassies, and a hospital. Functions in surrounding buildings bring people to each open space. This context of uses influences the program of activities they require for active participation.

Recreation has always been a basic functional role of all urban space, providing contact with nature in as many forms as possible. This was particularly necessary in the hot, humid nineteenth-century summers of Washington, before the advent of building air conditioning. In his 1900 annual report Chief of Engineers Theodore Bingham states, "They are the breathing spaces of a large city, and are used more by the poorer people in their daily life than are the large parks. Here children and nurses congregate, and here during the long hot summer those who can not leave the city go for a breath of fresh air or to find such a breeze as may be stirring and unable to penetrate the interior of the heated houses."[3] Thus, he says, the parks must be utilitarian, with fountains for refreshment and open plantings to allow breezes. As cities become denser in the current century, contact with nature will become more valuable for the health and happiness of the inhabitants. Fortunately, the City of Washington has an abundance of urban open spaces for this purpose.

There have been tremendous changes during the last two centuries in how downtown Washington, D.C., functions. The daytime population of employees has proportionately increased, whereas the nighttime population has decreased because many people live in outlying suburbs. Thus, all the open spaces in Washington except the residential squares are now used differently than they were at the end of the nineteenth century. The peak use is during lunchtime, and there is sporadic use throughout the business day. At night and on the weekends these spaces are deserted unless there are affiliated uses such as museums, hotels, theaters, restaurants, or shops. Encouraging these uses to locate on the squares would bring extended life to these public places. The best long-term solution is to incorporate residential uses around each space and establish a constituent population. As an example, this is occurring at McPherson Square with conversion of the historic United Mine Workers Building to condominiums.

Increasing use of the city's open spaces will require new programs and/or increased amenities. Successful open spaces in other cities—such as Pioneer Square in Portland, Oregon, or Copley Square in Boston, Massachusetts—sponsor a continuous program of concerts, festivals, and events to attract a wide spectrum of both the resident population and visitors. The Downtown DC Business Improvement District now sponsors noontime concerts on weekdays during the summer. This program could be extended to the weekends, along with events such as art fairs or exhibits. This would necessitate changes in the design form of the parks from passive to active spaces. Additional amenities in the form of fountains, sculptures, or memorials would also attract more users. At Bryant Park in New York City high-speed Internet access is being beamed into the eight-acre open space.[4] Anyone with an Ethernet card in his or her laptop computer can be online for free, enabling users to escape the confines of the office or library. As the Internet has exponentially expanded our communication and information opportunities, the wireless network enables Web browsing under the open sky in public spaces.

The multifarious functional roles of several old and new public spaces in Washington are indicative of future multiuse directions and accompanying changes in design forms. Eastern Market Square integrates a subway station with public and commercial uses. Union Station Plaza combines rail transit with shopping and entertainment. Market Square is an innovative combination of a memorial space with offices and residences. Pershing Square serves as a respite for office workers, while the adjacent Freedom Plaza is a contemporary public forum opposite the city hall.

Vehicular and pedestrian circulation is an important functional role. At the circles and squares of Washington the roads and paths form a complex nexus. In recent history the development of roads for automobiles was given preference over the development of paths for pedestrians. Control of automobile traffic is a constant necessity in the contemporary city. One of the best urban design achievements in Washington is the limitation on parking facilities under the parks. This National Park Service restriction, first imposed at Farragut Square, has been extended to all other federal reservations, and so far it has been upheld. The exhaust vents required for underground parking garages deteriorate air quality; the entrance and exit ramps are unsightly and hamper pedestrian access to the parks. Inducing people to use public transit rather than private automobiles has done much to protect the quality of the city in general and these open spaces in particular.

Public spaces serve an urban design role by providing relief from the density of the city. To be perceived as memorable, spaces must be defined by their architectural context or landscape design. One measure of the degree of spatial definition is the ratio of building height to the width of the open space, measured from wall to wall. The Renaissance architect Leon Battista Alberti, in his *Ten Books on Architecture,* recommended that this ratio be between 1:3 and 1:6.[5] At Farragut Square the ratios are approximately 1:3.2 and 1:4.6 in the short and long directions, respectively. These are within Alberti's recommendations and confirm our spatial perception that Farragut Square is a highly defined urban space. In comparison, the ratios at Stanton Square are approximately 1:1.4 and 1:2.1 in the short and long directions, respectively. These are outside Alberti's recommendations and confirm our own visual impression. The smaller squares with higher buildings are more highly defined than the residential squares with lower buildings. These spatial characteristics contribute to our mental images and experiences of these places.

The problem with spatial definition at all of Washington's squares and circles is the many street interruptions, resulting in short fragments of building walls that do not yield coherent spaces. This is more evident at the circular spaces. Another aspect of spatial definition is disruptions in the architectural frame, instances where buildings do not abide by the prevailing street wall in height or location. These problems can be countered by either a coherent architectural frame or a strong landscape design.

There are many urban design precedents for achieving spatial definition in public spaces with a coherent architectural frame. The Place des Vosges, Place Vendôme, and the Place des Victoires in Paris are the ideal models, with identical building facades on all sides in rectangular and circular spaces, achieved through monarchical control. Although this ideal is not possible in a democratic society, maintaining consistent street walls, building heights, and facade treatments through zoning and design review is possible. American examples of strong spatial definition are Rittenhouse Square in Philadelphia and Union Square in San Francisco, which have buildings from several eras. Monument Circle in Indianapolis is a highly defined circular space with quadrants of consistent curved facades of different design.

Landscape design can be effectively utilized to foster spatial definition within the park or plaza to compensate for problems with the architectural frame. The ground form can be shaped and reinforced by berms and terraces; low walls or fences can articulate the park from its context. At the ground level, hedges and shrubs are effective in defining small-scale spaces for walking or sitting. Evergreen trees are strong masses for shaping space, whereas deciduous trees create overhead canopies. Photographs of Washington's green open spaces in the nineteenth century illustrate this effective use of landscape elements to produce strong spatial definitions.

L'Enfant's Legacy

Washington, D.C., is fortunate to have a generous number of varied public open spaces that relate the built urban context to its natural setting. This ensemble of spaces and buildings is the hallmark that gives Washington a unique image of beauty and grandeur befitting the national capital. In this regard it compares most favorably with Paris, a city of grand, tree-lined boulevards and magnificent parks. As one drives and walks around the District of Columbia, the great wealth of avenues and parks is everywhere apparent.

L'Enfant's legacy to the nation's capital is the system of public open spaces, an invaluable resource for present and future residents and visitors to use and enjoy. Yet these public spaces face contemporary challenges from continued urban development and changing political and/ or social contexts. The changes in the physical form of public spaces as a result of politics, economics, design, engineering, and use have often resulted in serious compromises to their original purpose. To understand this evolutionary process and to learn from it in order to better shape the future of these places is one of the purposes of this book.

Many of the open spaces have been eroded in the name of traffic engineering; wider roads and altered configurations make pedestrian access to the parks difficult. Several of the circles have roads underneath them, adding noise and pollution to the setting. Although the land for the roads is owned by the federal government, they are improved and maintained by the District of Columbia, making these intrusions readily possible without federal oversight or intervention. At Logan Circle the citizens of the neighborhood prevailed, causing the excessive road widths to be reduced and the park reconfigured to its original size and shape. More of this kind of citizen activism needs to occur; the parks belong to the people, who should act to preserve their integrity and usefulness.

Many of Washington's public spaces have also suffered from undesirable commercial-development incursions. The building height is not a problem since this is limited by the 1910 Act to Regulate the Height of Buildings, and the spaces are large enough not to be shaded by tall buildings.[6] In fact, the density is good, for it brings more people to the area to potentially populate the spaces. The problem is architectural design, large banal repetitive facades of office buildings that detract from the visual quality of the parks or are incompatible with contextual historic buildings. To make matters worse, historic structures are often removed to make way for new buildings, or only their facades are preserved. New commercial buildings should both contribute to the spatial definition of a public space and provide public amenities such as stores or arcades.

This leads to the ultimate question: What is to become of Washington's public spaces in the future? As the legacy of the L'Enfant Plan, should they not be actively protected and preserved by the city and the nation? As early as 1868 Chief of Engineers Nathaniel Michler succinctly stated, "While adding so much to the appearance of the city, they at the same time largely contribute to the health, pleasure and recreation of its inhabitants."[7] Yet, in the present era both residents and public officials often take them for granted.

This historical analysis has demonstrated that the legacy of open space has already been significantly compromised, and further deterioration is probable. Preservationists in Washington should pursue protection of these public places since the L'Enfant Plan is now on the National Register of Historic Places as both a national and local landmark. Congress, local public officials, and city residents should actively work to preserve and improve this legacy of public open spaces.

Most of the city's urban spaces have been under the stewardship of the National Park Service for many decades. Some are well cared for and maintained; others have languished for lack of improvement or shrunk due to ill-considered traffic engineering. All of these spaces need a consistent program of maintenance and incremental improvement.

Neighborhood associations and citizen groups must continually work with the National Park Service to articulate the needs of the community for new park facilities or landscape improvements. The National Park Service has a vast number of public reservations in the city to maintain and improve, but a minimal budget. Active citizen groups can get things done by making their needs known through an improvement plan. These groups can also become proactive and raise their own funds through public-private partnerships. The recent improvement program at Meridian Hill Park is an excellent example of this cooperative effort.[8]

We live in an era when government is no longer able to provide all the public amenities that citizens need; corporate or foundation support must provide those not afforded by government. The Downtown DC Business Improvement District represents a 110-block area wherein landowners tax themselves to provide programs for safety, maintenance, marketing, streetscape improvements, transportation, and homeless services.[9] Working in conjunction with city agencies, they very effectively promote and improve the city's downtown to attract businesses and real estate investment. At Franklin Square a property owners' organization has provided funds for new lights, paths, and trees.

In 1997 the National Capital Planning Commission produced a comprehensive plan entitled *Extending the Legacy* to develop the monumental core of the city for the next fifty to one hundred years.[10] The primary objective was strengthening the open-space network of the monumental core. This would be accomplished by righting the wrongs of recent development related to expressways and railroads that have consumed precious land south of the Mall, separating it from the waterfront. Enhanced and continuous access to the waterfronts would add greatly to the system of open spaces and improve the vitality of pedestrian life in the city. In this respect the twenty-first-century plan is extending the legacy of previous visionary plans. However, the plan does little to integrate the other open-space system, the neighborhood parks and avenues, with the monumental core.

London, England, and Savannah, Georgia, are but two cities that have honored their legacy of public places through preservation of their networks of open spaces. The Mayfair and Bloomsbury sections of London have a multitude of green squares, many now surrounded by commercial and civic uses. Each one is superbly maintained and appointed with pedestrian amenities and historic markers. England's culture is different from Washington's, but Georgia's is similar. In Savannah the government restored each of its remaining twenty-one urban squares many years ago, and they have been maintained and actively used by residents and tourists alike. The squares and their historic architecture are the primary attraction in Savannah, the reason this city is a prominent tourist center.

Cultural changes regarding communication and information are occurring at a rapid pace. Technology is changing the physical and spatial structure of American cities much the same as the automobile changed our cities during the twentieth century. Some of these changes are already evident in the diminished use of public spaces for recreation and the increased use for illicit activity and crime. If our culture values the continued viability of public places, we need to consider their redesign for future use. Some redesign studies have been conducted in design studios at the University of Virginia School of Architecture.[11] Others have been undertaken by charette groups organized by the Washington, D.C., chapter of the American Institute of Architects, resulting in exhibitions and publications.[12] Both visionary and realistic design studies should be developed for each open space analyzed in this book.

In the words of the urban historian Spiro Kostof, "Public space as it is successively reshaped is an artifact of the collective passions that bind society: from civic protest or regimented ceremonies of consensus, to leisure pursued in an Arcadian idyll, or through the ritualized consumption of products and aestheticized environments. Even at its most trivial, the mere presence of a public realm is testimony to the insistence of our need periodically to rediscover the physical fact of community."[13] In many ways Washington, D.C., has historically set a high standard for expressing the nation's democratic ideals in the design of its public open spaces. The nation and city now need to make a commitment to continue this form of democratic realization into Washington's third century in order to honor and extend L'Enfant's legacy.

The federal government acquired the land area for avenues and streets in the new capital city from the original proprietors in exchange for city lots. These lands comprised rights of way from building line to building line for 20 avenues and 117 streets, more than 200 linear miles and 3,500 acres.[1] This area included the fifteen numbered squares and circles colored yellow on L'Enfant's plan located at critical avenue junctures. In addition, there were numerous oddly shaped pieces of land formed at the intersections between diagonal and orthogonal streets.

In 1791 the federal government purchased 541 acres in the newly laid out City of Washington from the original proprietors for use as federal reservations. Andrew Ellicott assigned a function to each of them, but not all developed as intended. This purchase was divided into seventeen parcels, called *reservations,* as listed below:

No. 1. Grounds of the President's House, Lafayette Square, and President's Park

No. 2. Grounds of the Mall and the Capitol, from First Street East to Fourteenth Street West

No. 3. Grounds for the Washington Monument south of Tiber Creek, between Fourteenth and Seventeenth streets

No. 4. Site for a university between Twenty-third and Twenty-fifth streets south of E Street on the Potomac River; currently the U.S. Navy Medical School

No. 5. Greenleaf Point at the juncture of the two rivers; now Fort McNair

No. 6. Intended as a market site at the juncture of New York and Virginia avenues; now part of the federal office precinct

No. 7. Market site between Seventh and Ninth streets on the Tiber Canal; used as a market until the 1930s, now the National Archives site

No. 8. Designated site for a national church between Seventh and Ninth streets and F and G streets; became the Patent Office Building site, now the site of the National Portrait Gallery and the National Museum of American Art

No. 9. Between Fourth and Fifth streets and D and G streets, possibly intended for the U.S. Supreme Court; now Judiciary Square

Nos. 10, 11, and 12. North of Pennsylvania Avenue, NW, between 2nd and 4½ streets, intended as bank and exchange sites; sold for private development by Congress in 1822

No. 13. Between Nineteenth Street East and the Anacostia River, B and G streets; intended for a hospital site, which it became along with the city jail site

No. 14. The U.S. Navy Yard on the Anacostia River south of M Street between Sixth and Ninth streets

Nos. 15 and 16. In the southeast quadrant between Fifth and Seventh streets and K and L streets; originally a market, now a playground

No. 17. Large tract called "town house square" along South Capitol Street[2]

In 1871 the U.S. Army Corps of Engineers Office of Public Buildings and Grounds surveyed all federal lands except military sites. The reservation list published in the 1872 annual report totaled ninety, an approximate area of 340 acres.[3] There was difficulty in enumerating all of the small triangles of land or parklets because of incomplete street improvements. Another survey, in 1884, listed 246 reservations—38 highly improved, 47 partially improved, and 161 vacant and unimproved—with an area of 408 acres.[4] This survey included a highly useful map with reservation numbers that did not correspond to the original 1791 numbers since many of those reservations had been for public buildings, not open spaces. An 1894 Army Corps of Engineers survey and map enumerated 301 reservations, which became the official park system of the city.[5]

Of concern in this study are the urbanized open spaces that presently exist within the area of the 1791 L'Enfant Plan. The extensive park lands along the Potomac and Anacostia Rivers, including Rock Creek Park, are not a part of this analysis. Other open spaces that have not been designed or developed, such as school or neighborhood playgrounds and traffic islands, also are not included. Hancock Park (number 3 on L'Enfant's plan), at the intersection of Maryland and Virginia avenues, is a vestigial space bordered by railroad tracks and a freeway ramp. Juarez Circle (number 4), at the intersection of Virginia and New Hampshire avenues, is a traffic circle underneath which the Whitehurst Freeway is tunneled. L'Enfant proposed that a naval column be located at Banneker Park, between Seventh and Tenth streets at the Washington Channel. Instead it has become a green space isolated from the city by the Southwest/Southeast Freeway. Barney Circle, at the southeast end of Pennsylvania Avenue, may be developed in the future as an eastern auto-oriented gateway.[6] Sheridan Circle and Meridian Hill Park have not been included since they are outside L'Enfant's original boundary for the city, now Florida Avenue.

This study began with a simple question: What happened to the open spaces designated on L'Enfant's plan for the city of Washington? L'Enfant numbered fifteen yellow squares on his 1791 plan, to be appropriated by each of the existing states for memorial use. Six have survived to the present.

This investigation led to a series of other questions. What happened to the other nine squares? Six were eliminated by Andrew Ellicott when he drew the official city map printed in 1792, and three never developed.

Ellicott neither numbered nor colored any of the squares. What happened to the unappropriated squares designated on L'Enfant's plan? There were at least thirteen of these squares, and all of them survive to the present. What happened to the three red public spaces on the plan? They are presently extant as Judiciary Square, John Marshall Park, and Garfield Park. Have there been other squares created since the 1791 plan? Only a few new urban spaces have been created since 1791. Rawlins Park was added by Andrew Ellicott; Franklin Square was created in the 1830s; Folger Park and Marion Park were created to serve their residential neighborhoods; Market Square and Freedom Plaza were redesigned with the redevelopment of Pennsylvania Avenue, NW, whereas Pershing Plaza was created anew; and Union Station Plaza was created when Union Station was built.

Table A.1 is an analysis of the public urban open spaces within the original planned area of Washington, D.C. comparing the 1791 L'Enfant Plan, the 1792 Ellicott Plan, the 1894 U.S. Army Corps of Engineers plan, and the 1998 American Automobile Association map.[7] They are grouped in categories of yellow, red, unappropriated, and new. Their general 1999 functional use is also designated.

From this analysis a list of significant urban open spaces in the City of Washington was developed for this study. This list is almost identical with the list of public reservations in the nomination of the L'Enfant Plan of the City of Washington, D.C., to the National Register of Historic Places.[8] East Potomac Park was deleted because it is not an urban park.

The historical maps illustrating the various public reservations were drawn utilizing data from Sanborn Company insurance maps.[9] The earliest maps were from 1888, but the first maps for outlying areas were from 1904. Baist and Company maps were analyzed for twentieth-century building uses and ground-plane configurations.[10] The 1999 maps for public reservations were drawn utilizing National Capital Planning Commission Geographic Information System data. Significant features on the maps have been updated to 2005.

Table A.1 Analysis of Washington, D.C., Urban Public Spaces

Public Space	Location	1999 use	1791 L'Enfant Plan	1792 Ellicott Plan	1894 Army Corps of Engineers Plan	1998 AAA Map	Reservation Number
Appropriated							
Yellow							
Undeveloped	Pennsylvania, 11th & 12th	n.a.	No. 1				
Mount Vernon Square	New York & Massachusetts	Square with old library	No. 2	x	x	x	8, 70–71, 175–76
Hancock Park	Maryland & Virginia	Urban park	No. 3	x	x	x	113
Juarez Circle	Virginia & New Hampshire	Traffic circle	No. 4	x		x	
Stanton Square	Massachusetts & Maryland	Residential square	No. 5	x	x	x	15
Undeveloped	Connecticut, 18th & 19th NW	n.a.	No. 6	x			
Undeveloped	Maryland & 14th NE	n.a.	No. 7				
Undeveloped	Delaware & Virginia	Expressway interchange	No. 8				
Thomas Circle	Vermont & Massachusetts	Monument circle	No. 9	x	x	x	65–67, 162
Undeveloped	Indiana, 3rd & 4th NE	n.a.	No. 10				
Undeveloped	South Capitol & P	n.a.	No. 11				
Undeveloped	Massachusetts & New Jersey	n.a.	No. 12	x	x	x	77
Undeveloped	Virginia & Potomac	Expressway interchange	No. 13	x	x		
Seward Square	Pennsylvania & North Carolina	Residential square	No. 14	x	x	x	38–43
Undeveloped	Rhode Island & 9th NW	n.a.	No. 15				
Red							
John Marshal Park	Pennsylvania & 4th NW	Urban park	Red			x	
Judiciary Square	D & F, 4th & 5th NW	Memorial square	Red	x	x	x	7
Garfield Park	Virginia & South Carolina	Residential park	Red	x	x	x	17

Unappropriated

Name	Location	Type				Pages
Eastern Market Square	Pennsylvania, 7th & 9th	Urban plaza	x	x	x	44–49
Washington Circle	Pennsylvania & New Hampshire	Circular urban place	x	x	x	25–27
Dupont Circle	Massachusetts & New Hampshire	Circular urban place	x	x	x	59–61
Scott Circle	Massachusetts & 16th NW	Monument circle	x	x	x	62–64
Logan Circle	Rhode Island & Vermont	Residential circle	x	x	x	152–54, 163–64
Farragut Square	Connecticut & K NW	Urban square	x	x	x	12
McPherson Square	Vermont & K NW	Urban square	x	x	x	11
Freedom Plaza	Pennsylvania & 14th NW	Urban plaza	x	x	x	32–33
Lincoln Square	Massachusetts & East Capitol	Residential square	B	x	x	14
Banneker Park	Washington Channel & 10th SE	Residential park (proposed naval column)	C	x		
Market Square	Pennsylvania, 7th & 9th NW	Urban plaza	x	x	x	35–36
Gompers-Burke Park	Massachusetts, 10th & 12th	Urban park	x		x	68–69
Barney Circle	Pennsylvania & Anacostia River	Traffic circle	x	x	x	55–56

New

Name	Location	Type				Pages
Pershing Park	E & 14th NW	Urban park			x	617
Rawlins Park	18th & 19th, E St NW	Urban park		x	x	13
Lansburgh Park	Delaware, I & M St SW	Residential park		x	x	
Folger Park	North Carolina, 2nd & 3rd SE	Residential park		x	x	16
Marion Park	E, 4th & 6th SE	Residential park		x	x	18
Franklin Square	H & I, 13th & 14th NW	Urban square			x	9
Union Station Plaza	Union Station	Urban plaza	x	x	x	334

NOTES

Introduction

Epigraph: Hannah Arendt, *The Human Condition* (Chicago: University of Chicago Press, 1958), 55.

1. Michael Webb, *The City Square* (New York: Whitney Library of Design, 1990), 29.

2. Alexis de Tocqueville, *Democracy in America,* trans. and ed. Harvey C. Mansfield and Delba Winthrop (Chicago: University of Chicago Press, 2000), 1:381.

3. John R. Vile, *A Companion to the United States Constitution and Its Amendments* (Westport, CT: Praeger, 1997), 127.

4. Richard Sennett, *The Fall of Public Man* (New York: Norton, 1974), 3, 4.

5. National Register of Historic Places, *L'Enfant Plan of the City of Washington, D.C.* (Washington, DC: National Park Service, 1997).

6. Quoted in Antony Jay, *The Oxford Dictionary of Political Quotations* (Oxford: Oxford University Press, 1996), 92.

Chapter 1. The L'Enfant Plan

Epigraph: Elizabeth S. Kite, *L'Enfant and Washington, 1791–1792* (Baltimore: Johns Hopkins Press, 1929), 34.

1. John W. Reps, *Washington on View: The Nation's Capitol since 1790* (Chapel Hill: University of North Carolina Press, 1991), 10.

2. Ibid., 1–2.

3. Saul K. Padover, ed., *Thomas Jefferson and the National Capital* (Washington, DC: Government Printing Office, 1946), 31.

4. Reps, *Washington on View,* 1–49.

5. Ibid., 2, 3.

6. In 1846 approximately one-third of the original District of Columbia was retroceded to the state of Virginia.

7. Constance McLaughlin Green, *Washington,* vol. 1, *Village and Capital, 1800–1878* (Princeton, NJ: Princeton University Press, 1962), 22.

8. Frederick Gutheim, *Worthy of the Nation* (Washington, DC: Smithsonian Institution Press, 1977), 19.

9. Ibid., 16.

10. L'Enfant may have consulted these city maps, but he also was inspired by his own experience of Paris and Versailles. He was also knowledgeable about the early American colonial capitals, such as Annapolis with its circles and diagonals, Williamsburg with its axes, and Savannah with its system of squares.

11. Padover, *Thomas Jefferson and the National Capital,* 59.

12. John W. Reps, *Tidewater Towns* (Williamsburg, VA: Colonial Williamsburg Foundation, 1972), 270.

13. Padover, *Thomas Jefferson and the National Capital*, 74.

14. Reps, *Washington on View*, 26.

15. Joseph R. Passonneau, *Washington through Two Centuries* (New York: Monacelli, 2004), 28.

16. Reps, *Washington on View*, 38.

17. Padover, *Thomas Jefferson and the National Capital*, 59.

18. Peter Nicolaisen, "Thomas Jefferson's Concept of the National Capital," in *Washington, D.C.: Interdisciplinary Approaches*, ed. Lothar Honnighausen and Andreas Flake (Tübingen: A. Francke Verlag, 1993), 115.

19. Reps, *Washington on View*, 28.

20. National Register of Historic Places, *L'Enfant Plan of the City of Washington, D.C.* (Washington, DC: National Park Service, 1997), sec. 8, pp. 11–12.

21. Peter Charles L'Enfant, *1791 Manuscript Plan for the City of Washington*, color facsimile (Washington, DC: U.S. Geological Survey, 1991).

22. Ibid.

23. Elbert Peets, "Washington as L'Enfant Intended It," in *On the Art of Designing Cities: Selected Essays of Elbert Peets*, ed. Paul D. Spreiregen (Cambridge, MA: MIT Press, 1968), 32.

24. Reps, *Washington on View*, 20.

25. Ibid., 7.

26. Elbert Peets, "The Background of L'Enfant's Plan," in Peets, *On the Art of Designing Cities*, 15.

27. Reps, *Washington on View*, 9.

28. Gutheim, *Worthy of the Nation*, 41.

29. Reps, *Washington on View*, 106.

30. John W. Reps, *Monumental Washington* (Princeton, NJ: Princeton University Press, 1967), 38.

31. Reps, *Washington on View*, 53.

32. James M. Goode, *Capital Losses* (Washington, DC: Smithsonian Institution Press, 1979), 142–43.

33. Green, *Washington*, 1:202.

34. Gutheim, *Worthy of the Nation*, 56.

35. Ibid., 68.

36. A[lbert] Boschke, *Topographical Map of the District of Columbia, Surveyed in the Years 1856–59* (Washington, DC: McClelland, Blanchard & Mohun, 1861).

37. Gutheim, *Worthy of the Nation*, 65.

38. Reps, *Washington on View*, 177.

39. Reps, *Monumental Washington*, 59.

40. Gutheim, *Worthy of the Nation*, 86.

41. Historic American Buildings Survey No. DC-668, *Plan of the City of Washington* (Washington, DC: National Park Service, 1993), 28 (hereafter HABS No. DC-668). For all HABS surveys, survey numbers rather than call numbers are referenced.

42. *Annual Report, Improvement and Care of the Public Buildings and Grounds in the District of Columbia, and Washington Aqueduct, O. E. Babcock, Colonel of Engineers, Bvt. Brig. General, U.S.A., Appendix HH, Annual Report of the Chief of Engineers for 1875* (Washington, DC: Government Printing Office, 1875), 4–5.

43. Gutheim, *Worthy of the Nation*, 90.

44. Ibid., 216–18.

45. HABS No. DC-668, 30.

46. Constance McLaughlin Green, *Washington*, vol. 2, *Capital City, 1879–1950* (Princeton, NJ: Princeton University Press, 1963), 281.

47. Gutheim, *Worthy of the Nation*, 241.

48. Ibid., 266.

49. Ibid., 314–15.

50. Daniel Patrick Moynihan, "Not Bad for a Century's Work," *Washington Post,* 23 November 1997, C7.

51. Maryann Haggerty, "Pennsylvania Ave. at the Finish Line," ibid., 30 March 1996, A1, A9.

52. Maryann Haggerty, "Momentum Is Building in Downtown Revival," ibid., 22 November 1998, A1, A20.

53. Marcy Gessel, "At 25, METRORAIL Still Overwhelmingly Popular," ibid., 29 March 2001, B5, B6.

54. Lyndsey Layton, "Crowds Could Derail Decades of Progress," ibid., 26 March 2001, A1, A12, A13.

55. Gutheim, *Worthy of the Nation,* 345.

56. National Capital Planning Commission, *Extending the Legacy* (Washington, DC, 1997), 5.

57. National Capital Planning Commission, *Memorials and Museums Master Plan* (Washington, DC, 2000).

58. National Capital Planning Commission, *Extending the Legacy,* 61.

59. National Capital Planning Commission, *Urban Design and Security Plan* (Washington, DC, 2002).

60. Roger K. Lewis, "The Use and Limits of Security Placebos," *Washington Post,* 24 August 2002, H5.

61. Reps, *Washington on View,* 5–6.

62. L'Enfant to Washington, 22 June 1791, in Kite, *L'Enfant and Washington,* 57.

63. L'Enfant, *1791 Manuscript Plan.*

64. Spiro Kostof, *The City Shaped* (Boston: Little, Brown, 1991), 99–101.

Chapter 2. Public Space and Democratic Ideals

Epigraph: Thomas Jefferson, *The Writings of Thomas Jefferson,* ed. H. A. Washington, vol. 8 (New York: Derby & Jackson, 1859), 5.

1. Hannah Arendt, *The Human Condition* (Chicago: University of Chicago Press, 1958), 22–78.

2. Stephen Carr, Mark Francis, Leanne G. Rivlin, and Andrew M. Stone, *Public Space* (Cambridge: Cambridge University Press, 1992), 45–46.

3. See ibid., 137–69.

4. *Congressional Record,* 44th Cong., 2nd sess., 23 February 1877, pp. 1877, 1876.

5. John R. Vile, *A Companion to the United States Constitution and Its Amendments* (Westport, CT: Praeger, 1997), 113–18.

6. *Annual Report, Director of Public Buildings and Public Parks of the National Capital, U. S. Grant III, Director, 1926* (Washington, DC: Government Printing Office, 1926), 33.

7. Alexis de Tocqueville, *Democracy in America,* trans. and ed. Harvey C. Mansfield and Delba Winthrop (Chicago: University of Chicago Press, 2000), 1:226.

8. *Annual Report . . . 1926,* 32–33.

9. *Annual Report, Improvement and Care of the Public Buildings and Grounds, and Care and Maintenance of the Washington Monument, in the District of Columbia, John M. Wilson, Lieut. Col. Corps of Engineers, Colonel, U.S.A.; and Oswald H. Ernst, Major, Corps of Engineers, Colonel, U.S.A., Appendix CCC, Annual Report of the Chief of Engineers for 1893* (Washington, DC: Government Printing Office, 1893), 4325.

10. *Annual Report, Improvement and Care of the Public Buildings and Grounds, and Care and Maintenance of the Washington Monument, in the*

District of Columbia, Thomas W. Symons, Major, Corps of Engineers, Colonel, U.S.A.; and Chas. S. Bromwell, Captain, Corps of Engineers, Colonel, U.S.A., *Appendix DDD, Annual Report of the Chief of Engineers for 1904* (Washington, DC: Government Printing Office, 1904), 3939.

11. Ibid., 2318.

12. Edward F. Cooke, *A Detailed Analysis of the Constitution* (Boulder, CO: Rowman & Littlefield, 2002), 122.

13. National Register of Historic Places, *Civil War Monuments in Washington, D.C.* (Washington, DC: National Park Service, 1978).

14. Christopher Shea, "The Brawl on the Mall," *Preservation,* January–February 2001, 39.

15. Philip Kennicott, "Monumental Questions," *Washington Post,* 30 May 2004, B2.

Chapter 3. The Mall

Epigraph: Charles Dickens, *American Notes* (London: Chapman & Hall, 1842), 1:281–82.

1. Peter Charles L'Enfant, *1791 Manuscript Plan for the City of Washington,* color facsimile (Washington, DC: U.S. Geological Survey, 1991).

2. Ibid.

3. John W. Reps, *Monumental Washington* (Princeton, NJ: Princeton University Press, 1967), 25.

4. Frederick Gutheim, *Worthy of the Nation* (Washington, DC: Smithsonian Institution Press, 1977), 44.

5. Pamela Scott, "'This Vast Empire': The Iconography of the Mall, 1791–1848," in *The Mall in Washington, 1791–1991,* ed. Richard Longstreth (Washington, DC: National Gallery of Art, 1991), 46.

6. James M. Goode, *The Outdoor Sculpture of Washington, D.C.* (Washington, DC: Smithsonian Institution Press, 1974), 314–15.

7. Reps, *Monumental Washington,* 35–36.

8. Gutheim, *Worthy of the Nation,* 51–52.

9. Pamela Scott and Antoinette J. Lee, *Buildings of the District of Columbia* (New York: Oxford University Press, 1993), 94–96.

10. Reps, *Monumental Washington,* 44.

11. George J. Olszewski, *A History of the Washington Monument, 1844–1968* (Washington, DC: Department of the Interior, 1971), 10.

12. Scott and Lee, *Buildings of the District of Columbia,* 100–102.

13. John W. Reps, *Washington on View: The Nation's Capitol since 1790* (Chapel Hill: University of North Carolina Press, 1991), 90.

14. David Schuyler, "The Washington Park," in *Prophet with Honor,* ed. George B. Tatum and Elizabeth Blair MacDougall (Washington, DC: Dumbarton Oaks, 1989), 293, 294.

15. Ibid., 295.

16. James M. Goode, *Capital Losses* (Washington, DC: Smithsonian Institution Press, 1979), 310.

17. Ibid., 306–8.

18. Scott and Lee, *Buildings of the District of Columbia,* 92–94.

19. Gutheim, *Worthy of the Nation,* 93, 92.

20. Reps, *Washington on View,* 66.

21. Goode, *Capital Losses,* 412–14.

22. Charles Moore, ed., *The Improvement of the Park System of the District of Columbia* (Washington, DC: Government Printing Office, 1902), 8–9.

23. Reps, *Monumental Washington,* chaps. 4 and 5.

24. Thomas Hines, "The Imperial Mall: The City Beautiful Movement and the Washington Plan of 1901–1902," in Longstreth, *Mall in Washington,* 81.

25. Moore, *Improvement of the Park System*, 41–42.

26. Ibid., 43–45.

27. Ibid., 47–48.

28. Ibid., 49–50.

29. Ibid., 51–52.

30. Reps, *Monumental Washington*, 136.

31. Ibid., 137.

32. Ibid., 91.

33. Goode, *Capital Losses*, 441–44.

34. Reps, *Monumental Washington*, 155–57.

35. Scott and Lee, *Buildings of the District of Columbia*, 103.

36. Ibid., 104.

37. Reps, *Monumental Washington*, 173–75.

38. Goode, *Outdoor Sculpture*, 393–94.

39. Gutheim, *Worthy of the Nation*, 217–18.

40. Goode, *Capital Losses*, 224–25.

41. Goode, *Outdoor Sculpture*, 243–48.

42. David C. Streatfield, "The Olmsteds and the Landscape of the Mall," in Longstreth, *Mall in Washington*, 135.

43. Goode, *Outdoor Sculpture*, 242, 249–50.

44. Roger K. Lewis, "U.S. Botanic Garden: On the Mall, a Hybrid of Form and Contents," *Washington Post*, 1 June 2002, H3.

45. Heather Hammatt, "Showcase of Stewardship," *Landscape Architecture*, July 2002, 18–19.

46. Historic American Buildings Survey No. DC-693, *West Potomac Park* (Washington, DC: National Park Service, 1993), 8 (hereafter HABS No. DC-693).

47. Historic American Buildings Survey No. DC-692, *East Potomac Park* (Washington, DC: National Park Service, 1993), 2–8.

48. Reps, *Monumental Washington*, 183–91.

49. Christopher Weeks, *AIA Guide to the Architecture of Washington, D.C.*, 3rd ed. (Baltimore: Johns Hopkins University Press, 1994), 64–65.

50. Gutheim, *Worthy of the Nation*, 172–82.

51. Scott and Lee, *Buildings of the District of Columbia*, 166–77.

52. Ibid., 209–12.

53. Ad Hoc Committee on Federal Office Space, *Report to the President* (Washington, DC, 1962).

54. Scott and Lee, *Buildings of the District of Columbia*, 108.

55. Ibid., 106–7.

56. Benjamin Forgey, "A Stroll down the Garden Path," *Washington Post*, 20 May 1999, C1, C5.

57. Michael Bednar, *The New Atrium* (New York: McGraw-Hill, 1986), 188–89.

58. William Marlin, "Mr. Pei Goes to Washington," *Architectural Record*, August 1978.

59. Scott and Lee, *Buildings of the District of Columbia*, 99–100.

60. Ibid., 97–99.

61. Donald Canty, "Masterful Placemaking beside the Mall," *Architecture*, November 1987, 42–48.

62. Suzanne Stephens, "Museum as Monument," *Progressive Architecture*, March 1975, 43–47.

63. Suzanne Stephens, "Modernism and the Monolith," ibid., July 1976, 70–75.

64. Michael Cannell, "Cardinal Rules," *Architecture*, July 2000, 60–64, 140–42.

65. Adrian Higgins, "Covering a Lot of Ground in a Little Space," *Washington Post,* 20 September 2004, C1, C2.

66. Canty, "Masterful Placemaking beside the Mall," 43.

67. Richard Longstreth, "Introduction: Change and Continuity on the Mall," in Longstreth, *Mall in Washington,* 14.

68. Benjamin Forgey, "Unwrapped Present," *Washington Post,* 4 July 2000, C1, C5.

69. Petula Dvorak, "Washington Monument Subtly Fortified," ibid., 1 July 2005, A1, A6.

70. Maya Lin, "Quite Simply, It Stands for the Fallen," ibid., 12 November 2000, B3.

71. John Beardsley, "Tin Soldiers," *Landscape Architecture,* February 1996, 152, 101.

72. J. William Thompson, "The Power of Place," ibid., July 1997, 63–70, 90–94.

73. Christopher Shea, "The Brawl on the Mall," *Preservation,* January–February 2001, 41.

74. Glenn Brown, *Memories* (Washington, DC: Roberts, 1931), 102.

75. Blake Gopnik, "Many Words, Little Eloquence," *Washington Post,* 23 May 2004, N1, N6.

76. Benjamin Forgey, "War and Remembrance," ibid., 25 April 2004, N1, N4, N5.

77. Heather Hammatt, "Dialogue of Memory," *Landscape Architecture,* December 2000, 48–51.

78. Shea, "Brawl on the Mall," 43.

79. J. Carter Brown, "The Mall and the Commission of Fine Arts," in Longstreth, *Mall in Washington,* 255.

80. Roger K. Lewis, "Sizing Up Grandeur: Big Walls That Diminish the Mall," *Washington Post,* 7 October 2000, G14.

81. National Capital Planning Commission, *Memorials and Museums Master Plan* (Washington, DC, 2000).

82. Linda Wheeler, "Making Room for John Adams," *Washington Post,* 29 October 2001, B1, B6.

83. HABS No. DC-693, 11.

84. Historic American Buildings Survey No. DC-678, *National Mall and Monument Grounds* (Washington, DC: National Park Service, 1993), 24.

85. Susan Levine, "Trampling the Nation's Front Lawn," *Washington Post,* 13 November 2000, A1, A6.

86. Susan Levine, "World Marches On; Issues Remain," ibid., 29 October 2000, C1, C9.

87. Arthur Santana, "Experts Say the Mall Can't Be Invulnerable," ibid., 20 March 2003, B5.

88. Moore, *Improvement of the Park System,* 25.

89. Longstreth, "Introduction," 16.

90. Richard Guy Wilson, "High Noon on the Mall: Modernism versus Traditionalism, 1910–1970," in Longstreth, *Mall in Washington,* 163.

Chapter 4. Capitol Square

Epigraph: Elizabeth S. Kite, *L'Enfant and Washington, 1791–1792* (Baltimore: Johns Hopkins Press, 1929), 55–56.

1. Peter Charles L'Enfant, *1791 Manuscript Plan for the City of Washington,* color facsimile (Washington, DC: U.S. Geological Survey, 1991).

2. Ibid.

3. Andrew Ellicott, *Plan of the City of Washington in the Territory of Columbia* (Philadelphia: Thackara & Vallance, 1792).

4. James M. Goode, *Capital Losses* (Washington, DC: Smithsonian Institution Press, 1979), 141–42.

5. Ibid., 290–92.

6. Pamela Scott and Antoinette J. Lee, *Buildings of the District of Columbia* (New York: Oxford University Press, 1993), 142–45.

7. Ibid., 113–19, 125–35. In order to maintain consistency, I have used Scott and Lee's account of the Capitol design and construction as the basis for this section.

8. William C. Allen, *History of the United States Capitol* (Washington, DC: Government Printing Office, 2001), 46, 54.

9. Richard Guy Wilson, "Historicization of the U.S. Capitol and the Office of Architect, 1954–1996," in *The United States Capitol*, ed. Donald Kennon (Athens: Ohio University Press, 2000), 134–68.

10. Allen, *History of the United States Capitol,* 445.

11. William C. Allen, "Seat of Broils, Confusion, and Squandered Thousands," in Kennon, *United States Capitol,* 3–4.

12. Allen, *History of the United States Capitol,* 162, 159.

13. B. B. French, *Report of the Commissioner of Public Buildings, Office of the Commissioner of Public Buildings* (Washington, DC: Office of Public Buildings and Grounds, 1866), 546–47.

14. *Report of Brevet Brigadier General N. Michler, Major of Engineers, U.S. Army, Public Buildings, Grounds, Works, Etc.* (Washington, DC: Government Printing Office, 1868), 7.

15. Allen, *History of the United States Capitol,* 340–44.

16. Ibid., 345.

17. Charles E. Beveridge and Paul Rocheleau, *Frederick Law Olmsted* (New York: Universe, 1998), 155.

18. Allen, *History of the United States Capitol,* 348.

19. Iris Miller, *Washington in Maps* (New York: Rizzoli, 2002), 134.

20. Charles Moore, ed., *The Improvement of the Park System of the District of Columbia* (Washington, DC: Government Printing Office, 1902), 38–39.

21. Elbert Peets, "Critique of L'Enfant's Plan," in *On the Art of Designing Cities: Selected Essays of Elbert Peets,* ed. Paul D. Spreiregen (Cambridge, MA: MIT Press, 1968), 45.

22. Scott and Lee, *Buildings of the District of Columbia,* 122–23.

23. Allen, *History of the United States Capitol,* 408.

24. Ibid., 386.

25. Ibid., 404.

26. Scott and Lee, *Buildings of the District of Columbia,* 136.

27. John W. Reps, *Monumental Washington* (Princeton, NJ: Princeton University Press, 1967), 164.

28. James M. Goode, *The Outdoor Sculpture of Washington, D.C.* (Washington, DC: Smithsonian Institution Press, 1974), 47.

29. Allen, *History of the United States Capitol,* 418–19.

30. Michael Bednar, *Interior Pedestrian Places* (New York: Whitney Library of Design, 1989), 131–32.

31. Allen, *History of the United States Capitol,* 453–55.

32. Goode, *Outdoor Sculpture,* 250–51.

33. Allen, *History of the United States Capitol,* 455–57.

34. David Lynn, *Enlarging of the Capitol Grounds* (Washington, DC: Government Printing Office, 1943), 17.

35. Ibid., 5.

36. National Capital Planning Commission, *Memorials and Museums Master Plan* (Washington, DC, 2000).

37. Goode, *Capital Losses,* 434–36.

38. U.S. Constitution, amend. 20, sec. 1.

39. Ronald Reagan, "Inauguration Speech," *Washington Post*, 21 January 1981, A34.

40. David Montgomery, "Out of Step with Democracy," ibid., 26 January 2002, C1, C5.

41. Spencer S. Hsu, "Capitol Fence Divides Officials," ibid., 3 April 2004, B1, B5.

42. Linda Wheeler, "Ugly Barricades on the Way Out," ibid., 13 January 2002, C1, C9.

43. Sylvia Moreno, "Capitol Trees Taking Their Leaves," ibid., 22 April 2001, C1, C9.

44. Allen, *History of the United States Capitol*, xiii.

Chapter 5. President's Park

Epigraph: Marie Beale, *Decatur House and Its Inhabitants* (Washington, DC: National Trust for Historic Preservation, 1954), 133.

1. Hametia Fielder King, "Historical Survey of Lafayette Square," report to John Carl Warnecke & Associates, San Francisco, 1963.

2. Ibid., 3.

3. Benjamin Ogle Tayloe, *Our Neighbors on Lafayette Square* (1872; reprint, Washington, DC: Junior League of Washington, 1872), 40.

4. Jeanne Fogle, *Proximity to Power: Neighbors to the President near Lafayette Square* (Washington, DC: Tour de Force, 1999).

5. Pamela Scott and Antoinette J. Lee, *Buildings of the District of Columbia* (New York: Oxford University Press, 1993), 162.

6. Tayloe, *Our Neighbors on Lafayette Square*, 24–31.

7. Beale, *Decatur House and Its Inhabitants*, 141.

8. Tayloe, *Our Neighbors on Lafayette Square*, 38.

9. Fogle, *Proximity to Power*, 60.

10. Ibid., 73–74.

11. Ibid., 26–27.

12. Ibid., 25, 38–41.

13. James M. Goode, *Capital Losses* (Washington, DC: Smithsonian Institution Press, 1979), 54–56.

14. Scott and Lee, *Buildings of the District of Columbia*, 164–65.

15. Goode, *Capital Losses*, 40–42.

16. Ibid., 99–102.

17. Sarah Booth Conroy, "Lafayette Square's Presidential Past," *Washington Post*, 16 October 2000, C2.

18. Fogle, *Proximity to Power*, 29–30.

19. Goode, *Capital Losses*, 24–26.

20. Scott and Lee, *Buildings of the District of Columbia*, 163.

21. Fogle, *Proximity to Power*, 5.

22. Historic American Buildings Survey No. DC-689, *White House Grounds and Ellipse* (Washington, DC: National Park Service, 1993), 5 (hereafter HABS No. DC-689).

23. David Schuyler, "The Washington Park," in *Prophet with Honor*, ed. George B. Tatum and Elizabeth Blair MacDougall (Washington, DC: Dumbarton Oaks, 1989), 293. The published Downing Plan does not include Lafayette Square; Historic American Buildings Survey No. DC-676, *Lafayette Square* (Washington, DC: National Park Service, 1993), 20 (hereafter HABS No. DC-676), shows the plan that was executed, similar to a Downing design, also shown on the 1903 Baist map.

24. Ibid., 19.

25. James M. Goode, *The Outdoor Sculpture of Washington, D.C.* (Washington, DC: Smithsonian Institution Press, 1974), 377–78.

26. HABS No. DC-676, 9.

27. Goode, *Outdoor Sculpture*, 372–73, 379.

28. Ibid., 374–75, 380.

29. HABS No. DC-676, 5.

30. Fogle, *Proximity to Power*, 91–93.

31. Ibid., 121–23, 212–13.

32. Goode, *Capital Losses*, 248–49.

33. Ibid., 259–62.

34. Charles Moore, ed., *The Improvement of the Park System of the District of Columbia* (Washington, DC: Government Printing Office, 1902), 64.

35. Michael Dennis, *Court and Garden* (Cambridge, MA: MIT Press, 1986), 82.

36. Elbert Peets, "Critique of L'Enfant's Plan," in *On the Art of Designing Cities: Selected Essays of Elbert Peets*, ed. Paul D. Spreiregen (Cambridge, MA: MIT Press, 1968), 56.

37. Scott and Lee, *Buildings of the District of Columbia*, 164.

38. Ibid., 161–62.

39. Fogle, *Proximity to Power*, 204–5.

40. Sue A. Kohler and Jeffrey R. Carson, *Sixteenth Street Architecture*, vol. 2 (Washington, DC: Commission of Fine Arts, 1988), 1–33.

41. Fogle, *Proximity to Power*, 210–12.

42. HABS No. DC-676, 10.

43. L. Morris Leisenring, "Lament for Lafayette Square," *AIA Journal*, February 1961, 23–32.

44. Sarah Booth Conroy, "The Savior of the Square," *Washington Post*, 21 August 1993, B3.

45. HABS No. DC-676, 11.

46. William Seale, *The White House: The History of an American Idea* (Washington, DC: American Institute of Architects Press, 1992), 23.

47. Scott and Lee, *Buildings of the District of Columbia*, 152–53.

48. Seale, *White House*, ix.

49. Ibid., 47.

50. Ibid., 67.

51. Constance McLaughlin Green, *Washington*, vol. 1, *Village and Capital, 1800–1878* (Princeton, NJ: Princeton University Press, 1962), 136.

52. Frederick Gutheim, *Worthy of the Nation* (Washington, DC: Smithsonian Institution Press, 1977), 53–55.

53. *Annual Report, Improvement and Care of the Public Buildings and Grounds in the District of Columbia, and Washington Aqueduct, O. E. Babcock, Colonel of Engineers, Bvt. Brig. General, U.S.A., Appendix GG, Annual Report of the Chief of Engineers for 1876* (Washington, DC: Government Printing Office, 1876), 4.

54. Goode, *Outdoor Sculpture*, 138.

55. HABS No. DC-689, 10, 11.

56. Goode, *Outdoor Sculpture*, 131–32.

57. Ibid., 133, 137.

58. Ibid., 292–94.

59. Scott and Lee, *Buildings of the District of Columbia*, 154–57.

60. Ibid., 157–58.

61. Christopher Weeks, *AIA Guide to the Architecture of Washington, D.C.* (Baltimore: Johns Hopkins University Press, 1994), 142–43.

62. Scott and Lee, *Buildings of the District of Columbia*, 207–8.

63. Ibid., 208–9.

64. Goode, *Capital Losses,* 32–33.

65. Fogle, *Proximity to Power,* 190–91.

66. Scott and Lee, *Buildings of the District of Columbia,* 171–72.

67. Goode, *Capital Losses,* 438–40.

68. HABS No. DC-676, 12.

69. Stephen C. Fehr, "Gridlock Predicted in Heart of Downtown," *Washington Post,* 21 May 1995, A1, A16.

70. David Von Drehle, "Fear Converts America's Main Street into a Sidewalk," ibid., 21 May 1995, A1–A15.

71. Benjamin Forgey, "Concrete Solutions to Concrete Barriers," ibid., 22 May 1995, D1, D9.

72. Stephen C. Fehr, "Throwing Pa. Avenue a Curve," ibid., 23 May 1996, A1–A23.

73. Benjamin Forgey, "Changing the Guard," *Landscape Architecture,* September 2002, 80–87.

74. Benjamin Forgey, "America's Avenue Again," *Washington Post,* 1 March 2003, C1, C5.

Chapter 6. Early Squares

Epigraph: J. B. Jackson, "The American Public Space," in *The Public Face of Architecture,* ed. Mark Lilla and Nathan Glazer (New York: Free Press, 1987), 278.

1. Historic American Buildings Survey No. DC-690, *Judiciary Square* (Washington, DC: National Park Service, 1993), 3 (hereafter HABS No. DC-690).

2. James M. Goode, *Capital Losses* (Washington, DC: Smithsonian Institution Press, 1979), 304–5.

3. Elmer Louis Kayser, *Bricks without Straw* (New York: Appleton-Century-Crofts, 1970), 116.

4. HABS No. DC-690, 4.

5. Ibid.

6. James M. Goode, *The Outdoor Sculpture of Washington, D.C.* (Washington, DC: Smithsonian Institution Press, 1974), 229.

7. *Annual Report, Improvement and Care of the Public Buildings and Grounds in the District of Columbia, and the Washington Aqueduct, Thos. Lincoln Casey, Lieut. Colonel of Engineers, Bvt. Colonel, U.S.A., March 3, 1877 until June 30, 1877, Appendix KK2 and 3, Annual Report of the Chief of Engineers for 1877* (Washington, DC: Government Printing Office, 1877), 7.

8. Pamela Scott and Antoinette J. Lee, *Buildings of the District of Columbia* (New York: Oxford University Press, 1993), 183.

9. *Annual Report, Improvement and Care of the Public Buildings and Grounds in the District of Columbia, and Washington Aqueduct, O. E. Babcock, Colonel of Engineers, Bvt. Brig. General, U.S.A., Appendix HH, Annual Report of the Chief of Engineers for 1875* (Washington, DC: Government Printing Office, 1875), 4–5.

10. Michael Bednar, *The New Atrium* (New York: McGraw-Hill, 1986), 12.

11. Goode, *Capital Losses,* 147, 146, 202–4, 220–22.

12. HABS No. DC-690, 14. The 1888 Sanborn maps do not show the locations of the school and the hospital. The 1876 park design shown in the HABS report was either not executed or changed, since it is at variance with the design depicted on the 1904 Sanborn maps. The 1904 design for the park has been drawn on the 1888 map.

13. Ibid., 6.

14. Nathan C. Wyeth, "Notes on the New Municipal Center," *Pencil Points,* September 1939, 578–83.

15. Claudia D. Kousoulas and George W. Kousoulas, *Contemporary Architecture in Washington, D.C.* (New York: John Wiley & Sons, 1995), 115.

16. Ibid.

17. Benjamin Forgey, "Lions of Valor: The Officers' Memorial," *Washington Post*, 12 October 1991, D1, D10.

18. Linda Wheeler, "Congress Approves U.S. Police Museum at Judiciary Square," ibid., 26 October 2000, B7.

19. National Register of Historic Places, *Mount Vernon Square Historic District* (Washington, DC: National Park Service, 1999), sec. 8, p. 1.

20. Michael Farquhar, "The Past Is Present," *Washington Post Magazine*, 23 March 2003, 8–11, 30–35.

21. Historic American Buildings Survey No. DC-682, *Mount Vernon Square* (Washington, DC: National Park Service, 1993), 4 (hereafter HABS No. DC-682).

22. Farquhar, "Past Is Present," 30.

23. HABS No. DC-682, 4.

24. Farquhar, "Past Is Present," 31.

25. *Annual Report, Improvement and Care of the Public Buildings and Grounds in the District of Columbia, and Washington Aqueduct, O. E. Babcock, Colonel of Engineers, Bvt. Brig. General, U.S.A., July 1, 1876 until March 3, 1877, Appendix KK1, Annual Report of the Chief of Engineers for 1877* (Washington, DC: Government Printing Office, 1877), 10.

26. Goode, *Outdoor Sculpture*, 524–25.

27. *Annual Report, Improvement and Care of the Public Buildings and Grounds in the District of Columbia, A. F. Rockwell, Colonel, U.S. Army, Appendix QQ, Annual Report of the Chief of Engineers for 1882* (Washington, DC: Government Printing Office, 1882), 2736.

28. Scott and Lee, *Buildings of the District of Columbia,* 196–97. The wealthy industrialist Andrew Carnegie funded hundreds of community libraries across the nation.

29. George J. Olszewski, *Mt. Vernon Square* (Washington, DC: National Park Service, 1970), 36.

30. Kousoulas and Kousoulas, *Contemporary Architecture in Washington, D.C.,* 59.

31. Lawrence Feinberg, "UDC Trustees Adopt New Downtown Campus Plan," *Washington Post,* 22 June 1978, DC1, DC3.

32. Benjamin Forgey, "A Long Way to Go: Giant Convention Center Takes a Baby Step," ibid., 4 October 1997, H1, H7.

33. Benjamin Forgey, "Up with Down at Convention Center," ibid., 29 March 2003, C1, C5.

34. Debbi Wilgoren, "New Portal to a City's Past," ibid., 11 May 2003, C1, C11.

35. Judith Evans and David Montgomery, "Convention Center: Nowhere to Grow," ibid., 26 May 1998, A1, A6, A7.

36. Neil Irwin and Dana Hedgpeth, "Library Wins in Current Site Plan," ibid., 16 July 2004, E1, E5.

37. Jackie Spinner, "D.C. May Let Developer Offer Plan for Old Convention Center Site," ibid., 2 July 2001, E4.

Chapter 7. Office Squares

Epigraph: Paul Zucker, *Town and Square* (Cambridge, MA: MIT Press, 1970), 1–2.

1. Frederick Gutheim, *Worthy of the Nation* (Washington, DC: Smithsonian Institution Press, 1977), 27.

2. Ibid., 86.

3. District of Columbia Municipal Regulations, title 11, Zoning, 2004, chap. 25, secs. 2510, 2512.

4. James M. Goode, *Capital Losses* (Washington, DC: Smithsonian Institution Press, 1979), 67–68.

5. John Clagett Proctor, "Farragut Statue Was Unveiled in 1881," *Sunday Star*, 3 May 1931, 81.

6. Historic American Buildings Survey No. DC-671, *Farragut Square* (Washington, DC: National Park Service, 1993), 2–3 (hereafter HABS No. DC-671).

7. *Annual Report, Major O. E. Babcock, Corps of Engineers, Commissioner of Public Buildings and Grounds* (Washington, DC: Government Printing Office, 1872), 7.

8. James H. Johnston, "A Field Guide to Washington's Civil War Memorials," *Washington Post*, 11 August 1999, H4.

9. James M. Goode, *The Outdoor Sculpture of Washington, D.C.* (Washington, DC: Smithsonian Institution Press, 1974), 101.

10. Paul Richard, "The Sculptor Who Knew Lincoln," *Washington Post*, 24 February 1990, C1, C9.

11. Goode, *Capital Losses*, 92–93, 152–53.

12. Ibid., 238.

13. HABS No. DC-671, 4.

14. Alfred E. Lewis, "Underground Parking Garage Proposed at Farragut Square," *Washington Post*, 7 January 1960, B4.

15. George J. Olszewski, *Farragut Square* (Washington, DC: National Park Service, 1968), 36.

16. Claudia D. Kousoulas and George W. Kousoulas, *Contemporary Architecture in Washington, D.C.* (New York: John Wiley & Sons, 1995), 68.

17. Ruth Marcus and John Mintz, "The Verdict's In: K Street's Out," *Washington Post*, 10 May 1987, D1.

18. *Annual Report* (1872), 7.

19. Goode, *Outdoor Sculpture*, 281.

20. Constance McLaughlin Green, *Washington*, vol. 1, *Village and Capital, 1800–1878* (Princeton, NJ: Princeton University Press, 1962), 186.

21. Historic American Buildings Survey No. DC-680, *McPherson Square* (Washington, DC: National Park Service, 1993), 2 (hereafter HABS No. DC-680).

22. Goode, *Capital Losses*, 82.

23. Ibid., 132.

24. *Annual Report, Improvement and Care of the Public Buildings and Grounds, and Care and Maintenance of the Washington Monument, in the District of Columbia, Oswald H. Ernst, Major, Corps of Engineers, Colonel, U.S.A., Appendix BBB, Annual Report of the Chief of Engineers for 1892* (Washington, DC: Government Printing Office, 1892), 3391.

25. Pamela Scott and Antoinette J. Lee, *Buildings of the District of Columbia* (New York: Oxford University Press, 1993), 202–3.

26. HABS No. DC-680, 5.

27. Kousoulas and Kousoulas, *Contemporary Architecture in Washington, D.C.*, 64–65.

28. Susan Straight, "Near White House, the Summit of Downtown Living," *Washington Post, Apartment Living*, 25 January 2003, 5, 7.

29. Aileen S. Yoo, "Tranquil Park by Day Is a Place of Sanctuary, Hope by Night," *Washington Post*, 22 September 1994, DC2.

30. Janice Armstrong and Deborah Burke, "Multi-Pronged Effort Reviving Franklin Square," ibid., 8 March 1990, 1.

31. Historic American Buildings Survey No. DC-673, *Franklin Square*

(Washington, DC: National Park Service, 1993), 2 (hereafter HABS No. DC-673).

32. Goode, *Capital Losses*, 66.

33. John Clagett Proctor, "Franklin Park Associated with Two Wars of Nation," *Sunday Star*, 26 April 1936, F-2.

34. HABS No. DC-673, 2.

35. Scott and Lee, *Buildings of the District of Columbia*, 195–96.

36. Christopher Weeks, *AIA Guide to the Architecture of Washington, D.C.*, 3rd ed. (Baltimore: Johns Hopkins University Press, 1994), 11.

37. Benjamin Forgey, "Lessons from Washington's Jewel of a School," *Washington Post*, 9 May 1992, B1, B3.

38. HABS No. DC-673, 3.

39. *Annual Report, Improvement and Care of the Public Buildings and Grounds in the District of Columbia, and the Washington Aqueduct, Thos. Lincoln Casey, Lieut. Colonel of Engineers, Bvt. Colonel, U.S.A., March 3, 1877 until June 30, 1877, Appendix KK2 and 3, Annual Report of the Chief of Engineers for 1877* (Washington, DC: Government Printing Office, 1877), 6.

40. *Annual Report, Improvement and Care of the Public Buildings and Grounds in the District of Columbia, John M. Wilson, Lieut. Col. of Engineers, Colonel, U.S.A., Appendix TT, Annual Report of the Chief of Engineers for 1886* (Washington, DC: Government Printing Office, 1886), 2078.

41. Goode, *Capital Losses*, 154–55.

42. George Burnap, *Parks, Their Design, Equipment and Use* (Philadelphia: Lippincott, 1916), 172.

43. Goode, *Outdoor Sculpture*, 280.

44. HABS No. DC-673, 4.

45. Ibid.

46. Armstrong and Burke, "Multi-Pronged Effort."

47. Ibid.

48. Benjamin Forgey, "Rooms for Improvement," *Washington Post*, 20 July 1996, B1.

49. Andrea Oppenheimer Dean, "Tall Order," *Architecture*, April 1991, 64.

50. Scott and Lee, *Buildings of the District of Columbia*, 217.

51. *Annual Report of Major O. E. Babcock, Corps of Engineers, Commissioner of Public Buildings and Grounds* (Washington, DC: Government Printing Office, 1873), 5.

52. Goode, *Outdoor Sculpture*, 466.

53. Linda Wheeler, "For This Wartime Major General, the Maneuvering Is Finally Over," *Washington Post*, 13 September 2001, VA8.

54. Gutheim, *Worthy of the Nation*, 148.

55. Ibid., 205.

56. Scott and Lee, *Buildings of the District of Columbia*, 216.

57. John H. Small Jr., "Some Small Parks in Washington, D.C.," *Landscape Architecture*, October 1918, 24–25.

58. Scott and Lee, *Buildings of the District of Columbia*, 216.

59. Historic American Buildings Survey No. DC-683, *Rawlins Park* (Washington, DC: National Park Service, 1993), 5.

60. National Capital Planning Commission, *Memorials and Museums Master Plan* (Washington, DC, 2000).

61. A[lbert] Boschke, *Topographical Map of the District of Columbia, Surveyed in the Years 1856–59* (Washington, DC: McClelland, Blanchard & Mohun, 1861).

62. J. L. Sibley Jennings, Sue Kohler, and Jeffrey B. Carson, *Massachusetts Avenue Architecture*, vol. 2 (Washington, DC: Commission of Fine Arts, 1975), 12–15, 16–20.

63. Historic American Buildings Survey No. DC-675, *Samuel L. Gompers Memorial Park and Reservation No. 68* (Washington, DC: National Park Service, 1993), 3.

64. Ibid.

65. *Annual Report, Improvement and Care of the Public Buildings and Grounds, and Care and Maintenance of the Washington Monument, in the District of Columbia, John M. Wilson, Lieut. Col. Corps of Engineers, Colonel, U.S.A., Appendix CCC, Annual Report of the Chief of Engineers for 1894* (Washington, DC: Government Printing Office, 1894), 3303.

66. HABS No. DC-675, 3.

67. Ibid.

68. Goode, *Outdoor Sculpture*, 277.

69. Jennings, Kohler, and Carson, *Massachusetts Avenue Architecture,*2:1–11.

70. Goode, *Outdoor Sculpture*, 276.

Chapter 8. Constituent City

Epigraph: Paul Kafka-Gibbons, *Dupont Circle* (Boston: Houghton Mifflin, 2001), 3.

1. Historic American Buildings Survey No. DC-684, *Scott Circle* (Washington, DC: National Park Service, 1993), 2 (hereafter HABS No. DC-684).

2. *Annual Report, Improvement and Care of the Public Buildings and Grounds in the District of Columbia, and Washington Aqueduct, O. E. Babcock, Colonel of Engineers, Bvt. Brig. General, U.S.A., Appendix BB, Annual Report of the Chief of Engineers for 1874* (Washington, DC: Government Printing Office, 1874), 10.

3. James H. Johnston, "A Field Guide to Washington's Civil War Memorials," *Washington Post*, 11 August 1999, H4.

4. J. L. Sibley Jennings, Sue Kohler, and Jeffrey B. Carson, *Massachusetts Avenue Architecture*, vol. 2 (Washington, DC: Commission of Fine Arts, 1975), 48–70.

5. James M. Goode, *Capital Losses* (Washington, DC: Smithsonian Institution Press, 1979), 91.

6. Jennings, Kohler, and Carson, *Massachusetts Avenue Architecture*, 2:71–77.

7. Goode, *Capital Losses*, 227–28.

8. James M. Goode, *The Outdoor Sculpture of Washington, D.C.* (Washington, DC: Smithsonian Institution Press, 1974), 288–89.

9. Ibid., 286.

10. Charles Moore, ed., *The Improvement of the Park System of the District of Columbia* (Washington, DC: Government Printing Office, 1902), 80.

11. *Annual Report of the Chief of Engineers, 1912, Appendix EEE, Report Upon the Improvement and Care of Public Buildings and Grounds, and Upon the Care and Maintenance of the Washington Monument and of the Highway Bridge Across the Potomac River, District of Columbia, and Upon the Erection of Monuments, Memorials, Etc., Washington, District of Columbia, Spencer Cosby, Major, Corps of Engineers, Colonel, U.S.A.* (Washington, DC: Government Printing Office, 1912), 3491.

12. Goode, *Capital Losses*, 127–29, 134.

13. HABS No. DC-684, 4.

14. Ibid.

15. Bill Black, "Taking Risks Paid Off for Tenants of the General Scott Apartments," *Washington Post*, 6 November 1982, E21.

16. John Clagett Proctor, "Massachusetts Avenue Tunnel Turns New Attention to Old Thomas Circle," *Washington Star*, 26 March 1939, C-4.

17. Goode, *Capital Losses*, 44.

18. Jennings, Kohler, and Carson, *Massachusetts Avenue Architecture,* 2:31–36.

19. Paul K. Williams, *The Neighborhoods of Logan, Scott, and Thomas Circles* (Washington, DC: Arcadia, 2001), 47.

20. Proctor, "Massachusetts Avenue Tunnel," C-4.

21. Pamela Scott and Antoinette J. Lee, *Buildings of the District of Columbia* (New York: Oxford University Press, 1993), 295.

22. Historic American Buildings Survey No. DC-687, *Thomas Circle* (Washington, DC: National Park Service, 1993), 3.

23. *Annual Report, Major O. E. Babcock, Corps of Engineers, Commissioner of Public Buildings and Grounds* (Washington, DC: Government Printing Office, 1872), 7–8.

24. Goode, *Capital Losses,* 180.

25. Goode, *Outdoor Sculpture,* 283.

26. Ibid., 284–85.

27. Jennings, Kohler, and Carson, *Massachusetts Avenue Architecture,* 2:37–47.

28. Scott and Lee, *Buildings of the District of Columbia,* 295–96.

29. Miles Maguire, "Thomas Circle Development Rejected," *Washington Times,* 13 June 1990, C1.

30. David S. Hilzenrath, "Plan for 14th St. Corridor Unveiled," *Washington Post,* 6 August 1988, F1.

31. Williams, *Neighborhoods of Logan, Scott, and Thomas Circles,* 7.

32. John Clagett Proctor, "Franklin Park Associated with Two Wars of Nation," *Sunday Star,* 26 April 1936, F-2.

33. Historic American Buildings Survey No. DC-339, *Logan Circle* (Washington, DC: National Park Service, 1993), 2 (hereafter HABS No. DC-339).

34. *Annual Report, Improvement and Care of the Public Buildings and Grounds in the District of Columbia, and Washington Aqueduct, O. E. Babcock, Colonel of Engineers, Bvt. Brig. General, U.S.A., Appendix HH, Annual Report of the Chief of Engineers for 1875* (Washington, DC: Government Printing Office, 1875), 5–6.

35. *Annual Report, Improvement and Care of the Public Buildings and Grounds in the District of Columbia, and Washington Aqueduct, O. E. Babcock, Colonel of Engineers, Bvt. Brig. General, U.S.A., July 1, 1876 until March 3, 1877, Appendix KK1, Annual Report of the Chief of Engineers for 1877* (Washington, DC: Government Printing Office, 1877), 12.

36. HABS No. DC-339, 4.

37. Ibid.

38. Goode, *Outdoor Sculpture,* 278–79.

39. Williams, *Neighborhoods of Logan, Scott, and Thomas Circles,* 13.

40. Ibid., 25, 29, 26.

41. Ibid., 17.

42. HABS No. DC-339, 5.

43. National Register of Historic Places, *Logan Circle Historic District* (Washington, DC: National Park Service, 1972).

44. Liz Spayd, "D.C. Gets New Historic District," *Washington Post,* 27 May 1994.

45. Linda Wheeler, "Commuters Lose Shortcut to Logan Circle Residents," ibid., 4 November 1980, C1, C4.

46. HABS No. DC-339, 3.

47. Linda Wheeler, "District Community Embraces Restorations," *Washington Post,* 13 June 1998, VN1, VN6.

48. Kafka-Gibbons, *Dupont Circle.*

49. National Register of Historic Places, *Dupont Circle Historic District*

(Washington, DC: National Park Service, 1978), sec. 8, pp. 1, 2.

50. *Annual Report of Major O. E. Babcock, Corps of Engineers, Commissioner of Public Buildings and Grounds* (Washington, DC: Government Printing Office, 1873), 5.

51. *Annual Report, Improvement and Care of the Public Buildings and Grounds in the District of Columbia, and the Washington Aqueduct, Thos. Lincoln Casey, Lieut. Colonel of Engineers, Bvt. Colonel, U.S.A., March 3, 1877 until June 30, 1877, Appendix KK2 and 3, Annual Report of the Chief of Engineers for 1877* (Washington, DC: Government Printing Office, 1877), 11.

52. Paul K. Williams, *Dupont Circle* (Charleston, SC: Arcadia, 2000), 19.

53. Michael Dolan, "A Short History of a Very Round Place," *Washington Post Magazine*, 2 September 1990, 24.

54. *Annual Report, Improvement and Care of the Public Buildings and Grounds in the District of Columbia, A. F. Rockwell, Colonel, U.S.A., Appendix SS, Annual Report of the Chief of Engineers for 1884* (Washington, DC: Government Printing Office, 1884), 2342–43.

55. Historic American Buildings Survey No. DC-669, *Dupont Circle* (Washington, DC: National Park Service, 1993), 4 (hereafter HABS No. DC-669).

56. Williams, *Dupont Circle*, 13.

57. Goode, *Capital Losses*, 112–14.

58. Scott and Lee, *Buildings of the District of Columbia*, 320.

59. Williams, *Dupont Circle*, 24.

60. HABS No. DC-669, 5.

61. Dolan, "Short History," 34.

62. Williams, *Dupont Circle*, 41.

63. National Register of Historic Places, *Dupont Circle Historic District*, 4.

64. HABS No. DC-669, 5.

65. Margaret Webb Pressler, "Down Under Resurfaces," *Washington Post*, 3 August 1996, F1.

66. HABS No. DC-669, 6.

67. Scott and Lee, *Buildings of the District of Columbia*, 319–20.

68. Thomas Bell, "Riggs Plans to Raze Dupont Circle Buildings," *Washington Post*, 17 May 1990, DC1.

69. District of Columbia Municipal Regulations, title 11, Zoning, 2004, chap. 15, sec. 1501.

70. "What About Dupont Circle?" *Washington Post Potomac*, 4 September 1966, 8.

71. Abhi Raghunathan, "Days of Knights at Dupont Circle," *Washington Post*, 25 July 2001, B3.

72. Manny Fernandez, "At Open-Mic Forum, a Yearning to Open Minds," ibid., 12 July 2003, B1, B5.

73. A[lbert] Boschke, *Topographical Map of the District of Columbia, Surveyed in the Years 1856–59* (Washington, DC: McClelland, Blanchard & Mohun, 1861).

74. "Old British Legation Faces Razing," *Washington Daily News*, 14 May 1946, 38.

75. Historic American Buildings Survey No. DC-688, *Washington Circle* (Washington, DC: National Park Service, 1993), 2 (hereafter HABS No. DC-688).

76. Goode, *Outdoor Sculpture*, 384.

77. HABS No. DC-688, 2.

78. B. B. French, *Report of the Commissioner of Public Buildings, Office of the Commissioner of Public Buildings* (Washington, DC: Office of Public Buildings and Grounds, 1865), 7.

79. *Annual Report, Improvement and Care of the Public Buildings and Grounds in the District of Columbia, John M. Wilson, Lieut. Col. of Engineers,*

Colonel, U.S.A., Appendix VV, Annual Report of the Chief of Engineers for 1885 (Washington, DC: Government Printing Office, 1885), 2506.

80. *Annual Report, Improvement and Care of the Public Buildings and Grounds in the District of Columbia, John M. Wilson, Lieut. Col. of Engineers, Colonel, U.S.A., Appendix TT, Annual Report of the Chief of Engineers for 1886* (Washington, DC: Government Printing Office, 1886), 2079.

81. Goode, *Capital Losses,* 20–21.

82. National Register of Historic Places, *Schneider Triangle* (Washington, DC: National Park Service, 1982).

83. *Washington Times Herald,* 8 November 1949.

84. Elmer Louis Kayser, *Bricks without Straw* (New York: Appleton-Century-Crofts, 1970), 284.

85. Anne H. Oman, "ANC, Developer Agree on Washington Circle Condo," *Washington Post,* 26 July 1979, DC5.

86. Benjamin Forgey, "Fortress Washington: Solid But Spare," ibid., 21 June 1997, H1, H8.

87. Michael Abramowitz, "Foggy Bottom Fights Creeping Development," ibid., 13 January 1990, E1, E16.

88. Dana Hedgpeth, "GWU Using Hotels to Expand Housing," ibid., 12 July 2001, E15.

89. David Montgomery and Stephen C. Fehr, "A Storm in Foggy Bottom," ibid., 26 September 2000, B1, B4.

Chapter 9. Capitol Hill

Epigraph: Robert Browning, "Up at a Villa—Down in the City," in *Men and Women and Sordella* (Boston: Houghton, Mifflin, 1886), 16–17.

1. Frederick Gutheim, *Worthy of the Nation* (Washington, DC: Smithsonian Institution Press, 1977), 90.

2. Ibid., 8.

3. Bill Thomas, "Fat Times on Capitol Hill," *Historic Preservation,* September–October 1987, 45.

4. Ruth Ann Overbeck, "Capitol Hill: The Capitol Is Just up the Street," in *Washington at Home,* ed. Kathryn Schneider Smith (Northridge, CA: Windsor, 1988), 31.

5. Peter Charles L'Enfant, *1791 Manuscript Plan for the City of Washington,* color facsimile (Washington, DC: U.S. Geological Survey, 1991).

6. Historic American Buildings Survey No. DC-677, *Lincoln Park* (Washington, DC: National Park Service, 1993), 2 (hereafter HABS No. DC-677).

7. B. B. French, *Report of the Commissioner of Public Buildings, Office of the Commissioner of Public Buildings* (Washington, DC: Office of Public Buildings and Grounds, 1865), 7–8.

8. James M. Goode, *The Outdoor Sculpture of Washington, D.C.* (Washington, DC: Smithsonian Institution Press, 1974), 86.

9. Ibid., 86.

10. "The Lincoln Monument," *New York Times,* 15 April 1876, 1.

11. *Annual Report, Major O. E. Babcock, Corps of Engineers, Commissioner of Public Buildings and Grounds* (Washington, DC: Government Printing Office, 1872), 13.

12. *Annual Report, Improvement and Care of the Public Buildings and Grounds in the District of Columbia, and Washington Aqueduct, O. E. Babcock, Colonel of Engineers, Bvt. Brig. General, U.S.A., Appendix BB, Annual Report of the Chief of Engineers for 1874* (Washington, DC: Government Printing Office, 1874), 6.

13. HABS No. DC-677, 3.

14. Ibid., 4.

15. George J. Olszewski, *Lincoln Park* (Washington, DC: National Park Service, 1968), 9.

16. Milton B. Medary, "Making a Capital City," *American Architect,* 20 May 1929, 663.

17. John W. Reps, *Monumental Washington* (Princeton, NJ: Princeton University Press, 1967), 176–77.

18. Olszewski, *Lincoln Park,* 42.

19. Goode, *Outdoor Sculpture,* 87–88.

20. Olszewski, *Lincoln Park,* iii.

21. Constance McLaughlin Green, *Washington,* vol. 2, *Capital City, 1879–1950* (Princeton, NJ: Princeton University Press, 1963), 126.

22. Linda Wheeler, "Hearing the Echo of Freedom's First Steps," *Washington Post,* 15 April 2001, C3.

23. Linda Wheeler, "Lincoln Park: Social Circles around Dogs," ibid., 8 February 1997, E1, E16, E17.

24. Olszewski, *Lincoln Park,* figs. 4–6, p. 19.

25. Ibid., figs. 11–13.

26. *Report of Brevet Brigadier General N. Michler, Major of Engineers, U.S. Army, Public Buildings, Grounds, Works, Etc.* (Washington, DC: Government Printing Office, 1867), 823–24.

27. *Annual Report, Major O. E. Babcock, Corps of Engineers, Commissioner of Public Buildings and Grounds* (Washington, DC: Government Printing Office, 1872), 13.

28. Goode, *Outdoor Sculpture,* 84.

29. *Annual Report, Improvement and Care of the Public Buildings and Grounds in the District of Columbia, and Washington Aqueduct, Thos. Lincoln Casey, Lieut. Colonel of Engineers, Bvt. Colonel, U.S.A., Appendix NN, Annual Report of the Chief of Engineers for 1880* (Washington, DC: Government Printing Office, 1880), 2341.

30. Pamela Scott and Antoinette J. Lee, *Buildings of the District of Columbia* (New York: Oxford University Press, 1993), 250–51.

31. Historic American Buildings Survey No. DC-686, *Stanton Park* (Washington, DC: National Park Service, 1993), 3 (hereafter HABS No. DC-686).

32. *Annual Report, Improvement and Care of the Public Buildings and Grounds in the District of Columbia, John M. Wilson, Lieut. Col. of Engineers, Colonel, U.S.A., Appendix WW, Annual Report of the Chief of Engineers for 1887* (Washington, DC: Government Printing Office, 1887), 2576.

33. *Annual Report, Improvement and Care of the Public Buildings and Grounds, and Care and Maintenance of the Washington Monument, in the District of Columbia, John M. Wilson, Lieut. Col. Corps of Engineers, Colonel, U.S.A.; and Oswald H. Ernst, Major, Corps of Engineers, Colonel, U.S.A., Appendix BBB, Annual Report of the Chief of Engineers for 1890* (Washington, DC: Government Printing Office, 1890), 2836.

34. HABS No. DC-686, 4.

35. Wendy Swallow, "Zoning Discrepancies Are Found in Newly Adopted Land-Use Plan," *Washington Post,* 26 January 1985, F1, F11.

36. Claudia D. Kousoulas and George W. Kousoulas, *Contemporary Architecture in Washington, D.C.* (New York: John Wiley & Sons, 1995), 182–83.

37. Diedre Davidson, "Stanton Park: Empowered on the Hill," *Washington Post,* 18 January 1997, E1, E4.

38. Historic American Buildings Survey No. DC-685, *Seward Square* (Washington, DC: National Park Service, 1993), 2 (hereafter HABS No. DC-685).

39. *Annual Report . . . 1890,* 2341.

40. HABS No. DC-685, 4.

41. Resident, telephone interview by Robert Zuraski, 30 January 2003.

42. James M. Goode, *Capital Losses* (Washington, DC: Smithsonian Institution Press, 1979), 162–63.

43. Ibid., 385–86.

44. *Annual Report, Improvement and Care of the Public Buildings and Grounds in the District of Columbia, John M. Wilson, Lieut. Col. of Engineers, Colonel, U.S.A., Appendix TT, Annual Report of the Chief of Engineers for 1886* (Washington, DC: Government Printing Office, 1886), 2079–80.

45. Scott and Lee, *Buildings of the District of Columbia*, 259–60.

46. Goode, *Capital Losses*, 392–94.

47. Historic American Buildings Survey No. DC-672, *Folger Park* (Washington, DC: National Park Service, 1993), 2 (hereafter HABS No. DC-672).

48. *Annual Report, Improvement and Care of the Public Buildings and Grounds in the District of Columbia, A. F. Rockwell, Colonel, U.S.A., Appendix SS, Annual Report of the Chief of Engineers for 1884* (Washington, DC: Government Printing Office, 1884), 2344.

49. HABS No. DC-672, 2.

50. *Annual Report . . . 1886.*

51. *Annual Report . . . 1890,* 2837.

52. Goode, *Capital Losses*, 394.

53. A[lbert] Boschke, *Topographical Map of the District of Columbia, Surveyed in the Years 1856–59* (Washington, DC: McClelland, Blanchard & Mohun, 1861).

54. *Annual Report* (1872), 25.

55. *Annual . . . 1886,* 2080.

56. Historic American Buildings Survey No. DC-679, *Marion Park* (Washington, DC: National Park Service, 1993), 2.

57. Ibid., 2.

58. L'Enfant, *1791 Manuscript Plan.*

59. National Register of Historic Places, *Capital Hill Historic District* (Washington, DC: National Park Service, 1976); John W. Reps, *Washington on View: The Nation's Capitol since 1790* (Chapel Hill: University of North Carolina Press, 1991), 7; Scott and Lee, *Buildings of the District of Columbia,* 246.

60. Goode, *Capital Losses*, 4–5.

61. *Annual Report . . . 1884,* 2344, 2351.

62. *Annual Report . . . 1887,* 2576.

63. *Annual Report . . . 1893,* 4326.

64. Historic American Buildings Survey No. DC-674, *Garfield Park* (Washington, DC: National Park Service, 1993), 2 (hereafter HABS No. DC-674), 4.

65. Ibid.

66. R. H. Baist, *Baist's Real Estate Atlas of Surveys of Washington, District of Columbia* (Philadelphia: G. W. Baist, 1960).

67. HABS No. DC-674, 5.

68. National Capital Planning Commission, *Extending the Legacy* (Washington, DC, 1997).

Chapter 10. New Public Places

Epigraph: Daniel Kemmis, *Community and the Politics of Place* (Norman: University of Oklahoma Press, 1990), 122.

1. Pamela Scott and Antoinette J. Lee, *Buildings of the District of Columbia* (New York: Oxford University Press, 1993), 140–42.

2. Historic American Buildings Survey No. DC-694, *Union Station Plaza* (Washington, DC: National Park Service, 1993), 4 (hereafter HABS No. DC-694).

3. Michael Bednar, *Interior Pedestrian Places* (New York: Whitney Library of Design, 1989), 84–85.

4. James M. Goode, *The Outdoor Sculpture of Washington, D.C.* (Washington, DC: Smithsonian Institution Press, 1974), 44.

5. HABS No. DC-694, 3.

6. James M. Goode, *Capital Losses* (Washington, DC: Smithsonian Institution Press, 1979), 444–47.

7. Christopher Weeks, *AIA Guide to the Architecture of Washington, D.C.* (Baltimore: Johns Hopkins University Press, 1994), 50.

8. Scott and Lee, *Buildings of the District of Columbia,* 142.

9. Historic American Buildings Survey No. DC-696, *Western Plaza* (Washington, DC: National Park Service, 1993), 2, 3 (hereafter HABS No. DC-696).

10. Goode, *Capital Losses,* 353–55.

11. Ibid., 170–73.

12. *Annual Report, Improvement and Care of the Public Buildings and Grounds in the District of Columbia, A. F. Rockwell, Colonel, U.S.A., Appendix SS, Annual Report of the Chief of Engineers for 1884* (Washington, DC: Government Printing Office, 1884), 2352.

13. *Annual Report, Improvement and Care of the Public Buildings and Grounds, and Care and Maintenance of the Washington Monument, in the District of Columbia, John M. Wilson, Lieut. Col. Corps of Engineers, Colonel, U.S.A., Appendix CCC, Annual Report of the Chief of Engineers for 1894* (Washington, DC: Government Printing Office, 1894), 3300.

14. Goode, *Outdoor Sculpture,* 366.

15. HABS No. DC-696, 4.

16. Charles Moore, ed., *The Improvement of the Park System of the District of Columbia* (Washington, DC: Government Printing Office, 1902), 29.

17. Benjamin Forgey, "The Hard But Happy Rebirth of a City's Hallmark," *Washington Post,* 29 December 2001, C1, C5.

18. Goode, *Outdoor Sculpture,* 367–68.

19. Michael Farquhar, "The City's Pretty New Face," *Washington Post,* 28 November 2000, A1, A6; John F. Kelley and Michele Clock, "1800s D. C. Governor Returning to Greatness," ibid., 2 January 2005, C5.

20. Goode, *Capital Losses,* 357–59.

21. Historic American Buildings Survey No. DC-695, *Pershing Park* (Washington, DC: National Park Service, 1993), 3 (hereafter HABS No. DC-695).

22. HABS No. DC-696, 5.

23. President's Council on Pennsylvania Avenue, *Pennsylvania Avenue* (Washington, DC: Government Printing Office, 1964), 38–47.

24. Ibid., 43–46.

25. Pennsylvania Avenue Development Corporation, *The Pennsylvania Avenue Plan* (Washington, DC, 1974), 29–30.

26. Stanislaus von Moos, *Venturi, Rauch & Scott Brown* (New York: Rizzoli, 1987), 116–21.

27. Carol M. Highsmith and Ted Landphair, *Pennsylvania Avenue: America's Main Street* (Washington, DC: AIA Press, 1988), 130.

28. James S. Russell, "Project Diary: Ronald Reagan Building and International Trade Center," *Architectural Record,* July 1998, 58–71.

29. HABS No. DC-695, 5.

30. William H. Whyte, *The Social Life of Small Urban Spaces* (Washington, DC: Conservation Foundation, 1980).

31. Stephen C. Fehr, "Luring People Back to D.C.'s Streets," *Washington Post,* 9 October 1998, B1, B8.

32. Cindy Loose, "Goal of Gay March Is Freedom Plaza," ibid., 15 June 1995, D5; Victoria Benning, "Calling for Equality to Begin at Home," ibid., 22

March 1999, B3; Pamela Constable, "Janitors Union Expands Its Campaign," ibid., 23 March 1995, B3; Keith A. Harriston, "Worldfest to Make Debut as Replacement for Riverfest," ibid., 28 May 1994, B3; Molly Sinclair, "Celebrating Their Golden Years," ibid., 19 September 1991, J7; Peter Baker, "Young Edisons Gather at Invention Convention," ibid., 29 July 1991, D3; Lynda Richardson, "Noon Rally Downtown Added to the Schedule," ibid., 26 June 1990, A12.

33. Goode, *Capital Losses,* 262–64.

34. Historic American Buildings Survey No. DC-691, *Market Square* (Washington, DC: National Park Service, 1993), 3.

35. Goode, *Capital Losses,* 262–64.

36. *Annual Report . . . 1884,* 2352.

37. *Annual Report . . . 1894,* 3300.

38. Goode, *Outdoor Sculpture,* 361.

39. Ibid., 358–60.

40. Goode, *Capital Losses,* 268–71.

41. Scott and Lee, *Buildings of the District of Columbia,* 175–76.

42. Michael J. Crosbie, "On the Avenue," *Architecture,* April 1991, 58–63.

43. Benjamin Forgey, "Market Square's Great Outdoors," *Washington Post,* 10 August 1991, C1, C6.

Conclusion

Epigraph: Spiro Kostof, *The City Assembled* (Boston: Bulfinch, 1992), 172.

1. Nathan Glazer and Mark Lilla, eds., *The Public Face of Architecture* (New York: Free Press, 1987), xiv.

2. Ibid., xiii.

3. *Annual Report, Improvement and Care of the Public Buildings and Grounds, and Care and Maintenance of the Washington Monument, in the District of Columbia, Theo. A. Bingham, Major, Corps of Engineers, Colonel, U.S.A., Appendix HHH, Annual Report of the Chief of Engineers for 1900* (Washington, DC: Government Printing Office, 1900), 3824.

4. Felix Gillette, "Web on the Green," *Landscape Architecture,* March 2003, 18.

5. Leon Battista Alberti, *Ten Books of Architecture,* trans. James Leoni (1755; reprint, Dover: New York, 1986), 173, first published as *De re aedificatoria* in 1485.

6. District of Columbia Municipal Regulations, title 11, Zoning, 2004, chap. 25, secs. 2510, 2512.

7. *Report of Brevet Brigadier General N. Michler, Major of Engineers, U.S. Army, Public Buildings, Grounds, Works, Etc.* (Washington, DC: Government Printing Office, 1868), 6.

8. Linda Wheeler, "Friends Help Meridian Hill Park," *Washington Post,* 4 June 1990, D5.

9. Downtown DC Business Improvement District, *Development Activity in Greater Downtown Washington, DC* (Washington, DC, 31 December 2002).

10. National Capital Planning Commission, *Extending the Legacy* (Washington, DC, 1997).

11. Washington Places, http://arch.virginia.edu/dcplaces.

12. Iris Miller, *Washington in Maps* (New York: Rizzoli, 2002), 158–61; Washington Chapter, American Institute of Architects, *Capital Visions* (Washington, DC, 1997).

13. Kostof, *City Assembled,* 172.

Appendix. Public-Space Analysis

1. National Register of Historic Places, *L'Enfant Plan of the City of Washington, D.C.* (Washington, DC: National Park Service, 1997), sec. 8, pp. 10–11.

2. Ibid., pp. 11–12.

3. *Annual Report, Major O. E. Babcock, Corps of Engineers, Commissioner of Public Buildings and Grounds* (Washington, DC: Government Printing Office, 1872), 22–25.

4. *Annual Report, Improvement and Care of the Public Buildings and Grounds in the District of Columbia, A. F. Rockwell, Colonel, U.S.A., Appendix SS, Annual Report of the Chief of Engineers for 1884* (Washington, DC: Government Printing Office, 1884), 2346–63.

5. *Annual Report, Improvement and Care of the Public Buildings and Grounds, and Care and Maintenance of the Washington Monument, in the District of Columbia, John M. Wilson, Lieut. Col. Corps of Engineers, Colonel, U.S.A., Appendix CCC, Annual Report of the Chief of Engineers for 1894* (Washington, DC: Government Printing Office, 1894).

6. Benjamin Forgey, "Backward to the Future," *Washington Post*, 16 July 2000, G1, G6.

7. Peter Charles L'Enfant, *1791 Manuscript Plan for the City of Washington*, color facsimile (Washington, DC: U.S. Geological Survey, 1991); John W. Reps, *Washington on View: The Nation's Capitol since 1790* (Chapel Hill: University of North Carolina Press, 1991), 39; *Annual Report . . . 1894*, public reservation map; American Automobile Association, *Visitors Guide to Washington, DC* (Heathrow, FL, 2000).

8. National Register of Historic Places, *L'Enfant Plan of the City of Washington, D.C.*, 7.3–7.9.

9. Sanborn Map and Publishing Company, *Washington Insurance Maps* (New York, 1888), vol. 1.

10. R. H. Baist, *Baist's Real Estate Atlas of Surveys of Washington, District of Columbia* (Philadelphia: G. W. Baist, 1960).

INDEX

Michael Bednar, a fellow of the American Institute of Architects, is a professor of architecture at the University of Virginia. He has had his own architectural practice in Charlottesville since 1972 and has worked with I. M. Pei and Partners in New York and Geddes, Brecher, Qualls, and Cunningham in Philadelphia. He taught at the School of Architecture at Rensselaer Polytechnic Institute from 1968 to 1972. His books include *Barrier Free Environments* (1977), editor; *The New Atrium* (1986), which was selected as the Architecture Book of the Year for 1986 by the Association of American Publishers; and *Interior Pedestrian Places* (1989). Professor Bednar has received fellowships from the Graham Foundation and the National Endowment for the Arts, among other honors. He resides in Charlottesville.